Grandfather *of the* Treaties

Also by Daniel Coleman

In Bed with the Word: Reading, Spirituality, and Cultural Politics
Masculine Migrations: Reading the Postcolonial Male in "New Canadian" Narratives
The Scent of Eucalyptus: A Missionary Childhood in Ethiopia
White Civility: The Literary Project of English Canada
Yardwork: A Biography of an Urban Place

Grandfather *of the* Treaties

Finding Our Future Through the Wampum Covenant

Daniel Coleman

Published by James Street North Books
an imprint of Wolsak and Wynn Publishers
280 James Street North
Hamilton, ON L8R2L3
www.wolsakandwynn.ca

Editor: Noelle Allen | Copy editor: Jen Hale
Cover and interior design: Jennifer Rawlinson
Cover image: *Interwoven Chain* by Richard W. Hill Sr.
Author photograph: Geoffrey Skirrow
Typeset in Adobe Caslon Pro, Calibri and Magister
Printed by Rapido Books, Montreal, Canada

10 9 8 7 6 5 4 3 2 1

The publisher gratefully acknowledges the support of the Canada Council for the Arts and the Ontario Arts Council. We also acknowledge the financial support of the Government of Canada through the Canada Book Fund and the Government of Ontario through the Ontario Book Publishing Tax Credit and Ontario Creates.

Library and Archives Canada Cataloguing in Publication
Title: Grandfather of the treaties : finding our future through the Wampum Covenant / Daniel Coleman.
Names: Coleman, Daniel, 1961- author. | Hill, Richard W., Sr., illustrator.
Description: Includes 28 black and white illustrations by Richard W. Hill Sr. | Includes bibliographical references and index.
Identifiers: Canadiana 20240489675 | ISBN 9781998408092 (softcover)
Subjects: LCSH: Wampum belts—Canada—History. | LCSH: Reconciliation. | LCSH: Canada—Ethnic relations—History. | CSH: First Nations—Treaties—History. | CSH: First Nations—Government relations—History.
Classification: LCC E99.I7 C62 2025 | DDC 305.897/554—dc23

For my mother, Bea Coleman, age ninety-six,
who has prayed faithfully for this book

Contents

List of Illustrations /ix
Foreword /xv

Part I Good Minds /1
Reintroducing the Linked Arms /11
Introducing Wampum /23
Introducing Myself /33

Part II Histories /45
Oral Histories of the Agreement /47
What Could "Covenant" Mean to Dutch and British Ears? /61
Tracing *Kaswentha*'s Flow /69
From Proclamation to Constitution /82
Race and the Other Theology: The Doctrine of Discovery /102
Distorting "Protection" /114
Canada Strong-Arms the Canoe /125

Part III Linking Arms: Face-to-Face Ethics /141
Clearing Ethical Space /144
Putting "First" Encounters Back in the Flow /162
Exhausting Inquiry /177
Undoing Unilateral Multiculturalism /196

Part IV Covenant Chain–Two Row Ecologies /208
The Family of Earth /212
Divided Home /231
Awe and Respect /253
Dish With One Spoon–Land Back /265
Linked Arms–Land Back /280

Part V Conclusion: Can We Restore the Linked Arms? /294

Gratitude /303
Glossary /306
Notes /315
Bibliography /352
Index /370

List *of* Illustrations

All illustrations and contextualizing comments are by Richard W. Hill Sr. unless otherwise noted.

Illustration	Description	Pages
In Relationship	Two Figures Holding Hands, from John Graves Simcoe Wampum Belt, National Museum of Natural History, Smithsonian Institution. Simcoe was Governor General of Upper Canada, 1791–94.	2, 9, 11, 30, 36, 72, 170, 235, 249, 280
Greeting	The tattooed arm of a Mohawk grasps the fore-arm of a man with a tattoo of the Dutch national symbol. This is the way in which arms of allies were linked in peace and friendship.	14, 47, 153, 269
Face to Face	Inspired by a Seneca hair comb, circa 1680, in the Metropolitan Museum of Art. Originally the antler hair comb had two European settlers facing each other. Rick Hill reclothed the figure on the left to represent the Haudenosaunee.	20, 61, 141, 158
Edge of the Woods	Whenever the Haudenosaunee met, they conducted a healing ceremony at the edge of the woods. Three sets of wampum strings were used to wipe the tears, clear the ears and unblock the throats of the visitors so that it was easier to come to one mind on the matters to be discussed.	23, 26, 144, 254
Looking for Himself	Daniel Coleman.	33

Disappearing Ink	While the Haudenosaunee depended upon wampum, memory and oral tradition, the settlers used writing to preserve their pledges. But history has shown that words on parchment seem to disappear as the European Crowns did not intend to keep their treaty obligations to the Indigenous nations.	33, 128, 189, 260
Interwoven Chain	The Two Row Wampum and the Covenant Chain have become interwoven in the memory of the Haudenosaunee. They both represent the hope that peace, friendship, trust, respect and Good Minds will flourish in the future generations.	45, 69, 162, 300
Two Paths	Dutch wooden shoes and Haudenosaunee decorated moccasins.	64
Sir William Johnson Treaty Icon	Sir William Johnson's Indian Testimonial icon, drawn by Henry Dawkins, circa 1770. It features the passing of the Peace Medal, likely from the 1768 Fort Stanwix Treaty. This icon was given to Indigenous allies of the Crown for safe passage between British forts.	78, 87
1764 Fort Niagara Treaty Wampum	Sir William Johnson designed this wampum for the Fort Niagara Treaty of 1764 to represent a large dish when its ends were brought together. By this, Johnson asked the twenty-four First Nations assembled at the treaty to consider the British forts as the new Dish With One Spoon from which they could obtain food, clothing and household goods given in peace and friendship.	82

House Divided	The European ships brought a belief system that divided the Haudenosaunee, weakening the People of the Longhouse as internal strife over those imported beliefs caused animosities to burst forth.	102, 231
Ship of Fools?	Part of the design of a porcupine quill–decorated leather pouch.	105, 196
Declaration of War Wampum Belt	Relationships became strained, or the Crown asked for military support, by the circulation of war belts, often containing the symbol of a hatchet or tomahawk. Delivering such a wampum belt was an invitation to enter war, as either an ally or an enemy. The invitation could be used and the wampum would have been returned.	114, 121
Rowing the River of Life	European settlers quickly adopted the use of bark canoes to travel the many rivers and lakes in the northeast. These men could be traders, diplomats or missionaries, seemingly determined to make their way into Haudenosaunee country.	125
Counting Strengths	English trader Wentworth Greenhalgh travelled on horseback for the English in Albany to count the number of warriors in the Haudenosaunee villages to the west. A Seneca artist crafted this hair comb to commemorate his visit to their village, circa 1677.	130
Welcome White Man	Prior to 1687, a carved antler man, who appears to be welcoming someone. Unearthed at a seventeenth-century Seneca village named Ganondagan (Victor, NY) that was destroyed during a French invasion.	133, 164, 177

The Arrival	Seneca view of Dutch man, in his three-cornered hat, buttoned-down waistcoat and leather boots. Antler hair comb, sixteenth century.	137, 179
Side by Side	The Dutch ship and the Mohawk canoe rest side by side, representing the message of the Two Row Wampum that each vessel contains the laws, beliefs and traditions of each society, being separated, yet equal in the treaty partnership.	148
The Council	Part of the design of a porcupine quill–decorated leather pouch.	199
Great Dish	The centre icon of the Dish With One Spoon Wampum is this graphic representation of the Dish, a metaphor for the bounty of Mother Earth. In the centre of that dish is a roasted beaver tail, said to be the most nutritious food that you could offer someone. The Dish was a reminder that we all have an equal share of what the earth provides to feed and heal ourselves.	203, 208, 265, 274, 276
Turtle Clan Effigy	Nicholas Etawacom (a.k.a. Etow Oh Koam), "King" of the River Nation, signed his agreement to a treaty by representing himself through his clan effigy, a symbol of the Turtle, in 1710. He was one of the "Four Indian Kings" who visited Queen Anne in England that year.	212

The Original Medicine Wheel	In the 1600s the Dutch made shell runtees, small disks with holes cut through them so they could be strung as necklaces. The design recalls the sacred circle of the Haudenosaunee and the symbol of the Four White Roots of Peace.	214
Deer Clan Effigy	One eighteenth-century Haudenosaunee diplomat marked his agreement to a treaty by representing himself through his clan effigy.	220
Bear Clan Effigy	Sagoyonquaroughtau or Sa Ga Yeath Qua Pieth Tow (Brant) signed a treaty document with his symbol of the Bear, 1710. He was one of the "Four Indian Kings" who visited Queen Anne in England that year.	228
Completing the Circle	Circular wampum medallion with porcupine quill–decorated edge, currently in Russian Museum.	240, 282, 303
Soaring Eagle	Seventeenth-century Dutch-made shell bird effigy, made to be hung from a necklace or sewn to clothing. In the Haudenosaunee Great Law of Peace, Eagle was said to land at the top of the Tree of Peace and to keep watch for any threats to the way of peace.	253
Two Rows	[no description]	285
Tree of Peace Arises	[no description]	294

Foreword

I first learned of the Two Row Wampum in 1970 when I was travelling to Haudenosaunee communities to photograph and interview our artists. Cayuga leader Jake Thomas had carved the image of the Two Row Wampum into the side of a large wooden bowl he had made. He shared a brief overview of what the two purple rows in the wampum represent.

This fired a lifelong fascination with the intelligence and diplomatic skills of my ancestors. It also depressed me a bit because I was already twenty years old before I had heard about it. What else didn't I know?

Working with Huron Miller (Onondaga), Corbett Sundown (Tonawanda Seneca) and Jake Thomas, my head was filled with the deeper meaning of that ancient wampum belt. Sadly, when I asked if I could see the actual belt, these mighty men grew quiet. Finally, they revealed that the original Two Row, along with many more wampum belts, had been taken from our hands by anthropologists and collectors and were locked away in museums far from our current council fires. All these men had to show me were replicas of the Two Row made of glass beads or dyed electrical wiring casings.

My fascination turned to anger and determination to recover these belts that my mentors said were sacred and held our history, our treaty agreements and, in a sense, our destiny. If we could not recover these wampum records, we would lose an important part of our identity, our sense of self. I set it as my personal mission to not look at the real wampum until they were back in our hands once again. I worked with Ray Gonyea (Onondaga), Peter Jemison (Seneca), Doug George (Akwesasne Mohawk) and Oren Lyons (Onondaga) to make that happen. It was a great victory for our People to have the Two Row and dozens of other wampum belts returned to our Confederacy to teach us.

So, the Two Row came into my life at the crossroads of that desire to learn and the consternation of my own colonized experience. We can't figure out where we are going if we don't clearly understand where we come from and how we got to where we are today.

Daniel came into my life about fifteen years ago. Like the Dutch and Mohawk ancestors, we had to find a way to communicate. We were both university professors and both had a sincere desire to see how the Two Row Wampum ideology might be a model for modern-day relations. We started a conversation about wampum meanings, human interactions and historical narratives, as professors often do.

Fortunately for both of us, I had assembled written interpretations of the Two Row Wampum from documents provided by Huron and Jake, as well as transcripts of a meeting of Haudenosaunee Chiefs from Grand River and Governor General Edward R. Schreyer in the 1980s. These brought deeper insight to the *Reader's Digest* version of the Two Row Wampum that I was hearing in our communities.

What fascinated me most about the narrative – the words held by the Wampum Belt – was that it explains the way by which the Dutch man and the Mohawk man came to one mind on what they could agree to. It was a negotiation, with both sides contributing ideas. They created mutual symbolism and meaning for subsequent generations to follow. It was a series of mini-agreements and prophesy about the future.

Enter Daniel and Rick seeking a way to relate to each other, to the intellectual work we were both doing, as well as seeking a way to manifest true reconciliation on a personal level. The Two Row Wampum became the centrepiece of our relationship, and we have explored together what it can mean to our current generation. Over the years, our conversations took us back to the canoe and the ship travelling down the river of life. We used the concepts between the two rows to develop a research paradigm. We worked with Grand River community members and graduate students to have them employ "Two Row Seeing" in their own research. These ongoing conversations led to the book you are now reading.

I welcome this publication because I think it will provide great insight for the other people descended from the many ships that arrived on our shores. It might help them rethink what it means to have inherited this Two Row Wampum agreement. It is about maintaining quality relationships and developing true friendship. It will also be important to the Haudenosaunee, as we see how peace was made and reflect on what each of us needs to do to maintain that peace. This is what Daniel and I have been able to accomplish – the kind of friendship imagined over four hundred years ago. I hope that Daniel's words and my drawings help you see what this friendship is like. Look back to look forward. Look at each other to find the real reason that peace, respect and friendship matter.

Rick Hill (Tuscarora)

Part I

Good Minds

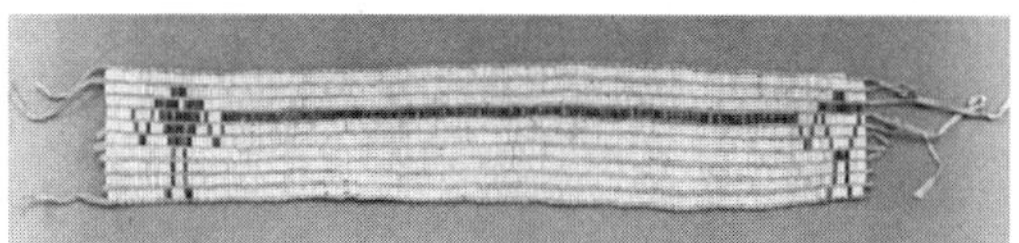

Tehontatenentshonteronhtáhkwa, "the thing by which they link arms," a.k.a. the Covenant Chain of Friendship. (Photo courtesy of Rick Hill)

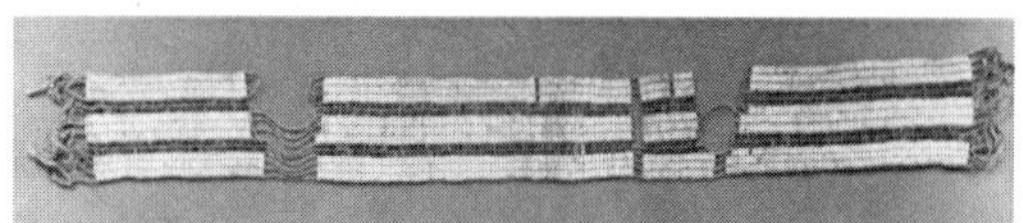

Tékeni Teyohà:te, "two roads or paths," a.k.a. the Two Row Wampum. (Photo courtesy of Rick Hill)

There's a church six and a half blocks from my house. It's called "Canadian Martyrs Catholic Church." Right beside it is Canadian Martyrs Catholic Elementary School.

I'm not Catholic, but in my Grade 10 public school class in Canadian history, I was taught about the Canadian martyrs. The first people declared saints in North America were the five Jesuits killed by the alliance of Peoples[1] the French referred to as the "Iroquois" in the 1640s.

The story of the Canadian martyrs is one of Canada's more sensational stories of origin. It's a story that tells of saintly priests and peaceful newcomers braving brutal savagery on their way to building homes, churches and civilization. It wasn't until I moved to Hamilton, Ontario, six and a half blocks from Canadian Martyrs Catholic Church, that I heard a different side of that same story. The people the Jesuits called "Iroquois" have a reserve just half an hour's drive south of here on the Grand River territory. Long before their ancestors met the Jesuits, they had formed an alliance of nations around a message of peace. They called themselves "Haudenosaunee," meaning "they are building the longhouse," and their social-political longhouse was made up of the *Kanyen'kehâka* (Mohawk), *Onyota'a:kâ:* (Oneida), *Onoñda'gega'* (Onondaga), *Gayogohó:no* (Cayuga) and *Onödowa'ga:'* (Seneca) nations. They lived in the region of the Finger Lakes in what is today upstate New York. The rivalry between the Huron-Wendat-Algonquin alliance, who traded furs with the French generally north of the Great Lakes, and the Haudenosaunee Confederacy, who traded with the Dutch and the English mostly south of the Lakes, escalated in the 1600s from occasional raids to open warfare as the rivalling European traders supplied arms to their Indigenous allies.

The story of the Canadian martyrs emerges out of that trade in arms and souls and furs. Like many action-adventure stories, it centres on violence, a story of innocent people attacked by savages, a story that troubles the heart and excites the mind. It's one of many such stories that energize colonial history.

There are, however, other stories. Since moving to live near Six Nations, I've heard the stories of how people in this exact region and time period made peace and lived in highly organized societies guided by sophisticated civil institutions. These stories do not get told as often in colonial history. They're rarely told in high school classes. Most Canadians have not heard them. Nonetheless, there is a stream of stories about Indigenous envoys stepping courageously toward unknown newcomers, carrying the articles of peace. This is a stream of stories about cross-cultural, inter-national peacemaking that have never truly ceased. They are stories that feed what Haudenosaunee People call "the Good Mind."

This book aims to retell these widely neglected stories of the Good Mind.

Let me begin with one recorded by the Jesuits themselves:

Kiotsaeton's Peace Mission

On July 5, 1645, several vessels shimmered through the heat haze toward the shoreline at Trois-Rivières. There, the Jesuits had a mission frequented by French settlers and soldiers, as well as their Huron-Wendat,

Montagnais (Innu) and Algonquin allies. When they saw the vessels approaching, the inhabitants rushed to the landing place to throw their arms around the neck of a long-lost villager, Guillaume Couture, who had been taken prisoner by the *Kanyen'kehāka* along with Jesuit Father Isaac Jogues almost three years earlier.[2] While Jogues had escaped with the help of the Dutch commissioner of trade, Arent van Curler, down on the Mohawk River, Couture had remained with the Mohawks and was only now being returned in exchange for a couple of Haudenosaunee prisoners.

This event constitutes a fragile moment when enemies took a breath and tried to create peace, a space for dialogue, in the spiral of violence. An Algonquin party of warriors had killed eleven Haudenosaunee warriors the year before.[3] But they had spared one of the Haudenosaunee from their hatchets. They had turned him over to their French allies, who had loaded him with gifts and letters anxiously proposing peace and sent him back to his home, hoping these gestures might avoid reprisals of war clubs and fire. In response to these gestures, the Haudenosaunee Confederacy had delegated a tall, gifted orator named Kiotsaeton to lead a peace embassy up the freshwater river from Mohawk country, past the lake the French named after Champlain, overland into the big river they named St. Laurent, then down the increasingly salty water to the enemy mission where the three rivers met.

As the boats neared the shore, the tall *Kanyen'kehāka* leader stood in the bow of his canoe.

"He was almost completely covered with Porcelain beads," writes Father Barthélemy Vimont, the Jesuit superior. "Colliers de pourcelaine" were his French words for the gleaming beads of wampum, fashioned from white whelk and purple quahog shells, then woven into patterned strings or belts, that the man carried upon his body.[4] Motioning with his hand for silence, Kiotsaeton, the glittering Haudenosaunee ambassador, called out, "My Brothers, I have left my country to come and see you. At last I have reached your land. I was told, on my departure, that I was going to seek death, and that I would never again see my country. But I have willingly exposed myself for the good of peace. I come therefore to enter into the designs of the French, of the Hurons, and of the Alguonquins. I come to make known to you the thoughts of all my country."[5]

Kiotsaeton opened his mission by mapping the ground and rivers he had traversed to get there. The importance of what he had to say was attested by the magnificent belts of beads he carried on his body; by the length and difficulty of his journey; the danger of the rapids; the portages from river to lake, to river; the darkness of the woods – by his fear that he might meet his own death in the land in which he had arrived. This peace mission was meant to quell the killing and violence between the Huron-Algonquin-French alliance and the Haudenosaunee Confederacy during what have come to be called the Beaver Wars over control of the fur trade.

Over the next week, from July 5 to July 12, 1645, Kiotsaeton and his colleagues were cordially welcomed with banquets and comfortable lodgings as they waited for Charles Huault de Montmagny, Governor of New France, to arrive and the peace talks to begin.

Once the governor arrived, everyone gathered in the shade of large sails that had been stretched over the courtyard in front of the fort, anxious for the embassy to start. At Kiotsaeton's request, he and his retainers sat with the governor and the Jesuits "as a mark of the affection that they bore to the French,"[6] while across from them sat the Algonquins and People Vimont calls the "Montagnais" (Innu) and the "Attikamegues" (Atikamekws were close allies of the Innu). On the other two sides of the rectangle, French villagers sat across from Hurons.

It matters where people sit. All must be able to see what happens on the ground cleared between them. All must be able to see each other's responses to what occurs in their midst. For the peace to take hold, all must hear what is said, make up their own minds, seek a common understanding. "In the center was a large space, somewhat longer than wide," writes Père Vimont, "in which the Iroquois[7] caused two poles to be planted, and a cord to be stretched from one to the other on which to hang and tie the words that they were to bring us, that is to say, the presents they wished to make us, which consisted of seventeen collars of porcelain beads, a portion of which were on their bodies. The remainder were enclosed in a small pouch placed quite near them."[8]

The Reverend Father's writing stammers over what to call these "words," these "presents," which is to say, these "colliers de pourcelaine." The *Kanyen'kehàka* called the belts "*kaswentha*."

Today, in English, we call them "wampum," a shortened version of the Algonquin word *wampumpeag*.[9]

It doesn't take long, though, for Father Vimont to describe how Kiotsaeton incorporated these "colliers" into the drama of his speech.

The tall *Kanyen'kehàka* ambassador took the first "collar" in his hand and began to pace the open rectangle. As he walked, he turned his eyes to the heavens, gazed up at the sun and performed an elevated form of speech that Vimont describes as song – "il fe mit à chanter" – and his Haudenosaunee colleagues chanted a choral response to each verse of the song.[10]

We are witnessing these opening scenes of the gathering at Trois-Rivières through Vimont's and L'Incarnation's words, so we can't know directly what Kiotsaeton sang. It could have been his *atónwa*, his self-identifying song or personal chant, by which he was introducing himself; it could have been that he was launching a version of the "Edge of the Woods," a ceremony for when people met at the edge of the clearing where villagers grew their fields of corn, beans and squash. Or Kiotsaeton could have been opening with what is known as the *Ohén:ton Karihwatéhkwen*, the "Words Before All Else," the Thanksgiving Address the Creator Tharonhyawá:kon had instructed the people to give throughout their lives, and especially at the beginning of important meetings.

Because the ambassador turned his eyes to the surrounding creation, to the heavens, to the sun, and because the members of his party chanted back at regular intervals, I'm inclined to think he was opening with the stanzas of the Words Before All Else, which proceed upward, offering thanks and greetings, first, to the lowly earth and water that nourish seeds and roots, then up to the plants, medicines, birds and animals that perform their differentiated duties. Higher yet – like Kiotsaeton turning his gaze upward to the heavens – the next stanzas greet and thank the sky, the winds of the four directions, thunderbeings, moon and sun. Next, the ceremonial speech recognizes the humans who have gathered at the meeting to put their minds together. And ultimately, the Creator of all. Each being is recognized, named and thanked until *etho kati nenyohtonhake ne onkwa'nikonra*, "that is the way it will be in our minds," commonly paraphrased as "now our minds are one." To affirm this joining of minds together, after each category of beings is recognized and thanked, those assembled sing out "*Henh!*," sometimes spelled in English "Huh" or "Tho," meaning "yes!" "agreed!," just as Kiotsaeton's companions did.[11]

The point of the Thanksgiving Address is to remind those gathered of the things on which they can easily agree. The earth, the land, is the source from which every life emerges. Gratitude to and for the interwoven lives that make up the fabric of creation clears and harmonizes our minds. Thanksgiving, respect and gratitude for the lives that make our own lives possible speaks the language of the heart in order to clear the mind.

One-mindedness, unity of mind, *ka'nikonhriyó'tshera't* comes from recognizing how all our minds, all our lives, rely upon the interdependent web of living things.

This was a good place for Kiotsaeton to begin his peace mission.

Having sung the opening words – whether by means of his *atónwa*, the Edge of the Woods or the Words Before All Else – that were needed to elevate Good Minds among his listeners, the tall ambassador held high the first wampum, which, he explained, conveyed thanks to the governor for liberating Tokhrahenehiaron, the Mohawk man who had been delivered the previous autumn from "the teeth of the Alguonquins" and sent back home to his People, bearing gifts, letters and tokens of peace. Kiotsaeton's thanks for the French effort to de-escalate the violence did not make him refrain, however, from chiding the governor for not sending someone to accompany the released prisoner on his perilous journey home.

Then, having concluded the first element of his oration, he hung the first strand of wampum on the cord that had been prepared to receive them – "for with [the Haudenosaunee]," explains Marie de l'Incarnation, "everything speaks and their actions are as meaningful as their words."[12]

Next, the embassy leader took a second wampum and fastened it around the arm of Guillaume Couture. The arm bound with wampum bespoke the care invested in Couture's return. This binding of the arm became a significant motif that was repeated in subsequent wampum scenes in the diplomat's drama. Reinforcing his gentle chastisement of the governor, Kiotsaeton noted that he had brought the Frenchman safely back, at great risk to himself; he had not sent him out, as the French had, into the forest alone. He had fulfilled more than the letter of the law for returning a prisoner; he had *cared* for the returned man, linked arms with him, as it were, through the raging rivers, the dark woods, the fears and nighttime dangers of travelling through unknown, enemy territory to ensure he arrived safely not just in body but also in heart and mind. As Kiotsaeton spoke, Vimont reports,

> He took a stick, and placed it on his head like a bundle; then he carried it from one end of the square to the other, representing what that prisoner had done in the rapids and in the current of the water, on arriving at which he had transported his baggage, piece by piece. He went backward and forward, showing the journeys, the windings, and the turnings of the prisoner. He ran against a stone; he receded more than he advanced in his canoe, because alone he could not maintain it against the current. He lost courage, and then regained his strength.[13]

"That is what was said by the second collar, which he tied near the first," Father Vimont explains, meaning that, at the end of this sequence, Kiotsaeton took the wampum from Couture's arm and placed it alongside the first wampum on the display cord for everyone to see and remember. Hanging the wampum marks the completion of an item of business, an *orì:wa*, almost like a scene change in his peacemaking drama. "In a word," the fascinated Vimont writes, "I have never seen anything better done than this acting."[14] Kiotsaeton's theatre set the peace negotiations in the context of struggle and distress. For, what needed to be addressed in those meetings were the challenges of the heart, the panic, the danger, the fight-or-flight, the stress of travel and of entering the unknown of other People's territory, their way of thinking, their suspicion and vulnerability.

Peace is a political matter. But it is first a matter of the heart, of the emotions, a matter of physical calm, a matter of minds assured that they are in a kindly or nurturing environment.

And so it went from wampum belt to wampum belt: "The fifth was given to clear the river" for the canoes of Kiotsaeton's embassy, writes the enthralled Jesuit. "He made use of a thousand gestures, as if he had collected the waves and had caused a calm, from Quebec to the Iroquois country. The sixth was to smooth the rapids and waterfalls, or the strong currents, that occur in the rivers on which one must sail to reach their country."[15] It was as if these wampum-word-presents conveyed stages of the journey, of passage through the land, which the journey of peace must navigate. The peace the actor-ambassador conveyed was not limited to humans alone. At each point, the mission of peace calms the land, clears the rivers, the rapids, the waterfalls – all understood as challenges to the message of peace.

Shinnecock scholar Kelsey Leonard, whose Algonquin-language People have lived for centuries where quahog inhabit the Atlantic seaboard and who still to this day fashion beads and wampum belts from these mollusks' shells, observes that the Shinnecock word for these creatures, *wunnáumwash*, means "speaks the truth." Why? Because "our speech should mimic our Mollusk relatives. Quahogs filter the pollution in our waters. They take out the bad and return to us water that is healthy to support life. Quahogs are life-givers. They are purifiers and truth-seekers. These processes of life produce truth and help us to conceptualize what justice means in our world – to speak the truth."[16]

Wampum words are held as sacred. Presenters of wampum guarantee the truth of their words by holding wampum in hand. Recipients of those words avow themselves to an honest response by touching and taking up the collar of truth-telling mollusk beads.

More than this, Kiotsaeton's wampum words were uttered within the understanding that speech circulates in a more-than-human world, clarifying, making peace, offering truths that can settle murkiness and calm disturbance in the land, ocean and rivers as much as in people's minds. He created a sequence of events and understandings his listeners had to acknowledge and to which they were invited to respond. As he completed his enacted song-speech for each wampum belt, the orator hung the truth-telling beads alongside the others on the cord: scenes in a drama, rituals in a ceremony, stones in a river, premises in an argument.

In this opening series, Kiotsaeton seems to have been enacting a version of the Edge of the Woods,[17] a ceremony that recognizes the hardship and danger of travel when people first meet at the place where the dark forest ends and the sunlit fields of corn, beans and squash that surround every village begin. The point of the Edge of the Woods ceremony is to clear the eyes, unblock the ears and moisten the throats of those who are just emerging from difficulty, who need to clear their senses so they can listen with attention and speak only from minds and hearts calmed by kindness. Each of Kiotsaeton's "collars," hung up on the cord for all to see, arose from Northeast Peoples' protocols for how to conduct important business between people.

Linking Arms

"The tenth was given to bind us all very closely together," Father Vimont pens in his report. "He took hold of a Frenchman, placed his arm within his, and with his other arm he clasped that of an Alguonquin. Having thus joined himself to them, 'Here,' he said, 'is the knot that binds us inseparably; nothing can part us.' This collar was extraordinarily beautiful."[18] This was an echo of the wampum Kiotsaeton had tied around Couture's arm. It's too bad Vimont doesn't describe the iconography of this extraordinary tenth collar, for Kiotsaeton's enactment of this sequence sounds like the *Tehontatenentshonteronhtáhkwa*, the wampum representing linked arms, the covenant to form inseparable friends and allies. Like brothers. It portrays People who have agreed to form a relationship founded on trust, friendship and respect.

"Even if the lightning were to fall upon us," the arm-in-arm Mohawk orator continued, "it could not separate us; for, if it cuts off the arm that holds you to us, we will at once seize each other by the other arm." Vimont supplies, "thereupon he turned around, and caught the Frenchman and the Alguonquin by their two other arms, holding them so closely that he seemed unwilling ever to leave them."[19]

In Kiotsaeton's tenth wampum, we have an instance of the central subject of this book, what several recent Indigenous leaders have referred to as the "Grandfather of the Treaties,"[20] which is now commonly referred to as the Covenant Chain of Friendship. Kiotsaeton's embassy to the French-Wendat-Algonquin alliance was one of hundreds of councils at which this wampum was agreed to between Indigenous Peoples, as well as with European newcomers, over the next two hundred years. It remains in place to this day. It's my hope that by renewing it among us today, we can rejoin the linked arms between us humans and build healthier relations with the lands and waters on which we all depend.

Chapter One

Reintroducing the Linked Arms

It matters which origin stories we tell and retell as we try to place ourselves in the land. I was taught the story of martyrs and savages in my high school class in Canadian history. I had never heard the stream of stories about linking arms until I moved to Hamilton, Ontario, in my thirties. It takes an adjustment of mind to begin to hear stories that differ from the ones to which we are accustomed. As I'll discuss later in this book when I introduce myself more directly, it took armed conflict in my neighbourhood and at the university where I work for me to begin to listen to the stories of how Indigenous Peoples made peace in the northeast part of this continent. I'd been hearing a little bit about wampum diplomacy ever since I arrived at McMaster University as a new professor in 1997, about ancient agreements known as the Covenant Chain of Friendship and the Two Row Wampum from the days of Europeans' first arrival in this part of the world, but these stories seemed remote to me until conflict over Indigenous land rights in my neighbourhood made them immediate.

Kiotsaeton's linking of arms with his enemies was taken straight from the Haudenosaunee vocabulary for family- and alliance-making. "Gripping each arm of the adoptee, one sponsor on each side, recalls the [Haudenosaunee] adoption ceremony," writes *Kanyen'kehâka* author Amber Meadow Adams about this scene. "The lightning Kiotsaeton describes represents a force even stronger than that of a falling tree, which is the force that can't break the rotiyaneshon's [chiefs'] grip on one another's arms."[1] She is referring, in the first instance, to the Haudenosaunee ceremony for adopting an adult, when a representative of the adopting family walks the adoptee, arm in arm, up and down the longhouse, singing *atónwa*, their personal song of thanksgiving.[2] And she refers, in the second instance, to the image of the linked arms of the fifty Haudenosaunee *rotiyaneshon* that make up the Confederacy Council, the chiefs who form a circle of joined arms to protect and uphold the Tree of Peace at the centre of their way of life.

Every one of Kiotsaeton's scenes, pictured in one of the belts of wampum hung up on the cord for all to see, represents a step in the Haudenosaunee ceremonial procedure for making peace and friendship.

And the French know it. For they, then, respond in kind with "presents," "collars" and oratory of their own. Marie de l'Incarnation reports that "Monsieur the Governor's presents were bestowed by Couture, who [familiar with Haudenosaunee ways from having lived among them for the last two years, spoke] in the Iroquois tongue and with the gestures and manners of that nation, *to correspond to those of the ambassador.*"[3] His first "present" was "to thank the one that made heaven and earth for being everywhere, and for seeing into our hearts, and for now uniting the mind of all the peoples." You could think of this as a French and Catholic approximation of the Words Before All Else. Couture's fifth wampum, following Kiotsaeton's order precisely, was "to make the river easy, the lake firm, and the way free so that the smoke of the fires of the French and the Algonkins may be seen." Peace in the environment opens the way to peace between nations. The eighth wampum offered by the French signified "a mark of the happiness we receive from their [Haudenosaunee] alliance with us and the Algonkins and from the fact that we shall eat together in peace," while the tenth, corresponding exactly to Kiotsaeton's tenth linking-arms wampum, was given "to assure them that the French will have the Hurons come as soon as possible so that they will put their arms down like the Agnerognons [Mohawks] and to show that we wish to be the friends of Ognoté [Oneidas] and that they will be Onontio's [the French governor's] children."[4] The tenth wampum indicated the French agreed to encourage their allies to drop their weapons of war and to link arms, like adoptees in one family, like chiefs in a confederacy, with the Haudenosaunee.

In Kiotsaeton's embassy to Trois-Rivières, then, we have an early European record of a practice that was widespread and well-established in the northeast of Turtle Island. Kiotsaeton's lavish gifts of wampum, each conveying a different part of his message, hung in view for all to see, review and repeat. All those assembled at the multilingual gathering could not fail to understand their meaning, even if they listened through the tongues of interpreters. When Couture responded, on behalf of the governor, with corresponding wampum after corresponding wampum, everyone could see if he missed anything, how faithful his response was, where he adapted and where he affirmed in full.

Any who doubted the sincerity or significance of these messages need only view the magnificence of the wampum "words" or "presents" that hung upon the cord. Kiotsaeton's "presents consisted of thirty thousand grains [beads] of porcelain," explains Marie de l'Incarnation, "that they had reduced to seventeen collars."[5] She doesn't say how many beads went into making the French wampum belts given to the Haudenosaunee in Couture's replies. Scholar Germaine Warkentin explains that coastal Pequots, who at one point dominated wampum manufacture from whelk and quahog shells, could make thirty-six to forty-eight beads per person per day.[6] If my math is right, the beads Kiotsaeton presented would have required 625 person-days, almost two years, to make, with no breaks or weekends off.

No wonder Europeans came to think that wampum was money. It was that precious.

Kiotsaeton's embassy to Trois-Rivières demonstrates how wampum covenants had shaped the culture of international diplomacy up and down the northeast by the time Europeans arrived and started to keep written records in America. These words, these presents, provided the council fire agendas for how to do diplomacy, how to make treaty between Peoples and how to record what was agreed upon for posterity.

"By repeatedly adopting the relational technique of wampum belts," writes Gilles Havard, research director at the National Centre for Scientific Research in Paris, "the French (and likewise the English in the colony of New York) demonstrated a capacity for adaptation that was in fact imposed on them; . . . it was vital to secure local allies." As a result, he says that for "nearly two centuries, the French [and, as we will see, the Dutch and British too] thus moved in a geopolitical sphere whose diplomatic practices were largely shaped by the Native Americans."[7]

The need for these principles and protocols was emphasized by troubles that came with Europeans, such as Chief Donnacona's kidnapping by Cartier in the 1530s and his eventual death in France, or the killings of Haudenosaunee men during their first encounter with firearms in Champlain's arquebus in 1609.

When they met Dutch merchants on the Hudson River in 1609, the same year Champlain killed some of their relatives, the Haudenosaunee looked to their long-established methods for making peace. Over the next four or five years of interaction with the Dutch, the Haudenosaunee developed wampum protocols to link arms with them. Same thing, later, when the British began to establish a colonial administration in New York in 1664. A hundred years later, when the British overtook New France, their officials assumed Haudenosaunee language, symbolism and protocols – wampum, spoken-word song-speeches, Thanksgiving Address, Edge of the Woods, Linking Arms – for how to conduct peace and treaty councils with Indigenous Peoples throughout the region. These protocols shaped British colonial practices right into the nineteenth century, after the British had defeated (or at least, outlasted) New France and then been forced themselves to retreat by the Revolutionary War and to reassemble their administration of a remaining British North America during the War of 1812.

Grandfather of the Treaties

"Haudenosaunee" (or "*Rotinonhsyón:ni*" in Mohawk, one of the six languages of the Six Nations) means "they are building the house," a symbol of peacemaking that is their own story of origin. Many years before Europeans arrived in the northeast of Turtle Island, these nations had been at war with each other. But through the influence of a Wendat man known as the Peacemaker, the former enemies linked arms with one another. They adopted each other as family. The house is said to have "added a rafter" as each nation linked its arms with the others, creating the household of the *Kayanerenhtsherakó:wa*, the Great Law of Peace. When the French arrived on the St. Lawrence River in 1534 and the Dutch on the Hudson River in 1609, the Haudenosaunee longhouse consisted of the Mohawk, Oneida, Onondaga, Cayuga and Seneca nations. Because the *Kanyen'kehàka* (Mohawks), the easternmost of the Haudenosaunee nations frequented these river systems, they were among the first Indigenous Peoples these early European mariners met. It is through the *Kanyen'kehàka* that the seafarers, and the British who followed in their wake, learned local diplomacy: how to approach People on Turtle Island peacefully, how to make cross-cultural, international agreements, how to build alliances and confederacies. When the *Skarure'* (Tuscarora) Nation migrated north from the Carolinas in the eighteenth century, they added a sixth rafter to the Longhouse of the Haudenosaunee, who have been known ever since as the Confederacy of the Six Nations.

Like many stories of origin, the story of peacemaking takes place in the teeth of its opposite. Civil life must be carefully built against the dark threat of distrust and violence. Part of the story told in this book is that the ideal of friendship and alliance pictured in the image of linked arms, and its betrayal, is so deeply embedded in Canadians' collective unconscious that it remains our country's constitutional – or even better, our *constitutive* – relationship. The covenant to link arms undergirds the Constitution (1982) of the country we call Canada, and, at the same time, it is a covenant powerfully evident in its repeated betrayal.

That's a complicated sentence, I know.

But covenants and their failure are constants in human experience. And the point of retelling the stories of both the original agreement, and its failure, is to haul the possibility of the first promise, even broken, back into the present, so we can't take either for granted – not the arrangement nor its failure. Retelling the story is a way of reanimating it, of returning us to good ways of thinking, to what Haudenosaunee people call *Ka'nikonhriyó'tshera't*, often translated into English as a "good mind." (Though "good mind" is very reductive of the layers of meaning in this word, which include wisdom, flexibility, magnanimity, self-discipline and generosity, as well as discernment, pragmatism, kindness, wit and a sharp sense of humour.) Repeating the story is a way to stop thinking of the original as frozen in the past, and therefore over and done with. Retelling puts it back in the flow of relationships that evolve over time, that are still possible today.

Because broken relationships – as any jilted lover, abandoned child or abused partner knows – are still relationships. Even if they trouble us. Especially if we repress them. We still live in the consequences of their betrayal.

The only way forward that I know of is to dust off the original ideals after each rupture, diagnose what went wrong, repair the harm that has been done and find ways to implement those missed possibilities in the everyday circumstances in which we live today. And to do this for the good of the future.

The good news is that this tradition of peacemaking stories is becoming better known today – and the different mindset it conveys is having wider and wider impact. Haudenosaunee leaders and speakers have retold this story of peace and its making right through the nineteenth and twentieth centuries. Some of the more recent retellings caught my attention when Haudenosaunee people proclaimed in April 2006 that Canadians needed to learn about the "Two Row Wampum" to deal with unresolved land disputes near the town of Caledonia, Ontario. The stories were retold again when Haudenosaunee people and their neighbours organized the "Honour the Two Row Campaign," in which they paddled canoes from Onondaga, New York, down the Mohawk River to the junction with the Hudson River near Albany, and from there down the Hudson to the United Nations in New York City between July 2 and August 10, 2013. Along the way, they spoke at meetings, information sessions and festivals in honour of the four hundredth anniversary of the ratification of the Two Row Wampum agreement between the Dutch and the Haudenosaunee. They insisted that it was high time to "repolish" the agreement now, in the twenty-first century.

More recently the story has been retold again in Canadian courts, such as on June 29, 2023, when Ontario Court Judge Gethin Edward cited the Two Row Wampum agreement to determine that Skyler Williams, charged by the Crown with mischief and failing to comply with a court injunction against blocking a developer from building homes on lands disputed by the Six Nations of the Grand River, was actually defending the Haudenosaunee public interest in accordance with Haudenosaunee law.[8] The story appeared again four months later in a Quebec Superior Court when on November 1, 2023, in a five-hundred-page judgment, Judge Sophie Bourque determined that "the Covenant Chain is an unextinct treaty of peace and friendship that contains a conflict resolution procedure, guaranteed by sec. 35(1) of the Constitution Act, 1982."[9] This second decision by a provincial court will need to be reviewed by the Supreme Court of Canada, since it has major implications for how we understand the Canadian Constitution, but it's a sign that after a long history of ignoring this storied tradition, the Covenant Chain–Two Row Wampum tradition is definitely making a comeback.

In this book, I retrace the ideals of good-minded relationships pictured in wampum belt representations of the *Tehontatenentshonteronhtáhkwa*, "the thing by which they link arms," and its supplement, the *Tékeni Teyohà:te*, "the two roads or paths."

These are complex, peacemaking concepts from Haudenosaunee languages such as *Kanyen'kéha* (Mohawk) that, when transliterated into English letters, look like very long words.

I know they are hard for English speakers to read and pronounce, but I think it's important to use them. Their very unfamiliarity to everyone who speaks a European language reminds us that they come from a different source, a different philosophy, a different worldview than the one Canadian and American societies usually look to for origins. They are not from the Enlightenment. Not from the traditions of Common Law. Or Civil Law. The Magna Carta. Or Christianity.

I call the set of protocols conveyed by the *Tehontatenentshonteronhtáhkwa* and *Tékeni Teyohà:te* the "Covenant Chain–Two Row treaty tradition," knowing full well that this does not capture the complex and evolving set of rules for conducting important agreements that have made some Indigenous leaders like Oren Lyons or Ovide Mercredi refer to it as the "grandfather of the treaties," while others have called it a "meta-treaty."[10]

"Grandfather of the treaties" emphasizes ancestry and genealogy, a multigenerational relationship that holds potential for the present day. Lawyer and long-time scholar of Haudenosaunee thinking and law Kayanesenh Paul Williams puts it this way:

> Euro-American [interpretations of treaties are flawed] by the thinking that a "treaty" is an individual transaction to be examined in isolation. *No.* In Haudenosaunee – and Anishinaabe, Wabanaki, and Crown-Imperial – terms, the individual transactions are part of a relationship. If the relationship is like a river of time, the individual transactions are like stones in its path, markers of particular events, and to focus only on them is to miss the whole point. The relationship is not a creature of English, French or Dutch law. It was created by taking the principles that brought the Haudenosaunee nations together in peace, *Kayanerenkó:wa*, and applying them to relations with the newcomers. To interpret that relationship "as the Indians would have understood it" requires knowledge of the legal system that is its ecosystem.[11]

The "ecosystem" of the treaties, the "river of time" – these phrases suggest the larger, evolving web of interdependencies in which individual treaty transactions occurred. To understand any given moment, we need to engage with it in the context in which it occurred, in the place or region from which it emerged and in its ongoing flow. I call this ecosystem, this flow, the Covenant Chain–Two Row treaty tradition.

Most Canadians, let alone Americans, have never heard of or seen the *Tehontatenentshonteronhtáhkwa*, most widely known as the "Covenant Chain of Friendship," or the *Tékeni Teyohà:te*, the "Two Row Wampum." Most have never seen images of these wampum belts such as those that appear in Rick Hill's photographs at the start of "Good Minds" or in his drawing on the cover of this book. The same was true for me until I moved to the region where the Six Nations Confederacy retains its largest population. I had never even heard of *kaswentha* (wampum belt), which, depending on who you ask, means "It flows," or "it holds something up (with flexibility, like a spine)," or "leftover ash, embers" in *Kanyen'kéha* language.[12]

It's important to realize that these fundamental principles for doing diplomacy, such as the linking arms by which Haudenosaunee Peoples adopted one another into a family of nations, had been developed long before Europeans arrived on Turtle Island. These principles flowed steadily from one treaty council to the next for hundreds of years. When Europeans arrived on the Atlantic coastlands and river systems, these rules of procedure were applied to negotiations with the newcomers from the moment of Cartier's landing in Gaspé in 1534 to the arrival of the Dutch on the Hudson River in 1609. They were also applied to the establishment of British colonial administration in New York in 1664 and onward throughout the War of 1812.

French, Dutch and British administrators, as well as Indigenous leaders from different nations and confederacies, consistently employed Haudenosaunee language and symbolism to make agreements of peace, cooperation and friendship. Because the Haudenosaunee Peoples were among the first Indigenous nations with whom the incoming Europeans had extended discussions when they arrived on this side of the ocean, their principles became the formal set of symbols and protocols for how Europeans learned to do diplomacy in North America. Of course, as the practice of treaty-making spread across the continent, different First Peoples in different regions introduced their own protocols and understandings to each distinct treaty's negotiations, but it nonetheless remains the case that the *colonial* officials – whether French, British, American or Canadian – would have heard the proposals and ideas of these various Indigenous leaders through the filter of their previous experience of Haudenosaunee protocols. That's why the Covenant Chain–Two Row tradition has been called the "grandfather of the treaties."

This means that Canada, as a jurisdiction,[13] emerged within the terms of Haudenosaunee ways of conducting important matters, and within Haudenosaunee procedures for building good minds and good relations. I have mixed feelings about speaking "as" a Canadian to Canadians in this book, but Canada as a nation-state has evolved into the legislative apparatus that determines what *juris* (laws) dictate human interactions with each other and with the environments in which I live. Of course, Haudenosaunee constitutional principles represent a profoundly different trajectory for what our nation-state might have become, and this is true in the emergence of the legislative structure of the United States as well.[14] Recovery of what Canada (and the U.S.) might have become is a major aim of this book.

If *kaswentha*, the name used to denote wampum belts, means "flow," like a river; if it's like a structure that holds things up, like a flexible spine; if it refers to embers that still glow in yesterday's ashes, then this evolving set of principles formed the jurisprudential ecosystem in which British North America and, therefore, Canada and the U.S. emerged as political and social bodies. These were the basic rules that had been originally set alight in Haudenosaunee civil, political and ecologically alert council fires long before Europeans arrived on Turtle Island. I think, therefore, that they not only set the groundwork for how "we" came to be here – newcomers and Haudenosaunee people alike – but that they point out good ways for us to live together here long into the future.

Linking Arms in the Face of Despair

The origin story of linking arms, later known as the Covenant Chain of Friendship, occurred right in the face of brutality. Very often, our colonial fascination with that early violence and treachery has buried the story of peacemakers like Kiotsaeton. Yet, despite its memory being actively suppressed by successive British and Canadian administrations, Canada and Canadians have never extricated ourselves from the Linked Arms, the officially agreed-upon relationship of the Covenant Chain and the Two Row Wampum, in which the groundwork for this country was laid.

But having suppressed this story, we Canadians live in a state of semi-consciousness. We are aware that things are wrong – aware that the land on which we live is bloodstained – yet unaware that it also carries the story of peace. The result is a state of haunted knowing *and* ignorance, knowing-and-not-knowing ourselves as Canadians; knowing-and-not-knowing where we live. When this haunted knowledge is too troubling, we revert to a state of "perverse ignorance," as Chickasaw scholar Eber Hampton names it, refusing to understand how we truly came to be here under the guise of denial.[15] In such a state, we can only replicate the violence our ancestors visited upon our unrecognized allies and friends.

Despite this denial and suppression – no, *because* of it – I have come to believe that the principles conveyed in the *Tehontatenentshonteronhtáhkwa* (Linked Arms, Covenant Chain) and *Tékeni Teyohà:te* (Two Row) can lead us back through the confusion of haunted knowing, of perverse ignorance, to the three principles at the heart of the Covenant Chain–Two Row treaty tradition, what Haudenosaunee people call *ka'nikonhriyó'tshera't*, the "even-tempered, quick, and well-fed mind" from which we can generate *ka'shatsténhsera*, the "force, capacity, and creative power" to build a culture of *skén:nen*, "peace, health, and harmony" – three principles that have sometimes been translated as righteousness, power and peace.[16]

This book, then, is for people who, like me, find themselves in the twenty-first century fighting despair on many fronts. Despair over how to repair the harm of our repressed and repressive past. Despair over a viable future. We would like to join the peace-seekers under the sails stretched over the courtyard at Trois-Rivières when, today, young Haudenosaunee stand by the barricades facing Canadian police to defend the remnants of their land. We would like to paddle on the crystal waters of the Fleuve Saint-Laurent that were greeted and thanked in Kiotsaeton's song. We long to clear them of the mercury and E. coli and particles of plastic that now choke anyone, human or animal, who drinks the water. Industrial Growth Society, powered by fossil fuels, is quickly generating rapid climate change with its extreme wildfires, freak hurricanes and unseasonable flooding. Global capital's hypermobility transmitted the quickly mutating Covid-19 virus around the world, throwing us, ironically (for all its mobility), into physical and social isolation. We fear revelations in the media of things we already know – that ground-penetrating radar will reveal thousands more unmarked graves of children buried on the sites of Indian Residential Schools, that another white policeman will be found innocent after taking the life of another young Black or Indigenous person, that more land defenders will be arrested at the site of another pipeline, real estate development or clear-cut old-growth forest.

There are so many causes for grief, for despair.

In times where despondency seems to have the upper hand, I am fascinated to know that wampum, Kiotsaeton's "colliers de pourcelaine," were invented to deal with grief, confusion and despair.

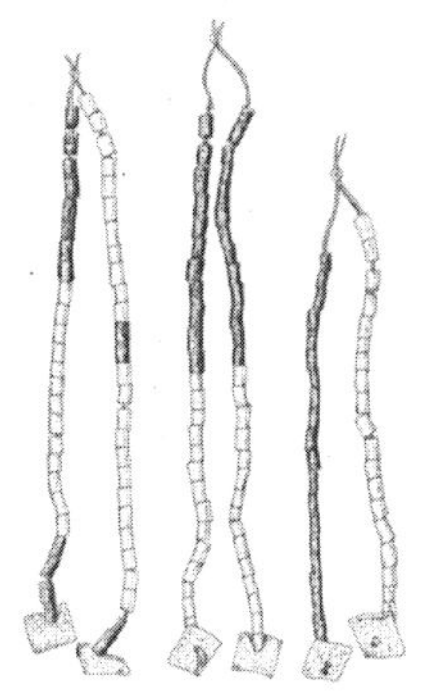

Chapter Two

Introducing Wampum

There is another story about peacemaking in this region that is much, much older than Kiotsaeton's visit to Trois-Rivières. This story is so old that nobody knows exactly when it occurred. Some have guessed a thousand years ago. Some even longer ago than that. I've encountered several versions, but the common thread of the story runs like this.

The people who lived south of Onyatarí:yo, the beautiful lake, lived in dark and troubled times. It was dangerous to leave your home for fear of war parties, raids, murder. Terrified villagers fashioned log palisades around their clustered longhouses. They chiselled the tops to sharp points to ward off anyone who might try to scale these rough walls. Fear and suspicion occupied the people's minds, despite the tallest and thickest defences. Tending the fields of corn, beans and squash, women kept an eye peeled to the margins of the dark woods, their children ready to flee to the palisades at the first flicker of human movement in the shadows. It is said that there were cannibals. No person could live secure. Death could arrive at any time.

There was a man, known as the "The One Who Lives Alone," Atotarhonh (sometimes spelled Atotáhrho or Tadodaho, depending on which language or translator you get the story from). This man's powers so bent him that his body was crooked, his skin as tough and dry as scales. His hair twisted and writhed like snakes. It was whispered that he had so much power that his mockery alone could kill you. Birds that flew over his isolated lodge on a hill by a swampy lake would drop like stones out of the sky.

Atotarhonh personified the terror of those times. His was the most dramatic example of the distorted, bitter minds that were widespread among the people in those days.

Just when things were most horrifying, a handsome Wendat man paddled a white stone canoe across the bright blue waves of the beautiful lake. On shore, he travelled on foot through the woods to the farm fields close outside the palisades of the longhouses south of Onyatarí:yo. Approaching town after fortified town, he boldly sang the songs of greeting, attracting sentinels to the edge of the woods, where he politely asked to meet each settlement's leaders. He suggested that people need not live in fear of one another. Despite generations of violence, he said, despite bloodletting and treachery between one community and the next, there were methods to avoid the endless cycles of vengeance and reprisal. The Creator had fashioned the beings on Mother Earth in such a way that human people could use their minds to reason together, to develop orderly techniques to discuss problems, to calm the panic within and develop *ka'nikonhriyó'tshera't* – a good, balanced mind. With this Good Mind, people could find the strength to build harmony with one another and live in peace.

He had a name, but he came to be so revered that the People ended up simply calling him the Peacemaker.

Central to the Peacemaker's message were the three principles known in *Kanyen'kéha* language as the good thinking of *ka'nikonhriyó'tshera't* that gives communities *ka'shatsténhsera*, the coherent power to get things done, and therefore produce *skén:nen*, peace. The way these principles relate to one another, and how people apply them, constitute the core principles of the Peacemaker's *Kayanerenhtserakó:wa*, which has become known as the Great Law of Peace.

The Peacemaker's ideas seemed too good to be true. Given the climate of fear and distrust, people were doubtful. They posed many questions and tests of his character, but he was patient and convincing, and eventually many villagers, beginning with an influential woman named Jigonsaseh in Cayuga or Tsikónhsase in Mohawk and later a male leader called Ayonwátha (meaning "He Keeps Awake," also spelled Aionwahta, Hayéwáthaˀ or Hiawatha), accepted the handsome messenger's ideas. These new principles burned brightly within them, and they joined the Peacemaker in spreading them among the five nations whose territories spread along the skinny fingers of lakes that defined the country south of Lake Onyatarí:yo. Some say it took years of itinerant travel and meetings, but people were gradually drawn to this message of peace. It tasted like nourishment, felt like a salve and grew more and more elaborate as the Peacemaker added new explanations and examples through his conversations with frightened, embattled people in nation after nation along his journey. Each time a new nation accepted the Peacemaker's ideas, they added a rafter to the Longhouse of Peace. But the house-building did not come easily.

The wizard Atotarhonh hated Peacemaker's message of *ka'shatsténhsera, ka'nikonhriyó'tshera't* and *skén:nen*. He feared what would happen to his power over people if they developed their own self-confidence and capacity, if they operated from good minds and character, and if they cultivated the ability to live in peace among themselves. He liked control. He wanted people to remain afraid of one another, afraid of him. He resisted Peacemaker's ideas of well-reasoned cooperation and discussion aimed at reaching consensus, because anxious, isolated people were easier to manipulate. He resented losing power over people like Ayonwátha, who was always wide awake and one of the Peacemaker's most energetic followers.

And so, darkly, disaster struck. It's an important part of the story. Rather than trying to tell it myself, I'll turn to an English translation, painstakingly made by Hanni Woodbury in the 1980s, of how chief John Arthur Gibson told it in Onondaga language, spelling Hayę̨hwathaˀ the Onondaga way, to the anthropologist Alexander Goldenweiser in 1912:

John Arthur Gibson's Story of Ayonwátha and the Origin of Wampum

Thereupon Hayę̨hwatha?'s daughter, the eldest, became ill and shortly she died. Thereupon Hayę̨hwatha? became mournful, at the loss of one of his daughters, two of whom survived, he having three children; but not long after that, the next one, in turn, became ill. Then Tekaihokę̨ and Tsha?tekaihwate? [leaders in the Mohawk village] decided they would help her to recover, as did the group of people who now helped by dispensing medicine by day and by night, supporting her to the extent that they were able, but in a short time, then, she died. Now, then, as to the chief, Hayę̨hwatha?, it broke his heart, and then Tekaihokę̨ and Tsha?tekaihwate? began to raise his spirits trying to console him . . .

Understandably, some Haudenosaunee people have distrusted ethnographers' transcripts like this one. I've heard Rick Hill, retired now from being Senior Research Coordinator at Deyohahá:ge: Indigenous Knowledge Centre at Six Nations Polytechnic, say that when he was first learning from traditional longhouse elders, they would say, "Don't write this down. As soon as you write it down, it loses its traditional authority."

"Now," he says, "I'm getting older. I tend to forget what I heard when I was young. I'm trying to write down as much as I can before I lose any more. I wish I had started writing sooner!" Jake Thomas before him had come to a similar view, creating controversy in the 1980s for performing and recording recitations of Haudenosaunee stories like this one in English. It's ironic, Rick observes, that the machinery of anthropology that did so much harm to Indigenous Peoples by removing Traditional Knowledge from Indigenous communities also produced the archives that are so necessary now for cultural memory and resurgence.

John Arthur Gibson continues:

Thereupon they decided, the young warriors, that they should divert Hayę̨hwatha?, and Tekaihokę̨ and Tsha?tekaihwate? sat down on top of

> the hill, and the crowd sat down there too as they began to play lacrosse, and while they were playing, Hayęhwathaˀ's young daughter, she was his last remaining daughter and she was pregnant, now she left taking a barrel along to go dipping water in the river; arriving at the river, she dipped water, turned back, and returned going back towards the house; but when she was half way home, they hollered loudly, saying, "Look at the animal that is flying," as they saw it coming down steadily from on high. Then in a little while it was flying very low. Thereupon the players and the crowd said, "It is beautiful, indeed [?[1]] let us catch it." Thereupon they ran, chasing it, the [?], and it went just where Hayęhwathaˀ's daughter stood. Then they ran there, chasing the bird, and they smashed into Hayęhwathaˀ's daughter, injuring her. In a very short time, she died, this, the last of Hayęhwathaˀ's three children. Thereupon Hayęhwathaˀ cried, saying "Now they are all gone, my children. So now I will leave, I will split the sky, going in an easterly direction [?] what happened to me."

In this passage, though the village community works together to distract the grieving father and surviving child with a game of lacrosse, the comfort of friends inadvertently tramples his last remaining family member. Ayonwátha splits the sky under whose unbroken expanse he and his family had previously lived. He stumbles off, alone, into the woods, heading blindly east. Not to the west, where the sun sets and day ends, but to the east where new cycles begin.

> Thereupon Hayęhwathaˀ departed going in an easterly direction; and he arrived at a place where he saw a cornfield and beside the field a lean-to; and when he got there he lit a fire. Thereupon he cut off a sumac branch, cored it, and cut it into short lengths, and then he strung up the sticks making several short strings. Thereupon he sat down next to the embers with his head bowed and gazed in front of him at the suspended rod, there where the short strands were strung up.

I imagine Ayonwátha in the shelter at the edge of the cornfield, sparking flint to dry grass and twigs, making a fire to warm his bones. Beside the flame, he watches, fascinated, as his hands carve brightly coloured sticks – red, green, yellow – of soft wood, sumac, into short lengths. His fingers work to keep themselves busy, the activity requires attention. His hands fashion an awl from something hard – oak, walnut or maybe antler – with the stone tip of his knife. They press the hard point of the awl to core out the soft inner pulp of each length of twig. Who knows how many hours later, he has a handful of twig tubes.

He watches his fingers take a length of sinew from his bag and thread it through these hollow tubes, securing each one with a knot, then adding another. After an unmeasured time, he sees he has fashioned multicoloured strands that he hangs over a rod, which he suspends between forked sticks thrust into the ground in the lean-to. It has taken hours to make each strand.

He has no idea how long he has occupied himself with cutting, coring, threading, tying off, suspending the strands. He stares at them as he completes each one and hangs them, wondering, on the rod.

Why is he doing this?

Indeed, while Ayonwátha is making these first wampum strings, the story falls silent about his grief – the deaths of his daughters, the split sky, the wandering through the woods. It is as if all these troubles are poured into the work of his hands, the concentration of his mind on sticks and strings and shapes and colours. His activity is instinctual. He does not seem to know why he did what he has done. It just happened.

He has been so occupied that he has not noticed the guardsman, who had been watching him from across the cornfield.

> Thereafter a man who was guarding the corn field sat down near the field by a log, and when he saw smoke rising from the lean-to, the man stood up, left, going slowly to the lean-to, and thought, "I will see who kindles the fire, causing smoke to rise." When he got near the house, he looked and saw a man inside the house; he was sitting near the fireplace, and in front of him was a suspended rod with short strands hanging down, and he was gazing at the hanging objects. Then the man moved away very slowly. Thereupon he returned, going straight to the place where the chief had his house, and arriving there, he said, "I will tell you about something surprising that happened . . ."

The sentinel of the cornfield reports to the village's headman what he had seen: the smoke rising from the lean-to, the stranger sitting within as if in a trance, gazing at strangely woven strings hanging from a rod. The foreigner's unresponsive state.

So the chief sends his sentinel along with another guardsman for backup, asking them to bring the stranger back to the village so he can explain himself. They go. But despite their speaking directly to Ayonwátha, despite offering the chief's invitation, even repeating it three times, the man remains impassive. Is he deaf? Why doesn't he respond?

They get a better look at the strands hanging from the rod in the lean-to. They think the sumac tubes are basswood. Then return to their village.

"He remains as before, inert," they tell their leader. "But the strands look as if they are made of hollowed-out tubes of basswood."

> Thereupon the chief said, "I know now what is needed, what it is that man is announcing with the short strands that are strung up. Now, I also will make them." Thereupon the chief cut off the tips of feathers and strung them up into short strands and said, "Now I am finished, the short strands are my words, and these will lead the man. This, moreover, is what you will take along, this. Thereupon you will hand him the short strands," he said, "and as you get there you will say to him, 'We have arrived with a message we have along inviting you to go to the chief's house, and this will lead you there, this short strand.' Thereupon you will hand it to him."
>
> Thereupon they departed going straight to the lean-to and as soon as they arrived, one of the men spoke, saying, "We have a message along, for he sent us to invite you to go to the chief's house. Moreover, this is what will lead you, the chief's word." When he handed it to him, the short strand, [Hayęhwathaˀ] immediately looked at it and began to speak, saying, "This is what is right and I accept it. Therefore I shall arrive at the chief's house, and he will ready himself."

The village chief intuits the meaning of Ayonwátha's strange behaviour. His intuition tells him to make a strand of wampum himself – this time adapting the hollow tips of feather shafts to fashion the tubes.

Those short strands initiate everything: in a moment of danger, the meeting of strangers, they initiate communication, invitation, council – civilization. They are the village's first step toward the Great Law of Peace. They seem to break the spell of the stranger's self-isolation and grief.

The short strand of feather tubes serves as a recognition of the sumac strands and creates a new kind of language. It forms a reply within this new language that conveys an invitation, a welcome.

In response, the stranger who had split the sky re-enters the possibility of civil society. He begins to speak calmly and reasonably. Just as the chief said, the short strands have become Ayonwátha's words, and they lead the grief-stricken man to their village.

> Then they assembled immediately and when they were ready and saw the man coming, the chief said, "Be prepared with a place for him to sit." Thereupon they made space, and when he arrived they showed him the seat that was ready, and there he sat down.
>
> Thereupon the chief stood up and said, "It is a wonderful thing that has happened, you arriving in the place where we live. Perhaps you have a message along; so that is what you will reveal, the kind of message you have, bestowing it unto us. So now we will listen well."
>
> Thereupon [Hayęhwatha?] stood up holding a short strand that was strung up and said, "Now today, is when we are meeting. So now you will all listen well to the kind of message I have along. This, indeed, is it:
>
> "Kanyę?ke Mohawk, our village, is where I come from; there the following amazing events took place. First, [the Peacemaker] arrived where we live, and he had news along of the Good Message, the Power, and the Peace."[2]

Reconnecting After Grief

According to Gibson's telling of this ancient story, then, wampum is invented by a man bewildered in grief. Ayonwátha creates the short strands without knowing what he is making. There is something about the process of making itself, the one-by-one, tube-by-tube work of his hands, that quiets his mind. And the chief, operating on instinct, mimics Ayonwátha's making, so that the strand he sends, adapted from materials he had ready to hand, enables him to convey respect for the man with the troubled mind. And that respect serves as an invitation to come and share his story.

One strand responds to another. Together they serve as a guide, an invitation, a response, a conversation, a sharing of understanding.

Ayonwátha joins the village headman at his council fire where all the people have gathered, and, holding the short strands he has made in his hands, he begins to tell his story. In John Arthur Gibson's telling, he starts not with the deaths of his daughters or his tortured heart and mind, but with the coming of the Peacemaker, with the message of *ka'shatsténhsera, ka'nikonhriyó'tshera't* and *skén:nen*.

The short strands in the grieving man's hands pace his story, as he recounts, hollow stick by hollow stick, the events that led him to this place and to this day. They are memory and reminder, order for his thoughts. They make a ritual, a ceremony of his journey of grief. As such, they enable civil conversation in a man whose mind had been confused by grief, which made him forget the protocols and become a threat to the security of a foreign village. The effort and concentration of fashioning these strands seems to have quieted the turbulence within Ayonwátha. Responding to the traveller's strands with strands of his own constitutes an imaginative listening from the chief, a willingness to enter into the symbol-making ritual of the stranger, that attracts Ayonwátha to conversation, invites him gently to break the self-imposed quarantine of devastation, to clear his troubled mind.

From this moment, *kaswentha* (belts or strings of wampum) evolved. At first Ayonwátha had used hollowed-out sticks, then the Oneida chief responded with lengths of feather tubes. Later in the Goldenweiser-Woodbury transcription, Gibson tells how Ayonwátha used freshwater mollusk shells instead of sticks or feathers to make the strands, and we know that, eventually, the Haudenosaunee traded with east coast Wampanoag Peoples so they could make "wampum" beads from the bone-dense white of whelk and dark purple of quahog shells that live to this day in the sand of the salt sea. These beads would have been the version of wampum witnesses like Father Vimont saw Kiotsaeton hang up on the cord one after another in 1645. When they saw how important wampum was to conversing with the Peoples of the northeast, the newcomers introduced materials of their own – porcelain, Venetian glass, which could be mass-produced – to make the beads. So the materials from which wampum is made have changed over time, but the original impetus, the original intent remains essentially the same:

To generate orderly, reasonable conversation between strangers, between those in grief and those who wish to hear their story and understand. To bring together those who have been separated with those who have gathered at the council fire. To generate a ceremony of condolence for those lost in grief. To inaugurate civil conversation during a time of suspicion, powerful emotion, unpredictable violence. Wampum clarifies. It is a truth-teller, so it has been used to declare war, just as it has been used to establish peace. Either way, it's about speaking clearly, ensuring both sides understand what's being said, opening the path to active, agile minds. It launches these things from an act of creative concentration as the bewildered, troubled mind fashions one hollowed-out twig or shell bead and then another, step by slow step, until the thoughts, the words, can settle into an orderly pattern, one that can be repeated, this time with "beads" made from the listeners' medium, as a kind of call-and-response, one strand responding to and inviting another. This is the origin and purpose of *kaswentha*.

Chapter Three

Introducing Myself

My crash course on wampum and the Covenant Chain–Two Row tradition was launched when I walked into work the morning of April 20, 2006. The beautiful spring morning was rinsed with birdsong and a light breeze that carried the green tang of buds swelling on tree branches. I crossed the bridge over Cootes Drive and, as I turned the corner at Mary Keyes Residence, I was startled to see thirty-some police cars parked behind the six-storey dormitory on the west side of the McMaster University campus.

The Police on Campus

Oh, I thought to myself, *the students have emptied the residences now that exams are done, and the police are using Mary Keyes for some kind of conference or convention.*

It wasn't until later in the day that Haudenosaunee colleagues told me that the two hundred Ontario Provincial Police officers who had raided the site of a land dispute near the town of Caledonia, half an hour south of campus, had been barracked at my university. During the early morning raid, OPP officers tased, manhandled and arrested Haudenosaunee elders, women and men at a real estate development called Douglas Creek Estates. This was land Six Nations folks insisted they had never given up. For a week or so, it was not safe for my Haudenosaunee friends and colleagues to cross the lines and come into their jobs on campus.

Until that day, I had felt that white Canadian academics like me who are inclined to support Indigenous justice do more harm than good by researching Indigenous topics. The barracks on campus changed my mind.

You see, I was born and raised outside of Canada, the son of Canadian evangelical missionaries who spent their working years living in Ethiopia.[1] We spoke in our family of "home," by which my parents meant Canada, but it was a home where I had never lived full time until I finished high school at a boarding school in Kenya in 1979.

High school had been rocky, to say the least. A military coup had removed Ethiopia's Emperor Haile Selassie from his throne in 1974, and the jostling between military divisions meant armoured personnel vehicles patrolled the streets at nights and people's corpses lay bleeding on the roadside in the mornings. The school I had gone to in Addis Ababa was suddenly confiscated by the junta for a military hospital, and so I went to live with family friends in Calgary, Alberta, while my parents searched for a spot in the closest boarding school for missionaries' children in Kenya. After completing high school in Kenya, I came to live in Canada at age eighteen. I was glad for safety, for predictable order, for calm.

At the University of Regina, I learned in an English 100 class that I liked reading and discussing stories, poems and plays. I had not known this about myself before, at least not in a serious way. I was the first person in my family to go from high school to university, and this kind of education was all new to me.

During my master's degree in the mid-1980s, I got a job teaching first-year English at what was then called the Saskatchewan Indian Federated College (today, First Nations University of Canada). I found Indigenous writers like Leslie Marmon Silko, N. Scott Momaday, Simon J. Ortiz, Lee Maracle, Jeannette Armstrong and Louise Erdrich compelling as I prepared my classes at the SIFC, and I considered doing a PhD in Indigenous literature.

But two things happened. First was the land dispute at Kanesatake with the nearby town of Oka regarding the town's decision to build a golf course over a stand of pines and gravesite that flared into an armed standoff against the Quebec police and the Canadian army. The standoff exposed what I had not previously seen: the long-running violence that simmered under Canada's façade of peace, order and good government. Indigenous Peoples were and are required to live in crushing injustice. The unmarked graves at residential schools, the lands expropriated by legal chicanery such as at Oka, the mercury poisoning the people at Grassy Narrows, the PCBs upriver at Akwesasne – these horrors were well-known in Indigenous communities.

Second was the widespread debate over cultural appropriation. Just as I was completing my master's degree in literature, a media firestorm spread across the country in the aftermath of the Calgary Winter Olympics of 1988. Calgary's Glenbow Museum had hosted an exhibition of Indigenous "arts and artifacts" during the Games. Its curators were shocked by the country-wide Indigenous protest against the exhibition. Many of the works on display, Indigenous folks said, were sacred objects, not "artworks."

The conflict revealed cultural incommensurabilities, different worldviews, that clashed in what was meant to be a moment of Canadian national celebration.

The context widened: Indigenous scholars and writers noted how white folks regularly raided Indigenous culture for their stories. Not only did these raids tend to misrepresent Indigenous people, but they also took up all the airspace so Indigenous artists, writers and thinkers had a hard time placing their work. As a result, during the cultural appropriation debates, nationally and internationally renowned white writers like W.P. Kinsella and Anne Cameron were publicly asked to stop writing Indigenous stories.[2]

This firestorm made me reconsider my ideas for a PhD topic. I decided that *respect* meant "keep out." I would be ready to support Indigenous justice as an ally, but I would not research Indigenous subjects or teach classes specializing in Indigenous topics. There is a long history of white scholars misappropriating Indigenous Knowledge and building their own academic careers as "Indian experts."[3] For this reason, Māori scholar Linda Tuhiwai Smith famously wrote, "'research' is probably one of the dirtiest words in the Indigenous world's vocabulary."[4] I did not want to become an exploiter of Indigenous culture and lifeways. Instead, I completed a PhD on the literatures of migration, a topic closer to my own experience of moving from Addis Ababa to Ontario and then Saskatchewan and Alberta. And it was with a PhD on migration writing in Canada, then, that I came to work at McMaster University.

Their "Problems" Are Our Problems

The police on campus in 2006 made me change my mind. Earlier that year, a group of young women from Six Nations Reserve, just a half-hour's drive south of Hamilton, had expressed concern about the Douglas Creek Estates housing development. The Haudenosaunee had long insisted that this particular stretch of land along Highway 6, which used to be known in the nineteenth century as the Plank Road from Lake Ontario to Lake Erie, had been removed from Six Nations by suspicious means back in the 1840s. The young women called for a resolution to the land dispute before building could continue. When distributing leaflets to passing cars didn't stop the bulldozers from entering the survey to begin construction, the protestors occupied the site and stood in front of the mammoth scraper blades, bringing work to a halt. They then set up lawn chairs around a firepit to guard against the return of the construction crews.

They did this in February, the coldest time of the year in this area. They were determined. They watched the steam rise as they exhaled into the sub-zero nights from their snowmobile suits and sleeping bags.

Predictably, the developer applied for and received a court injunction to have the occupiers removed, and, after the occupiers refused to leave, early in the morning of April 20, the two hundred Ontario Provincial Police officers armed with tasers, tear gas and M-16s arrived from their temporary barracks at my university to remove them by force. During the resulting melee, so many families from the reserve made their way onto the site that the police finally withdrew. After some months of stalemate, the Province of Ontario eventually purchased the site from the developer to hold it in trust until a resolution could be found.[5]

Almost two decades later and no resolution has emerged. Nor are any negotiations underway to find one.

The Caledonia conflict challenged my "keep out" approach to Indigenous relations. The university's hosting of the police on campus drove the point home: There is no safe, respectful place where we Canadians can stand in a kind of "serene contemplation" of the struggles of Indigenous Peoples as somehow "their problems" and not our own.[6] The ground we make our lives upon is shared ground – one social, economic and ecological home. There is nowhere in Canada outside our relationship with Indigenous Peoples. April 20, 2006, showed me that all institutions in our society, including apparently "neutral" ones like the university, are already invested in that relationship. There are no bleachers for spectators to watch from, uninvolved.

At my workplace, for instance, our university's awareness – or lack thereof – of this relationship is conveyed in our curricular choices; for example, the fact that local Indigenous languages or history are not seen as subjects necessary to Ontario's school or university curricula. That ignorance enables our university administration to barracks the police so they can then tase and beat and arrest Haudenosaunee people who were simply asking governments to clarify the provenance of disputed land. It is this ignorance that then expresses shock when the barricades go up to stop construction. This perverse ignorance produces the surprise of Canadian homebuyers who purchase a home in a development built on disputed land, within a land title registry system that does not track Indigenous interests, if anyone bothers to check. The same kind of oblivious denial characterizes other Canadian institutions, from our legal and medical systems to our chambers of worship and commerce, not to mention gas utilities, public parks or even grocery stores.

Each of these sectors of our lives is always and already invested in our relationship with Indigenous Peoples. If we drive a car or heat our homes, then we're invested in the pipelines that run through traditional Indigenous territories and threaten the watersheds. If we go to a Christian church, then we are connected to the Christian suppression of Indigenous languages and culture in the Indian residential schools, whether our particular denomination ran one of the schools or not. We can finesse the differences, say our denomination wasn't involved, that our church, or company, or university would never do that – but all these institutions occupy Indigenous lands and territories, and we continue to depend on resources drawn from them. Our very understanding of land – as an object you can own, as property, whose resources you can extract – denies Indigenous presence and Indigenous understandings of what it means to be a civilized society.

The Six Nations Polytechnic Partnership Belt given at the Champions for Change conference in 2014 to five universities, including McMaster, that joined the consortium that offers credit to students entering their institutions from SNP. The accompanying document explained: "In the Six Nations tradition, a Partnership is a relationship of respect, trust and mutual benefit. Each partner will receive a replica of a Covenant Chain Wampum Belt that features three human figures, one at each end representing SNP and our Post-secondary Partner, with a third figure in the middle representing the learners. This belt codifies the respectful and reciprocal nature of the partnership as it shows the fires of each institute connected by a path of peace, understanding, commitment and cooperation." (Wampum produced by Six Nations Polytechnic; photo credit: Georgia Kirkos, McMaster University Communications)

It's All About Relationships

Another experience occurred a year later that also helped me change my mind. I was asked by Haudenosaunee colleagues at McMaster University – Dawn Martin-Hill and Rick Monture – to serve as the Academic Co-Chair of McMaster's President's Committee on Indigenous Issues. The committee's responsibility was to serve as a liaison between Indigenous and university communities and to support the development of McMaster's Indigenous Studies Program. The committee had a community co-chair, Rebecca Jamieson, CEO and President of Six Nations Polytechnic.

Because of my earlier sense that respect means not doing research on Indigenous topics, all I knew about Haudenosaunee life was what I had read in the press about the Caledonia land dispute. I had served as faculty supervisor on Rick Monture's dissertation on a literary history of Six Nations, but I was very wet behind the ears when I attended my first President's Committee planning retreat at the Bear's Inn on the reserve.

I had been listening intently throughout the morning as people talked around the circle made up of the two professors, several contract lecturers and a couple of elders about challenges with staffing Indigenous Studies courses and the need for increasing the number of Indigenous professors at McMaster. I remember being startled when Dawn asked me what suggestions I had to offer. Aware of being new to the committee, I said, "It all depends on what the community sees as important."

At that, the elder in attendance from the Haudenosaunee Confederacy Council, Arnie General, leaned forward in his chair, clasped his hands over the head of his cane in front of him and said, "Well, I'm glad the professor has asked what we see as important. I think we've been making it pretty clear. We'd like our land back. All these other things are important – classes, languages, students and culture – but what we want is our land."

I had thought I was there to strategize with the committee about programs, curriculum, classes, students and scholarships. But Chief General cut through our university mindset to the heart of the matter: it's all about relationship – how we relate to land and therefore how we relate to one another. The reason to study, to learn, to communicate is to restore land to its rightful status and to establish just relationships on that land. We academics are so accustomed to living in the world of ideas; Arnie was reminding me and the others on the committee that we were from the university that facilitated the police who tried to remove Haudenosaunee people from their traditional lands. He was inviting me and the others on the committee into a real relationship, to link arms with him and the Haudenosaunee, to restore our original agreements with each other and with the lands where we live.

That was the first of many such invitations. A few months later, I attended the initial meeting to establish a new Indigenous research centre on the Grand River territory. Attending the meeting were Haudenosaunee leaders from Six Nations Polytechnic (Rebecca Jamieson, Linda Staats, Tracey Deer), community elders and recognized Knowledge Guardians (Hubert Skye, Lottie Keye, Ima Johnson, Tom Deer) and McMaster University faculty members (many of these Haudenosaunee themselves – Dawn Martin-Hill, Bonnie Freeman, Karen Hill, Rick Monture – while some of us non-Indigenous – William Coleman, not a relative of mine, and myself). The idea was that the centre would be housed and administered at Polytechnic, guided by traditional Knowledge Guardians and jointly seed-funded by McMaster and Six Nations Polytechnic.

The Knowledge Guardians suggested that the new Indigenous Knowledge Centre be named Deyohahá:ge:, which translates from the Cayuga language as "Two Roads or Paths."

Elders speak gently and quietly, and I had to lean forward to hear Lottie say the centre should work with the best of Haudenosaunee and Western methods to regenerate Six Nations knowledge for future generations. She and Ima and Hubert saw the ideas conveyed in the Covenant Chain–Two Row treaty tradition as essential to the operations of the Indigenous Knowledge Centre. It became our mandate to consider how the tradition of two peoples who had linked arms, two paths sharing the same direction, two vessels on the same river, might guide good relations between researchers based on the reserve and at the university.

Richard "Rick" W. Hill Sr., the Tuscarora artist and historian of Haudenosaunee cultural history, was appointed Senior Research Coordinator. And, in the years since 2007, he and Tanis Hill (administrator of Deyohahá:ge:, not a close relative of Rick) and I have hosted monthly seminars bringing together reserve-based and university-based scholars for conversations about the Covenant Chain–Two Row treaty tradition and how it might inform contemporary relationships between Haudenosaunee and Canadian people. Much of what I have learned about this tradition, then, has taken shape through our discussions in the monthly seminars of the Two Row Research Partnership.[7] Our seminar discussions have, in turn, been informed by the upsurge of Haudenosaunee thinkers' and writers' publications on Six Nations history, philosophy, law, environmentalism and culture of the last fifty years. These make up much of the bibliography for this book.

The point is that I have learned what I've learned about the Covenant Chain–Two Row tradition through these relationships that have extended almost two decades. Over those years, we've carried out different projects together, like creating a film to document the first ten years of Deyohahá:ge:'s existence, like Rick and I co-authoring an article on how the Covenant Chain–Two Row can guide university-Indigenous relations, or publishing a collection of essays by Deyohahá:ge:'s friends and neighbours about the history and ongoing influence of the Covenant Chain–Two Row Wampum tradition.[8] These relationships don't guarantee that what I have to say in this book "gets it right."

I am not some kind of expert. Nor am I an exception. I am not free from participating in the ongoing settler colonial system. Scholars like me, particularly social critics, can present ourselves as some kind of disembodied brains that float somewhere above the social system in which we are immersed. But: I drive a car. I own a home. I have a pension from working in a university. I pay taxes to the state that hires the police to raid the site of the land dispute. I walk around in a body and occupy space, land. I am grateful for my Christian upbringing, for the peace and prosperity I have enjoyed in Canada.

The Australian scholar Patrick Wolfe explains that "settler colonialism is a structure not an event."[9] If it's a structure of relations, rather than a past event, then I live within that structure and am not just an inheritor of past events.

I am an everyday person who is simply trying to find a better way forward from our current version of "Canada." An everyday person who thinks that you cannot absent yourself from a relationship that has utterly shaped your social and natural ecosystem simply by pretending it doesn't exist. Getting a court injunction each time that relationship asserts itself once again doesn't help.[10]

I am not an expert in constitutional law or a historian of colonial-era treaties. I am not a trained anthropologist with expertise in Haudenosaunee cultural or social systems. I've taken a *Kanyen'kéha* language class for beginners, but I'm only able to say a few greetings and introduce myself. My lack of fluency means I have no direct or sophisticated access to the oral history of the Covenant Chain–Two Row tradition whose protocols have been retained and passed down the generations by Haudenosaunee Peoples. As a neighbour, but not an insider to Haudenosaunee society and the ceremonial longhouse practices where cultural insight and ways of knowing are renewed and regenerated, I can only reflect upon and pass on what Haudenosaunee friends and colleagues have shared with me in their writing, conversations and public gatherings.

I identify with Ayonwátha, that figure at the edge of the cornfield, lost in the grief of what's happened, confused by the welter of traumatic history, a person whose sky has been split and has been lost in the dark woods and who intuits that the effort of threading one bead after another into a sequence will quiet the mind, open the path for new conversation, renew the effort to create words and conversation, the possibility of a liveable future.

I am a student of literature, a person fascinated by the power of words and stories. I am particularly interested in the Covenant Chain–Two Row Wampum tradition as a challenging companion to the Eurocentric book tradition that I love and in which I have been trained. I'm interested in what it means to learn to "read" the wampum narratives as ceremonial stories, as poetry, as jurisprudence, as a representation of the relationships our ancestors set out to clarify and establish.

I think of Kiotsaeton's dramatic speeches of 1645, retold by Père Vimont and Marie de l'Incarnation. I think of his brave greeting, "My Brothers, I have left my country to come and see you. At last I have reached your land. I was told, on my departure, that I was going to seek death, and that I would never again see my country. But I have willingly exposed myself for the good of peace." His words, and the hundreds of wampum speeches that resound throughout treaty council literature in the centuries that followed, are not just anthropological curiosities, but Canada's history plays, as far-reaching and complicated and profound as *Richard III* or *Henry IV*. History plays that chart a path to an alternative future.

I didn't grow up in Canada, and my ancestors only arrived here in the nineteenth century, but it doesn't matter when each of us newcomers came to Canada or America, whether our ancestors arrived on the ships with Jacques Cartier in 1534 or we arrived last week. Like the Dutch who ventured up the Hudson River into Haudenosaunee territory in the early 1610s, we may each be sailing in the vessel of our family background's unique set of culture, beliefs and laws – or we may think of ourselves as simply "Canadian" with no other homeland in our past – but by simply living here, we are sharing the river of life, the same interconnected environment that Kiotsaeton was urging his French and their Huron-Wendat allies to value and respect. My apparently fair-minded, supposedly neutral university still houses the police who raided Haudenosaunee territory – not in 1867 when Canada was being formed but now, in the twenty-first century.

So I've been made to realize that there is no neutral place where old, middle-aged or new Canadians can pose as uninvolved spectators of conflicts such as the one that is still simmering on the Plank Road lands at Douglas Creek Estates and its more recent iteration, 1492 Land Back Lane.[11] What I find fascinating about the Covenant Chain–Two Row treaty tradition is that, right from the beginning of wampum, it featured mutual involvement, an alliance based on call-and-response. The Oneida chief sending his strand of feather-tube beads in response to Ayonwátha's sumac ones. Couture responding, wampum by wampum, to Kiotsaeton's words.

No treaty is really an agreement if one party decides that the understanding, the interpretation, the application of that agreement is completely up to the other side. That would constitute a call with no response. This book is my attempt to respond, limited as I am, with words of my own and in the "porcelain" of my bookish, words-and-writing, English-language tradition. It's aimed primarily at my fellow Canadians, sitting on our side of the fire. I hope that it might spark others to respond, with words of their own. This book is my attempt as a white settler Canadian[12] to renew the possibility of alliance through trying to understand or interpret our original agreements, not from an official position, or even from extraordinary expertise, but from simply attending to the relationships that have come with the territory in which I live. Right here at the Head of the Lake, Onyatarí:yo, Ontario.

People who live in other regions will have other agreements, other treaty traditions to consider and renew. Any insights I have come from this place, from talking with friends and neighbours, from deciding not to ignore the huge amount of information hidden in plain sight. There are accounts of the Covenant Chain–Two Row treaty tradition everywhere, from the internet to the local library to government archives. It's really more a matter of choosing to learn than it is of digging up remote information.

The important thing is to testify to the relationship. The one that is ongoing. The one that linked arms in the face of violence and treachery. That sought a future built on Good Minds, the power to effect positive change, and to therefore set the terms for a culture of peace.

Haudenosaunee neighbours have given their lives to testify to this relationship. They persevered throughout generations of concerted efforts to suppress what they and their ancestors knew. Their determination has produced a new era in Haudenosaunee cultural resurgence. One that has blown open the doors of gatekeepers like William Fenton and produced an efflorescence of Haudenosaunee writing and expression that provides the potential for a renewed dialogue about the relationship between Haudenosaunee people and their neighbours. I could never have even imagined writing this book had this rich upsurge in Six Nations writing and thinking not provided the stimulus.[13]

This remarkable production of Haudenosaunee thinking and ideas calls for response. Like Kiotsaeton's delivery of seventeen collars of porcelain, this remarkable conveyance of words and presents calls for those of us gathered in the region to receive them, to turn them over in our hands and minds and to respond with words and gifts of our own. Learning about our basic agreements is a participatory thing, not reserved for "experts" – governments, lawyers or academic specialists. Otherwise, there will be no meeting of minds, no possibility of linking arms between neighbours, no direct agreement that has any power to generate peace, respect or friendship. My hope is that my effort in this book to learn about the Covenant Chain–Two Row way of making agreements will reintroduce readers to a method for making civil relations that was invented right here in the northeast of Turtle Island, one that made it possible for us to live here in the first place, and one that holds great potential for continuing to live here with good minds, friendship and peace.

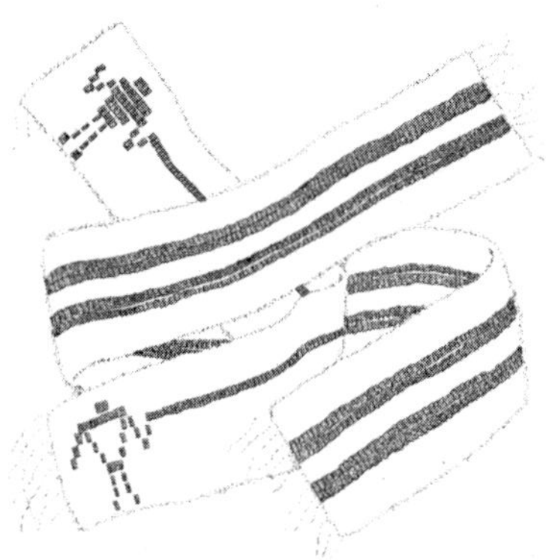

Part II

Histories

When they speak of the linked arms between themselves and Canada, Haudenosaunee speakers, activists and writers since the formulation of the Indian Act in the 1870s have emphasized the principle of two separate paths for Haudenosaunee and Canadian societies, sharing the same river, but never intersecting – the central principle of the Two Row Wampum. This image of autonomous paths for those who have linked arms helps resist Canada's ongoing efforts to disappear their Confederacy, culture, law and way of life.

Once Britain and – even more – Canada had decided that they could survive without the help of Indigenous allies, these colonial powers launched bureaucratic genocide campaigns against their former friends. They tried to disappear them as sovereign nations, as treaty partners with laws and cultures of their own, as Peoples, through "civil" methods such as "educating" their children, "protecting" them from colonial encroachment by "reserving" miniscule parts of their lands and "modernizing" their political institutions. The Haudenosaunee of the late nineteenth and early twentieth centuries saw that the Covenant of Linked Arms was being twisted into a deadly combination of assimilation and extermination, and they resisted these threats by insisting repeatedly on the autonomy of the two parties who had agreed to share the same river.

This is the version of the Covenant Chain–Two Row treaty tradition with which most people today are familiar.

As *Kanyen'kehàka* writer and researcher Amber Meadow Adams explained to me, the idea of separate paths for those who have linked arms has a precedent in the Creation Story. For in that story, the calm-minded Creator twin, Tharonhyawá:kon, known as the "Earth-Holder," soon realizes that his restless twin brother, Thawískaron, who is also known as "Flint," has the capacity to destroy or distort his beautiful creations, and that he must therefore protect the animals and plants and rivers he has made from his brother's troubling ways. Despite their being one family, despite having descended from the same Grandmother who fell to this earth from Sky World, Thawískaron tends to twist the beings of creation so that what was meant to support life and to make things flourish causes harm and destruction. Where Tharonhyawá:kon made juicy-tasting corn, Thawískaron makes thorns that prick your hands; where Tharonhyawá:kon made birds with bright feathers, Thawískaron makes bats with leathery wings and teeth; where Tharonhyawá:kon made smooth waterways for your canoe, Thawískaron throws in rocks and rapids that can break your vessel . . . or neck. So the One Who Holds the Earth places a river between his lodge and that of his brother to protect himself and his life-generating creations from his brother's harmful ways. Even in the cartography of Creation, Amber said, we see how people can have linked arms, can be of the same family and be involved in the same project of world-making, but it can become necessary to insist that they follow different paths, keep their culture, beliefs and laws – their behaviours and priorities – distinct. In this sense, she said, the Two Row Wampum is like an addendum or corrective to the Covenant of Linked Arms.

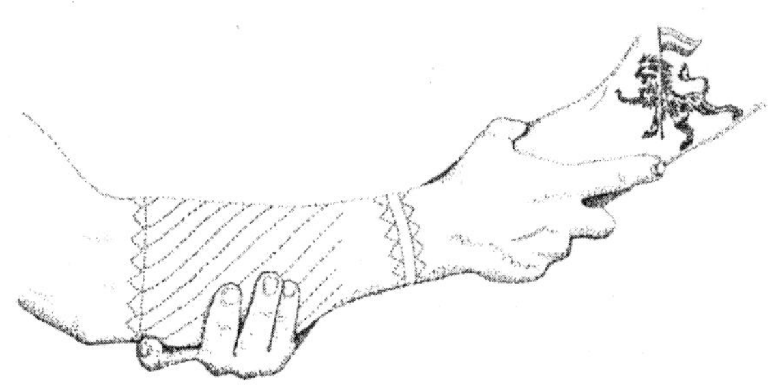

Chapter Four

Oral Histories of the Agreement

The thirty police cars at my workplace in 2006 pricked up my ears to news about the land reclamation at Douglas Creek Estates. In image after image, statement after statement in the news media, people involved with the reclamation pointed to the "Two Row Wampum" as the precedent for Haudenosaunee sovereignty in the face of intervention from the police, from Canada.

So, what is the "Two Row Wampum" agreement?

Jake Thomas's Oral Narratives of the Covenant Chain–Two Row

The most commonly quoted version of the agreement I encountered during and after the Caledonia land disputes in 2006 came from the speeches of Jacob "Jake" Thomas (1922–1998). An adjunct professor in Indigenous Studies at Trent University, a Cayuga speaker and a lifelong student of Haudenosaunee philosophy and culture, Thomas learned wampum history from his father, David Thomas, who in turn had learned it from his father.[1]

Below are two of Jake Thomas's orations in side-by-side format. I've chosen this two-column layout for a couple of reasons. First, I think seeing two versions side by side shows how consistent the principles laid out in Jake Thomas's two oral renditions are, despite his narrating them several years apart from one another and in rather different contexts. Second, this two-column format helps readers see that, while the main parts of the narrative are identical, minor points or phrases shift slightly from one rendering to the next. Even when both were spoken by the same person. This slight variation is typical of oral as compared to written narrative, because the setting of any speech makes the speaker emphasize certain elements of the traditional story to suit the moment or to catch the ears of the audience at hand, while the overall message remains the same. By presenting Thomas's two narrations side by side, even if they are by the same speaker and only seven or so years apart from one another, I'm wanting to highlight the *live* dynamics of oral narrative.

This approach will hopefully guard against the kind of forensic, "word-police" approach to interpretation that can make people grip a particular wording as if it were gospel. To hear these orations rightly, we need to hold the specific wording lightly, while we grasp the concepts or principles strongly.[2] We need to remember that the English version comes to us through translation, so the English connotations may be different from his Cayuga renderings, and, furthermore, his own Cayuga version is a translation at some point from the *Kanyen'kéha* Mohawk original, since it was Mohawks who first met the Dutch on what became known as the Hudson River. More than this, his oral speech has been translated again into writing, so that we cannot hear how he emphasized certain words, where he might have paused, nor can we read his body language, as Vimont read Kiotsaeton's in 1645. Wampum speakers choose their words very carefully, and they aim at verbatim accuracy, even as they are influenced by what they sense their listeners can understand, and so they shape their statements accordingly.

Jacob Thomas during a recitation of the Covenant Chain–Two Row agreement at Grand River in 1988. (Photo credit: Jacob Thomas Learning Centre)

The first of the two versions, printed in the left-hand column, was given to me by Rick Hill. He derived it from notes that Jake Thomas's friend Michael Foster[3] made during a recitation of the Covenant Chain–Two Row agreement that Thomas gave in Cayuga language to Edward Schreyer, Governor General of Canada, in the vice-regal setting of Rideau Hall in Ottawa in 1981. These were the days when Pierre Trudeau's government was preparing to "bring home the Constitution." Jake Thomas was one of nine Haudenosaunee leaders who made a delegation to the Governor General in order to remind the Crown's Canadian representative of the long-term relationship the Crown had formed with the Confederacy. Canada was about to affirm its Constitution, and the delegation knew it was a key moment when they might steer the newly-being-reconstituted Dominion away from denying its founding relationship and back to a renewal of the alliance with its independent Haudenosaunee neighbours that had been crucial to its own conception.

Grand River Chiefs meeting with Governor General Edward Schreyer to polish the chain, 1981. Vincent Walker, Onondaga; Jake Thomas, Cayuga; Oliver Jacobs, Onondaga; Peter Sky, Onondaga; Harvey Longboat, Cayuga; Barry Longboat, Seneca; Tom Longboat Jr., Secretary; Bob Jamieson, Translator; Allen MacNaughton, Mohawk. (Courtesy Rick Hill. Photo by Michael Foster. Thomas is second from left.)

The second version I am presenting here was jointly developed by Jake Thomas and a second Haudenosaunee leader, Huron Miller. I have placed this version in the right-hand column. It was first published in Rick Hill's article "Oral Memory of the Haudenosaunee" in 1992. This second recitation took place seven years after the first in a ceremony at Grand River in 1988, when eleven wampum belts were returned from the Smithsonian Institution's Museum of the American Indian/Heye Foundation to the Grand River Confederacy.[4] The 1988 return marks a key moment in the resurgence of Haudenosaunee knowledge and governance as a result of the work of Six Nations scholar-activists such as Oren Lyons, Kayanesenh Paul Williams, Chief Irving Powless Jr., Rick

Hill and others who asked public and private museums and archives around the world to return wampum that had been removed from the Haudenosaunee in the late nineteenth and early twentieth centuries.

Thomas's Recitation to Schreyer (1981)[5]

The One who dwells in the sky did not intend people who move about on earth to torment one another.

As the whites and the Onkwehonweh[6] began to see each other, they began to talk with one another about not being of one mind, and there was no love between them. People were not happy as they moved about, and often were trying to do away with each other.

It will put your minds at ease (that we still remember these words). We are being pressed down upon by our white brother.

When our white brothers first arrived in our lands, we completed the agreements. They made settlements nearby where our ancestors were living. The whites and Onkwehonweh began talking for quite some time about how they could make peace, when they joined their arms.

Thomas-Miller Version, from 1988 speech at Six Nations[7]

The Onkwehonweh of the Haudenosaunee made a treaty with the early Dutch when they came to this continent. The Onkwehonweh lived very happily, enjoying life the way the Creator intended. The Onkwehonweh was totally dependent on nature until the coming of the Dutch people. The Dutch learned the customs, art work, and how to get along with the Onkwehonweh. They became friends and decided to make a treaty and agreed to continue in friendship. Then the time came when the Dutch said, "We shall pronounce ourselves in friendship."

The white man said, "If we do not do something, it will always be this way. Is it possible to form an agreement so we can live in peace?"

The Onkwehonweh replied, "What you have in mind is good. The Creator did not intend that we would live in discord, and we should respect one another."

The Onkwehonweh called the Dutch "white people." The Onkwehonweh held a special council informing the people that the time had come for the white people and the Onkwehonweh to continue as friends so that all people may walk upon this earth in peace and love one another. Both races understood this kind of friendship and agreed that the day had come to make friendship.

The white man said: "We will do this right (make it right/legal), so both our people will know what we agreed on. First thing, we will each make records for ourselves, so the later generations will know this."

The Onkwehonweh replied, "He who dwells in the sky [The Creator] gave us wampum to keep track of things we want to perpetuate."

The white man responded, "I will do what is right for me, make it legal by writing it down. Thus people on both sides will know it."

They began to develop some rules to go by.

The Onkwehonweh said, "We now have an understanding about our friendship."

The whiteman replied, "I will put our friendship in writing."

The Onkwehonweh replied, "This is good, but one thing we must remember, paper will not last. We must find a way to make sure that the friendship will be passed on to the next generation."

They agreed.

The white man asked, "What symbol will we go by?"

The Mohawk man replied,

The whiteman said, "How is the Onkwehonweh going to describe our friendship?"

"First, we agree to have friendship and love as the Creator intended. In this way, we will have peace. This will be symbolised by the earth, the Creator's creation, and its happenings.

"Second, we'll take each other by the hand (take a hold of each other's arm)."

The Onkwehonweh replied, "We must thank the Creator for all his creations, and greet one another by holding hands to show the Covenant Chain that binds our friendship so that we may walk upon this earth in peace, trust, love and friendship, and we may smoke the sacred tobacco in a pipe which is a symbol of peace."

The white man then asked, "By what term of relationship will we go by? I will call you my 'child.'"

However, the Onkwehonweh replied, "This is not proper for a father can control the child. What do you think if we addressed each other as 'brother'?"

The whiteman said that he would respect the Onkwehonweh's belief and call him "son."

The Onkwehonweh replied, "We respect you, your belief, and what you say. You pronounced yourself as our father and this we do not agree with because the father can tell his son what to do, and can punish his son. We suggest that we call each other brother."

The Dutch man asked, "How will we seal the relationship?"

To which the Mohawk man replied, "We will seal the matter by taking each other by the hand. And we shall remain brothers for as long as the earth lasts."

They then took each other by the hand to confirm the love/respect for one another so that there will always be peace.

The Onkwehonweh stated,

The whiteman said, "The symbol of this Covenant is a three-link chain which binds this agreement made by us, and there is nothing that will come between us to break the links of this chain."

The Onkwehonweh replied, "The first link shall stand for friendship, the second will stand for our good minds, and the third link shall mean there will always be peace between us. This is confirmed by

"We will smoke the sacred tobacco that the Creator made for us, and pass a pipe around so that smoke will rise and pierce the sky. The Creator will then bear witness to our agreement.

"I will add iron to this to make a three-link chain. The first link will stand for friendship. The second link will stand for our both having good minds. The third link will mean there will always be peace.

us." The Onkwehonweh said, "This friendship shall be everlasting and the younger generation will know and the rising faces from Mother Earth will benefit by our agreement."

"The agreements will benefit (meaning they belong to) the faces deep underground (the generations to come that the Creator determined will be taking their place on the earth).

"We obtain our happiness from what he has planted, and there is no end to new life and to the faces coming from deep underground."

The whiteman said, "What symbol will you go by?"

The Onkwehonweh replied, "When the Creator made Mother Earth, man was created to walk upon the Earth to enjoy all nature's fruits, saying that no one will claim Mother Earth except rising faces which are about to be born. We will go by these symbols: As long as the sun shines upon this earth, as long as the water still flows, and as long as the grass grows green at a certain time of the year, that is how long our agreement will stand. Now we have symbolized this agreement and it shall be binding forever, as long as Mother Earth is still in motion. We have finished and we understand what we have confirmed and this is what our generation should know and learn not to forget."

"We both have our own authority – strength/power. We have our respective beliefs, from the same Creator. We have our respective laws. We do not have authority over each other or [each other's] kind of culture."

The Onkwehonweh stated, "The Creator gave us a canoe and you a boat (ship). We will take our vessels to the water and put them in the water, each in their distinctive way. Our people will follow the vessels in the water. We will place them a certain distance apart, but will line them up so they will always be parallel."

The white man stated, "This is an excellent way to represent our relationship."

The Onkwehonweh stated, "Now we have laid our vessels out, parallel to each other, so too it is with our beliefs. My beliefs will be in my canoe, yours will be in your boat. I will also put my laws in my canoe, and you will put your laws in your boat. Our authority, beliefs and laws will be dropped into our vessels. That is how people will know it, by the likeness to two paths."

The Mohawk man stated, "We will make a wampum belt of that likeness so people will know what

The whiteman said, "I confirm what you have said and this we shall always remember. What we do about our own ways of belief, we shall both respect having our own rights and power."

The Onkwehonweh replied, "I have a canoe and you have a vessel with sails and this is what we shall do. I will put in my canoe my belief and laws. In your vessel you shall put your belief and laws. All my people will be in my canoe, your people in your vessel. We shall put these boats in the water and they shall always be parallel, as long as there is Mother Earth, this will be everlasting."

we will go by. The Two Paths (wampum) is our way of keeping records. We both put our beliefs in our respective boats, and our people too.

"Perhaps in the days to come, some of your people would like to get into my canoe. But I don't think they would like the ways of my canoe." Moreover, he said that the canoe travels quite fast.

"Perhaps a number of my people would like to get into your large boat, because of its size. They might like being in your boat.

"People who get into your boat will be guided by it. Your people who will get into the canoe will be guided by the ways of the canoe."

The whiteman said, "What will happen if your people will like to go into my vessel?"

The Onkwehonweh replied, "If this happens, then they will have to be guided by my canoe."

Now the whiteman understands the agreement.

The white man asked, "What will happen in the days to come if a big storm comes up, and someone has a foot in each vessel, and the vessels are driven apart? I believe that person will fall between them."

The Mohawk man responded, "Yes, this will happen. We cannot take responsibility for this. Only the Creator has the power to save that person."

The whiteman said, "What will happen if any of our people may someday want to have one foot in each of the boats that are parallel?"

The Onkwehonweh replied, "If this so happens that my people wish to have their feet in each of the two boats, there will be a high wind and the boats will separate and the person that has his feet in each of the boats shall fall between boats, and there is no living soul who will be able to bring them back to the right way given by the Creator but only one – the Creator himself."

Both parties agreed, "People will be bound by what we have agreed upon. We will abide by our agreements as long as . . . the sun always makes it bright on earth; the waters flow in a certain direction; and the wild grasses grow at a certain time of year."

That is what they did when they made the agreement, and so our minds will continue to be. The white man affirms all that was agreed upon. The Onkwehonweh said they have made a wampum record, called the Two Paths, so our people would have the means to know what was agreed upon.

The whiteman said, "I understand. I confirm what you have said, that this will be everlasting as long as there is Mother Earth. We have confirmed this and our generations to come will never forget what we have agreed. Now it is understood that we shall never interfere with one another's belief or laws for generations to come."

It may happen in the days to come that dust will accumulate on our agreements – the symbols of our alliance. If that happens, it will be possible to polish them again, and wipe the dust from the agreements. We will renew our relationship and the agreements we have made. There will always be people to act as interpreters for us. We will appear the way we did when we first met. All of our people

The Onkwehonweh said, "What we agreed upon shall renew this every so often so that the Covenant Chain made between us shall always be clean from dust and rust. We shall renew our agreements and polish the Covenant and when we get together to renew our agreements we shall have interpreters. We will dress the same way as we met so that our people will know who we are.

shall always know of it. And there will be peace in the days to come.

I will put on my buckskin clothing, you will dress the same way you dressed when you first came to our people." They both confirmed this. So they completed the treaty of the two parties.

In the 1988 ceremony at Grand River, Jake Thomas would have been aware of a complicated audience that included Six Nations listeners, along with Foundation officials and influential scholars like William Fenton who had been opposed to the release of wampum from museums. Some of the audience may have been politely bored officials. Haudenosaunee members of his audience might have known the oral history of the agreements from family or clan sources, while others may have heard of these agreements previously but were only hearing them in any detail for the first time. Some of his audience who were fluent in Haudenosaunee languages questioned the rightness of Thomas's presenting the story of the agreement in English, while others did not have their ancestral languages and were grateful to hear the narrative in words they could understand. In the 1981 narration, the governor general, by contrast, not living in Haudenosaunee territory, or even particularly knowledgeable about Haudenosaunee history, would have needed context to understand Thomas's narrative. Here is how non-Indigenous academic Kathryn Muller describes the 1981 scene:

> As discussions surrounding the patriation of the Constitution unfolded between Canada and Great Britain, Schreyer met with some Haudenosaunee chiefs in his Rideau Hall residence in Ottawa to read the Friendship and Two Row wampums. Renowned chief and ceremonialist Jacob Thomas and his wife Yvonne had travelled from Six Nations to join their colleague and friend Michael K. Foster of the Canadian Museum of Civilization and they met others from Six Nations, Oneida of the Thames and Akwesasne at Rideau Hall, the governor general's residence . . . As the designated speaker for the event, Thomas lit his pipe upon arrival to help enhance the sincerity and power of his abridged wampum message;

> although Thomas had recently recorded a lengthy reading of the Two Row and Friendship belts with Foster, such meetings with government officials usually did not allow for such an intensive recitation. Thomas would therefore rely upon a shortened version prepared by his late father, Dawit [David], also renowned for his knowledge of traditional languages and culture. After the preliminary introductions, Thomas opened the proceedings with a shortened *Ganónhonnyonk*, or Thanksgiving Address, with Don Richmond acting as an ill-trained translator, and then moved on to the two belts.[8] The readings lasted only 33 minutes, and Thomas, as usual, read the Friendship belt first before moving on to the Two Row.[9]

If the left-hand version took a half-hour to present, the right-hand is even shorter. Perhaps because the left-hand version was recited to the governor general in Ottawa, it provides a wider context for the negotiations with the Dutch, alluding to conflict with incoming Europeans when Samuel de Champlain used muskets in a battle with the Haudenosaunee in 1609, the year Henry Hudson first ventured into their territory. Like Kiotsaeton carefully acting out each wampum in the message of peace he had been entrusted to bring to Trois-Rivières, Thomas would have been aware, on both occasions, of standing in the long line of speakers who had reviewed the terms of the Covenant Chain–Two Row treaty protocols before him.

These two speeches present step-by-step accounts of how the Haudenosaunee and the Dutch began "to talk with one another about not being of one mind, and there was no love between them." They found this situation unacceptable because the "One who dwells in the sky did not intend people who move about on earth to torment one another," so they met to "develop some rules to go by so they could make peace, when they joined their arms." Of course, the rules to go by had been previously developed in the Great Law of the Peacemaker.

The sequence and the concepts here are familiar to us from Kiotsaeton's speech to the French-Algonquin alliance in 1645, thirty or so years after the Haudenosaunee met the Dutch on the Hudson River.

Once it became clear that neither the St. Lawrence nor the combination of Hudson and Mohawk Rivers constituted passageways to the spice trade they had hoped to reach in Asia, Dutch traders following Henry Hudson's route began to explore the possibilities of trading for furs as an alternative to the spice trade.[10] We know from the papers of Lambert van Tweenhuysen, one of the founders of the New Netherlands Company, that Captain Hendrick Christiaensen and Jacob Eelckens were at the confluence of the Hudson and Mohawk Rivers in 1613–1614.[11] To establish trade, they needed to build friendly relations with the Haudenosaunee, whose confederacy controlled many of the river routes to the interior of the continent. The Dutch traders therefore took their bearings from the Haudenosaunee about how to conduct matters of business with local people. They learned to conduct these matters according to the key cardinal principles of *ka'nikonhriyó'tshera't*, *kentèn:ron* and *skén:nen*.

Thomas doesn't give the names of the orators who would have taken up the cleared space between the parties near the confluence of the Mohawk and the Hudson Rivers near present-day Albany. Compared to Kiotsaeton's day-long oration at Trois-Rivières, Thomas's half-hour recitations were conducted in shorthand. No time to hang seventeen "colliers de pourcelaine" on the wampum-display cord. No time for him to say if the Dutch, the next day, hung seventeen corresponding wampum on the cord to express their affirmation, one by one, of the pledges they were making. Thomas's short narrations have time only for a quick nod to the Words Before All Else, to linking arms, to the Covenant Chain, to the image of two paths travelling in parallel down the river of time linked by the three cardinal principles of trust, friendship and peace, and never assimilating or dominating one another.

Despite the shorthand, Jake Thomas's narrations still convey that the Creator wished for people to live in peace with one another, not just in the immediate present but for future generations. And to live in peace, they would have to link arms, to hold one another firmly, not as a father holds a child by the hand, but as equals – siblings, brothers. The agreement indicated that these distinctions needed to be respected and maintained, not just so that the Dutch and Haudenosaunee themselves could live with one another with good minds, united in friendship and peace in their own times, but so that, as Foster's translations of Thomas put it, "the agreements will benefit (meaning they belong to) the faces deep underground (the generations to come that the Creator determined will be taking their place on the earth)."

Treaties, inter-national, inter-cultural agreements, according to this principle, are for the future – for future generations; for children, and not just human ones; for timespans beyond our own. They are not present conveniences.

And here is the part that jumped out for me when I first encountered Jake Thomas's narrations of the Covenant Chain–Two Row Wampum way of making agreements: when asked how they would "symbolize" this durability, this future, the Haudenosaunee pointed to the steadily nurturing cycles of life around them – the sunshine, the flow of water, the green grass. The Western ideas of law that I'm used to don't tend to look, as Jake Thomas did in his 1981 oration, to these basic elements of the earth's ongoing life as the signs, reminders, guarantors of how long an agreement should endure: "We obtain our happiness from what [Creator] has planted, and there is no end to new life and to the faces coming from deep underground." Just as each element of earth's ecology plays its part in perpetuating the biome over millennia, so the wampum agreement lays out the parts we humans play in perpetuating multigenerational, interspecies life. "Now we have symbolized this agreement and it shall be binding forever, as long as Mother Earth is still in motion."

The rules of the agreement are consciously set within the context of what we in English call the "laws of nature." In Haudenosaunee thinking, these are the laws people must align themselves with in order to have a future.

Chapter Five

What Could "Covenant" Mean to Dutch and British Ears?

What would have shaped seventeenth-century Dutch traders' understanding of the agreement they were forming with the Haudenosaunee in Jake Thomas's oral histories? The idea of using intentionally ordered strings of beads to aid ceremony and memory would have been familiar to all the arriving Europeans from the widespread use of the rosary. The strings of beads Catholics use to keep track of their prayers shared many characteristics with wampum: they were both formed of beads organized in patterned strings to help steady the mind, keep track of ceremonies, communicate with others and the more-than-human world, including the Divine. Even though many Dutch of the period were departing from the rule of the Catholic Church – the northern provinces did so definitively and eventually became what we now call the Netherlands, while the southern provinces remained Catholic and became the country known as Belgium – they would still be familiar with these strings of beads. Sometimes worn as necklaces, rosaries were a common method, especially for the illiterate laity, to organize their thoughts as they fingered one bead for each Hail Mary prayer until they had completed a "decade." As Ayonwátha had found too, the faithful knew that the beads of the rosary helped calm the welter of emotions. The simple ordering of people's attention to one bead and then another settled the mind and restored peace in the heart. Each set of ten beads was separated by a different size or shape of bead to remind the devout to say the Doxology (in English: "Glory be to the Father, and to the Son, and to the Holy Ghost, as it was in the beginning, is now and will be forever, Amen") and then the "Our Father," before beginning a new decade of Hail Marys. Hendrick Christiaensen and Jacob Eelckens, two named leaders of the Dutch merchant expedition, would have been distinguished from rank-and-file sailors who were likely illiterate, as these merchant company officers needed to read and write in order to send reports home to their Van Tweenhuysen company employers. Their literacy would likely have been more functional than sophisticated, and it would not have been outside their frame of reference to consider bead systems for putting important ceremonies to memory.

Nor is it chance that assigned the word "covenant" to the Two Row–Covenant Chain agreement. For the word "covenant" in "Covenant Chain" has a rich resonance in seventeenth-century Protestant thinking, especially among Presbyterians and Reform-minded Dutch Protestants, as the religious studies scholar Louise Johnston has pointed out. Covenant thinking was intensified by the religious politics in Holland during and after the rebellion of William I, Prince of Orange, and other nobles against the Spanish-Catholic Crown. During this time, the rebellious lords in the low-lying lands along the North Sea complained that their region's needs got only belated notice from Spain and, when there was attention, it came in the form of Philip II's violent suppression of religious Protestants in their provinces. The populace was increasingly alienated from the Spanish rulers and the absolute authority of the Roman Catholic Church.[1]

Covenant theology grew as a fundamental rationale for the rebellion. This emerging doctrine taught that God formed covenants or agreements with people, as he had done first with Adam and then with Abraham in the Bible – to give them life in exchange for obedience. When Adam failed, God built a new covenant with Abraham in a subsequent time. English translations of the Bible render the Hebrew word for covenant, *berit*, meaning bond or fetter, as "testament." This Latin term, a translation of the Greek *diatheke*, "testament" or "covenant," was understood to divide the Christian Bible in two parts: the Old Hebrew Covenant (or Testament) and the New Covenant of Jesus, with the implication that God's covenants with humans evolved over time.[2] While some early Reform theologians considered God's covenants to be unilateral, increasingly they came to consider them to be bilateral – meaning that, rather than a vertical, unidirectional Great Chain of Being within which God imposes a covenant upon people through a hierarchy that descends through pope and/or king, to priests and aristocracies and then to common people, horizontal and bilateral (sometimes known as federal) covenant theology taught that the divine agreement with humans was two-way and conditional upon the consent of both parties: Jesus had committed himself to people, saying, "Anything you ask in my name, I will do," but he also demanded a mutual agreement, "If you love me, you will keep my commandments."[3]

Johnston highlights the impact of covenant theology on European politics by tracing the idea of political federalism between the northern provinces in the Netherlands to this covenantal bilateralism. She looks to the writings of the German-born philosopher Johannes Althusius (1557–1638), chief magistrate of the Calvinist city-state of Emden in the northwest corner of Germany near the Dutch border, to show how Reform theology became secularized into the argument for a republican state in which rulers and ruled understood themselves to be bonded in mutual compact. Althusius introduced his renowned work *Politics* (*Politica Methodice Digesta, Atque Exemplis Sacris et Profanis Illustrata*, 1603) with the following statement, which was radical for its time:

> Politics . . . is the art of associating [humans] for the purpose of establishing, cultivating and conserving social life among them. Whence it is called "symbiotics." The subject matter of politics is therefore association, in which the symbiotes (those who live together) pledge themselves each to the other, by explicit or tacit agreement, to mutual communication of whatever is useful and necessary for the harmonious exercise of social life.
>
> The end of political "symbiotic" mankind is holy, just, comfortable and

> happy symbiosis (living together), a life lacking nothing either necessary or useful.[4]

Althusius's book was reprinted in 1610 and 1614. His ideas were influential in Holland during the years of the ongoing struggle against Spanish-Catholic rule, precisely when Jacob Eelckens and Hendrick Christiaensen travelled up the Hudson River and formed the Two Row–Covenant Chain agreement with the Haudenosaunee (Peoples who had already organized themselves as a political confederation) near what became Fort Orange and later Albany.

Johnston points out that Althusius's ideas did not triumph without opposition. She observes that there was a resurgence of the monarchy in Holland in the later seventeenth century that overtook Althusius's formulation of symbiosis, reasserting the concentration of power in a central sovereign. Nonetheless, she quotes Charles S. McCoy and J. Wayne Baker's *Fountainhead of Federalism* to show how the Althusian concept of a federal or covenantal bond expanded from the seventeenth century onward in European thinking to suit many kinds of human association. As they put it, covenantal thinking spread the idea that "humans as symbiotes belong by nature to families as the most immediate and basic covenantal grouping. But people also form many kinds of private associations through agreements and compacts – craft guilds, academic societies, businesses and commercial associations." Thus, other public organizations such as towns, cities, provinces, confederations and the commonwealth were increasingly understood to "come together by covenant."[5]

Symbiotes

When the Dutch merchants and *Kanyen'kehá:ka royá:ners* met to establish their friendship, therefore, the evolution of this way of thinking from Reform Biblical interpretation to the wider worlds of economics and politics was underway, and it would readily have shaped Eelckens and Christiaensen's understanding of the compact they were forming with their new Haudenosaunee trading partners. For one thing, the Biblical context would have suggested to them the notion of the chain, since the concept of fetter or bond between parties was deep in the Biblical concept of what it means to form a "testament" or "covenant." And covenantal, symbiotic thinking would have suggested to them a horizontal, rather than a strictly vertical, Great Chain of Being. The model of a bilateral agreement between all manner of associations, from family to business, was fundamental to the emerging concept of covenant as they would have heard it debated back home in Holland. In addition, the symbiosis being struggled for was explicitly interreligious and departed sharply from the unilateral idea of papal power. Thus, they would not automatically have approached the negotiations with the Haudenosaunee under the aegis of papal bulls such as "Inter Caetera" – now commonly referred to as the Doctrine of Discovery – issued by Pope Alexander VI on May 4, 1493. This edict, issued the year after Columbus's first successful voyage and his encounter with Indigenous Taíno people in the Caribbean, stated that any land not inhabited by Christians was available for annexation and exploitation by Christian rulers – that is, brought into the "Body of Christ." The people who lived there must be converted to the Catholic faith. As legal historian Robert A. Williams Jr. has pointed out, the Doctrine of Discovery has its antecedents in medieval papal law during the period of the Crusades, when Pope Innocent IV reasoned that infidels who refused entry into Christ's body of the church displayed a lack of the mental capacity to reason and must therefore be compelled to submit to the authority of the church, which had the responsibility to look after their welfare in their childlike state.[6]

The Dutch merchants' home region was embroiled in a protracted war to free itself from this kind of unilateral religious view and to assert the right to form political and economic compacts across religious lines without requiring the conversion of others to the one true faith. The Dutch did not arrive in North America with the military might to impose their government or religion on the Haudenosaunee, and they also had a political theology that taught them to form secular, symbiotic compacts with others. More than this, the rise of covenantal thinking in Holland would have given them some experience of the notion of federalism and confederation, since the rebel states especially in the northern parts of the Low Countries had confederated with each other in opposing Spanish rule, so the merchants would have appreciated something of the political structure they encountered in the Haudenosaunee longhouse of nations that had been fashioned by Peacemaker and his associates.

We can get a better understanding of how Dutch thinking shaped their ability to enter into the Two Row–Covenant Chain agreement with the Haudenosaunee by comparison with the kind of relationships the French developed with the Iroquoian Confederacy during the same period. In *Cultivating a Landscape of Peace*, historian Matthew Dennis writes that the Dutch were "all business,"[7] while the French, powerfully influenced by the Jesuits and assuming the papal laws that governed Catholic thinking, aimed at conversion of Indigenous North Americans to the one true faith. The Jesuits would have considered conversion the more "humane" approach as compared to outright enslavement or annihilation.[8] According to Dennis, the early Dutch traders that worked in and around Fort Orange operated within a decentralized system of free trade, competing with one another so fiercely they would go out beyond the edges of the woods around their settlement to try to strike private deals with Haudenosaunee trappers and bypass rival Dutch merchants. If bribes didn't work, there are records indicating that Dutch traders even resorted to physical violence. At times, the Haudenosaunee were repelled by how Dutch merchants mistreated not just the Haudenosaunee trappers, but each other.[9]

By contrast, the French operated within a centralized trading system. Trade in New France was controlled by the Compagnie des Cent-Associés (the Company of One Hundred), so called because it involved one hundred subscribers, which was a church-dominated, private enterprise with a monopoly on trade granted by the king. Dennis says its investors acted out of religious devotion as much as a straightforward concern for profits. The presence and power of this centralized business-religious model among the French meant that trade and dealings with Indigenous people was much more calculated and self-conscious than in New Netherlands' free-trade environment.[10] By comparison with the Jesuits of New France, whose mission to convert Indigenous peoples caused such resentment among the Five Nations, Dennis explains that the Dutch showed little interest in converting the Haudenosaunee to Christianity. They sent almost no preachers or missionaries among them. The Dutch lack of missionary interest also meant that, unlike the Jesuits, they showed comparatively little ethnographic interest or knowledge of Haudenosaunee languages or cultural practices.[11] The Dutch participated in Haudenosaunee ceremonies and rituals of friendship such as wampum- and gift-exchanges and even the Condolence Ceremony, but Dennis concludes, "Dutch negotiators . . . took part in traditional and Iroquois social and political ritual, not out of any particular cultural sensitivity or appreciation but simply out of necessity, as the cost of doing business with the Five Nations."[12] Ironically, then, we have more accounts of Haudenosaunee rituals, practices and diplomatic protocols – think of the ethnographic detail about Kiotsaeton's visit to Trois-Rivières – in the *Jesuit Relations* than we do in Dutch colonial records.

Indeed, another historian of the period, Russell Shorto, suggests that New York City's current reputation for multi-ethnic, live-and-let-live tolerance and free enterprise can be traced to the freewheeling commercial ethos of early Dutch settlement on Manhattan Island and in Albany. Like Johnston, he traces this liberalism to Dutch religious history, noting that the city of Leiden, and particularly its university, was a mecca for religious refugees of many kinds in the early seventeenth century, including Jews and Puritans – this, because religious freedom had been fundamental to the emergence of the Dutch Republic; when Galileo had faced the Inquisition, his work was published at Leiden, and liberal thinkers like Descartes enrolled there too in 1630, with his work finding publication there in 1637.[13] Shorto says this secular, open market of ideas translated into a liberal attitude toward all kinds of regulation. He paints a picture of Beverwyck (the town that grew to a thousand inhabitants around Fort Orange – today, Albany) being composed of Germans, Swedes, French, English, Irish, Norwegians and Africans. There were so many kinds of currency in circulation in New Netherlands that the administration tried several times to establish wampum beads as a common coin for trade. He describes *Kanyen'kehàka* and Dutchmen fraternizing freely in Beverwyck, with Haudenosaunee boarding in Dutch homes, sitting by the fire over mugs of beer and buying cakes at the bakery. In 1659, Mohawk chiefs demanded a session in court to present grievances against Dutchmen who were taking advantage of Haudenosaunee traders. We should not assume, however, that given this "free trade," egalitarian, social ethos, there was no inequality; for there was slavery in the Dutch colonies, and patriarchy ruled the economy.[14]

So, while the Dutch traders may not have been prepared to understand women's particular responsibility for the land or the specific ways in which wampum echoed the story of how stringing the beads quieted Ayonwátha's mind and peacefully introduced him to distrustful Oneidas, and while the Haudenosaunee may not have been familiar with the idea of the private ownership of land or the kind of bare-knuckle enterprise that could make traders compete fiercely to gain advantage over each other, the shared desire for trade meant that there were avenues for mutual comprehension and agreement. The growing Dutch understanding of symbiotic or mutual covenant is significant among them. It helps us see how both parties had a framework for the idea of forming beneficial bonds between Peoples, and that they both understood the bonds they were forming had roots in the sacred, which in turn could shape relationships in everyday secular life. The European-Protestant word for this human-sacred kind of agreement was "covenant."

And this understanding did not die out with the Dutch, for as Shorto points out, when the English took over New Netherlands in 1664, they did not wish to interrupt the lucrative trade that came and went from the mouth of the Hudson River. They therefore left the Dutch laissez-faire practices pretty much in place, guaranteeing the rights of Dutch traders and religion in the New York City Charter and generally incorporating the existing multiethnic, multireligious population into the new English administration.[15] We should recall, too, that from Henry Hudson himself onward, many Englishmen in the late seventeenth and early eighteenth centuries had conducted business and made their fortunes in New Netherlands, and their loyalties were more to commerce than they were to one government or another. So it was not a major undertaking to transfer the covenant that had so benefitted Dutch business to the new English administration, but this is a story for another chapter.

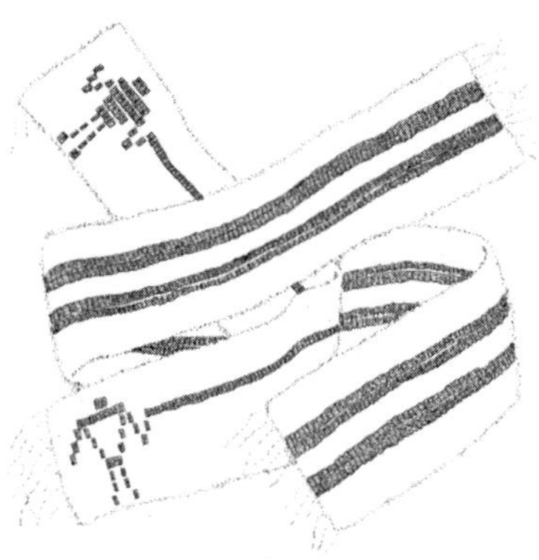

Chapter Six

Tracing Kaswentha's *Flow*

The emerging understanding of *reciprocal* covenants that I traced in the previous chapter means that the Dutch and Haudenosaunee, and later British and Haudenosaunee, especially in the period of the fur trade alliance–making, assumed the value of autonomy, rather than conversion or assimilation, *within* the alliances they agreed to. This is a key principle that runs throughout the Covenant Chain–Two Row treaty tradition: the treaty partners maintain sovereignty over their own governance and ways of life even as they link themselves together.

Jake Thomas's narrations of the Covenant Chain–Two Row agreement show that, while vowing to link arms in friendship, the Haudenosaunee and Dutch parties were aware that their different vessels carried different cultures, beliefs, laws and authorities on the river they wished to share, and they knew that these different systems or worldviews were important.

> "We both have our own authority – strength/power. We have our respective beliefs, from the same Creator. We have our respective laws. We do not have authority over each other or [each other's] kind of culture."
>
> The Onkwehonweh stated, "The Creator gave us a canoe and you a

> boat (ship). We will take our vessels to the water and put them in the water, each in their distinctive way. Our people will follow the vessels in the water. We will place them a certain distance apart, but will line them up so they will always be parallel. . . .
>
> "My beliefs will be in my canoe, yours will be in your boat. I will also put my laws in my canoe, and you will put your laws in your boat. Our authority, beliefs and laws will be dropped into our vessels. That is how people will know it, by the likeness to two paths."
>
> The Mohawk man stated, "We will make a wampum belt of that likeness so people will know what we will go by. The Two Paths (wampum) is our way of keeping records."[1]

This is the Two Row part of the agreement that has become most widely known in our times – the strong demarcation of difference, the autonomy of the two parties who are linking arms in this agreement. I think of it as a kind of protective clause of the Covenant Chain–Two Row treaty tradition. As Amber Meadow Adams reminded me, this protective arrangement was not developed in response to Europeans. Instead, it is a way of proceeding that traces back to the Haudenosaunee Creation Story and the necessity of separating the Creator Twins so that their different priorities and ways of going about things don't impede each other.[2] Eventually, the Twins decided to live on opposite sides of a river, with Tharonhyawá:kon ruling the daytime and Thawískaron active in the night.

They share the river of life, but they walk on different paths.

Perhaps it helps to think of this protective aspect of the Two Row as presenting a cross-section of the Covenant Chain – that is, it provides the content of the three white beads of peace, friendship and respect – for the section where the rope ties the two parties together.[3] To link arms, the Two Row explains, does not mean to assimilate or absorb each other. Just as sisters' families share their clan's longhouse and pass necessities back and forth across the fire, it is important to maintain the distinction of each family's side of the longhouse, even though it's all one extended family. Just as the fifty chiefs of the Confederacy have linked arms to protect the Tree of Peace at the centre of their way of life, the six different nations contribute to that alliance from the dignity and distinction of their own territory, language and culture.

To link arms, you don't give up or abandon who you are. You maintain yourself, your uniqueness, even as you influence each other. On the basis of this agreement, Haudenosaunee insist to this day that they are not Canadians or Americans, but citizens of their own Confederacy, their own canoe. Yet they have linked arms with the British Crown, and therefore with its political descendants in Canada and the U.S.

It is an important balance to keep, because the formal maintenance of difference, if it's overpoliced, can become a rationale for purity, for cultural apartheid or diplomatic eugenics. Jake Thomas's recitation indicates awareness of these concerns when he reports that the negotiators worried that "perhaps in the days to come, some of your people would like to get into my canoe. Perhaps a number of my people would like to get into your large boat, because of its size. They might like being in your boat." The two parties reason that, in such cases, the passengers in each vessel will need to follow the rules of the vessel they have chosen. But then the white man asked, "What will happen in the days to come if a big storm comes up, and someone has a foot in each vessel, and the vessels are driven apart? I believe that person will fall between them." His *Kanyen'kehá:ka* counterpart replies, "Yes, this will happen. We cannot take responsibility for this. Only the Creator has the power to save that person."

There you have it. It can look like an argument against mixing. An argument for racial and cultural purity. The absolute division of separate sovereignties.

But it's not.

We need to remember that Jake Thomas gave these recitations in a moment when Canada was patriating its Constitution, its juridical identity, and in a time when the Confederacy's foundational wampum belts were being slowly and reluctantly returned to the Six Nations Confederacy. Ever since the Indian Act of 1876, Canada had consistently disregarded the principle of symbiotic covenant. It manipulated and commandeered the passengers in the canoe, forced them to attend school in the ship, whittled away the capacity of the canoe to provide its members a livelihood, undermined its ability to govern itself and carried off its wampum records. The result is that the majority of Haudenosaunee people today live with one foot in each vessel, whether they want it this way or not. The space between the rows yawns dangerously and enticingly: the parties on each side could perhaps recalibrate and develop respect, even for those with one foot in each vessel, or they could let them drown in there.

As Rick Hill, who was raised and educated in the Euro-American ship and has worked all his adult life to regain and reinvigorate the ways of the canoe, has said about Thomas's wording for this delicate situation: "Only the Creator has the power to save those who find themselves treading water between the two vessels." It's all about realizing who we – whatever vessel carried our ancestors – were created to be. And then figuring out a healthy way to link arms, share the river, with the other side of the alliance.[4]

Canesatego's Narration in 1744

If Jake Thomas's recitations of the Covenant Chain–Two Row treaty tradition highlight the version that was negotiated with the Dutch in the early 1600s and give a fair amount of emphasis to the two separate rows, Onondaga orator Canesatego's recitation in 1744 was presented to British colonial officers during a period when he intended to emphasize the linked arms of the Covenant Chain – and especially how that covenant evolved over time. Canesatego's speech makes a regular appearance in commentaries on the Covenant Chain–Two Row tradition because it clearly traces the evolution of the agreement from Dutch to English treaty partners, while it also explicitly uses the imagery of a ship attached by rope and then chain to the nations of the Haudenosaunee shoreline.

Historian Robert Venables says that Canesatego was born in the 1680s, so he was about sixty years old – tall, strong, vigorous and broad-chested – when the Onondaga spokesman gave his speech to representatives of the colonies of Pennsylvania, Maryland and Virginia on June 26, 1744, at Lancaster, Pennsylvania. The orator's words were translated by the interpreter Conrad Weiser and later printed by Benjamin Franklin in *Indian Treaties Printed by Benjamin Franklin, 1736–1762.*[5] Canesatego's speech clearly outlines the Haudenosaunee understanding of their prior claims upon the country, on their functioning as "elder brothers" to the Dutch and English younger arrivals in the region, and especially their autonomy in their relationships:

> Brother
>
> You came out of the Ground in a Country that lies beyond the Seas, there you may have a just Claim, but here you must allow us to be your elder Brethren, and the Lands to belong to us long before you knew any thing of them.
>
> It is true, that above one hundred years ago the Dutch came here in a ship, and brought with them several Goods, such as Awls, Knives, Hatchets, Guns and many other Particulars, which they gave us; and when they had taught us how to use their Things, and we saw what sort of People they were, we were so well pleased with them, that we tied their Ship to the Bushes on the Shore; and afterwards, liking them still better the longer they staid with us, and thinking the Bushes too slender, we removed the Rope and tied it to the Trees; and as the Trees were liable to be blown down by high Winds, or to decay of themselves, we, from the Affection we bore them, again removed the Rope, and tied it to a strong and big Rock (here the Interpreter said, they mean the Oneida country) and not content with this, for its further Security we removed the rope to a big Mountain (here the Interpreter says they mean the Onondago Country) and there tied it verry fast, and rowll'd Wampum around it; and to make it still more secure, we stood upon the Wampum, and sat down upon it, to defend it, and to prevent any hurt coming to it, and did our best endeavours that it might remain uninjured for ever.
>
> During all this time, the new-comers, the Dutch, acknowledged our Right to the Lands, and sollicited us, from Time to Time, to grant them parts of our Country, and to enter into a League and Covenant with us, and to become one People with us.
>
> After this the English came into the Country, and, as we were told, became one people with the Dutch. About two years after the arrival of

> the English, an English Governor came to Albany, and finding what great Friendship subsisted between us and the Dutch, he approved it mightily, and desired to make as strong a League, and to be upon as good terms with us as the Dutch were, with whom he was united, and to become one People with us. And by his further care in looking into what had passed between us, he found that the Rope which tied the Ship to the great Mountain was only fastened with Wampum, which was liable to break and rot, and to perish in a Course of Years; he therefore told us, he would give a Silver Chain, which would be much stronger, and would last for ever. This we accepted, and fastened the Ship with it, and it has lasted ever since.[6]

Canesatego's account of the Covenant Chain emphasizes the continuous and evolving nature of the relationship between the treaty partners. The relationship was not, for example, marked by a permanent monument such as the monolith in Oneida country from which the People of the Standing Rock took their name. For it was a living, mobile covenant, a rope that needed reinforcement by the symbolic ritual of wampum exchange, that was progressively attached to different places along the riverbank and to nations in different parts of the Confederacy, and that continued to link the clasped arms of the signatories of the covenant even when regimes from far across the ocean changed hands. His reference to the governor of Albany's introduction of a silver chain (chains were used to measure water depth for ships on the river) to replace frayed rope or breakable wampum indicates how the linked arms of the fifty chiefs has been translated through British interpretation of the agreement into the links of a chain, an image Jake Thomas associated with the agreement with the Dutch a century earlier.[7] It also shows how the symbolism of the agreement developed through translation in a contact zone, where code-switching between Haudenosaunee and European languages and symbolism was essential to developing a shared understanding.[8]

Given the uncertainties of speech in such a dynamic contact zone, Canesatego makes it very clear that Haudenosaunee lands remain under Haudenosaunee jurisdiction: "During all this time, the new-comers, the Dutch, acknowledged our Right to the Lands, and sollicited us, from

Time to Time, to grant them parts of our Country, and to enter into a League and Covenant with us, and to become one People with us." The purpose of allowing the Europeans access to Haudenosaunee land was to facilitate their alliance, to welcome the "rafters" they brought to the Haudenosaunee longhouse. The Covenant made them like "one People." In case we think that these understandings were available only to diplomats on the Haudenosaunee side of the agreement, recall that Canesatego's speech was printed by Benjamin Franklin, the British colonial writer and philosopher who was later prominent in formulating the political foundations of the United States. It's hard to imagine how Franklin would not have been able to understand the meaning of the words he published: "You came out of the Ground in a Country that lies beyond the Seas, there you may have a just Claim, but here you must allow us to be your elder Brethren, and the Lands to belong to us long before you knew any thing of them."

Canesatego's speech to the British representatives from the Pennsylvania, Maryland and Virginia colonies, as published by Franklin, makes it clear that the agreement was familiar to Haudenosaunee and British representatives over one hundred years after the Dutch first arrived on the Hudson River, that they understood their alliance was an ongoing, evolving relationship that involved milestones that marked moments when the agreement had been polished and renewed. These moments of repolishing were aimed at ensuring that the agreement was consistent and continuous. The rope or chain that bound the two parties together functioned, then, as an extension of the arms joined in friendship, like a kind of telegraph of mutual protection, whereby people who have clasped arms can shake the rope or chain when they need to communicate with their friends on the other end, whether across the river or across the ocean or across the generations, so they can heed their partner's call.

Thus, the ever-renewing relationship required maintenance, even defence: "to make it still more secure, we stood upon the Wampum, and sat down upon it, to defend it, and to prevent any hurt coming to it." The tall Onondaga orator here alludes to the symbol of the Great White Mat on which the Peacemaker had instructed the Confederacy chiefs to meet. In 1912, John Arthur Gibson narrated this part of the *Kayanerenhtserakó:wa* this way: Now that the chiefs had all been assigned their titles and roles on the sides of the council fire, Peacemaker said,

> now it is accomplished, they have spread out the Great White Mat . . . for them, and they have placed the Great Long Wing . . . All the matters, the important issues, will come before you, at the place where you form a relationship group, you chiefs, the place where it is spread out, the object called the Great White Mat . . . and if it gets dark, then he shall pick up the Great Black Wing . . . , the Great Chief, sweeping the place where it is spread out, which means that if the argument becomes too intense – causing minds to spoil – then he shall stop it at once, and if they observe something crawling, just like a worm, to the place where it is spread out, the Great Chief will pick up the suspended pole, pry it out with the pole, and throw it back outdoors.[9]

Influenced by this symbol of the White Mat on which council meets, many wampum belts represent council fires (or nations) with a "lozenge" – diamond or square – of white beads. And the image of the wing and the pole to remove blemishes or threats to the clarity of the meeting initiates the idea of sweeping dust from wampum or polishing the purity of the silver chain. A version of the Friendship Belt exchanged between the Haudenosaunee and the Anishinaabe, for example, replaces the human figures at the two ends of the Covenant Chain with two white squares. The White Mat of Peace, too, sets the ground of the *Sewatokwa'tshera't* (Dish With One Spoon) belt, which is pure white, except for the purple lozenge at the centre, a dish with a white beaver tail in it, representing the provisions shared between the nations who had agreed to maintain the region in peace.[10] The ongoing adaptation of symbols and terms even extends to wampum itself, which, Canesatego admits, may break or rot over time, so the governor of Albany had suggested the more durable – and to the British, more precious – material of the silver chain.

It's a version of the *rotiyaneshon* negotiating with the Dutch and saying paper may not last. What's important is that the principles of the agreement are conveyed by durable symbols into the memories of future generations.

All of this to say that Canesatego's review of the Covenant Chain–Two Row treaty tradition with the embassies from Pennsylvania, Maryland and Virginia recognizes two row difference ("You came out of the Ground in a Country that lies beyond the Seas . . ."), but it emphasizes the linking of arms and the evolution of that agreement from place to place, from People to People, across time. His speech gives us a moment when he sweeps the wampum clean and repolishes it in his listeners' minds.

Canesatego's is one of many polishings of the Covenant Chain–Two Row treaty tradition recorded in colonial council meeting minutes. Historian Daniel Richter finds over a dozen between 1671 and 1691; Jon Parmenter lists eighteen of them between 1656 and 1744; while Robert Venables indicates that between 1613 and 1842 more than four hundred negotiations were carried out by the Haudenosaunee with the Dutch, the French, the English and the United States, and that "163 wampum belts associated with these negotiations have been identified and photographed."[11] After surveying the predominance of Haudenosaunee diplomatic protocols in early colonial treaty literature, Lenape legal historian Robert A. Williams Jr. concludes:

> The Covenant Chain functioned as a multicultural constitution in North America from 1677 until the middle of the eighteenth century. The scope of the Chain's influence within British America during this time was extensive. No tribe or tribal group appears more frequently or with such prominence as the Iroquois in the treaty literature of the colonial period. The multiracial and multicultural relationships established under the Iroquois Covenant Chain influenced events throughout most of the territory of England's mid-Atlantic colonies. . . . Iroquois influence through the Chain, either direct or indirect, was palpable throughout virtually the entire eastern North American diplomatic system.[12]

As we have seen, the chain of linked arms goes back in Haudenosaunee philosophy to the Peacemaker and the Great Law of Peace and even before that. Likewise, agreements such as the Dish With One Spoon were made with surrounding nations long before the arrival of the French on the St. Lawrence in 1534. So when Williams here gives a European starting date of 1677 for the constitutional function of the Covenant Chain concept and suggests the mid-1700s for its end date, I imagine he's positioning these as the bookends for the period of primary Haudenosaunee-Anglo treaty-making. But as we know, too, *kaswentha* carries the idea of flow and flexibility, like a river, and I am less ready than he is to truncate that flow to the late seventeenth and early eighteenth centuries.

Sir William Johnson's Version in 1748

Sir William Johnson (1715–1774), who received a royal commission as "Colonel of . . . the Six united Nations of Indians & their Confederates, in the Northern Parts of North America" and "Sole Agent and Superintendent of the said Indians" in February 1756, brought the Covenant Chain to even greater prominence.[13] Under Johnson's and his common-law wife Mary Brant's influence, Haudenosaunee ways of doing things formed the ground rules for treaty-making in the crucial period when Britain was trying to consolidate its administration, particularly after the fall of New France in 1760. Johnson lived on the Mohawk River, in a common-law marriage with Konwatsi'tsayén:ni Mary (Molly) Brant, *Kanyen'kehάka* from a prominent family in Canajoharie with whom he had eight children.[14] Mary was a reputed granddaughter of Deyohninhohhakarawenh, "King Hendrick," and sister to Thaientané:ken Joseph Brant. In marrying her, Johnson became intimately related to social and political power within Haudenosaunee society. He was given the name Warragehagey and is said to have been adopted into the Mohawk nation.[15] He became fluent in the *Kanyen'kéha* language. Through his powerful family connections, Johnson also became fluent in the principles of *Kayanerenhtserakó:wa*.

Johnson's career demonstrates that, not only did British officials *understand* the principles of the Covenant Chain–Two Row treaty tradition, they also officially *employed* this tradition themselves, using it to expand their network of Indigenous allies, first to overcome French rivalry, and later to try to stem American revolt. Less than four years after Canesatego's account of the Covenant Chain–Two Row agreement in Pennsylvania, for example, Johnson presented his understanding of the agreement. At this point, he had not yet come to cohabit with Mary Brant, and he was still a colonel over fourteen militia companies in New York before his appointment as Superintendent. In 1748, a party of French and their Indigenous allies had attacked and killed a scouting party of three "Christians" and three Mohawks and mutilated the bodies. The Haudenosaunee Grand Council planned to send an embassy to make peace and exchange prisoners with the French in Montreal. Johnson had sent a message to ask them not to go to Montreal, while he interceded with General Clinton, saying they stood to lose their Haudenosaunee allies if the British were not prepared to defend them. In the meantime, he requested an armed escort to attend a meeting at Onondaga with the Grand Council, so he could reinforce the relationship with the Haudenosaunee. In the presence of Ganughsadeagah,[16] and the other chiefs, Johnson said:

> Brethren of the five Nations I will begin upon a thing of a long standing, our first Brothership. My Reason for it is, I think there are several among you who seem to forget it; It may seem strange to you how I a Foreigner should know this, But I tell you I found out some of the old Writings of our Fore fathers which was thought to have been lost and in this old valuable Record I find, that our first Friendship Commenced at the Arrival of the first great Canoe or Vessel at Albany, at which you were much surprized but finding what it contained pleased you so much, being Things for your Purpose, as our People convinced you of by shewing you the use of them, that you all Resolved to take the greatest care of that Vessel that nothing should hurt her. Whereupon it was agreed to tye her fast with a great Rope to one of the largest Nut Trees on the Bank of the River But on further Consideration in a fuller meeting it was thought safest Fearing the Wind should blow down that Tree to make a long Rope and tye her fast at Onondaga which was accordingly done and the Rope put under your feet That if any thing hurt or touched said Vessel by the shaking of the Rope you might know it, and then agreed to rise all as one and see what the Matter was and whoever hurt the Vessel was to suffer. After this was agreed on and done you made an offer to the Governour to enter into

> a Band of Friendship with him and his people which he was so pleased at that he told you he would find a strong Silver Chain which would never break slip or Rust to bind you and him forever in Brothership together and that your Warriours and Ours should be as one Heart, one Head, one Blood & ca. and that what happened to the one happened to the other. After this form agreement was made our Forefathers finding it was good and foreseeing the many Advantages both sides would reap of it, Ordered that if ever that Silver Chain should turn the least Rusty, offer to slip or break, that it should be immediately brightened up again, and not let it slip or break on any account for then you and we were both dead. Brethren these are the words of our Wise Forefathers which some among you know very well to be so. Now Brethren understanding or hearing that the French our and your Common Enemy were endeavouring to blindfold you and get you to slip your hands out of that Chain, which as our Forefathers said would certainly be our destruction, I now out of a tender regard for your Safety and Welfare as well as Ours, conjure you not to listen any more to the deceitful French who aim at nothing more than to destroy you all if in their power; but stick fast to the Old Agreement which you will find the best. A large Belt of Wampum.[17]

Many of Johnson's recorded speeches conclude with this phrase: "A belt of Wampum" – meaning that, following Haudenosaunee protocol, he has prepared a wampum belt that he gives to his listeners as evidence of the veracity and reliability of his words. He is polishing the Covenant Chain.

Johnson's account closely echoes that of Canesatego, with its tracking of the relationship from the arrival of the original Dutch trading ship to the tying of an anchor rope at different sites down the Mohawk River until it was fixed at Onondaga, where the Confederacy had its central fire. He also describes the evolution from rope to silver chain and the injunction to "brighten" or polish its links. His reference to the "old Writings of our Fore fathers" takes us back to the part in Jake Thomas's oration where the *rotiyaneshon* noted that they kept track of things by wampum and that they were worried that "paper will not last," whereas the Dutch had said, "I will do what is right for me, make it legal by writing it down. Thus people on both sides will know it." That Dutch writing has been conveyed, according to Johnson, into the old writings of his English forefathers, and *that* writing is now being renewed in the wampum belt he gives to his listeners.

Johnson's narration is one more instance of the syncretistic, hybrid evolution of the Covenant Chain–Two Row tradition, whose records come to us in both vessels, down each path, oral wampum and written. With its emphasis on mutual protection "if any thing hurt or touched said Vessel" between the Haudenosaunee and the British against their common enemy, the French, we don't have Jake Thomas's division between the Onkwehón:we and the "white man," which sounds to modern ears like a racial category (i.e., the Dutch and then the English). Instead, in Johnson's rendering, we have a bond of "Brothership together and that your Warriours and Ours should be as one Heart, one Head, one Blood & ca. and that what happened to the one happened to the other." The overall principles of trust, the capacity to get things done and peace-between-friends remain the same, but the context shifts languages, vocabulary and matters of emphasis.

Tracing the Covenant Chain–Two Row tradition through Jake Thomas's narrations to the governor general and to people on the Grand River in chapter 4, and then from Canesatego's speech to the colonial representatives and onward to Johnson's narration "back" to the Haudenosaunee in this chapter, demonstrates more clearly than ever how this dialogue, this tradition of agreement-making, evolved through an *inter*-national, *cross*-cultural set of agreements and procedures. It had its origins in Haudenosaunee thinking, and it evolved. It had to do so, if it was to create linked arms in the intercultural, international contact zone – in a series of such contact zones. The rules of procedure and the overall objectives remained the same, but the contexts for conversation, the systems for keeping track and passing on the tradition flowed and required improvisation over time.

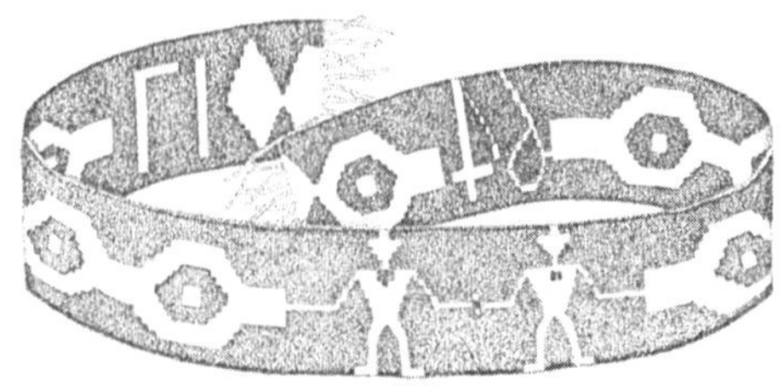

Chapter Seven

From Proclamation to Constitution

I've come to believe that the Haudenosaunee Covenant Chain–Two Row method for how to make civil relations set the groundwork for Canada's social contract, that it has structured this country's basic rules about who "we," its signatories, are and how we relate to one another.

As a key player in the contact zone of his times, Sir William Johnson, Imperial Indian Superintendent for the British, formulated the Royal Proclamation of 1763, Britain's self-defining statement of sovereignty in North America after the conquest of New France, on the basis of the Covenant Chain–Two Row Wampum relationship with the Haudenosaunee. In turn, the Royal Proclamation set the precedent for the protection of "aboriginal and treaty rights" in Sections 25 and 35 of Canada's Constitution Act (1982).

Section 25 reads:

> The guarantee in this Charter of certain rights and freedoms shall not be construed so as to abrogate or derogate from any aboriginal, treaty or other rights or freedoms that pertain to the aboriginal peoples of Canada including
>
> (a) any rights or freedoms that have been recognized by the Royal Proclamation of October 7, 1763; and

> (b) any rights or freedoms that may be acquired by the aboriginal peoples of Canada by way of land claims settlement.

Section 35 (1), reads, "The existing aboriginal and treaty rights of the aboriginal peoples of Canada are hereby recognized and affirmed."

Because of these statements, a whole legal industry has emerged since the "patriation of the Constitution" in 1982 with court case after court case working to define what "aboriginal" means, and what "rights" we're talking about. The need for clarification arises because Canadians have tended to read the Constitution in isolation, rather than as emerging from the ecosystem for agreement-making that had evolved from British engagements with Haudenosaunee diplomatic protocols and practices.

One form of isolation is to read these references to "aboriginal and treaty rights" as pertaining to Indigenous Peoples alone. Instead, they have more to do with ordering and regulating *Canadians* than they do Indigenous Peoples. And, for this reason, I'll begin with a focus on Section 25, which appears in the Charter of Rights and Freedoms.

After guaranteeing that every Canadian has freedom of conscience and religion; freedom of thought, belief, opinion and expression; freedom of the press and other means of communication; freedom of peaceful assembly and freedom of association;

After declaring democratic rights; the right to a fair trial; freedom of mobility, equality before and under the law without discrimination based on race, national or ethnic origin, colour, religion, sex, age or mental or physical disability;

After declaring the freedom to pursue remedies for any infractions upon these freedoms in court in either English or French language, the only two official languages each Canadian is entitled to speak and learn;

After identifying all these rights and freedoms, right there in the Charter of Rights and Freedoms – a statement so essential to what Canada says it is all about that it gets posted on the bulletin boards of classrooms across the country;

We find: the Two Row principle that no freedom in the Canadian vessel grants the right to abrogate (repeal or do away with) or derogate (detract or deviate) from any aboriginal or treaty right in the Indigenous vessel.

That is, the Charter of Canadian rights must respect and uphold the distinctive rights of those who ride in the distinctive Indigenous canoe.

To enjoy the rights and freedoms of the Charter a Canadian must respect the Indigenous "rights or freedoms that have been recognized by the Royal Proclamation of October 7, 1763." These rights and freedoms include the rights to share the river of life in peace, friendship and respect that had been formulated in the Covenant Chain–Two Row Wampum series of agreements, as well as the rights of each vessel to retain their "culture, beliefs, and laws" in their own canoe or sailing ship as they shared the river.

One river, two vessels. This configuration of relations is constitutive of "Canada."

This is why all Canadians – not just ones like me who live next door to Haudenosaunee territory – need to learn about and respect the Covenant Chain–Two Row tradition: it set the groundwork for our Constitution, which had everything to do with protecting what the Royal Proclamation called "unceded" Indigenous lands by "setting rights and responsibilities for settler colonial people," not, as is commonly thought, by presuming to rule over Indigenous Peoples, who were allies, not subjects, of the Crown.

This reading is borne out by two court cases that have recently affirmed the Covenant Chain–Two Row tradition as legally, constitutionally binding. The first is *R. v. Williams* (June 2023), in which Judge Gethin Edward of the Ontario Court of Justice determined that Skyler Williams should be discharged from the accusations of mischief and contravening a court injunction to stay off a disputed land development because by applying the principles of "Kuswentah, the Two Row Wampum," the judge determined that "Skyler Williams was carrying out his actions as a land protector in the context of these Haudenosaunee laws contained metaphorically within the canoe. Therefore, the public are the Haudenosaunee people. And this Court concludes that community would not conclude his actions in protecting their land was not in their public interest."[1] The second case is Quebec Superior Court decision *R. v. Monture and White* (November 2023), in which Judge Sophie Bourque, guided by lawyer Kayanesenh Paul Williams and the expert testimony of Amber

Meadow Adams, PhD in Haudenosaunee studies, alongside Chief Curtis Nelson of Kanesatake and the Mohawk Nation Council of Chiefs, sorted through the 360-year history of the Covenant Chain agreement between the Haudenosaunee and the British to determine exactly what I am claiming here: that the Covenant Chain agreement constituted a regularly renewed oral and wampum metatreaty that shaped Sir William Johnson's formulation of the Royal Proclamation, which in turn set the precedent for Section 35(1) and its recognition of Aboriginal and treaty rights. Here is Judge Bourque's statement from a section entitled "D.2.5 Conclusion on the constitutional status of the Covenant Chain":

> [1050] Amidst the turbulence of that era [of what British colonial historians have called the "French and Indian Wars"], two civilizations [the Haudenosaunee and the British] encountered one another and, in response to the challenge that this represented, they devised a distinctive mechanism to favour and govern a mutually beneficial relationship, the Covenant Chain.
>
> [1051] Through their entry into and subsequent renewals of the Covenant Chain, the parties intended to establish a lasting relationship characterized by both a military and friendship alliance. This alliance was to be guided by the principles of Haudenosaunee diplomatic protocol and included a conflict-resolution procedure.
>
> [1052] The Court concludes that the Covenant Chain is a treaty between the Haudenosaunee and the British, as recognized by s. 35(1).[2]

Judge Bourque's decision has already been appealed in Quebec court, and could very likely be sent on to the Supreme Court of Canada, since a provincial court's decision about a constitutional matter would need to be scrutinized by the Supreme Court.

However, while official bodies have the expertise to produce legal arguments like these about the precedential legal influences of the Covenant Chain–Two Row Wampum, from the provincial courts to the Supreme Court to the governor general and eventually to Parliament, nothing will change until a broad groundswell of public opinion calls for it. Movements like this will only happen, as Mohawk Native Studies and law professor Patricia Monture-Angus once said, when we understand law as something that touches our hearts and not just our heads. In a talk on "Legal Foundations of Haudenosaunee Assertions of Sovereignty," *Kanyen'kehàka* law professor Beverley Jacobs, who teaches at University of Windsor and is former president of the Native Women's Association of Canada, cited the now-deceased Monture-Angus on what's wrong with law in Canada, which is that we have taken the responsibility out of it. "It is not about your head where the answer lies," said Jacobs, quoting Monture-Angus. "It's about feeling, not about your head. Unfairness and anger are in your heart. The idea of objective law doesn't address this sense of feeling and fairness. Our responsibility is to put the heart back into law, *then* it can be about law and about justice again."[3] I hope my comments in this chapter can address the widespread *feeling* and knowledge of unfairness that Indigenous Peoples cannot avoid and of which more and more Canadians are increasingly aware. I hope they can help to generate from this feeling an increasing political will, a responsibility, to motivate our parliamentarians and court system to return to the good-mindedness, the spirit and principles of our founding agreements.

Our ancestors began by linking arms. They agreed to protect each other's interests and autonomy. They said these promises would last as long as the sun shines, the grass turns green and the rivers flow. These agreements have never been officially rejected by Canada or the Crown.[4] Canadians' awareness of not having lived up to them remains a palpable feeling of failed responsibility that contradicts the long history of parliaments and legislatures, courts and police, and even the army insisting on the status quo, insisting that each and every abrogation and derogation has been justified.[5]

Others better qualified than I, lawyers and law professors such as Patricia Monture-Angus (Kanyen'kehá:ka, Native Studies at University of Saskatchewan, now deceased), John Borrows (Anishinaabe, Indigenous Governance Program, University of Victoria), James Sa'ke'j Youngblood Henderson (Cheyenne, Native Law Centre of Canada, Saskatoon), Doug White (Kwulasultun, BC First Nations Justice Council), Beverley Jacobs (Kanyen'kehàka, Faculty of Law, University of Windsor), Kayanesenh Paul Williams (Onondaga lawyer, who serves as legal council for many

First Nations, including the Haudenosaunee Confederacy Council) and many others have been developing legal arguments in the courts, in legal philosophy and in jurisprudence for some time. But experts like these need a broad base of public support, they need the political will of a wide range of non-experts, to convince the governors general, supreme courts and the parliaments of our day to even entertain the arguments.[6] What I can do, as a non-specialist, is tell the story as best I can, tracing the consistent flow of Haudenosaunee principles that run through the history of Canada's formation, and leaving the forensic analysis and arguments to the specialists.

So, to go back.

Sir William Johnson and the Royal Proclamation

You could say that Johnson himself was a contact zone, positioned as he was in a *Kanyen'kehá:ka* family living in *Kanyen'kehá:ka* territory and functioning simultaneously as a businessman and as an emissary of the king. His role as "Sole Agent and Superintendent of the said Indians"[7] was primarily to build and enhance alliances with the Indigenous nations who had linked arms with the British, primarily the Haudenosaunee, over and against their rivals, the French and their allies, during the Seven Years War.[8] This mandate gave him a budget and direct line of communication with the Crown and the Lords of Trade that were not determined, in the first instance at least, by the colonial assemblies in New York, Connecticut, Nova Scotia, Pennsylvania, New Brunswick, Virginia, Massachusetts or the other British colonies. Very often the priority of retaining the good faith of Indigenous allies put him at odds with the land-hungry colonists.

This is important. As Crown Appointee in Northeastern America, he was, in a way, a precedent for our current vice-regal representatives, the governor general and provincial lieutenant governors. He was not a representative of the local colonial assemblies. He was not selected by them, and his term extended as long as the Crown chose to hold him in "his Majesty's Commission." His duty was to protect the Crown's interests in

America, and, during his times, the linked arms with Indigenous allies were central to those interests.

The images of the two human figures at either end of the Covenant Chain can lead us to personify the two sides as unified "individuals." But, of course, Six Nations was not one community but (at least) six, and the "British" were actually a series of colonies spread up and down the Atlantic coast, each with their own local assemblies, economies and priorities. Sir William Johnson represented the faraway "Crown," and his ability to negotiate between the varied interests of a widening network of Indigenous allies and those of the various colonies required a constant high-wire balancing act of compromise, tough enforcement of the Crown's priorities and dependence on a constantly shifting set of friends and enemies. As Rick Hill puts it, given Johnson's creative and skillful use of Haudenosaunee metaphors and cultural protocols, the Crown's Superintendent of Indian Affairs was the linchpin that held the Covenant Chain together.[9]

As France's power and influence declined in America after the capitulation of Quebec in 1760, he also had to navigate between long-term British allies such as the Six Nations and former enemy First Nations who had been trading partners of the French and with whom, as representative of the king, he now needed to link arms.

At the centre of his worries was his ability to retain the Crown's Indigenous allies by protecting their lands from being expropriated by British colonists.

Very often, therefore, Johnson found himself mediating in the tense clearing Kiotsaeton had occupied between a variety of parties, interests and alliances arrayed on all sides.

Given his explicitly international, cross-cultural, diplomatic role, Johnson busily extended the principles of the Covenant Chain–Two Row treaty tradition with which his *Kanyen'kehá:ka* family had made him so familiar. His wife, Mary (Molly) Brant, served as a cultural mediator, helping him understand where the Haudenosaunee were coming from and what he needed to say to address their frame of mind. At the same time, she helped her *Kanyen'kehá:ka* relatives understand what the Crown (and Johnson) were trying to achieve. His relationship with her was an intimate link in the chain with the Haudenosaunee. He worked intensively to link arms with a wide variety of Indigenous nations and colonial administrations throughout his tenure as superintendent from his appointment in 1755 until his death in 1774. He was central, for example, to advising the king on the drawing of what came to be known as the "Proclamation Line" that forbade colonists from settling on Indigenous lands west of the Appalachian and Allegheny ranges, as well as the important recognition of allied Indigenous nations' rights to "unceded lands" in the Royal Proclamation.[10]

The British colonies' security immediately following the withdrawal of France from the region remained delicate. Fraudulent purchases of Mohawk land such as the Kayaderosseras and Canajoharie patents had been ratified by New York colonial courts, angering the Kanyen'kehá:ka, who were the king's staunchest allies in the region. The nations to the west who had previously traded with the French were affronted when British soldiers and traders occupied French forts or trading posts without recognizing these nations' sovereignty or offering trade benefits to match what the French had previously offered. Under Seneca and Ottawa (*Odawa*) co-ordination, what has come to be called Pontiac's War (1763) flared up when Ojibways took Fort Michilimackinac and Ottawas laid siege to Fort Detroit. Senecas cut off Niagara with a deadly attack at Devil's Hole and killed garrisons at British posts throughout the Ohio country, south of Lake Erie. The Delawares and Shawnees aimed to take Fort Pitt.[11]

Johnson therefore campaigned with the Lords of Trade in Whitehall to solicit official statements from the king that would shore up British administration in the region by placating their allies, both long-established ones and the new ones Britain was hoping to attract, especially through protecting their land from "frauds and abuses." Due to Johnson's advice and urging, therefore, King George III published the Royal Proclamation, dated December 24, 1763, declaring that it is "essential to our Interest and the Security of our Colonies, that the several Nations or Tribes of Indians, with whom we are connected, and who live under our Protection, should not be molested or disturbed in the Possession of such Parts of our Dominions and Territories as, not having been ceded to, or purchased by Us, are reserved to them, or any of them as their Hunting Grounds." There are many details to comment on here. Such as the use of the word "nations" to refer to Indigenous Peoples or tribes. This usage flies in the face of those who would claim that early colonial powers such as Britain did not think of groups of Indigenous Peoples as nations, and that they therefore did not consider treaties they made with them to be "nation-to-nation" agreements.[12]

Next, the Proclamation distinguishes between Nations or Tribes "with whom we are connected" and those who "live under our Protection" – otherwise why list them separately? Kayanesenh Paul Williams points out that the first written treaty between the Crown and the Haudenosaunee made at Fort Albany almost a hundred years earlier, on September 23 and 24, 1664, "distinguished between people 'belonging to any of the Sachims' of the Haudenosaunee, on the one hand, and 'Indians under the protection of the English,' on the other."[13] A century later, this terminology distinguished allies such as the Haudenosaunee, with whom the British had been long connected, from the Western nations, whose participation in the fur trade had been previously protected by the French, and whose access to the trade would now, after the departure of the French, be protected by the English. In both cases, the Crown notes that lands not previously "ceded to, or Purchased by Us, are reserved to them."

The language of "ceded" and "unceded" territories so common in today's discussions about Indigenous lands traces to the Royal Proclamation.

Indeed, as Haudenosaunee anger over the Kayaderosseras and Canajoharie Patents showed, the British stood to lose whatever allies they had gained over land losses. The Proclamation thus proclaims:

> And whereas great Frauds and Abuses have been committed in the purchasing Lands of the Indians, to the great Prejudice of our interest, and to the great Dissatisfaction of the said Indians; in order therefore to prevent such Irregularities for the future, and to the End that the Indians may be convinced of our Justice, and determined Resolution to remove all reasonable Cause of Discontents, We do with the Advice of our Privy Council,

> strictly enjoin and require that no private Person do presume to make any Purchase from the said Indians of any Lands reserved to the said Indians, within those Parts of our Colonies where We have thought proper to allow Settlements; but that if, at any Time, any of the said Indians should be inclined to dispose of the said Lands, the same shall be purchased only for Us, in our Name, at some Publick Meeting or Assembly of the said Indians to be held for that Purpose by the Governor or Commander in Chief of our Colonies respectively, within which they shall lie; and in Case they shall lie within the Limits of any Proprietary Government, they shall be purchased only for the Use and in the Name of such Proprietaries, conformable to such Directions and Instructions as We or they shall think proper to give for that Purpose.

Here we see what the Proclamation meant by "protection." The Crown took upon itself the role of protecting Indigenous nations from British colonial land speculators and their unscrupulous land grabs by asserting that, henceforth, any exchanges of land must occur at public meetings or assemblies with the "said Indians" and that these meetings be convened by the governor or commander-in-chief of the colony in question. The requirement of these public meetings replicates the series of regular Covenant Chain–renewing councils the British had held with the Haudenosaunee in Albany, ever since they replaced the Dutch administration in New York in 1664.[14]

The point of these injunctions was to avoid any more private swindles, such as the one William Johnson tried unsuccessfully to reverse in 1763 after a number of Canajoharie Mohawks had been enticed to sign away a block of land. Johnson attended the March 10 judicial inquiry convened by the Justices of the New York colony to investigate the affair. The witnesses from Canajoharie indicated that they had been induced by alcohol and bribes to sign away their nation's land, and that the survey of the patent in question had been cooked in the purchasers' favour.[15] Cayenquiragoa, one of the main spokespeople from Canajoharie, rose to speak:

> I am heartily glad that so many Justices are now present to hear and bear testimony of what we have said. I have mentioned to you that such

proceedings may prove bad, as you know that we are now all in Alliance & Friendship with all Indians, must it not appear very bad and cause the other Nations to laugh at us, should you who are our next Neighbours, and with whom we have always been friends act such a part, and appear to be at Variance with us who are the heads of the Six Nations.[16]

Cayenquiragoa suggests that it will not be attractive to potential allies among the Western nations to ally themselves with the British if they see that the Six Nations, with whom the British are connected, have been swindled and taken advantage of by their supposed friends; that the British authorities were unable to protect their existing Indigenous friends – let alone would-be friends – from the greed of their own colonial subjects. Then he enjoins the Justices of the colonial assembly to repolish their end of the Covenant Chain–Two Row agreement. His people are familiar with the practice of dusting and refreshing the wampum, he says, but

for our parts we are not used to Silver, and cannot brighten the Chain which we are apprehensive begins to be weak from the Rust it has contracted, We must therefore entreat you to brighten and preserve the same in order to prevent it from breaking –

I cannot too often repeat our desire that the Chain might be preserved on your parts, which may otherwise occasion our Fire to go out both here and at Onondaga . . .

We Love the Covenant Chain as we do our Lives, and we do the same by our Lands, which we are determined to dye by, rather than give up.[17]

It's clear that Cayenquiragoa sees Mohawk maintenance of their relationship to their lands as consistent with maintenance of the covenant with the British. "Protection," in this context then, means mutual protection of the covenant. Each side of the linked arms must requicken their side of the agreement. "We must therefore entreat you to brighten and preserve the same in order to prevent it from breaking." This principle, whereby the parties to the alliance keep their own house in order, hearkens to the above-mentioned Treaty of Albany of September 25 and 26, 1664, when the British colony of New York was just being established. In that first written treaty between the Haudenosaunee and the British, Colonel George Cartwright, the commanding officer at Albany, agreed with the "Maquaes" (Mohawks) and "Synicks" (Senecas), the keepers of the eastern and western doors of the Confederacy, to maintain order within their separate jurisdictions. Any Dutch, English or Indigenous person living under the governance of the British fort who committed a crime would answer to the Officer in Chief at Albany, while any "Indians belonging to any of the Sachims" would answer to the "Sachims."[18] Cayenquiragoa therefore calls upon the British to brighten the silver chain that represents their version of the agreement. In the case of the Canajoharie lands, this means protecting their Indigenous friends and allies in the colony's own courts by restraining Britain's colonial sharpsters. It means British colonial governments getting their own house in order. Linked arms requires preserving separate spheres, clear zones of jurisdiction.

The Covenant Chain is brightened by keeping members of one's own vessel from trying to take the properties of the other.

It means, to flash forward, that the rights and freedoms of the Crown's subjects must not abrogate or derogate "from any aboriginal, treaty or other rights or freedoms," especially their rights and freedoms upon lands "not having been ceded to, or purchased by Us" – the "Royal We" that Canadians today refer to as the "Crown."

Indeed, the Royal Proclamation extends this kind of protection from land to other economies derived from land, such as the trade in furs for tools, guns, ammunition and other supplies: "And We do, by the Advice of our Privy Council, declare and enjoin, that the Trade with the said Indians shall be free and open to all our Subjects whatever; provided that every Person, who may incline to trade with the said Indians, to take out a Licence for carrying on such Trade from the Governor or Commander in Chief of any of our Colonies respectively, where such Person shall reside." The trade anticipated here is to be between "the said Indians" and "all our Subjects" who must "take out a Licence," again, under the supervision of the Governor or Commander in Chief of the colony in which that subject resides. Here the Proclamation distinguishes the "said Indians" from "all our Subjects," indicating that protection does not mean subjection. The "said Indians" are not "Subjects." The two paths remain distinct. This usage is repeated in the injunction against settlers occupying land West of the "Proclamation Line" of the Appalachian-Allegheny mountain range: "We do hereby strictly forbid, on Pain of our Displeasure, all our loving Subjects from making any Purchases or Settlements whatever, or taking Possession of any of the Lands above reserved, without our especial Leave and Licence for that Purpose first obtained."[19]

I am aware that for readers who aren't specialists in law, let alone Constitutional law, my pages here about the Royal Proclamation may feel like a hair-splitting game over words. But each of these words and phrases – "Nations," "ceded," "protection," "said Indians," "subjects," "with whom we are connected," "Lands reserved for the Indians" – have been and will continue to be pored over whenever Canada seeks to address the basis of its relationship with Indigenous Peoples. As Lord Dunning put it, in his judgment for the Privy Council in 1981 during the lead-up to the Constitution Act (1982), the Royal Proclamation, as a founding precedent for the 1982 Constitution, functions as a Magna Carta, "an Indian Bill of Rights."[20] To trace its function as a bill of rights, we need to understand how the terms and ideas of the Covenant Chain–Two Row tradition flowed from one of these transactions to the next.

And, to trace the flow of legislative jurisdiction from the Royal Proclamation to the British North America Act to the Constitution Act of 1982, we need to be aware of the significant expansion of Covenant Chain–Two Row principles that occurred immediately after the Royal Proclamation. This is the period after the Seven Years War and its echo in Pontiac's War of 1763, when, in the words of Kayanesenh Paul Williams, "the Proclamation was part of Sir William Johnson's peacemaking toolkit."[21] Johnson immediately set about the task of extending the Covenant Chain to the "Western nations" who had shown the British how tenuous their hold was upon the trading territories relinquished by New France. He had fifty copies of the Royal Proclamation printed in preparation for a whole series of meetings with Indigenous nations.[22] The most immediately important of these was the Treaty of Niagara, where he invited twenty-four nations, comprising over two thousand delegates, to join (or renew) the Covenant Chain–Two Row relationship. The Haudenosaunee Confederacy were in attendance, including the Six Nations plus the Haudenosaunee members of the Seven Nations of Canada (including Kahnawà:ke, Kanesatake, Akwesasne and Oswegatchie). So also were the Anishinaabe ("Chippewaes," in Johnson's list), Ottawas, Potawatomis, Crees ("Christineaux"), Algonquins, Nipissings, Hurons, Sauks and Foxes.[23] We can get a sense of how significant the treaty-making at Niagara was through Kayanesenh Paul Williams' reminder that "the traditional territory of those nations is a third of present-day Canada. And the land treaties, in much of that territory, do not supersede the Proclamation: they coexist with it."[24]

Rufus Grider's redrawn seal of Sir William Johnson, circa 1890. (Image from Milton W. Hamilton, ed., *The Papers of Sir William Johnson*, vol. 13 [Albany: University of the State of New York, 1962], 98.)

Extending the Covenant Chain relationship to these other nations was crucial to establishing peace in the region – it was necessary to both the British and their Haudenosaunee allies and to the concept of "protecting" the land for future generations. Consistently, Johnson's lexicon for making these alliances came from the concepts and symbolism of the Haudenosaunee Covenant Chain–Two Row tradition. The personal wax seal, for example, that he used to certify the written testimonials that he issued to confirm new allies' formal ties to the Crown borrows the image of the Circle Wampum from the Haudenosaunee Great Law and refashions it into a chain grasped by seven arms ("six unclothed arms and his clothed one"[25]). This chain surrounds a set of symbols that include the tree of peace, the pipe, the hill at Onondaga with smoke rising from its council fire, a sailing ship and a canoe – all symbols from the Haudenosaunee diplomatic lexicon. For the treaty meetings at Niagara in 1764, he had a version of the Covenant Chain Wampum specially designed for distribution to the twenty-four nations gathered there.

The Treaty of Niagara and the Extension of the Covenant

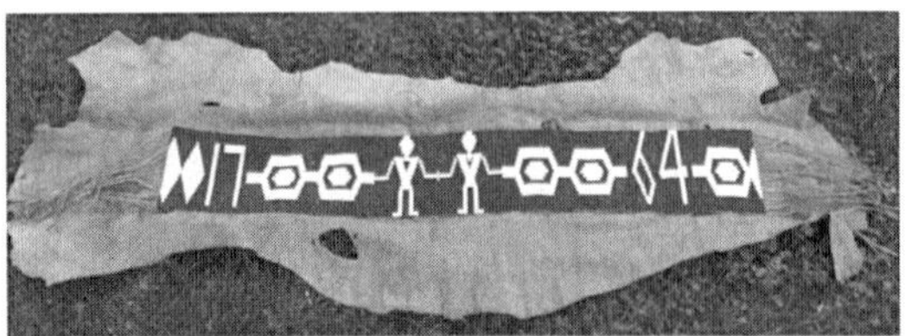
The 1764 Covenant Chain Wampum Belt; replica commissioned by Nathan Tidridge and created by Ken Maracle, March 8, 2014. (Photo by Nathan Tidridge.)

We can see the ongoing evolution of Covenant Chain–Two Row peacemaking in this 1764 Covenant Chain Wampum's addition of European numbers to the image of linked arms (the lozenges or squares representing linked, distinct fires of the various nations). Anishinaabe historian Alan Corbiere, one of the descendants of the "Ojibways" who attended the Treaty of Niagara, has traced how wampum belts such as this one begin to incorporate letters and numbers from European languages as they become instruments for European diplomacy in North America: "The 1764 Covenant Chain wampum represents a syncretic blend of symbols between two literary traditions," he writes. "In fact this belt should be approached as a document that evolved from prior treaties and wampum belts. The symbols used and the talk contained therein suggest a tradition akin to British common law, in which the compilation of various rulings on various torts had eventually led to a system of common law based upon precedents that lawyers, judges, and others in the legal profession could consult and debate in order to resolve a dispute or issue, in a manner informed by prior decisions and actions."[26]

For his part, Rick Hill sees the designs as evoking the Covenant Chain, but also adding a reference to the Dish With One Spoon Wampum, whereby Johnson was advocating that the British forts be considered as outlining the Great Dish, the region where the Indigenous allies would come for presents, foods and clothing from the king. Hill suggests that Johnson was trying to change the image of the fort from being seen as a military intrusion to representing a meeting ground where allies linked arms. If the 1764 Treaty of Niagara belt was connected end to end to form a circle, he suggests, the design is complete, with a dish shared by two confederacies as seen in the linked diamonds and human figures. In this way Johnson is making allies of former fur trade adversaries, uniting them to return to the tradition of sharing from the Dish, both in the woods and at the forts.[27]

Johnson's syncretic wampum inspired others. Sometimes, rivalling others.

Thirty years later, for example, after the Revolutionary War, George Washington used similar wampum iconography to record and ratify the Treaty of Canandaigua with those Haudenosaunee who remained in the territory claimed by the newly independent thirteen colonies. The Canandaigua Treaty belt, commissioned by Washington in 1790, showed thirteen states linking arms with the Haudenosaunee. By the time of Canandaigua in 1794, the member states had increased to fifteen. Rick Hill reads this belt as conveying Washington's desire to make peace with the nations he tried to exterminate in 1779, addressing Seneca land concerns and creating ways by which American-Haudenosaunee friendship could be reaffirmed.[28] It was, among other things, a bid to court Haudenosaunee friendship away from the alliances Johnson had built in the 1760s. In instances such as these, colonial authorities such as William Johnson and George Washington show they knew that, if they were to survive on Turtle Island, they would need to present these agreements in a form that their allies would perceive as holding the highest ceremonial gravitas. We can get a sense of how important wampum was to early colonial diplomacy when Anishinaabe legal philosopher John Borrows writes that Johnson spent over thirty-eight thousand pounds sterling, an astronomical sum at the time, on the wampum and other gifts he distributed in 1764.[29]

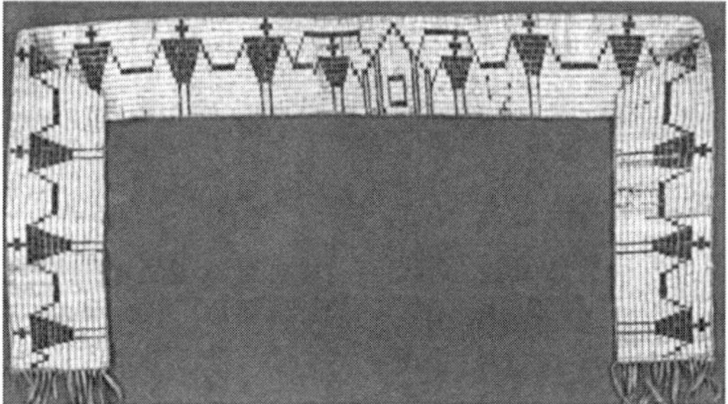

The 1794 Canandaigua Treaty Belt (also known as the George Washington Belt) is six feet long and composed of thirteen figures holding hands connected to two figures and a house. The thirteen figures represent the thirteen states of the newly formed United States of America. The two figures and the house symbolize the Haudenosaunee. The two figures next to the longhouse represent the Mohawk (easternmost of the Six Nations) and the Seneca (Keepers of the Western Door). (Source: Six Nations Legacy Consortium Collection and the Six Nations Public Library, http://www.onondaganation.org/culture/wampum/george-washington-belt/)

In the years after 1763–1764, Johnson worked energetically to expand the Covenant Chain–Two Row Treaty relationship, to "extend the rafters" of peace and friendship from its conceptual home in Haudenosaunee diplomatic culture west to the Ohio country, south to the Carolinas, all along the Great Lakes and St. Lawrence to the Atlantic coast. He confirmed Covenant Chain treaties with the Wabanaki Confederacy in Nova Scotia in 1766.[30] And he convened a treaty of alliance between the Haudenosaunee and the Cherokee at Johnson Hall in 1770.[31]

Johnson's Covenant Chain–Two Row approach to Indigenous relations powerfully shaped British policy in North America for seventy crucial years, writes Amber Meadow Adams, through the defeat of the French colonial regime in New France, the formalization of British colonial administration in the period that followed, and leading into the American War of Independence. By the time of his death in 1774, he had built a bureaucracy peopled largely by his own family members, so that his approach was followed over several generations by son-in-law Daniel Claus, his deputy based at Montreal; his nephew and son-in-law Guy Johnson, his successor in 1775; his son Sir John Johnson, who took over the Imperial superintendency until his death in 1830; and his grandson William Claus, who became a Deputy Superintendent General.[32] There's no doubt that Johnson, his wife Konwatsi'tsayén:ni Mary Brant and his descendants played crucial roles in spreading the Covenant Chain–Two Row understanding of treaty-making far beyond Haudenosaunee country by means of the Royal Proclamation and its regional affirmations, making the Haudenosaunee protocols central to how the British conducted treaties in many places.

Johnson's spreading of the Covenant Chain–Two Row set of protocols allows us to see how this way of agreement-making became the "grandfather of the treaties." It also helps us see how it functioned as a grandparent of the Canadian Constitution.

This account does not depend on Johnson being an unblemished champion of Indigenous relations. It's important to remember that the relationships I am tracing in this part of this book were negotiated and ratified by flawed and contradictory people in the midst of compromised and compromising circumstances, just as they are today. For one thing, even though Johnson campaigned for the Royal Proclamation's protection of Indigenous lands, he himself acquired hundreds of thousands of acres of land in *Kanyen'kehà:ka* territory.[33] To farm these extensive land holdings, he imported white indentured labourers and enslaved Black people.[34] He made his personal fortune through business facilitated by his contracts both as colonel of the Six Nations and the New York militia and as Superintendent of Indian Affairs. The thirty-eight thousand pounds sterling he spent on wampum for the treaty meetings at Niagara in 1764 didn't come from his own pocket. As agent and superintendent, he had a budget line from the Crown that he used to buy favour among both settlers and Indigenous people.[35]

Furthermore, as a strategist for British colonial policy, his cards were not always clearly on the table when he treated with Haudenosaunee and other Indigenous Peoples. In the midst of planning for the Treaty of Niagara, for example, where he hoped to gather Western nations with Haudenosaunee allies, he wrote privately to General Gage on February 19, 1764, "In my opinion a Treaty of Offensive & Defensive Alliance would be the best, as we would then have a right to claim their assistance on occasion, & they would hardly ever desire ours for any thing other than Arms & Ammunition which it would be our interest to give them in a War with each other. That we should enter into this with each Confederacy against the other, which would put them more on their guard hereafter."[36]

Statements like this look like classic colonial divide-and-conquer tactics. Hardly the peace that arises from a whole-hearted linking of arms. But then, he's saying this about the new alliances he was seeking to create with former allies of the French and enemies of the Haudenosaunee. And he's saying these words to another British officer. Who knows what he would have said to Konwatsi'tsayén:ni Mary Brant or her Canajoharie *rotiyaneshon* and *yakoyaneshon* relatives?

Several months earlier, he had written to other British administrators in "Memoranda Concerning Indians," November 10, 1763, "Such Indians as are yet our Friends [are] to be kindly used and make it their Interest to continue so, *until we are better able to do without them*, otherwise they may turn our Enemies before Spring."[37]

Doesn't sound like "as long as the sun shines, the rivers flow and the grass turns green" to me.

So it's not easy to nail down the contact zone that is Sir William Johnson. Perhaps, like many others who negotiate in the space between two vessels, he wavered. However we evaluate his true commitments, his place in the Imperial gravy train made him and his policies the objects of resentment for many colonists. He got wealthy on Indigenous lands, while his colonial neighbours were forbidden access to the same resources and relationships through which he built his fortune. Eventually, his campaign to rule Indigenous lands out-of-bounds for his fellow colonists made him and his family the enemies of the patriots, and Mary and the children had to flee after his death to British North America when his estate was overtaken by American troops during the Revolutionary War.

Johnson's case makes it clear, therefore, that the principles conveyed in the ecosystem of the Covenant Chain–Two Row tradition don't arise from a sterilized scenario of good guys with squeaky-clean motivations.

Which does not mean its principles aren't good principles. They still shine whenever treaty partners use the great wing to sweep away the dust that arises from corrupt values and hidden motives from the White Mat of wampum where councils meet to discuss the continuance of peace, when we brighten the chain that links different people, even those of uncertain virtue, into the common cause of *skén:nen*. It is in response to mixed characters like Johnson and their less-than-stellar motivations acting on behalf of the Crown that Canadian courts, trying to reconcile different interpretations of historical treaties have developed the concept of the "honour of the Crown." Judge Bourque cites *R. v. Badger* (1996), for example, to remind us that "the honour of the Crown is always at stake in its dealing with Indian people. Interpretations of treaties and statutory provisions which have an impact upon treaty or aboriginal rights must be approached in a manner which maintains the integrity of the Crown. It is always assumed that the Crown intends to fulfil its promises. No appearance of 'sharp dealing' will be sanctioned."[38]

So the Constitution of Canada names the Royal Proclamation as the precedent for recognizing "aboriginal and treaty rights" in Canada. And, as I've tried to show in this chapter, the Royal Proclamation built this foundational statement about Britain's own sovereignty upon the Covenant Chain–Two Row principles by which differentiated parties live respectfully in two parallel roads as they link arms to mutually protect their alliance and the lands on which they live. These principles, then, shaped the Royal Proclamation, which is, to cite Justice Laskin in *Calder* (1973) citing Lord Dunning, "analogous to the status of Magna Carta which has always been considered to be the law throughout the Empire."[39]

This is why my rights as a Canadian to a fair trial without discrimination or my freedom to assemble or to move freely around the country cannot derogate or abrogate from the "aboriginal and treaty rights" that also appear in the Charter of Rights and Freedoms. The distinctive relationship between my rights and Indigenous Peoples' rights are foundational to the Constitution of Canada.

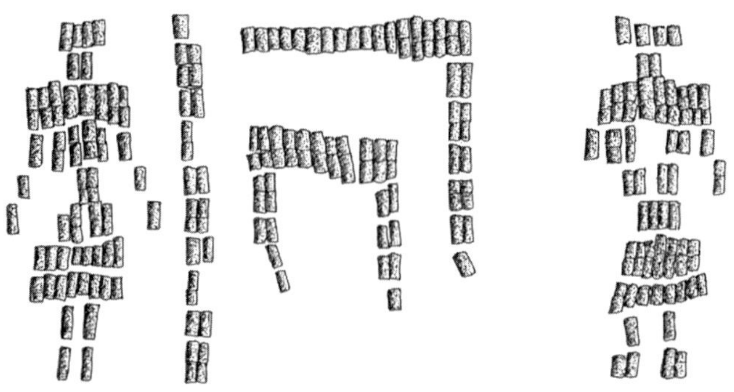

Chapter Eight

Race and the Other Theology:

The Doctrine of Discovery

If principles of the Covenant Chain–Two Row tradition formed the spine or vertebrae on which the Royal Proclamation was built, and if the Royal Proclamation placed a "Bill of Indian Rights" in the Charter of Canadian Rights and Freedoms, what happened? Why are the rights outlined in Sections 25 and 35 – "aboriginal," treaty and land rights – so much under contention and debate all these years later?

It would be easy to assume that it's a matter of ignorance or forgetting: the powers that be simply don't know – or have deliberately forgotten – about the old tradition and the agreements they made.

But it's clear that they do know.

The British Crown, U.S., Canadian and Haudenosaunee governments all continue to refer to the Covenant Chain protocols, even in the twenty-first century, whenever they wish to remind themselves or each other of the basis on which our relationships were formed. For the 2010 commemoration of the three hundredth anniversary of the diplomatic mission of the "Four Indian [Mohawk] Kings" to the court of Queen Anne, for example, Queen Elizabeth II presented a set of silver handbells to the Mohawk Chapel in Brantford, Ontario. The bells were engraved with the words "The Silver Chain of Friendship 1710–2010."[1] Such a gesture makes me assume that the queen had not forgotten. Yet, as Rick Hill reminded me when he read this passage, the Grand River Haudenosaunee had been involved in the major land dispute in Caledonia since 2006, and the queen did not see fit to intervene. Or yet again, in the very year in which she sent the handbells with their reminder of the Silver Covenant Chain of Friendship, the Haudenosaunee Nationals Lacrosse team attempted to board a flight to England to compete in the 2010 World Men's Lacrosse Championships and were denied a boarding pass because the Haudenosaunee passports they carried were deemed not valid for international travel. The queen, as a loyal friend and ally, did not intervene.

In Canada, after Prime Minister Stephen Harper's government offered an official apology for the intergenerational harms caused by the Indian Residential School system in 2008 and launched a Royal Commission Inquiry into the continuing traumatic effects of the schools, the Covenant Chain–Two Row Wampum was reviewed at the Crown-Assembly of First Nations gathering of January 24, 2012, to remind everyone that the agreement needs repolishing.[2] "To signify the importance of the long-standing relationship between First Nations and the Crown, then AFN National Chief Shawn A-in-chut Atleo presented a Silver Covenant Chain of Peace and a Friendship Belt to Prime Minister Harper and the governor general of Canada, the Right Honourable David Johnston. He explained,

> The Covenant Chain belt represents one of the earliest treaties between the Crown and First Nations peoples and established the foundation for First Nations–Crown relationships for generations thereafter. The belt shows that the Crown is linked by a chain to the First Nations peoples of this land. The three links of the chain represent a covenant of friendship, good minds, and the peace that shall always remain between us. The covenant chain is made of silver symbolizing that the relationship will be polished from time to time to keep it from tarnishing. This was the basis of the Nation to Nation relationship between the British Crown and the First Nations who became their allies in the formation of Canada."[3]

So the Canadian government has been reminded. Many times. Yet, Prime Minister Harper also had nothing to say about the land dispute in Caledonia and even stated publicly that the governor general had no say over Indigenous affairs – despite the governor general being the representative for the Crown in Canada with whom the Covenant Chain agreement had been made and renewed in the Royal Proclamation.

Likewise, in his opening remarks at the Tribal Nations Conference held at the White House on November 13, 2013, President Barack Obama evoked the Covenant Chain–Two Row agreement:

> I know we've got members of the Iroquois nation here today. And I think we could learn from the Iroquois Confederacy, just as our Founding Fathers did when they laid the groundwork for our democracy. The Iroquois called their network of alliances with other tribes and European nations a "covenant chain." Each link represented a bond of peace and friendship. But that covenant chain didn't sustain itself. It needed constant care, so that it would stay strong. And that's what we're called to do, to keep the covenant between us for this generation and for future generations.[4]

These twenty-first century examples show that the Covenant Chain–Two Row tradition of agreement-making is not forgotten at the highest levels of our various political orders, even if it is little known among everyday citizens and its current applications have been largely ignored by British, American and Canadian legislatures and parliaments. It seems to be instead remembered as a quaint idea or symbol, not as any kind of binding law, policy or procedure. And, as the political cycle that replaced Stephen Harper with Justin Trudeau, and Barack Obama with Donald Trump, then Joe Biden and then Trump again demonstrates, the four-or-so-year cycles of our North American political systems enable an ebb and flow in political memory from recognition to disavowal, depending on the priorities of the day.

This wax and wane of awareness on the part of politicians is why I follow Indigenous thinkers and legal scholars like John Borrows, Rick Hill and Kayanesenh Paul Williams in tracing the flow of the Covenant Chain–Two Row tradition as a continuous narrative that runs in jurisprudence through the Royal Proclamation to the Constitution. The wax and wane shows why questions of Indigenous self-determination, citizenship and rights need to be addressed in permanent "constitutional" jurisprudence, rather than cyclical "parliamentary" recognition. It is also why in Canada, under the arrangements of a constitutional monarchy, we have a form of authority known as "the Crown," a political authority that keeps track of interests that are of long duration, considerations of the welfare of peoples and lands that extend beyond the mandate of one government or the next. Because the four- or five-year pendulum swing of electoral politics is too volatile and self-interested to sustain consistent respect for this foundational relationship, the Haudenosaunee have consistently appealed to the figure of authority with which they linked arms long ago, the Crown and its local descendants, the governors general and their provincial parallels, the lieutenant governors, to polish the chain of that relationship.[5] It's in the long flow of Canada's own Constitution that we can see the ongoing relevance of the tradition we have traced from Kiotsaeton with the French and Algonquins as well as the *rotiyaneshon* and the Dutch onward to Canesatego and Sir William Johnson.

So why don't we Canadians today understand that Canada's long-term legal structure depends on Indigenous principles for linking arms across parallel, sovereign pathways?

My big-picture-perspective answer would say: we don't understand these things because of how colonial expansion distorted our collective understanding of ourselves in the world – how it twisted Europeans' ability to perceive and relate to non-European people, let alone to other, more-than-human inhabitants of the "new" world, as equals. And this distortion extended to and still influences the Crown and its representatives.

Distorted Worldviews

The inability of Europeans to see non-Europeans as equals, as covenantal symbionts, extends *way* back. And its effects are still very much under contention today.

Up to this point, this book has traced the consistent flow of principles within the Covenant Chain–Two Row treaty tradition that shaped agreement-making between Indigenous Peoples in the northeast and then with incoming Europeans from the moment Europeans arrived in North America. To trace the principles of this tradition, we've needed to extend back long before that arrival to the tradition's antecedents in Haudenosaunee law and cosmology.

But, of course, no cross-cultural encounter is shaped purely by one tradition, one way of thinking, one way of proceeding. Europeans, too, had precedents that they brought with them across the ocean. They had long-established protocols and expectations of how to proceed that shaped their thinking and behaviour too.

Earlier, I traced a fairly new set of ideas that emerged through the secularization of covenant theology that would have been known to seventeenth-century Dutch and English merchants when they arrived in the northeast of Turtle Island. But it is important to remind ourselves that these new ideas of reciprocity, where participants derive equal benefits from contracts, operated in and against the longer-running laws and assumptions derived from the unilateral assumptions of Catholic theology collectively known to us today as the Doctrine of Discovery.

On Friday, April 1, 2022, in the presence of 190 delegates, survivors and supporters, the Vatican's Pope Francis apologized and asked for forgiveness for the Catholic Church's role in the Canadian Residential School system. "It is chilling to think of determined efforts to instill a sense of inferiority," the Spanish-speaking pope said in Italian, "to rob people of their cultural identity, to sever their roots, and to consider all the personal and social effects that this continues to entail: unresolved traumas that have become inter-generational traumas."[6] Many of the Indigenous delegates, who had been working for many years to secure the pope's apology, were deeply moved by his sincere statement of contrition. Many other people, Indigenous and not, saw it as one more among many apologies that add up to so many empty words. A more important move, many said, would be for the pope to officially revoke the Doctrine of Discovery.

The Doctrine of Discovery gets its name not directly from papal law, but from a line of thinking and history of legal precedents identified in an 1823 court case, *Johnson v. McIntosh,* in which United States Supreme Court Chief Justice John Marshall justified the American nation-state's "exclusive right to extinguish the Indian title of occupancy, either by purchase or by conquest" on the basis of the European "law of nations." Marshall explained:

> On the discovery of this immense continent, the great nations of Europe were eager to appropriate to themselves so much of it as they could respectively acquire. Its vast extent offered an ample field to the ambition and enterprise of all; and the character and religion of its inhabitants afforded an apology for considering them as a people over whom the superior genius of Europe might claim an ascendency . . . But, as they were all in pursuit of nearly the same object, it was necessary, in order to avoid conflicting settlements, and consequent war with each other, to establish a principle, which all should acknowledge as the law by which the right of acquisition, which they all asserted, should be regulated as between themselves. This principle was, that discovery gave title to the government by whose subjects, or by whose authority, it was made, against all other European governments, which title might be consummated by possession.[7]

Here Marshall identifies the counter-story, a long Euro-American line of thinking, that is hostile to the story of linked arms of the Covenant Chain–Two Row treaty tradition that we have been tracing throughout this book. It does so by vanishing Kiotsaeton, Canesatego and the *rotiyaneshon* on the Hudson River in Jake Thomas's oration – not to mention Sir William Johnson and the thousands of treaty council delegates between Cartier's arrival in 1534 and Marshall's decision in 1823 – from the agreements they made in northeastern America and replaces them with the competition between European nations for Indigenous lands. "All" in Justice Marshall's statement refers exclusively to Europeans. And it does this by means of a legal-political-religious hallucination: in Marshall's words, "the character and religion of [America's] inhabitants afforded an apology for considering them as a people over whom the superior genius of Europe might claim an ascendency."

This is very cynical reasoning: Indigenous Peoples' character and religion "afforded an apology" so the "superior genius of Europe might claim an ascendency." "Apology" not so much for wrongs committed, as in the pope's apology, but "apology" as in an argument providing the reasons or evidence for something, in this case, Europe's "superior genius."

But how did this evaluation of Indigenous Peoples' supposed religious inferiority get turned into the "obviousness" of the Supreme Court judge's "superior genius of Europe"? Justice Marshall's thinking along religious and legal lines takes us back to the medieval Catholic Church's earliest encounters with powers outside of Christendom.

In his tracing of this brutal and tragic story, Lenape legal historian Robert A. Williams Jr. hearkens back to Pope Innocent IV and the letters he sent in the year 1246 to Güyük, grandson of Ghengis Khan, at his coronation over the Mogul Empire. Williams says Innocent was "the first great medieval legal theorist who attempted to systematically address the question of the legal rules that might govern Christian relations with non-Christians."[8] In his letter, Innocent informed Khan Güyük that Jesus Christ had made his disciple Peter responsible to gather all people into the "body of Christ" – a metaphor for the church – and from Peter that responsibility had passed down the line of succession from pope to pope. It was therefore Pope Innocent IV's responsibility to protect everyone's access to the Kingdom of God on earth, including anyone living within the Khan's empire who might convert to the "true faith." The Mongols' military advance toward Europe had violated what Innocent IV presumed to be divine natural law, and he therefore warned the Khan to desist, stop persecuting Christians and "conciliate by a fitting penance the wrath of divine Majesty."

Of course, the newly crowned Khan scoffed at Innocent's message, asking how the pope could be sure he was God's sole agent on earth, since the Mongols' military successes could not have occurred if "contrary to the command of God." Innocent replied that he was now even more concerned about the condition of the Mongols' souls. Having heard the truths of Christianity, they could no longer plead ignorance of the true faith when God called them to judgment.[9]

Williams observes that in these letters we see articulated the basic worldview that shaped Christian-European thinking for the next millennium: all people everywhere are enjoined to become part of the body of Christ, the church. Christ gave the "keys of the church" to the pope, whose fatherly responsibility it is – in Greek and Latin "pope" means "papa" – to bring all people into the body of Christ. The pope then passed on this responsibility to his agents throughout the world, including the Jesuits in New France, who became known as martyrs for sacrificing their lives in the mission to draw all people into the body of Christ. Those who reject this divine law demonstrate their unthinking condition, and it behooves the patriarch of the Church and his agents to compel them, even against their childish obstinacy, to take their place within the body of Christ. "The manifest irrationality of heathens and infidels who rejected the Pope's message," Williams explains, "patently demonstrated the need for papal remediation. According to Innocent, his office required him to call upon Christian princes to raise armies to punish serious violations of natural law, and to order those armies to accompany missionaries to heathen lands for purposes of conversion. 'If the infidels do not obey, they ought to be compelled by the secular arm and war may be declared against them by the Pope and not by anybody else.'"[10] On this basis, subsequent popes could and did appoint Christian kings and princes in papal bulls such as *Dum Diversas* (1452), *Romanus Pontifex* (1455) and *Inter Caetera* (1493) to subjugate "Saracens" and other non-Christian peoples so as to compel their conversion to Christian Europeans' conceptions of reason and truth.[11]

This distorted worldview could even justify chattel slavery as a way to compel people into the body of Christ. In his impassioned description of the disembarkation and auctioning of 235 Africans at the port of Lagos, Portugal, on August 8, 1444, for example, the king's royal chronicler, Gomes Eanes de Azurara, weeps at the heart-rending scene of Africans from the region known as Guinea emerging from the holds of the ships, exhausted and traumatized. He sheds tears when he sees them forcibly parted from their loved ones when the princely investors prepared to depart with their percentage of the human "goods" they had purchased. Azurara's tears, however, are lightened by the role he insists his master, Prince Henry, the Infante, went on to play in saving their souls:

> For of the forty-six souls that fell to him as his fifth, he made a very speedy partition of these for his chief riches lay in his purpose; for he reflected with great pleasure upon the salvation of these souls that before were lost. And certainly his expectation was not in vain; for . . . as soon as they understood our language they turned Christians with very little ado; and I who put together this history into this volume, saw in the town of Lagos boys and girls (the children and grandchildren of those first captives, born in this land) as good and true Christians as if they had directly descended, from the beginnings of the dispensation of Christ, from those who were first baptized.[12]

Black American theologian Willie James Jennings observes that in rationale such as this, we witness the distortion of Christian worldview into what he calls a "Christian imagination," one that *displaced* bodies from the distinct lands and landscapes in which they identified themselves by measuring them according to an abstract and transportable "*racial scale*" wherein proximity to whiteness served as a marker of civilize-ability.

We see this racial scale operating clearly when Jesuit Alessandro Valignano (1539–1606), who had arrived as Catholic vicar-general in Japan in 1579, assessed South Asian and Japanese people by the scale in his *Sumario* (1580): "There is this difference between Indian and Japanese Christians . . . for each one of the former was converted from some individual ulterior motive, and since they are blacks, and of small sense, they are subsequently very difficult to improve and turn into good Christians; whereas the Japanese . . . are white and of good understanding and behavior, . . . they frequent the churches and sermons, and when they are instructed they become very good Christians."[13]

Over and over again throughout Europe's encounter with non-Europeans, Jennings observes, we see the emergence of a theology "in a pedagogical form that constantly reimagines the world and especially native subjects by gauging their intelligence and intellectual capacities." Ever since, he observes, whiteness has functioned as a marker and arbiter of civilization, aesthetic beauty and proportion, and therefore good judgment and reason. This theological imagination, he says, "transform[ed] the New World into one large, ever-expanding classroom" in which "native peoples of the world received a Christianity exaggerated in evaluative habit and poised to merge brutality with intellectual formation."[14]

This is how we get caning in classrooms as being "for your own good." It was simply a more intimate version of invading Crusaders conquering you and your people for your own salvation. It is also how the notion of mutual covenant can be twisted by a paternalism that assumes it knows what is best and how to "protect" and "benefit" the supposedly weaker member of the alliance.

"By what term of relationship will we go by?" Jake Thomas reports the Dutch saying when the Two Row agreement was being formulated on the Hudson River. "I will call you my 'child.'" Seeing the problem right at the start, the Onkwehón:we replied, "This is not proper for a father can control the child. What do you think if we addressed each other as 'brother'?"

Jennings offers numerous instances of how the paternalism of what he calls a "pedagogical racial scale" worked in statements by explorers and missionaries such as Christopher Columbus measuring Carib peoples in a scale from black barbarity to white civility or the earlier example of Jesuit Alessandro Valignano. Measured according to this universally applicable racial scale, Jennings explains, "People would henceforth (and forever) carry their identities on their bodies . . . From the beginning of the colonialist moment, being white placed one at the center of the symbolic and real reordering of space."[15] This racial scale coloured the global map of what he calls the Christian imagination.

And, in case we are tempted to blame this worldview on the Roman Catholic Church alone, Robert A. Williams Jr. reminds us of how the same line of thinking informed politico-legal instruments generated in English colonial law just as readily as in papal law. The Second Charter of Virginia of 1609, for instance, confirmed the rights of the Virginia Company to occupy an extensive domain within Indigenous lands in America known by the British as Virginia.[16] In its approval of this arrangement the English Crown affirmed:

> We, greatly commending, and graciously accepting of, [the Company's] Desires for the Furtherance of so noble a Work, which may, by the

> Providence of Almighty God, hereafter tend to the Glory of his Divine Majesty, in propagating of Christian Religion to such People, as yet live in Darkness and miserable Ignorance of the true Knowledge and Worship of God, and may in time bring the Infidels and Savages, living in those Parts, to human Civility, and to a settled and quiet Government; Do, by these our Letters Patents, graciously accept of, and agree to, their humble and well-intended Desires.[17]

Note that this Virginia Charter was tabled the same year that Henry Hudson first arrived in Haudenosaunee territory in what became New Netherlands. At the same time that covenant thinking made an opening for reciprocal alliance formation in the minds of some incoming Protestant traders in one region, the religious racial scale promoted a worldview of unilateral Euro-Christian superiority to the Indigenous Peoples they were meeting in the minds of others.

This religious rationale for European invasion and domination of Indigenous lands informed the line of legal precedent Marshall evoked in the Doctrine of Discovery. It's why his judgment could assume that "the superior genius of Europe might claim an ascendency." It's why Indigenous land and Peoples could be dismissed from his account of a supposedly international "law of [European] nations." According to this religious racial scale, the farther you were from white, the less Christian (or civilized) you seemed to be, and the less Christian-and-therefore-civilized you were, the more reasonable it was to justify the confiscation of your lands and your forced re-education and servitude.

By this unilateral calculus running through emerging colonial law, *our (white)* greed was for *your* own (*less-than-white*) good.

You could say that the development of this paternalistic, racist worldview foreclosed many European Christians' ability to see a civilized world beyond the one they were busily remaking in their own image. Many of our ancestors were diminished in their ability to meet others *as others* – as equals within their own systems – whether that was other places or other people. They could not see them as having their own valid worldview, cognition, way of life. Everything was filtered by their own European-Christian worldview, a worldview that still operates today. This is why

Indigenous Peoples seeking reparations from the Catholic Church have asked not just for an apology from the pope for the Residential School system but a repudiation of the Doctrine of Discovery altogether.[18]

Think of how such a worldview would skew the perceptions of any European participating in the flow of linked-arms treaty-making. As Haudenosaunee orators such as Kiotsaeton chanted the stanzas of the Thanksgiving Address at the start of each meeting, all would have affirmed, "*Henh*, now all our minds are one." But the European minds would not have been one with their Haudenosaunee allies. And you can see this when the speaker for the French, Couture, responds to Kiotsaeton's first item, the *Ohén:ton Karihwatéhkwen*. The next wampum, Couture's Jesuit scribes report, "is to thank the One that made heaven and earth for being everywhere, and for seeing into our hearts, and for now uniting the mind of all the peoples."[19] Rather than achieving one-mindedness by greeting and thanking the horizontal, interdependent web of beings on which all life depends, including the Creator, the Christian imagination unites the minds of "all" peoples with reference to a single, anthropomorphized Authority, the "One that made heaven and earth" and who "sees into people's hearts" and is "everywhere." This European conception of how to align one's mind via gratitude refers to a single sovereignty whose vision is unlimited and whose power is not located, but everywhere. Unity, here, and the idea of a good, "civilized" mind, does not arise from understanding oneself-in-horizonal-interrelation, but from deference to a single, unilateral, undividable, transcendent Authority. This is the worldview that runs in tension in European thinking with that of covenantal reciprocity.

Instead of affirming that "now, all our minds are one," Europeans in the "new" world have long been seduced by the old, unilateral distortion: "Now, your minds are ours."

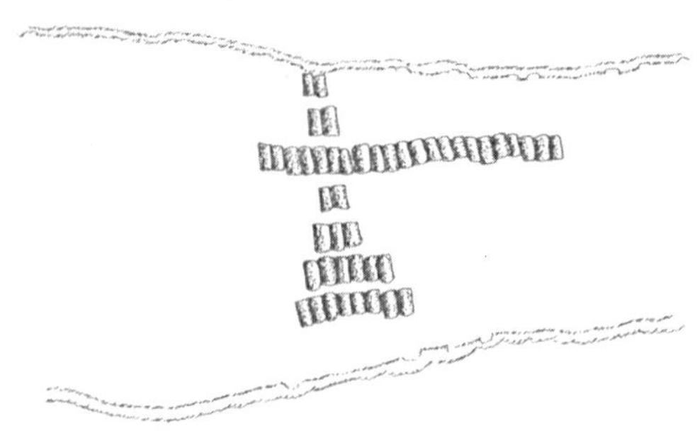

Chapter Nine

Distorting "Protection"

The unilateral worldview conveyed in the series of papal laws now referred to as the Doctrine of Discovery shaped European colonial encounters with non-Europeans, competing with the reciprocal and horizontal principles that were emerging in covenant thinking when the Europeans met the Haudenosaunee. The jostling of these principles within colonial thinking has twisted the British-Canadian understanding of the mutual protection of linked arms that the king had reaffirmed in the Royal Proclamation in 1763. The British North America Act (1867), for example, which established the Dominion of Canada a century later, only mentions Indigenous Peoples once, and, at that, only in a minor subheading (24) of Section 91.

Section 91 begins, "It shall be lawful for the Queen, by and with the Advice and Consent of the Senate and House of Commons, to make Laws for the Peace, Order, and good Government of Canada in relation to all Matters not coming within the Classes of Subjects by this Act assigned exclusively to the Legislatures of the Provinces." Okay, we might say, this is the British-Canadian Dominion setting its internal house in order, just as the Crown was trying to do back in 1763, for instance, by regulating settlers' desire for Indigenous land. Just as the Crown in 1763 tried to protect its long-term interests at the time by asserting limitations on the local colonies' access to Indigenous land, so in Section 91, the Crown in the new Dominion sets out to determine separate realms of jurisdiction between the local colonies, now provinces, and the federal Crown's long-term interests.

But then – and to my mind, startlingly – after everything the Royal Proclamation had said about how "our Interest and the Security of our Colonies" depends upon the Indigenous nations "with whom we are connected" and how Indigenous neighbours "who live under our Protection . . . should not be molested or disturbed in the Possession of such Parts of our Dominions and Territories as, not having been ceded to, or purchased by Us, are reserved to them, or any of them as their Hunting Grounds," Section 91(24) of BNA asserts that "exclusive Legislative Authority of the Parliament of Canada extends to . . . Indians, and Lands reserved for the Indians."

That's it. No comment on how the Crown's own security moved from protecting Indigenous land *from* colonial frauds and abuses to legislative authority being *extended to* "Indians, and Lands reserved for Indians."

What might "extended to" mean?

Commenting on 91(24), for example, University of Victoria law professor Brian Bird explains that "prior to Confederation, the British Crown assumed the responsibility 'to define and reconcile the relationship between First Nations and others' by ensuring the welfare and protection of Aboriginal Peoples in the face of colonial expansion."[1]

"This responsibility of the British Crown found its inheritor," he continues, "in the federal Crown at Confederation by virtue of s. 91(24) of the Constitution Act, 1867."[2] Reading forward from section 91(24) to the Constitution Act (1982), he observes the "obligation upon the federal government to exercise its exclusive legislative jurisdiction *over* Aboriginal Peoples in Canada in order to fulfill the constitutional promise embedded within [Constitution Act 1982] s. 35(1), namely the affirmation and recognition of aboriginal and treaty rights."[3] I italicize his use of the word "over" because I think it is a paternalistic distortion he and many others have derived from Section 91's assertion that "exclusive Legislative Authority *extends to* . . . Indians, and Lands reserved for the Indians."

"Extends to," not "over."

This distortion mistranslates the Royal Proclamation's legislative authority "to restrict colonists' access to Indigenous lands" into authority "over Indigenous people and their lands." In *The Clay We Are Made Of*, *Kanyen'kehàka* historian Susan Hill provides a backstory to the British tendency to distort the concept of "protection." In the 1701 "Nanfan Treaty" (after John Nanfan, then Governor of New York) signed in Albany, the Haudenosaunee gave the British rights to build forts and extend trade into hunting grounds that extended west to Lake Michigan in exchange for British "protection" of their hunting and fishing from the French and their Indigenous allies who also hunted and fished in the region. "Protection" in this context would have meant mutual protection of their shared economic interests in the region.[4]

It matters what story we tell. Section 91(24) extracts "protection" away from the treaty-making tradition of the *Tehontatenentshonteronhtáhkwa* and *Tékeni Teyohà:te* that shaped the Royal Proclamation and displaces it into the narrative of the Doctrine of Discovery. It takes the Royal Proclamation out of a primary relationship with the culture, beliefs and laws of the canoe and puts it firmly and solely in the culture, beliefs and laws of the ship. In the process, Section 91(24) distorts the idea of "protection."

This distortion turns allies and friends – "those with whom We are connected" – into subjects. Rather than protecting Indigenous land by restricting colonists' access to land as outlined in the Royal Proclamation, and rather than maintaining separate jurisdictions for mutual "protection" as outlined in the 1664 Treaty of Albany, it asserts the Canadian Crown's unilateral rule over Indigenous Peoples themselves and *their* rights to land. More than this, it assumes that the duty to "protect" Indigenous lands turns those lands into Crown lands, which the Crown (and later, its Canadian representatives) will administer on behalf of Indigenous *subjects*.[5]

This distortion reduces independent Indigenous allies with lands of their own into supplicants at the Crown's table, which today controls 89 percent of all the land within the physical borders of Canada. This 89 percent is known today as "Crown land."

A major reason why the Covenant Chain–Two Row precedents for

Canada's constitution have been dismissed, then, is because the understanding of race, as put forward in the Doctrine of Discovery, shaped British and Canadian legislators' worldviews in the period of Canada's formulation. This worldview could not admit (or allow) Indigenous civil, diplomatic procedures as sources for something so sophisticated as the Canadian Constitution.

They therefore tended to isolate each transaction of treaty-making away from the centuries-long Haudenosaunee principles of how neighbouring nations could protect each other, and the land itself, by linking arms.

This practice of compartmentalization allowed Ontario courts, in cases such as *Bear Island* (1974) and *Chippewas of Sarnia* (1999), for example, to rule, in the words of the latter, "that the procedural requirement for purchase of Indigenous land 'at some public Meeting or Assembly . . .' was repealed [in the Quebec Act of 1774]. Thus, at the relevant times there was in existence no positive law prescribing the manner in which aboriginal rights could be ceded to the Crown."[6] Decisions like these read one transaction against another, seeing the provisions of the Quebec Act as cancelling out those of the Royal Proclamation. In so doing, they contradict Lord Dunning's insistence, cited at the close of the previous chapter, that "the aboriginal peoples of Canada shall continue to have all their rights and freedoms as recognized by the royal proclamation of 1763."[7] And of *Calder* (1973), which states, "The Proclamation must be regarded as a fundamental document upon which any just determination of original rights rests."[8] Isolated into these separate decisions, the provisions for Indigenous rights laid out in the Royal Proclamation are sometimes repealed, sometimes enduring in Canadian law.

If you look at these various moments across time, you see two things: the variation *and* the consistent recurrence of the question of what it means for Indigenous Peoples to have linked arms with the Crown while retaining their autonomy as nations, to be allies without being subsumed as subjects.

In a letter dated April 5, 1909, for example, Canada's Minister of the Interior Frank Oliver, serving in Wilfrid Laurier's government, assured *Royá:ner* John Smoke Johnson, the Deputy Speaker of the Six Nations

Confederacy Council, that Ottawa did not claim authority over Six Nations. "It is the policy of the Canadian Government," wrote Oliver,

> to recognize its relations with the Six Nations of the Grand River as being on a different footing from those with any of the other Indians of Canada. The Six Nations Indians of the Grand River came to Canada under special treaty as allies of Britain, and the policy of the Canadian government is to deal with them having that fact always in view. . . . The system of tribal government which prevailed among the Six Nations on their coming to Canada was satisfactory to the Government at that time, and so long as it is satisfactory to the Six Nations themselves so long it will remain satisfactory to the Government of Canada.[9]

Statements such as Oliver's echo assessments like that of Governor John Graves Simcoe, who had reviewed the records of Britain's agreements with the Six Nations when he came into office more than a hundred years earlier in 1791 and assured the leadership of the Six Nations that these "authentic papers prove that no King of Great Britain ever claimed absolute power or sovereignty over any of your lands or territories."[10] Statements like these do not indicate that the federal government has legislative authority *over* Indigenous Peoples or their lands. Oliver's and Simcoe's letters sound like they clearly understand the principles of the Covenant Chain–Two Row treaty tradition.

And yet, fifty years after Oliver's letter, an Ontario court judge could review the same records of Six Nations' relations with the British Crown and conclude the opposite: "In my opinion," Justice King wrote, in *Logan v. Styres* (1959), "those of the Six Nations so settling on such lands [in British North America], together with their posterity, by accepting the protection of the Crown then owed allegiance to the Crown and thus became subjects of the Crown. Thus, the said Six Nations Indians from having been the faithful allies of the Crown became, instead, loyal subjects of the Crown."[11] Somehow "those with whom We are connected" in the Royal Proclamation had become "our loving Subjects"; the "elder brothers" outlined in the Covenant Chain–Two Row had been rendered "sons."

It was a forced conversion.

American journalist and writer Upton Sinclair once wrote, "It is difficult to get a man to *understand something*, when *his salary depends on his not understanding it*."[12] Ever since the War of 1812, when their reliance on Indigenous allies for their own protection receded, the colonial governments of North America, whether British, American or Canadian, have depended upon *not* understanding the Covenant Chain–Two Row agreement. Our extraction economies, the same ones the Royal Proclamation had been trying to protect Indigenous Peoples from, depend on us not being able to interpret it.

To me, this is what stands out in the long-running disputes over the extent of the Haldimand Tract, the land granted to the members of Six Nations who maintained their alliance with the British Crown throughout the American War of Independence. While many Confederacy leaders advised staying neutral during the Revolutionary War, seeing the conflict as an internal matter between British fathers and British colonial sons, some, including members of the Johnson household like Konwatsi'tsayén:ni Mary Brant and her brother Thaientané:ken Joseph Brant, who had become a captain in the British Army, interpreted the Covenant Chain to mean that the Six Nations must fight alongside the British Crown.[13] They were able to convince the majority of the Haudenosaunee to join them. When the tide turned in the patriots' favour, American troops under Generals Sullivan and Clinton swept through Haudenosaunee country in 1779–1780, burning cornfields and homes.

The Haudenosaunee refugees gathered at the border, unsheltered and starving, near Buffalo Creek, while Mary Brant, widowed after Sir William Johnson's death in 1774, with her brother Joseph Brant negotiated with their British army colleagues for a new homeland. Joseph visited some of the lands of their traditional beaver hunting grounds and, finding them suitable, suggested that the British arrange for them to resettle along the Grand River that ran down the peninsula between Lakes Erie and Ontario. Accordingly, Frederick Haldimand, Governor General in Chief of the Province of Quebec and Territories, as well as General and Commander of the British forces in North America, arranged to purchase the Niagara Peninsula from the Anishinaabe Mississaugas, who had settled near the Credit River since the Beaver Wars a century earlier.[14] He then set aside a large tract for the Haudenosaunee allies in the following proclamation:

> Whereas His Majesty having been pleased to direct that in consideration of the early attachment to his cause manifested by the Mohawk Indians, and of the loss of their settlement [in New York] which they thereby sustained – that a convenient tract of land under his *protection* should be chosen as a safe and comfortable retreat for them and others of the Six Nations, who have either lost their settlements within the Territory of the American States, or wish to retire from them to the British – I have at the earnest desire of many of these His Majesty's faithful *Allies* purchased a tract of land from the Indians situated between the Lakes Ontario, Erie and Huron and I do hereby in His Majesty's name authorize and permit the said Mohawk Nation and such others of the Six Nation Indians as wish to settle in that quarter to take possession of and settle upon the Banks of the River commonly called Ours [Ouse] or Grand River, running into Lake Erie, allotting to them for that purpose six miles deep from each side of the river beginning at Lake Erie and extending in that proportion to the head of the said river, which them and their posterity are to enjoy for ever.[15]

Protection, again. And contrary to Justice King, not subjects but *allies*.

On the strength of this tangible recognition of their contribution to protecting the British cause and of the resulting devastating loss of their traditional homelands in upstate New York, a large group of Six Nations, consisting of about five thousand people, went to live under the king's protection in the newly reduced British part of North America. It was land they knew, since it was in the Beaver Hunting Grounds they had negotiated with the British in the 1701 (Nanfan) Treaty of Albany, and the willowed riverbanks and forests of maple, black walnut and white pine reminded them of the homeland they had lost along the Mohawk River. Once they crossed the Niagara border after the Haldimand Proclamation, the Six Nations looked forward to resettling on land where they could restore their Confederacy government and continue in friendship with the British Crown as laid out in the Covenant Chain–Two Row treaty tradition.

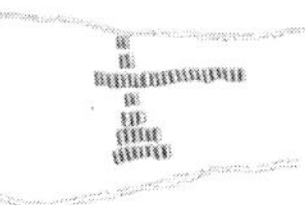

Removed from the Ongoing Flow

However, right from the start, when the Six Nations were establishing themselves on the Haldimand Tract along the Grand River, Six Nations leaders ran into interference from the British authorities. Haldimand had not conducted a survey of the tract granted to the Six Nations, so Lieutenant Governor John Graves Simcoe, the first civil rather than military chief administrator of Upper Canada (though he had a military background), set out to clarify the actual extent of the Haldimand lands. His investigations determined that the Mississaugas had not "owned" the lands at the headwaters of the Grand River and therefore could not have sold them to the British.[16] The result was that the Simcoe Patent of 1793 cut the Haldimand lands by one-third, or three hundred thousand acres.

Haldimand's "protection" of a homeland for the Haudenosaunee on the Grand River from its source to its mouth turned out to be not from its source to its mouth. *Here we go again*, the *rotiyaneshon* would have thought, *Kayaderosseras and Canajoharie all over again.*

The Six Nations Confederacy protested immediately. They turned to Captain Brant because of his familiarity with British protocols from his time in Sir William Johnson's household, his facility in English from his training at Moor's Charity School in Lebanon, Connecticut, and his years serving as a captain in the Indian Department of the British Army. Since he had not been named one of the Confederacy's official fifty chiefs, the Confederacy Council gave him a special designation as a "Pine Tree" chief, authorizing him to negotiate with the British so they could do things like lease out some of the Haldimand lands to raise funds for community infrastructure such as schools, roads and farms.

It was a tricky assignment because Brant had British friends from his army days who were some of his readiest purchasers or leasers of Six Nations land. And they brought skills and services the people needed – grain mills, schooling, blacksmith shops. It was not always clear if Brant was acting as a former officer of the British army, who had received his own grant of land (on the shore of Lake Ontario where the city of Burlington is today), which he could buy or sell as he chose like any other army officer, or if he was acting as an agent for the Six Nations Confederacy Council, whose lands were understood to be "protected" from land-hungry speculators by the Royal Proclamation's declaration that all Indigenous land negotiations must be brokered by the Crown.

Looking back, it seems that both the British colonial regime and Brant himself may have been confused by these distinctions.

Add to this that other settlers and refugees from the war simply squatted on parts of the Haldimand lands. It is not always possible to tell who had made official arrangements with Brant and who were simply squatters, nor to say with certainty when Brant overstepped the authority he had been given by the Confederacy chiefs.

In the midst of these uncertainties, Brant and the council subdivided the Haldimand lands into five blocks. Brant then set about making arrangements with settler friends and acquaintances to sell, lease or rent out over three hundred thousand acres of land – another third of the Haldimand lands. The leasees or purchasers would pay yearly installments to government-appointed trustees. These trustees would invest the funds and use the interest to pay annuities to the Grand River Haudenosaunee. By this means, the Confederacy Council could do the work of government: help their people build homes, villages, farms, roads and schools.

These transactions were stymied repeatedly by British uncertainty about how to deal with their Six Nations allies. As a mass of five thousand people, the Haudenosaunee constituted a large block of Upper Canada's population, at a time when Upper Canada's number of Loyalist refugees from the Thirteen States totalled around ten thousand.[17] Despite losing their homes and lands in New York, the Six Nations were a significant military and political force. In accord with Covenant Chain–Two Row protocols established in New York, the Haudenosaunee insisted they had come to Canada as independent allies, not subjects, of the Crown. They had their own laws and government and did not see why they should be subjected to British laws. They relied on the Covenant of Linked Arms to protect their interests by arranging for Crown-appointed trustees who would monitor the revenue from their leased lands and ensure a good return on the funds these trustees would hold in trust on behalf of the Six Nations. Throughout, Brant and the Haudenosaunee determined to keep a close eye on the Crown's arrangements with these funds, especially when various colonial governors took different views of whether their lands could be rented, leased or sold.

In a letter to the governor dated December 10, 1798, for example, Brant wrote to clarify the exact nature of the Six Nations' tenure on the Grand River. He explained that the Haudenosaunee understood the lands to be "indisputably our own, otherwise we would never have accepted the land, yet afterwards it seemed a little odd to us that the writings Gov. Haldimand gave us after our settling on the lands, was not so compleat as the strong assurances and promises he made to us at first." Now, Brant reports, the Haudenosaunee "have even been prohibited from taking tenants on [the land], it having been represented as inconsistent for us, being but King's allies, to have King's subjects as tenants."[18]

Brant's letter shows how difficult it was to maintain the Covenant Chain–Two Row's two principles of linked arms *and* autonomy from the Revolutionary War onward. The colonial government's shifting interpretations about how to "protect" Indigenous land transactions meant repeated intrusions upon Six Nations lands and governance. In 1835, for example, the Crown approached Six Nations about developing the Plank Road from Lake Ontario through to Lake Erie. This strip includes the land where Highway 6 now runs through the Haldimand Tract and where today's disputed Douglas Creek Estates and McKenzie Meadows (a.k.a. Kahnonstaton and Land Back Lane) developments are located. The Six Nations leaders at the time agreed to lease a mile-wide path through their territory for the road, but refused to surrender the land. Lieutenant-Governor John Colborne agreed to the lease, but his successor, Sir Francis Bond Head, reinterpreted all Indigenous leases as sales.

In 1841, the colonial government declared that it had negotiated a "general surrender" of even more land, signed in Kingston by a small number of Confederacy chiefs, which reduced the Grand River territory to about 5 percent of the original Haldimand Tract. The Haudenosaunee Council immediately sent petitions to colonial authorities, alleging that those who signed the surrender had been coerced and intimidated by the Indian agent and that the majority of chiefs had not signed the agreement. An inquiry was commissioned in 1843, but in an eerie echo of the New York Assembly's upholding of the Kayaderosseras and Canajoharie Patents almost one hundred years earlier, the colonial authorities upheld the purported surrender. After 1845, despite protests from Six Nations, the Plank Road and surrounding lands were sold to third parties.

During the same period of the 1830s and 1840s, Six Nations lost 369 more acres to build towpaths, dams and locks for the short-lived Grand River Navigation Company. They also lost $160,000 of their trust funds when the lieutenant-governor skipped the small detail(!) of securing the Confederacy Council's consent to purchase stocks in the Navigation Company. The idea was to produce revenue for the Haudenosaunee from usage fees on the canals and locks. Unfortunately, the emergence of steam-powered railways in the same period bankrupted the scheme. This and other money, which had been taken from the Six Nations trust funds and invested in such enterprises as the Welland Canal, Upper Canada College and McGill University, was never returned.[19]

In each of these cases, we have instances where paternalistic ideas of "protection," of how to "help" and "improve" the situation of the Haudenosaunee, meant interference by the colonial governments in the Haudenosaunee canoe, and the result is that, between 1784 and 1847, the Six Nations territory was reduced from over nine hundred thousand acres of land to twenty-two thousand acres on the south side of the Grand River.

All of these reductions were deemed fair and square by the colonial powers right up to this day. All of them show how distorted the guise of "protection" had become.

If you study any single transaction, you will find a paper trail of bureaucratese that rationalizes, loopholes and justifies every extraction. The lands "which them and their posterity are to enjoy for ever" have been reduced to 5 percent of Haldimand's original grant.

Chapter Ten

Canada Strong-Arms the Canoe

For many Canadians, Canada threw off colonial domination with the establishment of the Dominion of Canada in 1867. We call that turning point "Confederation." Right from the start, the confederation of four colonies in British North America shunned federation with other participants significant in their formation, whether those of the Six Nations Confederacy, other Indigenous nations with whom they had allied themselves or the Red River Métis.

Indeed, the new Dominion immediately fell in step with Doctrine of Discovery thinking, over Covenant of Friendship thinking, and worked to dismantle its relations with these already-established confederated neighbours.

It's telling that one of the first moves the new Dominion made was to "advance" the lives of Indigenous Peoples in every conceivable domain. Having distorted *protection* from restrictions on settler colonial access to unceded Indigenous land into the appropriation of all undeeded land as Crown land, and then restricting Indigenous Peoples' access to it, Canada then went on to create the Indian Act (1876), which asserted the federal government's power to determine everything from who qualified as "Indians" to who they could marry, where they could travel, how they could sell farm produce, whether they could attend university or if they could drink alcohol. The Indian Act was and is paternalistic racism made into law.

Alarmed at the hostile "protection" of Indigenous Peoples being developed by the Dominion's first government, the Confederacy Council at Six Nations invited twenty-one First Nations to a ten-day "Grand Indian Council" at Ohsweken in June 1870. There, line by line, and clause by clause, they rejected the new country's provisions for their dissolution as autonomous and sovereign, self-determining nations.[1]

It's not unreasonable to compare this crucial moment in the emergence of Canada to the moment in the Creation Story when the Twins struggled violently with each other's views and priorities for the kind of world they were trying to create. At such a time, when an aggressive vision threatens to destroy the peace, it becomes important not to paper over differences by blandishments about common ground. If one of the parties refuses to retract its aggressive claws, it's important to draw some boundaries. It becomes necessary to keep the peace by barring one party from invading the other. To peacefully share the river, to go on living in the Dish With One Spoon, you may need to insist the parties keep to separate paths.

Accordingly, one of the *rotiyaneshon* active in the Grand Indian Council, Chief William Jacobs from Grand River, wrote in 1872 to the Superintendent of Indian Affairs in Ottawa with the following reminder of the *Tékeni Teyohà:te* elements of the Covenant Chain–Two Row tradition (all spellings from original transcript):

> You sail your own Boat and we'll paddle our own canoe Side by Side. I was not to enter in your craft and you was not to enter in my canoe. Gale and calm we must be side by side . . . when the pail face man saw my laws he says to the read man's face your laws of the Six Nations is good that your forefathers made for you we will always keep our laws separate from your laws.
>
> The pail face man said to the read fase I don't understand the way of your cannoe ruls the Six Nations chief said I don't understand the ways of your boat ruls the pail fase said to the read man I don't understand the

> Birch cannoe ruls if I enter in it it might [up]sett the Read man said to the pail face that is the ruls and laws the great Spirit gave us.[2]

Respect begins with a recognition that different Peoples, different parties, may have different priorities, different objectives, different philosophies of life. They may not understand the rules by which each other's vessels, each other's social systems, work. There are different assumptions, different values to be attended to – these need to be discussed, not swept under the carpet, if understanding is to emerge.

Despite reminders such as this, however, it was as if the newly emerging Dominion of Canada saw the Covenant Chain–Two Row series of agreements as a threat to its own ambitions. It therefore wished to repress its memory. For, if the Haudenosaunee had seen their "protected" lands carved away under the British administration, they saw their independence as self-governing Peoples directly attacked under Canadian administration.[3]

Canadian interference in Six Nations affairs intensified in the late nineteenth and early twentieth centuries. Maybe because this is the period when Canada was struggling to establish itself as a fully fledged state independent of Britain. Although Canada's Parliament was founded in 1867, its status as a nation among global nations developed only gradually. The emerging Dominion worked hard to join international institutions such as the International Labour Organization and the newly established League of Nations in the 1920s as part of its efforts to sign its own international trade agreements. It further disentangled its legislative powers from Britain with the signing of the Statute of Westminster in 1931 and then discontinued the need to turn to the Privy Council in London as its final court of appeal in 1949.

While these changes emerged on the international front, Canada worked internally to establish uniform legislative and juridical powers within its own borders – including a universally applied Indian Act that its federal, centrist leaders hoped would conclusively override Haudenosaunee and all other Indigenous claims for sovereignty or self-determination. This, despite the Royal Proclamation's distinction between "Indians with whom we are connected" and "subjects," despite Governor Simcoe's

1791 statement that "no King of Great Britain ever claimed absolute power or sovereignty over any of your lands or territories," or Minister of the Interior Frank Oliver's promises in 1909 that Six Nations would remain self-governing. Essentially, Ottawa worked to eliminate the understanding of arms linked between Peoples who walked on independent paths. Primary in this effort was the goal of extinguishing Indigenous self-governing autonomy. Seen from this light, Canada's colonization policy was much more aggressive than Great Britain's had been.

Citizenship as Elimination

One way to extinguish Indigenous jurisdiction was to disappear Indigenous people and Peoples[4] entirely, to scrub out one of the two paths and to do this civilly – meaning, by the pen if possible rather than the sword. Through bureaucracy and policy rather than blunderbuss – through bureaucracy and policy *as* blunderbuss. If there were neither Indigenous people nor Peoples, then the new nation-state would not have to abide by the various treaties the British Crown had made with them. To achieve this disappearance, Canadian authorities tried to compel Indigenous Peoples to become assimilated Canadians by "enfranchising" them – by converting them into Canadians who had no distinct treaties with the British Crown.

I know this sounds benign to many people. If the larger story of settlers in America is about entering into democracy and getting the right to vote, why wouldn't Indigenous individuals want the chance to determine who is in government?

After all, it was seen as good for others who had been excluded. Canadian women, for example, fought in the 1920s to get the vote. For them, getting the franchise meant, quite literally, being recognized as *people* who could participate in the affairs of the nation-state. That's why the case they took to the Privy Council in London became known as "the Persons Case" of 1929 – the case hinged upon them being recognized in law as "persons."

More recently, for Canadians who have escaped dictatorships or who have lived as stateless refugees, gaining access to citizenship and the right to choose one's own government means having a voice in the political order. It means the blessings of the Charter of Rights and Freedoms and a say in government for people who had experienced such arbitrary hazards as war at home, desperate interethnic conflict in refugee camps, haphazard policing in the no man's land between national borders and the unpredictable currents of humanitarian "charity." There are good reasons why many Canadians think enfranchisement is something everybody in the world would want.

But for Indigenous Peoples like the Haudenosaunee, to accept the "blessing" of enfranchisement would mean extinguishing themselves as a People. It would mean relinquishing their status as allies of the Crown, citizens of their own country, as autonomous equals to any colonial state with its rules for citizenship and sovereignty.[5] Significantly for us all, it would mean rejecting their original instructions to participate as citizens in the natural orders of *Yethi'nihstenha Onhwentsyakekha'*, our Mothering Earth, which must take priority over the human laws established by nation-states like Canada.

If Indigenous Peoples rejected enfranchisement, as most Haudenosaunee have consistently done since before Canada became a country, then Ottawa devised a second method to extinguish their autonomy, and this was to go over their heads and designate them as wards of the state whose lives would be "protected" under a brutal regime of laws that evolved from the British colonial Civilization of Indian Tribes Act (1857) to the many reiterations of the Indian Act, first tabled as law in 1876. As it evolved through various amendments and iterations over the years, the Indian Act has contained too many mechanisms of intervention and control to list here, but suffice it to say that it has contained clauses that controlled everything from women's status, their reproductive and marital rights, mandatory residential schooling for children, a pass system for anyone leaving their reserve and the edict that getting an education as a teacher, lawyer, church minister or doctor eliminated a person's "Indian" status.

Most grievously, the Indian Act eliminated traditional governments and established the Ottawa-controlled-and-beholden band council system. Imagining today's band councils as First Nations "governments" is basically like getting a group from within to do the work of what used to be called Indian agents.

It's not much of a covenant if the figure at the other end of the Covenant Chain wampum was placed there by the figure on our side.

Canada Invades

Just as Canada's dominion as a nation-state emerged gradually, so also did its consolidation of control over Indigenous Peoples. While the new government worked to negotiate what have become known as the eleven "numbered treaties" spreading north and west from northern Ontario and through the prairies between the 1870s and the 1920s, Six Nations remained self-governing outside the dictates of the Indian Act for almost fifty years, until 1924.

Two pieces of legislation at the close of the First World War made explicit Canada's growing intention to intervene in the Haudenosaunee canoe. This effort had become even more pointed under the regime of the poet and civil servant Duncan Campbell Scott, who was appointed Deputy Superintendent of Indian Affairs in 1913. In a move reminiscent of Six Nations' Covenant Chain-inspired support for the British during the Revolutionary War and the War of 1812, a good number of Grand River men volunteered for the Canadian army during the First World War. Canada's Soldier Settlement Act of 1917 granted land to returning veterans. This provision applied to Haudenosaunee veterans, but in their case, they were granted properties taken, not from Crown lands, but from the tiny 5 percent that remained of Six Nations' collectively held Haldimand lands. These grants were made, again, without consultation with the Confederacy Council.[6]

Over and over again in the history of Canada's efforts to impose "one law for everybody," the unique history of Indigenous land – in this case, the story of how the Grand River lands were granted to the Haudenosaunee as allies, not subjects, of the Crown – throws a crowbar into the universalizing bulldozer's treads. Ottawa's expropriation of more Grand River land through the Soldier Settlement Act sparked even more pan-Indigenous political organizing in twentieth-century Canada. Following upon the Grand Indian Council's work from 1870 onward, returning Six Nations (Mohawk) veteran F.O. Loft worked to establish the League of Indians in the 1920s,[7] an organization that evolved into the Indian Brotherhood of Canada, and eventually the Assembly of First Nations.

Speaking in the pale man's voice, Chief Jacobs had warned, "I don't understand the Birch cannoe ruls, if I enter in it it might [up]sett." The Soldier Settlement Act constitutes one of many instances when ill consideration of the birch canoe's rules meant upset, not just for Indigenous Peoples and Indigenous lands, but for trust, the good-minded ability to act appropriately and peace within Canada more broadly.

In a second legislative imposition in 1920, Deputy Minister Scott put forward Bill 14, an amendment to the Indian Act, another effort to enfranchise Indigenous people, again without their consent. In the short life of Canada by that time, the strategy to use enfranchisement to eliminate both Indigenous Peoples and the treaty arrangements they had made with the British Crown had gone back and forth. Sir John A. Macdonald's Conservative government extended voting rights to Indigenous people in 1885 and Wilfrid Laurier's Liberal government excluded them from it again in 1898.[8] Scott brought a renewed determination to the enfranchisement scheme, especially with reference to Six Nations. In a letter insisting on the importance of Bill 14 written to Confederacy Council Chief David Hill, June 11, 1921, Scott wrote, "With reference to enfranchisement I may say that the policy of the government is to carefully protect and educate the Indians and to thus contribute towards their civilization in order that they may eventually be merged in the general body of citizenship. If this in any way conflicts with the aspirations of the Indians whose faces are set against ultimate destiny, it can only be regretted."[9]

Scott's assimilationist policy represents an outright attack upon Two Row philosophy. Paternalistic distortion of the concept of "protection" and the idea of enforced "civilization" is central to this attack.

Completely dispensing with the idea of dignified respect between two separate but cooperative, civilized nations travelling the same river and refraining from interfering in each other's internal arrangements, Scott's approach to Indian Affairs became nothing less than a policy of social Darwinist extinction. Social Darwinism borrows sloppily from evolutionary theory to suggest that the differences between human societies, too, can be plotted, like any other species, along the timeline according to which those that were naturally weaker or inferior would give way to others better suited to win the competition for survival. Considered through a Darwinist lens, Indigenous people's susceptibility to urban European diseases such as tuberculosis or smallpox confirmed that they would gradually vanish as a People, while more robust Europeans would naturally step in to fill the empty landscape.[10]

Scott considers their disappearance "destiny" – it's not hard to hear the echo of American "manifest destiny" here – and his policy of protection aimed to hurry that destiny along through physical and cultural genocide.

It had been part of the Indian Act requirements since the 1890s that Indigenous people's children be (re)educated in a national Residential School system, but it wasn't until Scott's administration that the RCMP actually invaded Indigenous Peoples' homes and forcibly removed children to the schools. Over the years of his enforcement, Scott suppressed reports informing him that 50 percent of the students died from malnutrition, overcrowding and tuberculosis; nonetheless, he insisted that the policy continue.[11] It was under Scott's tenure that Indigenous spiritual and cultural practices such as sun dances on the prairies and potlatches among West Coast Peoples were vigorously forbidden;[12] and it was also under his tenure that the oldest continuously running participatory democracy in the world, the Confederacy Council of the Haudenosaunee, which traced its formation back to the Peacemaker, Jigonsaseh, Ayonwátha, Atotarhonh and the others, was officially abolished in October 1924.

Deskaheh Levi General's Delegation to London and Geneva

In response to the aggression of the Soldier Settlement Act of 1917 and of Bill 14 on compulsory enfranchisement in 1920, the Haudenosaunee hired a lawyer (a practice that was barred for status Indians under the Indian Act) to send a historical-legal petition to the Canadian government that would remind Ottawa of the Covenant Chain–Two Row relationship – of the Six Nations' status as "friends" and "allies," not "subjects" of the Crown. Both this petition and a second one, when the first failed, were reviewed and rejected by Scott, who, as Deputy Superintendent of Indian Affairs, was the prime minister's advisor on such matters.[13]

Because of the failure of these petitions in Ottawa, many of the members of the Confederacy Council grew increasingly frustrated. Some Grand River people doubted the council's ability to protect Six Nations interests and, having been egged on by the Indian agent, began to wonder if the Haudenosaunee should accept the band council system as Canada's reinterpretation of the Crown's guarantee of "protection."[14]

The majority of residents were incensed at Canada's aggression and therefore appointed Levi General, who held the Cayuga chief's title of Deskaheh, to take their concerns to the king in England. They had formed the Covenant Chain–Two Row agreement with the king and his representatives, such as William Johnson, and not with the new and aggressive series of Canadian governments. They therefore insisted upon re-polishing the chain with the British Crown – a practice they have continued to this day.[15]

"(Prince of Wales' visit to Canada) at the Mohawk Chapel, Brantford, Ont., Oct. 20 [1919]." (Credit: Doughty, A. / Library and Archives Canada / PA-022253)

In October 1919, Edward, Prince of Wales, had visited Six Nations on the Grand River, where he was greeted by the Haudenosaunee, made an honorary chief and given the name Da-yon-hem-se-ia. We know that the Covenant Chain–Two Row agreement was reviewed during the proceedings because the very end of a Two Row Wampum hangs over the edge of the table where the signatories are seated in the photographs taken at the ceremonies at Victoria Park, Brantford, October 20, 1919.[16]

As they began in the next year or two to plan Deskaheh's delegation to London, the Confederacy chiefs may have hoped that Prince Edward's recent reminder of the 250-year-old understanding between the British and the Six Nations would gain them a hearing at Buckingham Palace. Instead, Scott and the Canadian government were able to pre-empt Deskaheh from getting an appointment with King George on the basis that entertaining his delegation would interfere with a dispute internal to Canada. Scott urged, "If Government fails to take the fullest measures consistent with justice and fairness to suppress this agitation, it will weaken our administration of Indian Affairs in Canada."[17] He also asked the Department of External Affairs to block Deskaheh's passport so he could not travel to Europe. But the Confederacy Council foiled his plans by issuing a Haudenosaunee passport of their own and hiring an American lawyer (since a Canadian one was disallowed by Canadian law) to accompany Deskaheh on his journey.[18] Having foreseen the possibility of being refused in London, Deskaheh took his delegation to the newly formed League of Nations in Geneva, hoping that, if Six Nations could gain acceptance as a member state, they could attract international support against Canada's aggression.[19] "We want none of your laws and customs that we have not willingly adopted for ourselves," Deskaheh said in a speech summarizing his mission's central concerns. "You have adopted some of ours – votes for women, for instance. . . . We could be happier today, if left alone."[20]

Levi General (Deskaheh) in regalia in Geneva, 1923. (Source: Collections du Centre D'Iconographie de la Ville de Genève, photo number Icon P 1968-18-2, photo taken by Fred Ottiger)

The ancient agreement to link arms was being warped by Canada into genocidal paternalism, and the best defence he and the Confederacy Council back home could think of was to insist on separate paths to protect them from this new upstart Dominion.

What happened between 1922 and 1924 constitutes an episode little known by the Canadian public but utterly revealing of the Haudenosaunee commitment to the Covenant Chain–Two Row relationship. In Canada, the government stepped up the campaign to depose the Confederacy government and to subject Six Nations to the band council system of the Indian Act, while in Europe, Canada worked to block the Haudenosaunee bid for membership in the League of Nations. In Europe, Deskaheh's unheard petition to the British Crown evolved into a mission to find a sponsor required by the Assembly of the League of Nations to hear their case for membership in the League as a sovereign nation. In December 1922, the RCMP conducted a three-day raid on the Grand River territory, ostensibly in search of liquor.[21] Primary among their targets was the home of Deskaheh, even though he was widely known as a teetotaller.[22]

So often, the wampum principles of how to discuss matters together are undermined by overpersonalizing the story, by oversimplifying the issues at stake by turning them into a story of good guys versus bad guys. If Canada could show that Deskaheh drank, if his mission could be turned into an ego trip or represented as a stubborn man who bulldozes the will of others, perhaps it could turn other Grand River people in favour of Ottawa's band council system.

Meanwhile, what was at stake was the autonomous jurisdiction of those who had linked arms with the Crown as allies, not subjects, who lived on lands protected by but not ceded to the Crown.

Indeed, seen in this light, the Six Nations Confederacy's claim for status as an independent nation was stronger than Canada's, since the Haudenosaunee had negotiated international treaties before Europeans arrived in North America. They had their own clearly defined self-governing population and territory, while Canada at this point still had to have Britain ratify international treaties. Nonetheless, the Six Nations, because of diplomatic pressure among members of the League of Nations exerted by Canada and Britain, were unable to find a necessary sponsor for their bid to join the League.

And to ensure that they were unable to mount any future efforts to assert international claims to sovereignty, on October 21, 1924, Colonel C.E. Morgan, a former colonial administrator in South Africa, arrived on the Grand River with an armed detachment of RCMP to officially close the Confederacy Council house and supervise elections for a new band council.[23] His arrival was a Canadian echo of the papal bulls that justified the invasion of Christian kings into "pagan" territories in order to convert their Peoples into European ideas of civilized people.

The Canadian government urged some unhappy reserve residents to express frustration with the traditional leadership and the failure of Deskaheh's mission[24] and used it to give Morgan and his men the excuse of removing what they dismissed as an outdated system of government. The resulting "election," however, put the lie to the idea that the change was welcomed by the people of Six Nations, for it was boycotted by the majority of eligible voters, with only twenty-seven ballots being cast by the entire population on the reserve for the thirteen positions on the new council. Viewing the band council as Ottawa's puppet intended to manipulate the Grand River canoe,[25] most reserve residents to this day continue to avoid voting, with turnout for band council elections averaging a mere 15 percent of the Grand River population.[26]

The 1924 imposition of the band council system marked the armed invasion and colonization of the Six Nations by Canada,[27] which then got its own admission as a full member of the League of Nations the following year.[28] This is what I mean by strong-arming the canoe. Most Canadians are proud of our reputation for "peace, order, and good government." But most Canadians aren't thinking of this armed invasion of our friends' and allies' territories.

Or, we say we didn't know.

Indeed, these actions might suggest that the Canadian government had so far repressed its own memory of the Two Row-Covenant Chain agreement that it didn't itself realize how much it had departed from the Covenant of Linked Arms and Two Paths. We might think it had become ignorant of the legal relationship it had inherited from the wampum exchanged with the Dutch and the British. But the fact that the wampum belts stored in the Grand River Council House were taken during the raid and not returned when asked for indicates that the Canadian government knew very well what wampum signified and did not want any reminders of the broken relationship to remain in Haudenosaunee hands.[29]

Nonetheless, the Six Nations Confederacy Council has never stopped meeting, and to this day it retains the support of the majority of Haudenosaunee on the Grand River. It does its business, however, without the resources it needs to govern. Ever since the British and then Canada decimated the Haldimand Tract and expropriated the Six Nations' trust funds, the council has had little money to carry out its daily business on the reserve.[30] The simultaneous existence of two forms of government on the reserve has distorted the Linked Arms and the Two Paths. Canada insists that its arms are linked with its own imposed creation, the band council, as if this were the original circle of chiefs surrounding the Tree of Peace. Having stripped resources and funds from the traditional Confederacy Council, on the one hand, and empowered the band council, on the other, it has shifted arms by a sleight of hand, and if you're confused by the number of hands and arms in this sentence, so is anyone who wants to get governance work done at Six Nations.

One (White) Law for Everybody

The fallout from this episode of Canada's invasion of Six Nations and replacement of its Council of Chiefs with a band council funded and regulated by Ottawa is loudly echoed one hundred years later in the most recent set of road barricades at the land dispute of 2019/20 known as 1492 Land Back Lane. In this most recent of many such cases over the years, Foxgate Developments gave the Six Nations Band Council $352,000 and 42.3 acres of land elsewhere in exchange for their "public support" for the development on the former Plank Road lands.[31] The Confederacy Council, of course, was not involved in this agreement, and the land defenders point to the arrangement as yet another moment when Canada's band council operates more to enable Canadian extraction than it does Haudenosaunee governance.

Back in 1924, Deskaheh was forbidden re-entry into Canada after the delegation to Geneva. It was unspoken revenge for the bruise he had landed on Canada's international reputation. Not only was he refused entry, but his family was not allowed to exit Canada and visit him in Buffalo across the border. There, he raised immediate public protest of Canada's takeover in the radio speech he delivered in Rochester, New York, March 10, 1925. "The governments at Washington and Ottawa have a silent partnership of policy," he said. "It is aimed to break up every tribe of red men so as to dominate every acre of their territory. . . . Over in Ottawa, they call that policy 'Indian advancement.' Over in Washington, they call it 'assimilation.' We who would be the helpless victims say it is tyranny." He then urged his non-Indigenous listeners to write their governments and "ask them to tell you when and how they got the right to govern people who have no part in your government and do not live in your country but live in their own. They can't tell you that."[32]

They can't because neither Canada nor the U.S. has ever rejected the Covenant Chain–Two Row treaty relationship. Dig as you might, there are no divorce papers to be found. And the Haudenosaunee have continued to insist that we remember these original covenants.

In 1954, for example, after the United States' House Concurrent Resolution 108 proposed the termination of treaty relationships with Native Americans, specifically pointing to relationships with the Indigenous Peoples of New York, the Haudenosaunee sent delegates to Washington, D.C., with replicas of the Covenant Chain and Two Row Wampum Belts to remind the American government of the centuries-old agreements they had never rescinded.[33] In subsequent years, in 1959 and again in 1970, members of the Six Nations on the Grand River territory re-entered the council house closed by Colonel Morgan and his men. They aimed to restore the Confederacy government, but once again, they were ejected by police.[34]

The 1970 attempt to restore the Confederacy Council's authority came in the wake of the Pierre Trudeau government's "White Paper" on Indian Affairs of 1969. In essence, this paper was another instance of the British 1857 Gradual Civilization Act and the subsequent Canadian Gradual Enfranchisement Act of 1869, for it aimed to incorporate Indigenous Peoples as regular citizens of Canada and extinguish the treaties. Jean Chrétien, Trudeau's Minister of Indian Affairs, wrote a letter to the Six Nations Confederacy Council dated November 17, 1969:

> I know that the Six Nations "Iroquois" Confederacy considers itself a "sovereign nation" and does not recognize the right of the Canadian Government to make any legislation affecting it. But I must say I consider the position of the Confederacy to be invalid.
>
> By definition the sovereignty of Canada precludes the sovereignty of the Iroquois Confederacy. It is impossible to have a nation within a nation. Our nation is Canada and the Indian people of Canada are Canadians. Incidentally, I believe it is true that those Indians who adhere to the Confederacy at the same time take advantage of the many provisions of the Indian Act and many of the programs and services now extended by my Department. By those actions, they contradict their presumption to sovereignty.
>
> You of the Confederacy were born here, you live here, you are Canadians.[35]

Here, Chrétien cites no evidence for his opinion. He must be relying on the racist Doctrine of Discovery and the European Law of Nations, for his letter contains no references to the Covenant Chain–Two Row tradition, nor does it refer to the Royal Proclamation, to Frank Oliver's or Governor Simcoe's assurances that Six Nations should continue to govern itself, to Deskaheh's mission to the League of Nations, or the failure of earlier efforts to force Six Nations to become Canadians. Nor does it mention the draining of the Six Nations trust funds or the massive reduction of its land base. The letter simply asserts Six Nations' incorporation into Canada as an accomplished fact.

It took only twelve days for the Confederacy Council to respond in a letter of November 29 signed by Mrs. Garnett Thomas, secretary for the Confederacy:

> We consider this letter to be another example of Canadian tyranny and aggression against the Iroquois nations.
>
> . . . The Department of Indian Affairs has not the right to swallow us up. Whether Jean Chretien likes it or not, we are here and we are sovereign by our divine constitution and anything contrary has again upheld the Canadian tradition of not having honored the treaties of native people.
>
> If the definition of Canadian sovereignty is precluded by the ingenious legislation of assimilation and genocide – and its ability to ignore the rights of North American native people, then this shameful evidence will proclaim to the world the advent of a Canadian sovereignty built on the heartbreak and tears of the Six Nations North American Confederacy of the Great League of Peace, of our children and of those children yet unborn.
>
> We are waiting to meet the representatives of the Crown and not a Questionable third party.[36]

This is where a twisted understanding of "protection," a warped paternalism that reduces independent allies to "wards of the state," has brought us. Fifty years later, we remain pretty much at the same impasse. Successive Canadian governments, in defiance of the Covenant Chain–Two Row protocols and of the Royal Proclamation, presume that Haudenosaunee residents of the Grand River and of other Haudenosaunee reserves are subjects of Canada. This, because they have been subjected to Ottawa's band council governance.

Each invasion becomes a precedent for the next until we now have a long record, a narrative flow, of recurrent conflict and even violence between the Haudenosaunee and their neighbours, all feeding a deepening climate of resentment and distrust. We are a far cry from the peace, good-mindedness and unified empowerment that comes from mutual respect.

Part III

Linking Arms: Face-to-Face Ethics

The approach of Kiotsaeton's embassy to the shore at Trois-Rivières raised no fear or alarm. This, because the people on shore would have heard from advance runners about the flotilla of vessels paddling upriver, and, as the boats got closer, they would have heard Kiotsaeton's party singing long before their vessels threaded their way through the clumps of reeds and nosed into the wet earth of the riverbank. For, before the people gathered under the sails in front of the fort, where Kiotsaeton later hung his seventeen collars of porcelain one after another on the cord with each phase of his dramatic speech, he would have already enacted the first three "words," the opening phases of a protocol the Haudenosaunee call the "Edge of the Woods."

It is never safe to approach another People's home, their village, hunting territory or farmlands, without announcing your peaceful intentions. This had been the anomaly presented by Ayonwátha in the lean-to near the Oneida village where the cornfields lay at the edge of the woods. The making of the first wampum took place in the time before *Kayanerenhtserakó:wa*, before the Law of Peace had been established among the warring nations.

Once the Great Law had been established, however, as *Royá:ner* John Arthur Gibson explained, any Haudenosaunee travelling into other People's lands, and any of them receiving foreign people into their territories, would have expected to enact the first three phases of the Edge of the Woods, consisting of the Prologue (On the Journey), Near the Thorny Bushes and Wiping Their Tears.[1] Father Vimont had been impressed with Kiotsaeton's opening word-song, his Prologue, which conveyed the danger and difficulty of his journey. Not just his fear for his life at the hands of the French-Algonquin allies, but the struggles of travel through forests, past rapids and upcurrent in the unfamiliar salt water of the big river. In this first segment, On the Journey, the Mohawk spokesman presented to his listeners the exposure and emotional exhaustion demanded by the travails of his travel. The Prologue dramatized his party's vulnerability.

Hearing of his difficulties, it was then the part of his hosts to perform Near the Thorny Bushes. In his oration to Goldenweiser, Gibson chanted the next phase in Onondaga language:

> ne' ęyųtattsístayéha··s
> teyo'nyúkwá·kta··'
> né'tho tęyųtatitę·hé·nyú··'
> oihokú'á··
>
> They will kindle a fire for them,
> at the thorny bushes
> [and] there they will console them
> [with the] "few words."[2]

In this second segment, the villagers greet those who arrive at the edge of the woods, or, in Kiotsaeton's case, at the shore of the river, after the rigours of travel. The visitors' journey through the dark woods is never easy, for the bushes may be thorny and tear the travellers' skin, the woods are often filled with danger, the terrain uneven, the rivers swollen with rain or the snows deep. The villagers see the travellers' exhaustion, their weariness, their relief, and they "console" them. They themselves have slept in their own beds, eaten corn soup with their families by their own fires, but they picture to themselves the struggles and labour their visitors have come through, and they comfort them.[3]

The tenderness of this ceremony of meeting sets the tone, the gestures and mood, for how to greet visitors who emerge from the woods or the river needing hospitality.

The third phase of this ceremony of greeting is known as Wiping Their Tears (or the Requickening). The rigours of travel, like Ayonwátha's grief-stricken stumbling through the woods, can dull a person's sensory capacities, and, before any serious or important discussion can begin, it is important to "requicken" the senses. In this first part of Wiping Their Tears, called *né áhsę nikawénakeh* in Onondaga, the villagers therefore wipe the tears from the travellers' eyes. They clear their ears and unblock their throats so that they can speak clearly again. It is a reciprocal ceremony, so the second part of the Requickening has the travellers performing the same gentle gestures for their hosts: the speaker for the travellers takes the softest deerskin to wipe their hosts' eyes, to quiet the din in their ears, to clear the lump in their throats. There is a string of wampum to represent each of these three gestures. The aim, for both parties, is to recognize the pains and struggles that hinder *ka'nikonhriyó'tshera't* – nimble, intelligent, balanced minds – to touch them kindly, and thus enable them once again to see and hear and speak clearly.

This is the ceremony for approaching the delicate, vulnerable space at the Edge of the Woods.

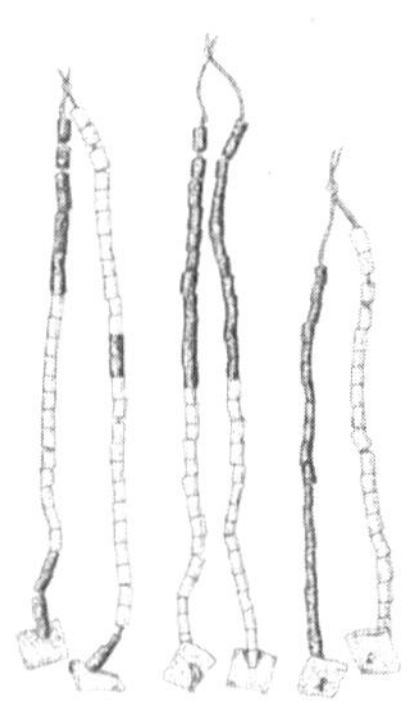

Chapter Eleven

Clearing Ethical Space

In an essay titled "Approaching the Clearing," the Canadian environmentalist poet and philosopher Don McKay speaks of how nature gives us our first lessons in philosophy, how it shapes our minds, how living in the physical world *is* our first philosophy.[1] He describes, for example, walking in the woods and coming upon a clearing:

> a pool of light where the trees relent, a place that combines seclusion with openness. As we approach, we tend to slow down and shut up, partly because of a possible deer or fox, and partly out of respect for the presence which always seems to gather in a clearing. Each has its own presence, its own tone. I suspect that sense of presence is the true ancestor of our notion of place, before arbitrary naming and the grid.
>
> So we enter tentatively, craning our senses, much as a deer or fox would. It is as though we had entered our own listening. When we pause here, taking off our packs, getting out the water bottles and binoculars, it is in a spirit of cohabitation rather than ownership.[2]

It's not hard to imagine a similar tentative, alert-and-listening respect being crucial when warriors approached Jigonsaseh's clearing in the

Dish-With-One-Spoon lands between nations. Or when Kiotsaeton's party approached the shoreline near the village of Trois-Rivières where people were anxiously wondering if Couture had survived among the Haudenosaunee and if he might safely return. Whether you are a warrior, a deer, a fox, a returner of prisoners or a man stumbling in grief through the woods after the loss of your family, the edge of the clearing is a volatile and vulnerable space, as risky as it is compelling.

The Edge of the Woods ritual, with its three phases of On the Journey, Near the Thorny Bushes and Wiping Their Tears, was and is a key site in Haudenosaunee body-thinking. And McKay's description of the feeling that arises when someone enters a clearing helps us non-Haudenosaunee imagine how the People of the Longhouse ritualized the experience of that site in their philosophy and cultural practices. Indeed, this heightened moment is discernible, not just by people from the ship, but by any alert, embodied being who enters the clearing. The Edge of the Woods represents a distinct kind of encounter, where arrivees are made conscious that they do not know the rules, where locals watch every move of the travellers to determine friend or foe, safety or flight. At the margin of the woods, the hair stands up on the back of the neck, the fur rises around the ruff. Anyone who enters is thrown off balance. They are unsure of the adequacy of their customary knowledge, assumptions and even language. Coming upon a clearing stimulates alertness and silence, McKay suggests, the impulse to slow down and shut up.

Or it doesn't. There are always those who are oblivious to their surroundings. But for those who are attending to themselves in the world, the clearing opens a moment of heightened awareness.

A major part of this awareness comes from stepping out of the shelter of the thicket and into open space. We become uncomfortably aware that we may be seen before we see who or what sees us. Their eyes may see us as prey, as friend, as threat or – we hope – as welcome guest. We can't yet know. Antonio Machado, the Spanish schoolteacher and poet, captures the essence of this experience in a powerful, short poem:

The eye you see is not
an eye because you see it;
it is an eye because it sees you.[3]

Without a consciousness of the clearing, if we aren't aware of entering unfamiliar space, we can be so absorbed with our own thoughts, our own assumptions, our own experiences, our own worldview that we fall under the delusion that we are the only ones who see the situation as it truly is. We extrapolate our single field of vision, our interpretation of the world, over everyone. We universalize our own perspective. We obliviate.

Commenting on the universalizing assumptions of the word "we" in the above paragraph – and at other moments in this book – Amber Meadow Adams reminded me that Haudenosaunee grammar doesn't assume this kind of generalization. Her comments took me back to the introductory class in *Kanyen'kéha* that I took more than ten years ago. There, our teacher Tom Deer taught us about dual and plural pronouns and how each of these can be inclusive or exclusive. So, for example, he observed that Mohawk language speakers can add different word-stems to refer to four distinct kinds of "we": dual inclusive *teni-* ("you and I"), the plural inclusive *tewa-* ("you and I and some other persons"), dual exclusive *iakeni-* ("we two and not the person addressed") and the plural exclusive *iakwa-* ("we three or more without the person addressed").[4] For me, this is one of those crucial instances where simple language usage tells you so much about the philosophy of a People. The all-absorbing "we" of English that readily speaks for others as if they were members of the first-person collective isn't available in Mohawk. *Kanyen'kéha* speakers don't absorb others into their own perspectives in that unmarked way. Mohawk language doesn't have a royal "we."

Against Innocent IV's assertion that Mongols must be incorporated by force if necessary into the collective "we" of the body of Christ, Mohawk pronouns anticipate a wide array of distinct relations to the collective "we."

The clearing is more clearly marked and observed in Haudenosaunee language.

But for those of us whose European pronouns are not so alert, *we* are not shy to assert *our* interpretation, *our* understanding, *our* parameters, over the space of encounter and its participants. We tend to think our science is the universal science, our religion the all-inclusive faith, our laws the obvious, objective, universal laws.

Stepping to the edge of the woods can back us (plural, exclusive "us Canadians and not those with more precise pronouns") up from this kind of self-generalizing assumption. It can help us to recalibrate, to reassess who is looking, who is being seen, what we truly know. It makes us aware of dynamic otherness, of life and agency beyond our own. This makes it what the Onondaga Chair of the Chanie Wenjack School for Indigenous Studies, David Newhouse, calls "Guswenta space" (wampum space), an ethical space, an alert and volatile space in which our interactions with others, our awareness of how our own behaviour is interpreted by other beings, our assumed universalism, comes into focus.[5] It is what Gae Ho Hwako (Norma Jacobs) calls in Cayuga language "*ǫ da gaho dę:s* (the sacred meeting space) between the ship and the canoe, where we originally agreed on the Two Row and to which we must return today."[6]

At the edge of the clearing, we are challenged by our ability to respond to others – our response-ability.

I want to emphasize how, at its crux, the visual iconography of the Covenant Chain–Two Row Wampum highlights this heightened, ceremonial, ethically charged space. Whether in the rows of white beads that fill the space between the two purple rows or in the line of purple beads representing the rope or chain that stretches between the two human figures in the Covenant Chain, we see featured an image of two parties meeting across a clearing. "The Creator gave us a canoe and you a boat," said the Mohawk leaders in Jake Thomas's recitation to Governor General Schreyer. "We will take our vessels to the water and put them in the water, each in their distinctive way. Our people will follow the vessels in the water. We will place them a certain distance apart, but will line them up so they will always be parallel." Over the years of listening to Haudenosaunee people talk about the Two Row-Covenant Chain tradition, I've come to see that this visual distance between distinctive vessels constitutes a clearing of ethical space between parties that is deeply important to the Haudenosaunee philosophy of how to build lasting relationships – how to create *skén:nen, ka'shatsténhsera* and *ka'nikonrio.* It is central to the thinking that generated the Covenant Chain–Two Row treaty-making tradition in the first instance, and it has continued to run through Haudenosaunee efforts to repolish and renew that silver chain with British, Canadian and American partners ever since.

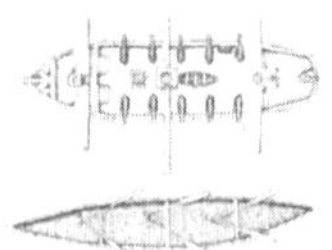

Ethical Space

One of the first things that struck me when I first learned about the Covenant Chain–Two Row agreement is that, like pronouns in *Kanyen'kéha*, it affirms relationships at the same time that it marks differences. The two parties agree to link arms, tie the rope, between their separate vessels, to respect a space between them, not for segregation but to build the long house, to set the ground rules for friendship. As Johanne McCarthy (Onondaga, Beaver clan) put it during one of our Two Row Research Partnership meetings, the Covenant Chain–Two Row set the "house rules" for anyone wanting to live here.[7] It's important to remember that all the dual and plural inclusive and exclusive Haudenosaunee pronouns I mentioned are different kinds of collective-making "we." What this approach to the collective does is protect each other's distinctive dignity. Often in such circumstances, our Euro-Canadian instinct is to look for similarities and play down differences so as to find common ground, to enfranchise the other party *within our system.*

The *Ohén:ton Karihwatéhkwen* Thanksgiving Address works to establish unified, good minds – you could say civilized society – by recognizing and thanking the ecosystem of distinct lives on which ours depend. By contrast, the line of thinking represented by the Doctrine of Discovery tries to establish "one mind" by insisting everyone must submit to the unilateral law of which Christian popes and kings were the champions or guardians.

Nonetheless, the wisdom, even the necessity, of attending to differences to build good relationships is not just a Haudenosaunee idea. There are thinkers from the Western sailing ship who have reflected on its wisdom too. According to them, a better way to seek what we often think of as common ground is to attend to different parties' ways of understanding their encounter with the same space, the same phenomenon. I've already described how the experience of the Edge of the Woods, the encounter in the clearing, became formalized in Haudenosaunee thinking and political ritual, so now let me trace how a similar experience has been described in European philosophy.

While there are any number of thinkers a person could turn to from the canon of European philosophy for a discussion of the importance of the encounter with difference, let me trace it in the thinking of Emmanuel Levinas. This twentieth-century Jewish-French philosopher never indicated awareness of the Covenant Chain–Two Row tradition or of the Haudenosaunee understanding of the Edge of the Woods, as he developed influential ideas about how human sentience actually emerges through the ethical challenge of encountering what he called the "face of the other": "Thought begins with the possibility of conceiving a freedom exterior to my own," he wrote. "To think a freedom exterior to my own is the first thought. It makes my very presence in the world. The world of perception shows a face."[8]

It is as if he is describing the experience of stepping into the clearing. Without this awareness of stepping into a world of beings outside my own perspective, he says, I would have no reason to distinguish my own thoughts, to identify myself. Levinas suggests that what stimulates us to order our impulses into what we call *thoughts* is dialogue. Beginning to think, moving from impulse to reason, happens when we realize that others outside ourselves have their own impulses and thoughts, independent of our own. The encounter with difference helps us conceive of ourselves.

"It is this shattering of indifference," Levinas writes, "this possibility of one-for-the-other, that constitutes the ethical event."[9] His wording suggests that when we enter a clearing, when we encounter the face of an other, we Western universalizers cannot proceed on autopilot, we cannot assume everything is already familiar. Transitions, moments of encounter, make us tentative and alert; we cannot be indifferent and unaffected. The face of the other challenges our presumptions. You could say that what makes Canesatego's or Kiotsaeton's or Johnson's Covenant Chain–Two Row encounter ethical, in Levinas's remarkable phrase, is the "shattering of indifference" – the shattering of the assumption of no difference.

Of course, people respond in different ways to the unfamiliarity of the clearing, the site of encounter. Some flee the discomfort. Some stand curiously, wondering at what they see, what they feel. Some, like Innocent IV, indicate their desire to incorporate it into the familiar terms of Christendom, violently if necessary. Some, like Don McKay, "enter their own listening," while others talk nervously on autopilot like Azurara did in the slave market to translate the horror he witnessed into something more palatable.

The Dutch in Jake Thomas's narrative went on autopilot when they called the Haudenosaunee "sons," but the Haudenosaunee exercised a freedom of their own, to use Levinas's diction, one that was exterior to Dutch assumptions about how the new family should be organized, and the newcomers' attempt to project non-difference was repelled.

Indifference – the assumption of non-difference – is a ruse of power, the privilege of assumed sovereignty. You might call it a "civil" ruse, for it quietly imposes uniformity, the assumption of one law, one worldview, upon everybody. As compared to Champlain's violent way of obliterating Haudenosaunee difference with his firearm, the Canadian government has tried many times to enact "civil" *in*difference – to obliterate Indigenous difference – whether through the Gradual Enfranchisement Act of 1869, the Indian Advancement Act of 1884 or Pierre Trudeau's White Paper of 1969. And it is still a common ruse to this day. The dismissal of difference is a deliberate kind of not-seeing that we enact when we say we are "protecting" the other, as if they were a child.

Making them a ward of the state. Insisting their children attend our schools, in our language. That we will manage their trust funds. That their unceded lands will be managed as "Crown lands." We will look after their welfare.

A true encounter with the other, however, insists that the I, that *other* I, is an I because their eye sees me. They see through these claims and have I's of their own, their own opinion about my assumed sovereignty, the adequacy of my self-knowledge.

In "The Ethical Space of Encounter," Cree philosopher Willie Ermine suggests that we need to reopen the clearing in today's society. He discusses the importance of reopening "a space between two entities, . . . a space between the Indigenous and Western thought worlds. The space is initially conceptualized by the unwavering construction of difference and diversity between human communities. These are the differences that highlight uniqueness because each entity is moulded from a distinct history, knowledge tradition, philosophy, and social and political reality."[10] Ermine reminds me of Chief William Jacobs writing to the Superintendent of Indian Affairs in 1872: "I don't understand the way of your cannoe ruls," the Six Nations chief said. "I don't understand the ways of your boat ruls the pail fase said to the read man." Yet successive British and Canadian governments tried multiple times to completely assimilate the Haudenosaunee canoe. As Ermine puts it, the resulting "sordid and cumulative conditions of socio-political entanglement" have created "an irritable bond of communities and trans-cultural confusion at its worst that is now the Canadian experience."[11]

Think of the irritable bond, to put it lightly, that binds Canadians' and Indigenous Peoples' very different kinds of shame over D.C. Scott's "protection" as enacted in the Indian Residential School system. For Indigenous people, there is the complex shame of having been subjected to physical, sexual, psychological and cultural degradation; of children's questions about why their parents could not protect them from being kidnapped in the first place; and the schools' multigenerational effects in loss of language and culture, substance abuse or family dysfunction – cultural and spiritual identities left unmoored. For Canadians, the sordid shame of being citizens of an abusive country, of having the institutions of our society's loftiest ideals – the nurturing of children, the reverence of religion, the values of peace, order and good government – exposed as mechanisms of pedophilia, brutality and cultural genocide; of realizing belatedly how widespread ignorance and *in*difference among Canadians about what was happening to Indigenous children and families was sanctioned by government policy, religious certitude, school curricula and media disinterest. All this, just in reference to the Residential School system. We could as easily identify other irritable bonds arising from the draconian "protections" of the Indian Act, the history of unresolved land claims, undrinkable water on First Nation reserves, the unconscionably high number of Indigenous people incarcerated in *our* Canadian correctional system. The list goes on. Using English's plural inclusive pronoun, Ermine says, "We are now so badly entangled in our political and social lives that the principles of our existences as autonomous human communities have become blurred in that intercultural confusion."[12] The closure of the Confederacy Council house, the machinations to undermine Deskaheh's delegation to the League of Nations, the expropriation of the Six Nations' trust funds, the imposition of the band council system, all in the effort to force the Haudenosaunee to become "Canadian Indians." These are among the many ways in which Canada has tried to obliterate the white beads of *skén:nen* (peace), *ka'shatsténhsera* (good minds) and *ka'nikonrio* (friendship, respect) between the two rows that have created the resulting confusion in which we now live.

The purpose of opening a clearing between the "two solitudes,"[13] to use Ermine's words, is not to build silos or a Berlin wall, but to open a ground where people can actually meet and learn from one another: "the idea of the ethical space, produced by contrasting perspectives of the world, entertains the notion of a meeting place, or initial thinking about a neutral zone between entities or cultures. The space offers a venue to step out of our allegiances, to detach from the cages of our mental worlds and assume a position where human-to-human dialogue can occur. The ethical space offers itself as the theatre for cross-cultural conversation in pursuit of ethically engaging diversity and disperses claims to the human order."[14]

Ermine calls this ethical meeting place "a theatre," and by doing so reminds me of Kiotsaeton pacing as he sang and gestured in the square between the French, the Algonquins and the Hurons. It reminds me of the fragile, dangerous space Ayonwátha traversed when the wise Oneida chief sent his matching wampum of feather shaft tubes to the edge of the cornfields.

Informed by long Haudenosaunee experience in spreading the Great Law of Peace, the Covenant Chain–Two Row agreement very clearly laid out this kind of ethical space where the travellers and hosts could step out of their habitual mental worlds and into a clearing, a theatre, as Ermine puts it, where explicitly cross-cultural conversation could take place. The space between the two rows, the stretch of chain between the two human figures, graphically represents this ethical space, this clearing, where both parties can enter their own listening, can feel the gaze emanating from the face of the other, can come to first philosophy, a consciousness of themselves.

It is in this dialogical, *kaswentha, ǫ da gaho dę:s* space that any legitimate idea of Canada was constituted.

Entanglements

But how, after all these troubled and troubling years, after the distorting influence of patronizing racism and the unilateral imposition of Euro-Western universalism, can we regain this first philosophy, this experience of the fragile, unfamiliar ethical space that is represented in the Covenant Chain–Two Row treaty tradition? How we can repolish the covenant? How do we sweep clean the white mat of peace? After four hundred and some years of side-by-side living, the entanglements and distortions of the relationship between the colonial and Haudenosaunee vessels are woven not just into the public domains of law and government, but right into the intimacies of people's homes and families.

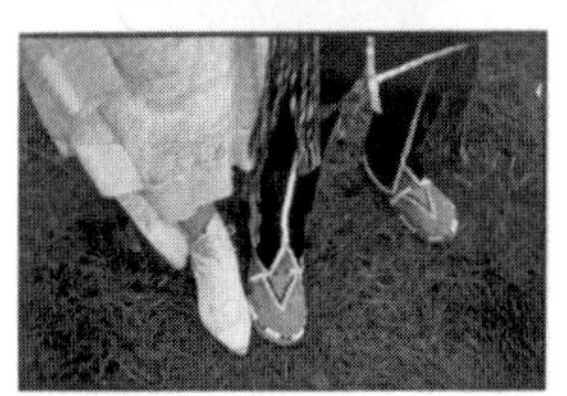

Jolene Rickard. *Two Canoes*, 1988, Chrome print, 11 x 17 inches. (Photo courtesy of Jolene Rickard and the Burchfield Penney Art Center)

Tuscarora historian, artist and curator Jolene Rickard, a professor of Art at Cornell University, pictures these intimacies in a photo collage called *Two Canoes* that alludes to the Two Row in its image of two parallel tree trunks growing side by side in the same soil. But where we would expect to see the interlaced roots of the two tree trunks, we see instead the feet of a moccasined groom and a European bride.

Rickard says that the collage's title comes from her grandfather, "who always said the Indian canoe is too swift for white culture. You had to decide which way you were going to go." The photo of the bride and groom, she says, was taken at the wedding of a white woman "who is very into her colonial background" and an Indigenous man "who is also very into his past." The bride was therefore dressed, Rickard says, like a nineteenth-century woman while the man was dressed for the present, and his natural, traditional, but still popular moccasins contrast with her artificial, pointed and fashionable shoe.[15] Rickard's collage asks many questions about how to reconsider the ethical space of the Covenant Chain–Two Row in our times: How long can two trees grow side by side in the same ground, cross-pollinating and intertwining their roots, before they blend into some kind of hybrid? Is it reasonable and workable to expect people to share the same region, the same river, for hundreds of years and for them not to eventually cross over into each other's vessels? Will one of the two eventually become engulfed in the other? Or will the inevitable entanglements cause people who have one foot in each vessel to fall into the water between the two?

Rickard's reference to the wedding may suggest that people have entered into these entanglements willingly, but it also brilliantly alludes to the ways in which the intimate entanglements have been complicated by Canadian law. One of the most invasive of these laws appears in Section 3 of the 1876 Indian Act, where the new Canadian government attempted to define what an Indian is:

> The term "Indian" means
>
> *First. Any male person of Indian blood reputed to belong to a particular band;*
>
> *Secondly. Any child of such person;*
>
> *Thirdly. Any woman who is or was lawfully married to such person.* (italics in original)

Let's remember that before this act, there were Indians only in India. Mesmerized by the goal of reaching Asia, Columbus had mistaken the Caribs he had met in Cuba as "Indians," and the name had spread throughout Europe to refer to the people who inhabited what for Europeans was a "new" world.

So it is quite literally the case that in settler colonial laws like this, the category of "Indian" was being invented as a legal category. This is how law can make a race where it didn't previously exist.

In the process of inventing legally recognizable "Indians," the Indian Act ordained that a woman's personhood depended on the status of the man she married: if she married a man with Indian Personhood, she became Indian, whether her parents were Indian or not. If she married a man without Indian status, she became non-Indian, regardless of her ancestry. Likewise, the children of these marriages, as the second clause indicates, derived their status from their father. The application of these rules reveals how nonsensical this could be: for example, if an Indigenous woman in Canada married an Indigenous person from the U.S., who could not have Indian status in Canada, she became a "non-Indian." "Indian" is thus a property determined by the Canadian state, not by ancestry or by Indigenous forms of affiliation or kinship.

We encounter even further complications when we remember, too, that Haudenosaunee families are organized matrilineally. So when Section 3 of the Indian Act imposed the practice of determining Indian Personhood by patrilineage, by either being a male with status, being the child of such a male or being married to one, it interfered not only with Haudenosaunee family belonging, but also with political participation in the Haudenosaunee canoe. Six Nations children receive their clan identities through their mother, and Clan Mothers traditionally invite leaders from among their extended family to represent their clan among the Confederacy Council's circle of fifty chiefs. Without a clan, a Haudenosaunee person has no tie to any chief to represent their concerns on council.

By measures such as this, Canada invaded and attempted to absorb the Six Nations, not just by closing the Confederacy Council house, but also by creating the conditions for generations of clanless children to be detached from the traditional Confederacy Council system. It legislated their political participation *toward* the Ottawa-imposed band council.

These are the kinds of "oblivious" unilateral invasions that happen when one enters the clearing of another culture with indifference, with no concern for agency, practices or freedoms exterior to one's own.

And, once started, the entanglements continue to multiply. Indigenous women agitated against the gender discrimination of Section 3 in the 1970s and 1980s, arguing that it contradicted the guarantees of gender equality in the Canadian Charter of Rights and Freedoms. Ottawa attempted to correct the problem with Bill C-31, a Bill to Amend the Indian Act (1985), which detached status from marriage. So Indigenous women who had previously lost Indian status by "marrying out" could apply to regain it, and non-Indigenous women who had gained status by "marrying in" could lose it. It also restored Indian status to the children of Indigenous women who had married non-Indigenous men.

But it's extremely difficult to untangle an entanglement after the fact. How many generations later would the descendants of mixed marriages be able to reclaim Indian status? Should the reclamations go on indefinitely? Bill C-31 set an arbitrary number: two generations later. If the children of women who had married out, marry out themselves, their children do not have status, creating a "second-generation cutoff."

What this means, in practice, if not in name, is that recent Canadian law has introduced a racial blood quantum measure – eerily echoing the Nuremberg laws of 1930s Nazi Germany on how many grandparents constituted Jewishness – for who is an "Indian" and who is not.

One reason to limit the generational transfer of Indian status to two was that Ottawa would not afford more funding or land for reserves to meet the needs of unlimited numbers of new, status-holding "Bill C-31ers." This situation is precisely what the Six Nations *rotiyaneshon* had anticipated when they tried to build a trust fund after their arrival on the Grand River in the 1780s. They had worked with their British allies to re-establish a land base and set aside funds so that they could care for the "faces waiting in the ground to be born." If Ottawa could not afford to meet these needs, it's because their British colonial forebears had squandered these protections.

The 1985 Amendment meant there were potentially thousands of Canadians who might claim status and access to band councils' restricted funds and land. Seeing a way to escape the embarrassing and impossible task of judging each generational case for who is and who is not an Indian, Ottawa has appealed, in the years since 1985, to a distorted interpretation of "self-government" in order to insist that band councils must establish their own status-determining committees. The result is that Indigenous Peoples themselves have been forced to judge one another's blood quantum as an arbiter of which vessel will carry them down the river of life.[16]

The Covenant Chain–Two Row treaty protocols had warned how the relationship would become distorted if the idea of equity between siblings ("brothers") was replaced by that of patriarchy, the system by which fathers hand down orders and entitlements to their children. The seventeenth-century Haudenosaunee *rotiyaneshon* seem to have anticipated the irritable bonds that Willie Ermine observes and that are demonstrated in the sordid entanglements created by the Indian Act. They therefore encouraged their European treaty partners to see the wisdom of building their relationship in ethical space, a clearing or open space between two freedoms, where peace, friendship and good-minded respect could flourish.

Looking back from the convolutions these interventions in the Indigenous canoe have produced, we may wish our sailing ship ancestors had known what we know now. "To know in truth is to allow one's self to be known as well," writes the Quaker master teacher, Parker Palmer. The English word "truth" comes from the Germanic word "troth," he explains, which means "a covenant with another, a pledge to engage in a mutually accountable and transformative relationship, a relationship forged of trust and faith in the face of unknowable risks." He could be describing *Tehontatenentshonteronhtáhkwa–Tékeni Teyohà:te* philosophy when he goes on to say, "Truth involves entering a relationship with someone or something genuinely other than us, but with whom we are intimately bound . . . Truth requires the knower to become interdependent with the known. Both parties have their own integrity and otherness, and one party cannot be collapsed into the other."[17] It sounds like Palmer is looking, as he writes these words, at Newhouse's Guswenta space, at the three white beads and the chain on the wampum that links the two parties. He reminds us that a true experience of the clearing, an experience of troth, challenges the known and familiar. Unless we assume indifference, this experience makes us question whether the things we know, our patterns of action, protocols for behaviour, have prepared us for this encounter. It is a moment of vulnerability.

Ceremonies for Ethical Space

And this vulnerability is precious and powerful. Nothing kills vulnerability like fear, so it's important to have protocols or ceremonies for approaching the unfamiliar and for dealing with our fear of the unknown, our discomfort at the edge of the clearing. This is precisely what wampum, in this case the Covenant Chain–Two Row Wampum protocols, established: a ceremony for maintaining a good mind in the face of the unknown, in the face of difference.

Such a meeting begins with the participants very conscious of mutual fear, of the danger there is when people meet at the woods' edge and feel the gap between them. The purpose of the meeting is to address this fear, to create a protocol or ceremony to deal with it: "It will put your minds at ease (that we still remember these words)," said Jake Thomas, quoting the seventeenth-century *rotiyaneshon*. The recent book *Ǫ da gaho dę:s: Reflecting on Our Journeys / Gae Ho Hwako (Norma Jacobs) and the Circles of Ǫ da gaho dę:s*, edited by Timothy Leduc, evokes ceremonial space to calm the fear and harm that so often troubles the space between the Two Rows of the ship and the canoe. The book is composed of chapters written by Haudenosaunee and non-Haudenosaunee people who participated in a series of *ǫ da gaho dę:s* teaching circles led by Cayuga, Wolf Clan, Longhouse Faithkeeper Gae Ho Hwako (Norma Jacobs) in her role as Elder-in-Residence at Wilfrid Laurier University's Brantford Campus. Each section of the book opens with Gae Ho Hwako's teachings from Haudenosaunee traditions, especially the Thanksgiving Address and the Two Row Wampum. Her chapters are then followed by *skowanaht* (Mohawk) / *ęsęhsgwaowhaneh* (Cayuga) expansions of the teaching that are contributed by participants in the circle who take up matters they learned from Gae Ho Hwako and expand upon them from their own reflections.[18]

"*Ǫ da gaho dę̱:s*," explains the book's glossary, is Cayuga language for

> the sacred meeting space where we can communicate with one another and be really clear about who we are in our relationships. As our conversation evolves, we come to a real understanding of what the other means. This is what we refer to as *ganigǫhi:yo* (a good mind), which is needed to come to *ǫ da gaho dę̱:s*. This sacred space is where the ship and the canoe originally agreed upon the Two Row Wampum, and today it is the place to which we must return in order to talk about the impacts we have experienced because of its violation.[19]

Gae Ho Hwako explains, "We have forgotten about *ǫ da gaho dę̱:s* (the sacred meeting space) between the ship and the canoe . . . Ceremony is important to all our Two Row relations, as it is a way of knocking at the door of another with a good intention to be respectful and caring." This ceremonial awareness affects not just interhuman relations, she goes on to say, but ecological ones as well: "Every place is sacred, and we need to ask permission in order to respectfully come into it. Being respectful to what is already there is beneficial for those who are in that environment, and thus it is a way of being that is really important for building relationships between people and creation."[20]

The Covenant Chain–Two Row way of making agreements establishes symbolic, ceremonial *ǫ da gaho dę̱:s* spaces that are designed to put the fearful and tentative participants in a state of mind where the extraordinary can take place. References to time scales beyond the range of human life (as long as the earth shall last, the Creator will bear witness, the future generations that will rise from the earth), the identification of memorable symbols (the linking of arms, the three iron or silver links of the chain) and the performance of symbolic acts (the smoking of the pipe whose tobacco smoke lifts to the Creator above the realm of earthly life, hanging the wampum up for all to see after each scene or phase of the agreement) – all these are elements of a ceremony that is meant to elevate human minds from our everyday fear so we can experience something out of the ordinary. Or, to put it differently, to help us step back from habitual practice and obsessions to see the importance of having good minds in the present moment in order to set the terms so we can continue in a healthy way into the future.

Ceremony has the potential to create an interlude, to create a clearing. When we enter it with openness and intention, ceremonial suspension removes us from operating on the "autopilot" of our usual assumptions and conceptions.

Perhaps it was the translation over time of *ǫ da gaho dę:s* into a business or political "treaty" that dulled non-Haudenosaunee people's capacity to experience the extraordinary in the space between the rows. In his book, *Linking Arms Together: American Indian Treaty Visions of Law and Peace, 1600–1800*, Lenape historian Robert A. Williams Jr. talks about how "Europeans . . . regarded the drawn-out naming ceremonies, rituals, and gift-giving that Indians routinely performed at treaty councils as time-consuming diversions from the conduct of vital matters of trade, diplomacy, and survival on the colonial frontier." Listening to long and elaborate speeches conducted in languages they either didn't understand, or understood only dimly, would have bored many colonial delegates, especially underlings like clerks, who didn't get to make decisions, but were tasked with writing down the commitments established at each meeting. "The European scribes who produced the voluminous treaty literature of the Encounter era rarely commented on the visions that animated their Indian treaty partners in giving a tribal name to a colonial official, smoking the calumet of peace, or presenting a gift of eagle feathers. For Europeans, these were the 'usual ceremonies' that had to be tolerated if one wanted to do business with the strange and alien-seeming tribal peoples of North America."[21]

It is not hard to imagine how the ceremonial sensibility of the Covenant Chain–Two Row Wampum, then, can be lost in the written history of the agreement derived from these scribes' records. Brushing past the "usual ceremonies" or the presentation of a seventeenth wampum – in a notation such as "Gives a Wampum" – the colonial functionaries often focused on what the covenant bound each party to do, especially the parts that assured them of Haudenosaunee protection against other Indigenous nations or exclusive access to Haudenosaunee trade. It usually skipped over who the covenant bound each party to be.

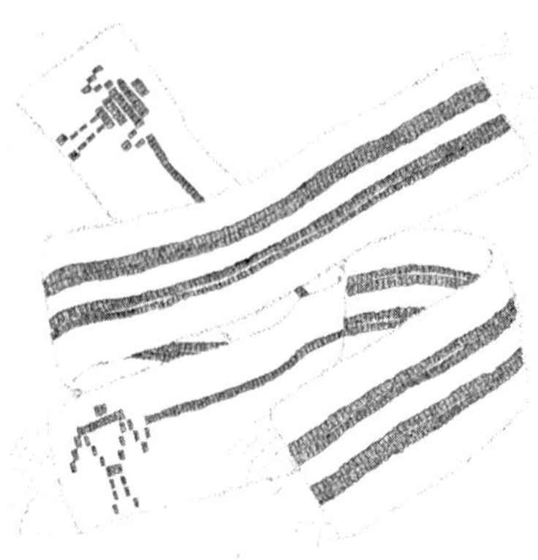

Chapter Twelve

Putting "First" Encounters Back in the Flow

But is it not naive to dream that we can re-enter such a clearing after all these years during which Britain, Canada and the U.S. have disavowed the Covenant of Linked Arms with the Haudenosaunee and other Indigenous allies? Is it not a delusion, this late in the game, to try to reanimate this respectful, ethical space after Canada bulldozed the agreement to protect one another with the scraper blades of the Indian Act, residential schools, reserves and the designation of "Crown land"?

What is the point in trying to reimagine some long-ago, pristine encounter?

Māori scholar and writer Alice Te Punga Somerville warns that settler colonials repeatedly indulge two destructive fantasies: first, the fantasy of terra nullius (from Roman law, meaning "nobody's land") that the land was empty when our ancestors arrived in the "new" world and, second, the fantasy that every encounter with Indigenous people is a "first encounter." By the former, she refers to the active amnesia that scrapes away the long history of Indigenous Peoples' sophisticated cultures and civilizations – anybody hear of Aztecs? Incas? The Great Zimbabwe? – with the blade of the Doctrine of Discovery. According to this self-justifying deception, if there were inhabitants, they were "savages," subhumans, living lives in an uncultivated "state of nature" that were, in seventeenth-century political philosopher Thomas Hobbes's much-quoted phrase, "nasty, brutish, short."[1] So the land might as well have been empty because, according to the Christian version of this line of thought, it lay unproductive under the ignorance of unredeemed infidels and pagans, and according to the social Darwinist version that emerged in the nineteenth century, these primitive people would not survive the stern demands of cultural evolution anyway. This is the first of Te Punga Somerville's colonial myths.

The second one dreams that *every* meeting with Indigenous folks is the first one.

Year after year, generation after generation, settler colonials act as if the Indigenous people we are meeting just emerged out of terra nullius for the very first time. Or, to put it differently, that the present meeting does not follow from previous ones. There are no previous encounters, agreements. We're starting from scratch. Take Simcoe's reduction of the Grand River tract by one-third on the basis that the headwaters of the Grand River were not "owned" by the Michi Saagiig Anishinaabe, for example. The recourse to the survey scrapes clear the Nanfan Treaty of 1701 whereby, evoking the Covenant of Linked Arms, the Haudenosaunee agreed to support British replacement of French trading forts during what have been called the "French and Indian Wars" in exchange for British protection of Haudenosaunee rights to continue to hunt, trap and fish throughout territory they had long made their living in, across the Niagara Peninsula and all the way to Lake Michigan. This area included the headwaters of the Grand, so the British had already agreed to protect Haudenosaunee life on this land long before Haldimand's proclamation.

The myth of first encounter removes the present encounter from history and imagines each new one as original. Each transaction gets isolated from the chain of previous meetings and agreements.

Take, for another example, Justice King, in *Logan v. Styres* (1959), determining that the Six Nations submitted to being subjects of the Crown when they accepted living under the "protection" of the British on the Haldimand lands. It's as if the concept of protection had no antecedents.

Or Jean Chrétien in 1969 determining the same thing and citing no precedents for his determination.

Again and again, each encounter, each transaction, is imagined to be the first one, an original, unrelated to the long history of encounters I refer to as the Covenant Chain–Two Row treaty tradition.

Perhaps we allow ourselves this delusion because Canada as a nation has worked so hard to convince itself that Indigenous Peoples "disappeared" long ago as their own Nations, as political and sovereign entities. Which meant that we didn't need to know anything about the history of our relationships with them. So when they reassert their presence, their current existence today, we are embarrassed to realize we now know next to nothing about them. We don't know what language they speak. We Canadians don't know whether Indigenous neighbours are Saulteaux, Salish or Seneca, because we can't distinguish these nations from each other anyway. It is as if they had been frozen in an uncharted past, a separate planet, and now they have sprung, improbably, into the modern present, right in our midst.

Repeatedly, people who buy homes in the disputed lands around Caledonia, Ontario, will say in the media that the Land Back reclamations come "out of the blue," as if no one had ever raised a concern about these lands before. Each time they do, they are repeating the myth of first encounter.

The Resilient Myth of First Encounter

This fantasy of first encounter is remarkably resilient. We Canadians may meet people who tell us they are from the Six Nations, or some such number, but that means nothing to us, so we remember it as "First" Nations, and we don't know the difference between "Six" and "First" anyway. Nothing in our education or upbringing made us aware of the history of the Peacemaker, so we don't know how their models of governance influenced our ancestors' ideas about the importance of responsible government, how to make a confederation from widely distinct populations, how to create law and peace in a time of chaotic violence.

Ayonwátha threading wampum into strings at the edge of the woods was not on the syllabus for the classes we took – not in art, psychology, literature, history, law, political science or international relations – so we don't know of the wampum records of the Mohawk, Oneida, Onondaga, Cayuga and Seneca confederation in the first place, let alone how wampum functioned in international diplomacy between the Haudenosaunee, Wendat, Anishinaabe and other Indigenous nations – or with our own settler colonial ancestors. We do not even know how to pronounce their nations' names, much less explain how our own Constitution was shaped by the Covenant Chain–Two Row tradition, which in its turn was shaped by principles from their Great Law of Peace.

Each encounter, decade after decade, generation after generation becomes an amnesiac *first* encounter. "How!" we say, holding up our hand. "How should we open this meeting? Should we burn a smudge, to start things off? Should we do some kind of land acknowledgement? Which nation did you say you come from? Did that territory used to be around here or somewhere far away?"

The harm of repeated first encounters is that it indulges the habit of *in*difference. It sanctions a dogged ignorance, a persistent illiteracy. "I don't know" grows into an excusable habit. This pattern demonstrates how the habit of indifference is the ruse of power and privilege. And the unaccountable harm of privilege is blissful, repeated obliviousness – the privileged don't know how ignorant we are, nor how much harm our indifference can wreak.[2]

Indifferent to the distinction of the Confederacy Council system, Canadians unconsciously follow the thinking advanced by Pope Innocent IV nearly eight hundred years ago, believing that inclusion is good for everybody – whether inclusion in the body of Christ or the political body. Let's include Indigenous Peoples, just like other citizens. Whether they like it or not.

And we are startled when they take offence. "What's wrong with them?" we wonder. "Why are they so prickly? Are they trying to avoid paying taxes? Yes, there have been some wrongs in the past, but why don't they just get over it?" We're hurt and offended that they don't like us, don't want to join our family – don't like it when we try to welcome them, as if they were our own "sons." The premise of indifference, a fundamental plank in the platform of Enlightenment understandings of human equality, blinds us to what's buried in plain sight and that was abundantly clear when Kiotsaeton met the French and Algonquins in 1645 or Canesatego met the representatives of the British colonies in 1744: the canoe and the ship are not the same. Differences are important. Attending to them is important to building good relationships. It's a self-blinding practice to pretend they aren't. And self-blinding practices handicap us on every level: physical, mental, emotional, ethical and spiritual.

So how do those of us who wish to repair the relationship with Indigenous people return now to the clearing at the woods' edge without simply repeating another instance of the myth of first encounter? How do we regain that self-knowledge, that vulnerability, the apprehensive anticipation of the difference that may lie in the clearing, in the unknown? How do we refresh our openness to learning again, to retaining what we learn, to seeing what is buried in plain sight all around us?

Willie Ermine, whose article on "The Ethical Space of Encounter" I quoted earlier, speaks of how a "calculated disconnection through the contrasting" of Indigenous and Western thought-worlds and the "creation of two solitudes" can open ethical space. But doesn't this effort to widen the gap between the two risk freezing these solitudes into permanent separatism? And isn't disconnection a different version of how colonization works – seeing the others as Others, as savage, as absolutely outside any definition of the civilized and therefore as justification for wiping them off the face of the earth and occupying the land they weren't using properly anyway?

If there is a danger in the amnesia of repeated first encounters, then too there is an opposite danger in overemphasizing differences: that of freezing others into incomprehensible otherness. In a 2011 interview posted on YouTube in the Different Knowings video series, Indigenous American literary scholar Chad Allen warns:

> I think we should be careful about overfetishizing radical distinctiveness and . . . it's a hard thing to think about. On the one hand, celebrating difference and distinctiveness; on the other hand, celebrating links, commonalities, common humanity, common experience of the planet, of

> the cosmos – and thinking between those two poles, I think – is quite difficult and understandably it's strategic. There are times when, especially for activist purposes [you] mobilize radical distinctiveness for certain purposes; other times that's not very strategic at all, and you need to mobilize: "Here's how we're all similar. Here's what we have in common. Here's what we can learn from each other." My fear with something like "different knowings" would be to hold it up and reify this idea of the radical, that it has to be *so* different.[3]

You could say that the danger of wishing to return to the clearing is that we may freeze the clearing and therefore lose the kind of strategic flexibility Allen speaks about – the option to emphasize Two Row difference, when needed, and the linked arms, the common purpose, of the Covenant Chain, when appropriate. We may stunt the natural growth and change that any relationship involves by freezing all the participants in their first positions, as if we were perpetually repeating that first encounter.

And this is a real danger, not just in the attitudes with which Canadians approach Indigenous neighbours, but in Canadian law. I've referred frequently in this book to Sections 25 and 35 of the Canadian Constitution, which indicate that "Aboriginal and treaty rights" are derived from the Royal Proclamation. But because these rights were not defined in the Constitution itself, subsequent Canadian courts have taken on the challenge of trying to do so.

Let's pause on this for a second: the effort to clarify what those rights were and how they should be interpreted today has been taken up, not in or with Indigenous councils, such as the Confederacy Council, but in *Canadian* courts. This, despite the fact that the Royal Proclamation ordered that any discussion of Indigenous lands must occur "at some Publick Meeting or Assembly of the said Indians to be held for that Purpose by the Governor or Commander in Chief of our Colonies respectively." Instead, the Canadian approach to interpreting the Constitution's "aboriginal and treaty rights" has been to try to address these matters in exclusively Canadian courts, where the entire procedure of argument, evidence-making and precedent-quoting has been framed within the thought-world of British common (or, in Quebec, French civil) law. As Kayanesenh Paul Williams has said, "The treaty relationship is the hinge between nations." Accordingly, this relationship must be worked out together, not just in one partner's councils or courts. Indeed, "treaty" can only "exist in the legal systems of the nations on either side of the council fire. Yet in court, partly because the cases are populated by Euro-American lawyers, judges and their governments, and despite admonitions that 'the treaties should be interpreted as the Indians would naturally have understood them,' it is Euro-American values, laws and interests that determine the outcomes."[4]

Without meeting *with* Indigenous Peoples and seeking to understand "aboriginal and treaty rights" in dialogue between Western worldviews and Indigenous ones, Canadian efforts to understand our own Constitution are hamstrung.

For example, *The Queen v. Van der Peet* (1996) has become renowned for trying to define Aboriginal rights by developing a "Distinctive Culture Test." In this court case, Dorothy Van der Peet, a member of the Stó:lō Nation in British Columbia, had sold some salmon caught by her common-law partner to a white neighbour and had been charged with having unlawfully sold fish caught under a food-only fishing license. Basically, the charge insisted that the Aboriginal right to fish for food or ceremonial purposes did not extend to commercial sales. The case went back and forth in the provincial court, being appealed once and then having the appeal overturned. At issue was whether the law preventing sale of the fish infringed Van der Peet's Aboriginal rights under Section 35(1).

The Supreme Court of Canada eventually determined in a seven-to-two decision that in order to qualify as an Aboriginal right an activity must be an element of a practice, custom or tradition integral to the distinctive culture of the Aboriginal group *before Europeans arrived.*[5] The court found that the exchange of fish for money or other goods did not constitute a practice, custom or tradition that was integral to Stó:lō culture as it existed before contact with Europeans. In essence, *Van der Peet*'s "distinctive culture test" ruled that, to qualify as "Aboriginal," a practice must be proven to have pre-existed first encounter with Europeans.

Anishinaabe legal scholar John Borrows admits that this case and others following from it have established a valuable recognition in Canadian law that identifies Aboriginal rights not only in the prior occupation of the land, but also in "the prior social organization and distinctive cultures of Aboriginal peoples."[6] So far, so good – I guess. This aspect of the decision denies terra nullius. It acknowledges that somebody was here, that communities, laws, society were here before Europeans arrived.

Borrows also observes, however, that the distinctive culture test tends to "freeze" aboriginality in a "once upon a time" prehistory and refuses to recognize the contemporary life of Indigenous cultures and their ongoing exchanges with all kinds of neighbouring nations, including European colonials. He cites Judge Beverley McLachlin (later, after 2002, Chief Justice of Canada) saying, in her dissenting opinion on the case, "Aboriginal rights find their source not in a magic moment of European contact, but in the traditional laws and customs of the Aboriginal people in question . . . One finds no mention in the text of s. 35(1) or in the jurisprudence of the moment of European contact as the definitive all-or-nothing time for establishing an Aboriginal right."[7]

The problem, in my layman's understanding, is that the pressure to clarify Aboriginal rights by reference to pre-contact practices makes repeated returns to the myth of "first encounter" necessary to the Canadian legal system. We can only understand what is "Aboriginal" about Aboriginal rights by freezing what's distinctive about Indigenous life in the moment before the initial encounter with Europeans – which would mean, for example, that no distinctively Aboriginal practices could be identified from treaties worked out during the fur trade. Or, closer to my point in this book, the distinctive culture test separates off Kiotsaeton's culturally syncretistic meeting with the French and Algonquins from the much older Covenant Chain–Two Row Wampum treaty tradition that had been practised for centuries before the arrival of the French, Dutch or British. It isolates the international practices of Indigenous diplomatic negotiations with Canadian and American nations from their Haudenosaunee precedents.

So there are dangers in trying to return, even in our imaginations, to the original vulnerable, ceremonial clearing at the Edge of the Woods.

Essentially these are the dangers of freezing "true Indigeneity" in the past, in an authenticity that can only be imagined before that first encounter, and therefore in a fantasy of pure, incommensurable difference with which there can be no dialogue or understanding. As Terry Goldie observed in *Fear and Temptation: The Image of the Indigene in Canadian, Australian, and New Zealand Literatures*, contemporary Indigenous Peoples, after generations of entanglement in settler colonial occupation, can rarely pass our settler-colonial-designed distinctive culture tests, and therefore they become "deindigenized, no longer valid."[8]

Having got into the business of trying to define Indian status in the Indian Act and Bill C-31, Canada can't seem to get out of it. Ironically, in our country's effort to respect difference, to recognize Aboriginal rights as essential to Canada's Constitution, we can overfetishize radical distinctiveness and freeze Indigenous people into being Canada's unchanging, constitutive "other" – the other on which our Constitution depends, but who cannot live as present, autonomous People.

Requickening the Chain of Encounters

This book's retracing of *kaswentha* is aimed at breaking the strategic amnesia of the colonial myth of first encounter. Remember that *kaswentha*, in *Kanyen'kéha* language, evokes the flow, the spine of vertebrae, the still-glowing ashes from the council fire. Retracing the flow reminds us that Aboriginal and treaty rights are recognized in the Canadian Constitution, which names the precedent for that recognition in the Royal Proclamation, which in turn refers to Indigenous nations who are "essential to our Interest and the Security of our Colonies" and "with whom We are connected." British representatives of the Crown, such as William Johnson, had crafted that wording for the King's Proclamation about the linked arms on the basis of his knowledge of the Covenant Chain–Two Row series of agreements between the Haudenosaunee and the Crown. On the king's behalf, he had extended the linked arms of the Covenant Chain to Indigenous nations from Cherokee to Ohio and from Anishinaabe to Wabanaki Peoples.

The tradition or protocol for making these agreements was already long-established in Haudenosaunee wampum diplomatic practices. None of these meetings or transactions could qualify as first encounters. Rather, they were and are part of an ongoing relationship.

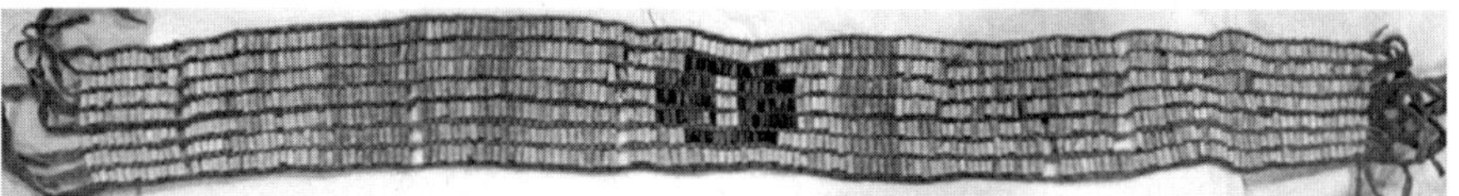

Sewatokwa'tshera't: The Dish With One Spoon. (Photo courtesy of Rick Hill)

It's clear from the French-Algonquin exchange of wampum and prisoners at Kiotsaeton's embassy, or Canesatego's rehearsal of the century-long evolution of the Covenant Chain relationship with the British, that these important meetings at the edge of the woods were not first encounters. The evolving symbolism of wampum iconography itself demonstrates that none of these meetings were firsts, none were unprecedented moments of origin. Kiotsaeton was conscious, when he hung the porcelain collars over the cord in the meetings at Trois-Rivières, that his listeners gathered in the shade of the sails in front of the fort would have recognized images in the wampum from previous meetings, such as when his ancestors made the Dish With One Spoon agreement at the formation of their Confederacy and subsequently with surrounding nations. At the formation of the Great Law of Peace between the former enemy nations, the Peacemaker had said:

> It will turn out well for us to do this: we will say, "We promise to have only one dish among us; in it will be a beaver tail and no knife will be there." Thereupon the chiefs confirmed that so it shall happen. Thereupon [the Peacemaker] said, "Now we have completed the matter; we will have one dish, which means that we will all have equal shares of the game roaming about in the hunting grounds and fields, and then everything will become peaceful among all of the people, and there will be no knife near our dish, which means that if a knife were there, someone might presently get out, causing bloodshed . . ."[9]

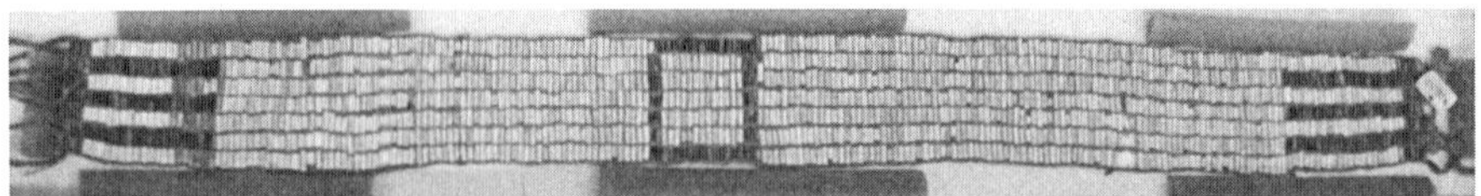
Huron Peace Belt (1612). (Photo by Rick Hill)

The iconography of the dish, the lozenge at the centre of the Dish With One Spoon where people meet around the fire to share food in peace, reappears throughout wampum iconography. It reappears, for example, in the Huron Peace Belt of 1612. Rick Hill writes that this belt was given to the Haudenosaunee by the Huron-Wendat ancestors of those who met at Trois-Rivières in an effort to reduce hostilities that were being fuelled by competition for the emerging fur trade. Shortly before this belt was made, Hill explains, French trader Étienne Brûlé had visited the Huron villages in 1611 and remained with them through the winter. He realized that the Huron had better furs than both the Algonquin and Haudenosaunee. They also had better access through trade to other Indigenous nations to the west. Hill figures that these factors may have compelled the French to make allies of the Huron rather than the Haudenosaunee, launching the brutal "Beaver Wars" that resulted eventually in the vanquishing of the Huron. Of this 1612 belt, Hill writes, "The central square designates the Huron Nation. Purple lines at each end designate people, and the white background symbolizes peace, meaning the people of both nations walk in peace together."[10] He imagines that the Huron Peace Belt was an effort to avoid the warfare they saw coming. It's not hard to see the symbolism of the Dish With One Spoon, of the council fire as a lozenge in the landscape of peace, being echoed in the Huron Peace Belt.

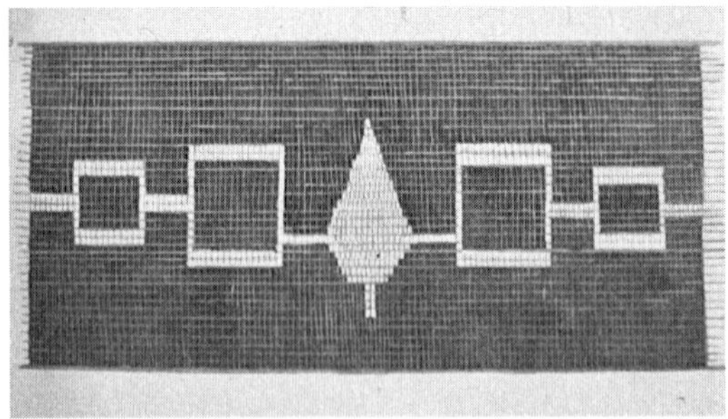
The "Hiawatha" Belt. (Photo by Rick Hill)

These lozenges (sometimes square and sometimes diamond shapes) appeared regularly in wampum and were often linked together by a line of white beads to symbolize alliance-making as a path of peace between the council fires of the nations. This imagery is central to the depiction of the Six Nations Confederacy itself in what has come to be known as the Hiawatha (Ayonwátha) Belt, which pictures the chain of linked arms as a path of peace connecting the lozenges of Five Nations into a single Confederacy, with the Onondaga Nation tending the Tree of Peace at its centre. It is this same image of the path of peace that we see extending as a rope or chain between the outstretched arms of the two figures at the ends of the Covenant Chain wampum. And again, it is this same path of peace, one representing the path taken by each vessel, that we see unfolding in parallel in the Two Row Wampum.

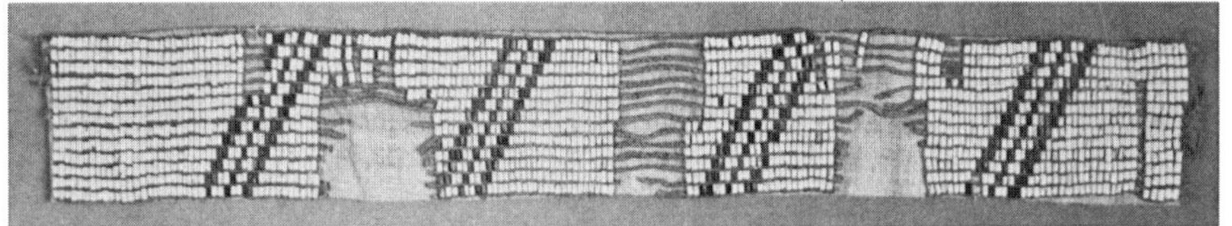

First Sighting of the People with Pale Faces Belt. (Photo courtesy of Rick Hill)

There is, too, a wampum precedent to the Two Row's use of parallelism. The friendship and mutual aid represented by parallel paths (or lines of beads) can be seen in what some have called the oldest wampum representing relations between the Haudenosaunee and Europeans. The Haudenosaunee had retained a record of their encounter on the St. Lawrence River with Jacques Cartier and his sailors in 1535 in a wampum known as "First Sighting of the People with Pale Faces." Rick Hill explains that this belt presents four sets of diagonal "rafters" or "braces" that hearken to Haudenosaunee protocols for welcoming new nations into the Iroquoian longhouse by linking arms with them and thus adding "another rafter" to the Longhouse of Peace. Both the written French record and the oral memory of the wampum recall the devastating illness suffered by the French mariners (likely scurvy) that was treated with herbal medicines supplied by the Haudenosaunee hosts. Hill writes, "The thick diagonal lines in the wampum belt represent the St. Lawrence Natives (possibly Mohawks) who stand in support of their weaker allies, as if they were holding them up."[11] The parallel lines protect but do not intersect, do not touch. Accordingly, the Haudenosaunee hosts supported and protected their travel-weakened visitors, but they did not interfere with their internal governance or practices. The iconographic echo of non-intersecting parallel lines or parallel paths between the Two Row and the First Sighting of the People with Pale Faces reveals that the meeting with the Dutch on the Hudson River was not a first encounter.

Nor is the rope or path of peace between nations on the Covenant Chain, let alone the Hiawatha Belt, a first encounter.

Kiotsaeton's was not a first encounter. Nor was Canesatego's. They were not original, isolated transactions.

The Royal Proclamation was not a first encounter. Not a point of origin.

Nor was Section 91(24) of the BNA, let alone Sections 25 or 35 of the repatriated Constitution.

The colonial powers have made many efforts to scrape the land bare, to wipe history's memory. To insist that *this*, this Proclamation, this Advancement Act, this Haldimand Proclamation, this White Paper of 1969 – *this moment* is the starting point.

From the imposition of the Indian Act and the magical transposition of Indigenous lands into "Crown lands" to the closing of the Confederacy Council house and the imposition of the band council system – it's all enabled by the myth of first encounters. By the hidden ways in which the path has been scraped clean.

And the scraping keeps being repeated. When my own university hosts the Ontario Provincial Police who are *protecting* developers' rights, rather than Haudenosaunee rights, to land that has been contested since the 1840s, I am made aware that this is another perceived first encounter.

When Canadians are shocked that ground-penetrating radar has found the remains of over two hundred Indigenous children at Kamloops Indian Residential School in June 2021,[12] I am aware of another first encounter. Every time someone expresses surprise that as many as four thousand Indigenous women, girls and queer folk are either missing or murdered and remain uninvestigated, we are in the presence of the myth of first encounter.[13]

The persistent myth of perpetual first encounters reduces us Canadians to a naive, childish and wilfully ignorant state.

When we see the brutal effects of our uninformed actions, when we awaken belatedly to myriad problems that plague our relationship with Indigenous neighbours, and not just neighbours, but with the lands on which we live – blockades at railroads or pipelines, dysfunction in families and band councils, unresolved land disputes, a Department of Indian Affairs (under ever-changing names) that fights against, rather than advocates for, Indigenous concerns – we throw up our hands at the complexity of the situation, blame Indigenous people for the problems our country's blundering has foisted upon them, or dismiss the whole situation, wondering why they can't "get over it" as we do.

All the while, there remains a time-tested procedure for building healthy relationships, for generating the trust needed to enable our shared capacity for action, for finding enough shared purpose to operate together in peace. The treaty tradition already exists, but the terra nullius, the Doctrine of Discovery and the myth of first encounters have caused Canada repeatedly to disregard it, to isolate each encounter from the long-term flow of relationships that remains ghosted in our own Constitution.

We need to re-enter the clearing at the edge of the woods, but with an awareness that in this space we have worked out arrangements and differences before. We need to renew the ceremonial space of an honest encounter with those who set the terms for how to link arms, how to develop mutual aid, in the first place. This means relearning the principles and rules that have been conveyed repeatedly and insistently throughout the Covenant Chain–Two Row treaty tradition.

Thankfully, this is precisely the direction in which recent court decisions are moving. In *The Queen v. Monture and White* (2023), Quebec Superior Court Judge Sophie Bourque writes, "Since *Van der Peet*, knowledge about Indigenous peoples' life in Canada has tremendously evolved . . . Canadian society is starting to grasp the pressing need for a renewed relationship in which reconciliation is central."[14] Rather than seeing Aboriginal rights as frozen in a pre-contact past, Judge Bourque puts forward a new formula for determining these rights: "1- [The Court] will require first to identify the collective right that the [Indigenous] Applicant invokes; 2- Then, the Applicant will have to prove that such a right is protected by his or her traditional legal system; and 3- Finally, the Applicant will have to show that the litigious practice or activity in question is an exercise of that right."[15] Commenting on the second point above, the judge explains, "If the Court is of the opinion that some continuity in time is essential to establishing constitutional rights, the 'magic moment' of European contact is no longer relevant to determine the existence of an Aboriginal right. The reference to traditional legal systems will be sufficient to ensure continuity. Each claim should be dealt with on a case-by-case basis."[16] To put it differently, *R. v. Monture and White* puts today's encounters back in the *kaswentha* flow. Rather than pretending that each encounter is a first encounter, this case concludes, "[1051] Through their entry into and subsequent renewals of the Covenant Chain, the [Haudenosaunee and British] parties intended to establish a lasting relationship characterized by both a military and friendship alliance. This alliance was to be guided by the principles of Haudenosaunee diplomatic protocol and included a conflict-resolution procedure,"[17] and that therefore, "[1100] The court concludes that the Covenant Chain is an unextinct treaty of peace and friendship that contains a conflict resolution procedure, guaranteed by sec. 35(1) of the Constitution Act, 1982."[18]

The Attorneys General of Quebec and Canada immediately appealed the case, so it remains to be seen if Canada's Section 35(1) recognition of "aboriginal and treaty rights" will remain situated in the flow of the Covenant Chain. But *R. v. Monture and White*, as well as the aforementioned Ontario ruling of *R. v. Williams* (2023), marks a moment of profound shift in Canadian jurisprudence from the long-held Canadian approach of treating each interaction as a first encounter by placing Canada's constitution back in the flow of its precedents in the Covenant Chain–Two Row treaty tradition.

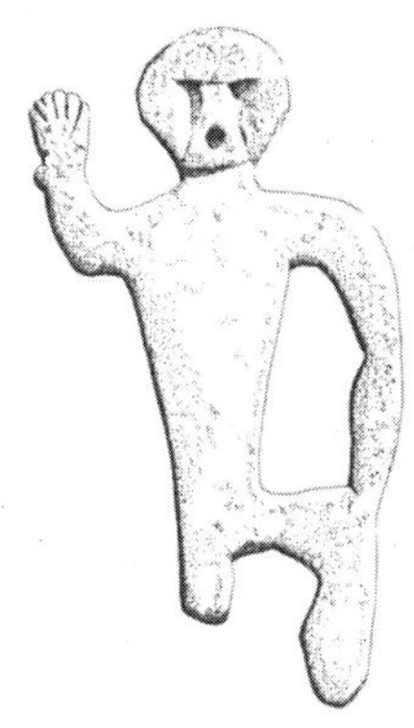

Chapter Thirteen

Exhausting Inquiry

Over the past half-century, from the period of Canada's centennial in 1967 to the "bringing home" of the Constitution in 1982, and throughout the period of constitutional fatigue after the failures of the Meech Lake and Charlottetown Accords that extends from the 1990s to the present, Canada has repeatedly commissioned research teams to survey the state of Indigenous lives in Canada and to offer analysis and recommendations on how to improve Canada's founding relationship. It's an exhausting thing to read these commissions and inquiries – not just because they are detailed and lengthy (RCAP alone is over four thousand pages!), but because cumulatively, they make depressing reading. So my challenge in this chapter is to read these depressingly predictable reports' negligent-to-negligible results and to help readers see them – or not so much *them*, as the ways they are (not) dealt with – as important and revealing.

The Hawthorn Report (1966–1967) and the Penner Report (1983) leading up to the Meech Lake and Charlottetown Accords, and then the RCAP (Royal Commission on Aboriginal Peoples, 1996), the TRC (Truth and Reconciliation Commission, 2015) and the MMIWG (National Inquiry into Missing and Murdered Indigenous Women and Girls, 2019) that followed the failures to ratify the Constitution are deflating because reading these studies one after another reveals how persistent and anaesthetizing the old myth of first encounters truly is. Despite these reports' lists of devastating findings over the past sixty years about the brutal circumstances of Indigenous lives within the borders of Canada, Canadians still respond to the grizzly details about the number of unmarked graves identified at residential schools in 2021 or the scale of emotional, physical and sexual abuse at those schools with complete shock.

Many Canadians say they had never heard before that the extermination of languages and cultures was not just the practice of a "few bad apples" in that school system, but that it was in fact our government's explicit intention. Until the Missing and Murdered Indigenous Women and Girls Report was released in 2019, many Canadians had no idea that the disappearances of thousands of Indigenous women, girls and queer people had never been investigated, let alone brought to court. Because they have gone largely uninvestigated, we don't know how many people have been murdered or gone missing (the *Canadian Encyclopedia* refers to reports as low as fifteen hundred and as high as four thousand). Over and over again, Canadians appear to be hearing about Indigenous people's experiences of genocide and genocidal intent "for the first time."

Think of the uproar there would be if we found the unmarked graves of two hundred Polish-Canadian children or that somewhere between fifteen hundred and four thousand Scottish-Canadian girls, women and queer people had disappeared and never been investigated.

But these injustices have been the subjects of official inquiry, at the very least, since the Hawthorn Report in 1967. So we have to ask ourselves: why can't these repeated inquiries dismantle once and for all the shock of first encounter, of repeatedly hearing these stories of injustice as if for the first time? More than this, why don't they help Canada do something about them?

I am reminded here of Azurara's tears to comfort himself at the brutal parting of Africans from their families at the slave port of Lagos in 1444 by telling himself a story of redemption that was supplied by his conviction that, ultimately, the violence he witnessed would be for the weeping families' own religious good. His unself-questioning confidence that ultimately his worldview knows best what will be good for the enslaved Africans is the same kind of certitude that rationalized not only the Indian Residential School system, the reserves and the Indian Act, but the system of inquiries and commissions themselves that are meant to investigate their ongoing effects. It's a powerful unself-questioning assumption that can ask the patron, the prince, the parliament or Crown to set the terms for an investigation, to appoint its commissioners and then to decide in the end which of their recommendations it will actually take up.

Canadian Paternalism

In 1964, the government of Lester B. Pearson appointed UBC professor of anthropology Harry B. Hawthorn to collect a team of researchers to study conditions in Indigenous communities across Canada. The resulting report addresses Canadian paternalism directly, indicating that "paternalistic provision of services with only a modicum of Indian participation has contributed to widespread civic apathy in Indian communities"[1] and that "the problem of Indian dependency, we were told on a number of occasions, was created by years of federal ineptitude and paternalism."[2]

A revealing moment occurs, however, when the Hawthorn researchers suggest what needs to happen to "decolonize" (their word) this paternalism.

First, the report suggests, Indigenous people should no longer be treated as "citizens minus" – minus self-determination; minus many standard citizen rights because of restrictions in the Indian Act; minus the right to consult with lawyers; minus freedom of movement; minus many of the provisions that provincial governments provide to their citizens such as education, healthcare, economic participation or social services. Instead, Hawthorn recommends Indigenous people should be "regarded as 'citizens plus'; in addition to the normal rights and duties of citizenship, Indians [their term] possess additional rights as charter members of the Canadian community."[3]

Charter members! That sounds like a potential return to the original allyship outlined in the Covenant Chain–Two Row treaty tradition.

But get ready to scratch your head when Hawthorn indicates what a decolonized, charter membership as citizens-plus involves: "not only striking changes in the relationships of Indians to federal and provincial governments, but also dramatic improvements in the capacity of Indians *successfully to accommodate themselves to the requirements of an impersonal, bureaucratic, technological society undergoing constant change*."[4]

I pause on this statement because it highlights the patronizing unilateral assumption that persists through effort after effort to address the troubled relationship between Canada and Indigenous Peoples: the self-contradictory assumption that the removal of paternalistic restrictions will give Indigenous Peoples the dubious gift of full participation *within the existing order of things* – and this order of things is Canada's version of the Industrial Growth Society, usually masked as an impersonal "economy."[5] The assumption of social "progress," premised on the Hobbes-to-Locke theory that societies evolve and improve according to the sophistication of the tools and political arrangements they develop for turning nature's elements into products for human comfort, is not an idea exclusively held by either right-wingers or leftists.[6] It is the ready assumption of Canadians from all manner of political or ideological perspectives, including the writers of the Hawthorn Report.

A decolonized future for Indigenous people, according to Hawthorn, demands they "accommodate themselves to the requirements of an impersonal, bureaucratic, technological society," and they can do this by becoming full citizens, even *super*-citizens – citizens plus – in an unquestioned Industrial Growth Society. Hawthorn does not envision alternative Indigenous economies, does not imagine that Indigenous Peoples may not wish to accommodate themselves to an impersonal, bureaucratic, technological society, or that bureaucratized technologies may themselves be producing self-cannibalizing, diseased economies that may consume all our futures – Indigenous and non-Indigenous alike.[7] In this sense, then, Hawthorn does not see the value *for all Canadians* of an autonomous, alternative Indigenous canoe.

And neither did the Pierre Trudeau government, which soundly rejected Hawthorn by having Minister of Indian Affairs Jean Chrétien propose the infamous White Paper two years later in 1969. The White Paper aimed to wipe history's slate clean so that Indigenous people would be simply absorbed into Canadian citizenship, minus Hawthorn's distinctive *plus*. Although the White Paper spurned Hawthorn's distinct Indigenous charter group status, its presumption that decolonization means full integration into Canada's Industrial Growth Society is a different version of Hawthorn's paternalism.

In either case, "inclusion" and even "decolonization" means Indigenous people must abandon their primary understanding of how they are to live in the world. They must abandon their original instructions as Indigenous Peoples and become "Canadians."

The White Paper's disregard of Hawthorn and its recommendations reveals a pattern that repeats itself in government responses to report after commission after inquiry after report over the next half-century: regardless of the expense in money, time and community consultation, the reports are repeatedly ignored. Instead of empowered ambassadors like Canesatego or William Johnson linking arms between Indigenous governments and the Crown, these inquiries deploy deliberately disempowered researchers and commissioners to meet with Indigenous communities and send their recommendations to the Crown, whose parliamentary representatives may or may not heed their guidance.

Indigenous leaders' responses to Hawthorn had been cautiously optimistic, but the affront caused by the White Paper's attempt to annul the linked arms and subsequent treaties generated furious political organizing by Indigenous peoples in Canada. The White Paper's attempt to obliterate their distinct relationship with the Crown intensified Indigenous resolve to insist upon honouring that relationship. Rather than being some kind of assimilated citizens, or even "super-citizens," Indigenous Peoples increasingly insisted that they are, have always been, autonomous paddlers of their own canoe. Not "citizens plus," not "Canadians," but nations who had made nation-to-nation agreements with the Crown and, later, with its emerging representatives in the Dominion of Canada.

This was the central point of the Penner Report of 1983, tabled the year after the patriation of Canada's Constitution. You could say Penner was an effort to give substance to Sections 25 and 35's recognition of Aboriginal and treaty rights. According to this report, what it calls "Indian First Nations" had formed nation-to-nation agreements with the British Crown and thus the Crown in Canada, and they therefore have an inherent right of self-government. They were not granted this right by the Crown, but by the Crown's recognition in the Royal Proclamation that they already had this right. The few Canadians who have read (the executive summary of) the Royal Commission on Aboriginal Peoples of 1996 associate the "inherent right of self-government" with the RCAP, but it is in the Penner Report thirteen years earlier that we see a clear recognition by government commissioners that Indigenous rights pre-existed the authority of the Crown in North America, and thus, constitute inherent, rather than delegated, rights to self-government. This Special Committee on Indian Self-Government – commonly referred to by the name of its chair, Liberal MP Keith Penner, and composed of members of the House of Commons from the three major political parties – was created "to review all legal and related institutional factors affecting the status, development and responsibilities of Band Governments on Indian reserves."[8]

Oops!

We were just talking about nation-to-nation agreements between self-governing nations whose legal rights pre-existed those of the Crown, right? But here, inserted into the wording of the Penner Commission's mandate from the then–Pierre Trudeau government, is the figure of the Ottawa-made "Band Government" or band council. In Six Nations' case, that is the form of government imposed by the RCMP in 1924 that officially displaced the Confederacy Council as the "nation" with which Canada had previously discussed its founding agreements. Right from the start of Penner's mandate to review all the "legal and related institutional factors" affecting Indigenous governance in Canada, we have the unilateral exclusion of Haudenosaunee (and other nations' traditional) government.

In an investigation about *self*-government!

The Haudenosaunee knew this, and a special delegation was assembled to correct the Penner Commission's distorted mandate before the commission got too far down the tracks. The minutes of the June 30,

1981, meeting list the delegates as Bob Antone, Venus Walker, Bruce Elijah, Loran Thompson, Mike Myers and Robert Jamieson. They went separate from members of the Assembly of First Nations, some of whose members don't share the same history of sharp division between traditional government and the band council system.

Lucky for us, there is an easy way to be a fly on the wall of the Haudenosaunee delegation's meeting with the Penner Committee, because Kayanesenh Paul Williams and Chief Arihote Curtis Nelson included its transcription in Appendix III of *Kaswentha,* their three-hundred-page contribution on the history of the Two Row Wampum to RCAP in 1996. In this transcript, MP John Manley observes that "the whole concept of the two-row [wampum] is something that we as a committee are going to have to wrestle with." And he asks for clarification on its implications: "It seems to me that you want to see the confederacy as a nation in the international community rather than a nation within the structure of Canadian federalism. Am I wrong in seeing it that way or not?" Segwalise Mike Myers of the Haudenosaunee delegation echoes Deskaheh Levi General a half-century earlier when he replies, "No, you are correct. We are not part of Canada. We have never desired to be a part of Canada, and we have no future plans to be part of Canada."[9] When asked by MP Frank Oberle if this forecloses forever the idea of the Haudenosaunee being partners to Canadian Confederation, Myers replies:

> The Creator made us and put us on the earth, and chose that we would be in this particular part of the universe. The language we speak is specific to northeast North America; you cannot take our language out of here and put it down to the Amazon, it will not make sense down there. We cannot go to the southwest deserts; we cannot talk about that environment, except superficially. All of our way of life, all of our existence, our ceremonies, the way our councils operate, the whole basis of our existence is placed here. That is what the Creator gave to us. Canada is not the Creator. So we cannot join that; we cannot become a part of that.[10]

Just as the Covenant Chain–Two Row treaty tradition referred nation-to-nation agreements to the more-than-human time frame of the environment – "as long as the grass turns green, the rivers run, and the sun rises" – Myers refers to the bioregion in which the Haudenosaunee Confederacy emerged. This eco-regional placement recalibrates Western ideas of law and treaty. These are not simply human-made agreements that suit the convenience of people. They are based on the laws and rhythms of nature, a particular place, a particular ecosystem, and they reflect and take into account the relationships that exist in that place and environment. Myers explains that these laws cannot be simply transplanted to the environs of the Amazon or deserts of the Southwest. Likewise, Haudenosaunee arrangements cannot simply be transferred to the prairies or the coasts of Nova Scotia, the Arctic or British Columbia. Each bioregion needs to consider the sovereignties of its particular People and environment.

Local constitutionalism – *located* or *grounded* constitutionalism – determines which human laws are most relevant and appropriate to the set of relationships that constitute any ecosystem, but this constitution does not imply exclusionary rights, for the laws of nature begin with relationships, with interdependency as the *Ohén:ton Karihwatéhkwen* (Thanksgiving Address) reminds everyone, with finding peaceful ways to share the river. The Two Row supplement to the Covenant of Linked Arms emphasizes the importance of clear distinctions between Indigenous and Canadian powers and authorities, while the Covenant Chain element reminds us that we grip one another's arms; we are interdependent.

The Haudenosaunee delegates informed the Penner Committee that this is the true precedent for Section 35 of the Canadian Constitution. When asked why the Confederacy would not sign the Declaration of First Nations put forward by the Assembly of First Nations and espoused by many First Nation witnesses to the Penner Committee, Oneida member of the Haudenosaunee delegation Bob Antone explained that the Declaration had been composed largely by band councils, who are considered by the Haudenosaunee, especially after the band council system had been forced on them in 1924, to be branches of the Canadian government's Indian Act system. Furthermore, the Declaration presented Aboriginal rights as derivative rather than inherent. "I think it is very clear," Mr. Antone noted,

> that the treaties and aboriginal rights that we have and that we envision as the Haudenosaunee lie very clearly in the Two Row Wampum and in the covenant of the Haudenosaunee. That is where the origins of aboriginal rights are. In many cases that we have seen with Indian nations in this country they have begun to say that treaties gave Indians rights. That is not true. If treaties gave Indians rights, what did we have before there were treaties? Did we have nothing? Treaties might have given us benefits for us to enjoy, but our rights as the Haudenosaunee lie within the Covenant of the Haudenosaunee. That is where our rights come from.[11]

The delegation's visit to the Penner Commission certainly affected what the commissioners ended up saying.

Arguing against the common dismissive "view held by non-Indians that political structures were unknown to Indian people prior to contact with Europeans," the finally submitted version of the Penner Report asserts that "most First Nations have complex forms of government that go far back into history and have evolved over time."[12] The report's primary example are the Haudenosaunee, who are presented as having a "code of laws, generally expressed in positive admonitions rather than negative prohibitions, [which] governs both official and civil behaviour. Laws are passed by a bicameral legislature, made up of senior and junior houses. A council of elders oversees the general course of affairs." After this brief sketch of Haudenosaunee constitutionalism and governance, Penner regrets that in 1924 "the Canadian government suppressed the Haudenosaunee government by jailing its leaders and refusing to give it official recognition . . . The system of 'band councils' mandated in the Indian Act was installed in its place."[13]

The Haudenosaunee delegates who met with the Penner Committee must have been pleased to see this impact of their carefully prepared presentation. They had shown the committee the wampum they had brought with them, along with government letters and other legal documents illustrating and instantiating their relationship; first with the Dutch and then the British, as allies and friends, but never subjects. They must have seen some gleam of hope when they saw the Two Row Wampum gracing the cover of the government-commissioned report whose first recommendation was "that the federal government establish a new relationship with Indian First Nations and that an essential element of this relationship be recognition of Indian self-government."[14] This promising statement was followed by the second recommendation: "The Committee recommends that the right of Indian peoples to self-government be explicitly stated and entrenched in the Constitution of Canada. The surest way to achieve permanent and fundamental change in the relationship between Indian peoples and the federal government is by means of a constitutional amendment. Indian First Nation governments would form a distinct order of government *in* Canada, with their jurisdiction defined."[15]

Oops again! How can this order of *self*-government be conducted *in* Canada? Wasn't the exchange between John Manley and Segwalise Mike Myers clear when Myers confirmed, "You are correct. We are not part of Canada. We have never desired to be a part of Canada, and we have no future plans to be part of Canada"?

The Penner Report continues: this order of government would be guided by the treaties, which would be negotiated in a bilateral process, between independent governments or nations. "It is not the rights of Indian people that are ill-defined," Penner clarifies, "but the recognition of these rights in Canadian law that has been ill-defined."[16] Perhaps what we have here is a 1980s restatement of the practice of protection outlined in the Royal Proclamation – the Crown's protection of Indigenous rights (and land, I would add) from its own colonial administration's encroachment, this time in the form of law?

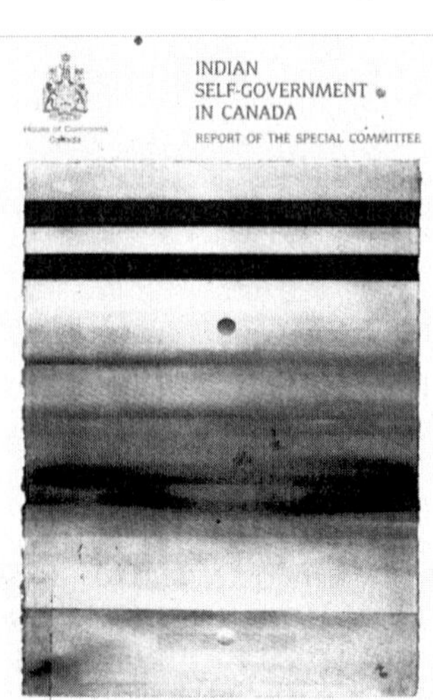

"Two Row Wampum," Front Cover of Penner Report (1983).

The problem is that it's very difficult to keep Eurocentric paternalism from reinstating that protection within its own assumed jurisdiction, from placing that supposed *self*-government back *in* Canada, within the bureaucratic arrangements of the nation-state.

What needs regulating, again, is not Indigenous nations, but Canada's unilateral assumption of power over First Peoples. Penner goes some way to seeing this point. And it symbolizes its strong(er) recognition of Indigenous jurisdiction by reproducing a painting of the Two Row Wampum on its front cover (see previous page) and offering the following narrative about its meaning on its back cover.

> The Two Row Wampum
> When the Haudenosaunee first came into contact with the European nations, treaties of peace and friendship were made. Each was symbolized by the Gus-Wen-Tah or Two Row Wampum. There is a bed of white wampum which symbolizes the purity of the agreement. There are two rows of purple, and those two rows have the spirit of your ancestors and mine. There are three beads of wampum separating the two rows and they symbolize peace, friendship and respect.
>
> These two rows will symbolize two paths or two vessels, travelling down the same river together. One, a birch bark canoe, will be for the Indian people, their laws, their customs and their ways. The other, a ship, will be for the white people and their laws, their customs and their ways. We shall each travel the river together, side by side, but in our own boat. Neither of us will try to steer the other's vessel.
>
> The principles of the Two Row Wampum became the basis for all treaties and agreements that were made with the Europeans and later the Americans. Now that Canada is a fully independent nation, perhaps it will be possible to strike up the Two Row Wampum between us, so that we may go our ways, side by side, in friendship and peace.
>
> – excerpted from presentations to the Special Committee by the Haudenosaunee Confederacy and from *Wampum Belts* by Tehanetorens
>
> The cover painting is a two-row wampum belt on a landscape. But it is more than the representation of an object. Like the Haudenosaunee artist who made the belt, I am part of a process of carrying an idea through history – the idea symbolized by the two-row wampum. The belt shouldn't be forgotten in a museum, because it expresses an idea, and an idea can't be killed. This report is part of the same process of carrying the idea forward,

and the painting expresses my hope that the report won't be set aside and forgotten either.

Leo Yerxa, artist

Despite Yerxa's hope, and just like what happened with the Hawthorn Report, Canada completely ignored its own Penner Commission's report on Indigenous self-government. In their eagerness to bring Quebec into full participation in Canada's 1982 Constitution, the federal and provincial leaders who formulated the Meech Lake Accord of 1987 agreed to recognize Quebec's constitutional status as a "distinct society," and completely overlooked Canada's other founding members, Indigenous Peoples. Meech Lake included no consideration of the Penner Commission's recommendations about enacting orders of Indigenous self-government *in* Canada, let alone within their own jurisdictions. Over the subsequent years of social and political upheaval, from Cree NDP MLA Elijah Harper's refusal to sign the accord, through the confrontations between the Sûreté du Québec and Canadian Army with armed Mohawks over land rights between Kanesatà:ke and the town of Oka (1989–1990), and to the eventual failure of the Charlottetown Accord (1992) – which *did* include provisions for a "third order" of government run by Indigenous Peoples alongside federal and provincial ones – the Canadian appetite for Constitutional debate exhausted itself. Prime Minister Brian Mulroney, who had been at the helm through all these events, had fallen so far out of favour that his Conservative party was reduced to only two seats in Parliament in the election of 1993, and the Liberal government of Jean Chrétien that succeeded them campaigned on the promise not to revisit Constitutional reform. The result was a clear message to Quebec nationalists and to Indigenous leaders – Canadians voters had no more appetite for working out a new constitution that would retune the relationships between the country's three founding groups: Indigenous, French- and English-speaking Peoples.

The intensity of the confrontation between the Sûreté du Québec, the Canadian Army and the Mohawks at Oka, did, however, register in public awareness the deep rift that divided Canadians from their Indigenous neighbours, especially the Haudenosaunee. Back in January 1991, a few months after the end of the violent standoff and before Charlottetown was defeated in a referendum, the Mulroney government had commissioned a Royal Commission on Aboriginal Peoples (RCAP), which was asked to "make recommendations promoting reconciliation between aboriginal peoples and Canadian society as a whole."[17] With a $60 million budget, RCAP was asked to conduct a cross-country study of how – you guessed it – to "break the pattern of *paternalism* which has characterized the relationship between Aboriginal peoples and the Canadian government" and "to suggest how Aboriginal peoples [can] resume their status as self-governing and self-reliant nations *in* the Canadian federation."[18]

Reconciliation, (Always) in Canadian Terms

Like Hawthorn and Penner, then, the effort to address paternalism is contained, ultimately, within "Canada," within Canadian paternalism, within unilateral Canadian jurisdiction. Imagined this way, Canada cannot enter into discussion with an equally empowered government, nation or system of law; it can only do so with its partner already absorbed within itself. The key term of that absorption appears in a word that reappears in RCAP and has risen in usage ever since: "reconciled" – Indigenous rights, Indigenous legal traditions, Indigenous self-government must be *reconciled* with the existing system in Canada. In a pattern that will be echoed in what we might call the "reconciliation era," RCAP gestures toward freeing its process of inquiry from paternalism by putting Indigenous leaders at the helm of the inquiry process; in this case, by appointing four Indigenous along with three non-Indigenous commissioners.[19] By December of 1993, the RCAP commissioners had visited ninety-six communities and held 178 days of hearings. They had asked community leaders, scholars and other experts to study and submit reports on over three hundred issues.[20] The resulting five-volume, four-thousand-page report, tabled in 1996, remains the most comprehensive study of the lives of Indigenous peoples across the country, and it covered a wide range of issues.

Like RCAP, the TRC and MMIWG are reconciliation-era, large-scale studies, commissioned by the federal government and led by widely respected Indigenous experts who crossed the country consulting with urban- and reserve-based communities to produce reports so detailed and thoroughly researched that they look more like encyclopedias than the word "report" suggests. The TRC, in particular, received significant media coverage over its public hearings, hosted from coast to coast to coast, at which survivors of the Residential School system finally had a chance to tell the stories of physical, sexual and emotional abuse that had been ignored and suppressed for so long. The TRC constitutes a moment when sanctioned Canadian ignorance lost many of its sanctions.

RCAP's major recommendations include: new legislation, especially a new Royal Proclamation, stating Canada's commitment to a new relationship accompanied by laws setting out a treaty process and recognition of Aboriginal nations and governments. Echoing Penner, the commission recommends the establishment of an Aboriginal order of government with authority over matters related to the government and welfare of Aboriginal peoples and their territories, whether they live on reserves or in urban communities. This exercise of authority could be empowered by creating an Aboriginal parliament, which would oversee the expansion of the Aboriginal land and resource base. RCAP promotes setting aside land for a self-governing Métis nation, and many initiatives in Indigenous communities to address education, health and housing, as well as other social needs, including the training of thousands of Indigenous health professionals over a ten-year period, building an Indigenous Peoples' university and putting child welfare under Indigenous nations' authority.

After Oka made it hard for Canadians to deny the violence that runs through the relation between Indigenous Peoples and Canada, RCAP used the term "reconciliation" to highlight the serious changes that Canada would need to make if it were to avoid band-aid solutions for deep, festering wounds.[21] RCAP follows Penner in confirming that Aboriginal rights recognized by Section 35 do not exist by virtue of Crown title but are inherent and sui generis.[22] Figuring out how to build new and healthy nation-to-nation relations therefore requires mutual, not delegated, recognition: "Aboriginal nations do not require federal legislation to exercise constitutional authority to function as governments. But in the complex arrangements of a modern federal state, guidance is needed to make relations between governments operate effectively. Governments need to 'recognize' each other in order that their authority is respected."[23] According to RCAP, this mutual recognition would need to be worked out between three distinct orders of government *in* Canada: Aboriginal, provincial and federal. Each of the "governments making up these three orders are sovereign within their several spheres and hold their powers by virtue of their inherent or constitutional status rather than by delegation. They share the sovereign powers of Canada as a whole, powers that represent a pooling of existing sovereignties."[24] With recommendations such as these, RCAP could as easily have featured the Two Row Wampum on the covers of its five volumes as had Penner. Across its four thousand pages, RCAP promotes the separate authorities of the Indigenous canoe and Canadian sailing ship, even as it respects the Covenant Chain that binds them in a relationship of sharing.

RCAP was released in 1996 in a period when Canadians had lost their taste for Constitutional reform. It was five volumes long, adding up to thousands of pages, and like many encyclopedias that used to be published in multiple volumes, it sat on the shelf, only being lifted down from time to time to check dates or names or historical episodes; and, like many online encyclopedias, it's now available for keyword searches to help you find these episodes or names faster. TRC and MMIWG operate in much the same way. Each of these reports constitutes remarkable, impressive research into the everyday conditions of Indigenous people's lives, deaths and disappearances. They offer analysis and explanations, translations of complex Indigenous histories and concepts into readable English (and French). They offer hundreds and hundreds of recommendations for what can be done to change the situation. RCAP offered 440 of them, TRC made 94 "calls for action" and MMIWG presented 231 "calls for justice."

The terminology gets stronger, angrier as the "recommendations" remain unaddressed.

A few have been engaged. Most not. The latter two commissions' unsoftened use of the term "genocide" expresses their growing frustration over Canadian reluctance to address the ongoing brutality and oppression that characterize Canada's relationship with Indigenous people. Aside from painful, tiny steps grudgingly taken in Canadian courts – always with Indigenous Peoples having to take these matters to trial and most often with Indian Affairs defending the status quo rather than advocating change – Canadians have not "recognized" a new relationship nor have we "reconciled" ourselves to the idea, let alone practice, of Indigenous sovereignty or self-determination.[25] Despite the success of the TRC, in particular, in exposing to a broad spectrum of Canadians the long history and continuing effects of the brutal suffering Indigenous children underwent in the Indian Residential School system, it's not hard to detect in these later reports a palpable despair that meaningful changes will occur. The MMIWG, for example, notes that "there has been very limited movement to implement recommendations from previous reports. What little efforts have been made have focused more on reactive rather than preventative measures. This is a significant barrier to addressing the root causes of violence. Further, insufficient political will continues to be a roadblock across all initiatives."[26] Therefore, although "we have been mandated to provide recommendations," write the commissioners, "it must be understood that these recommendations, which we frame as '*Calls for Justice*,' are legal imperatives – they are not optional."[27]

Unsurprisingly, a Two Row understanding of autonomous self-determination undergirds RCAP's, TRC's and MMIWG's vision of a better future beyond the multigenerational suffering caused by the Indian Residential School system and the violent deaths and disappearances of Indigenous women, girls and queer people. "We call upon the Government of Canada, on behalf of all Canadians," says the TRC, following a proposal originally put forward in RCAP, "to jointly develop with Aboriginal peoples a Royal Proclamation of Reconciliation to be issued by the Crown. The proclamation would build on the Royal Proclamation of 1763 and the Treaty of Niagara of 1764."[28] By evoking the Royal Proclamation and Treaty of Niagara, the RCAP and TRC deliberately place the present desire for "re-conciliation" back in the *kaswentha* flow – one that is centuries old. Sir William Johnson's Niagara conference was central to the British Crown's effort to expand the alliance referred to in the Royal Proclamation from its original Haudenosaunee signatories to a broad coalition of Indigenous nations. The RCAP and TRC reject the myth of first encounters by calling for a New Royal Proclamation that will

> reaffirm the nation-to-nation relationship between Aboriginal peoples and the Crown. The proclamation would include, but not be limited to, the following commitments: i. Repudiate concepts used to justify European sovereignty over Indigenous lands and peoples such as the Doctrine of Discovery and *terra nullius*. ii. Adopt and implement the United Nations Declaration on the Rights of Indigenous Peoples as the framework for reconciliation. iii. Renew or establish Treaty relationships based on principles of mutual recognition, mutual respect, and shared responsibility for maintaining those relationships into the future. iv. Reconcile Aboriginal and Crown constitutional and legal orders to ensure that Aboriginal peoples are full partners in Confederation, including the recognition and integration of Indigenous laws and legal traditions in negotiation and implementation processes involving Treaties, land claims, and other constructive agreements.[29]

Some of these recommendations are beginning to be acted upon as I write this. As of June 21, 2021, the "Act respecting the United Nations Declaration on the Rights of Indigenous Peoples [UNDRIP]" has received Royal Assent and is now the law in Canada. But the work to "reconcile" it with Canada's legal system, particularly UNDRIP's third and fourth articles, "the right to self-determination and to freely determine political status and freely pursue economic, social and cultural development" and "the right to self-government relating to internal and local affairs," remains to be done.

It's not hard to see the pattern that recurs in these reports and commissions on the relationship between Indigenous people and Canada: The government appoints an arm's-length commission or committee to investigate problems in the relationship, and after lengthy study and consultation the commissioners recommend that Canada reject its colonial and paternalistic attempt to assimilate Indigenous people as "children" in the Canadian sailing ship and that it recognize Indigenous Peoples, instead, as independent "siblings" who govern their own canoe. Successive reports present Indigenous Peoples as nations with whom our colonial ancestors negotiated the original Covenant Chain that bound British North America to Indigenous allies in charter agreements that in turn shaped the constitution of Canada. Yet, these reports are repeatedly stymied by the assumption of their mandate: to *reconcile* Indigenous autonomy *within* the Canadian Crown's unilateral sovereignty.

This kind of unilateral reconciliation – an impossible contradiction – can never give us a healthy pathway forward, not for our relationships with each other as People nor for our relationships with the natural environments we share. There is a revealing moment in MMIWG, in which the commissioners note the high incidence of sexual violence against Indigenous women and resource extraction. They cite a report by the Women's Earth Alliance and the Native Youth Sexual Health Network on the correlation of high incidences of sexual abuse of women and girls and resource industries' tendency to build all-male work camps near remote Indigenous communities: "The industrial system of resource extraction in Canada . . . is based on the raping and pillaging of Mother Earth as well as violence against women. The two are inextricably linked. With the expansion of extractive industries, not only do we see desecration of the land, we see an increase in violence against women. Rampant sexual violence against women and a variety of social ills result from the influx of transient workers in and around workers' camps."[30] Ironically, this statement hearkens chillingly to Hawthorn's assertion that Indigenous people will need to "accommodate themselves to the requirements of an impersonal, bureaucratic, technological society."[31] We can only become aware of how violent that "accommodation" can be when we link the legal system that legitimizes and fuels Industrial Growth Society's violation of the earth with the violation of Indigenous women, girls and queer people. That's when we can begin to see the underlying, ongoing patterns that link them together. TRC shares this understanding of how a violent approach to land is part of the brutal mentality that rationalized a violent approach to Indigenous schooling. This insight informs TRC's insistence that "reconciliation between Aboriginal and non-Aboriginal Canadians, from an Aboriginal perspective, also requires reconciliation with the natural world. If human beings resolve problems between themselves but continue to destroy the natural world, then reconciliation remains incomplete."[32]

Here, we are returned to the land as witness, the natural world as participant (or victim), the earth as family place, as registrar of the agreements living beings make with one another about how to live together in a place. Reviewing the series of predetermined encounters produced by disempowered commissions whose "recommendations" and "Calls to Justice" have repeatedly been ignored by governments and the citizens who elect them and reading these in relation to the flow of agreements that stretch all the way back to the formulation of the Covenant Chain–Two Row Wampum treaty tradition helps us see that if Non-Indigenous Canadians are ever to reconcile ourselves to where we live, if we are ever to "settle" legitimately in North America, we need to learn that it is in our own interest to protect the autonomy and distinctiveness of Indigenous ways of living and knowing. Not only because of the inherent rights of Indigenous Peoples, but because the *difference* of these ways from the assumptions of Industrial Growth Society may allow us Canadians to seek advice from them about how to develop new founding principles, new ground rules for a constitution that can understand the crucial relation between constitutional law and the laws of nature, between our fundamental national institutions and the ecology of human and more-than-human relations on which our future lives depend.

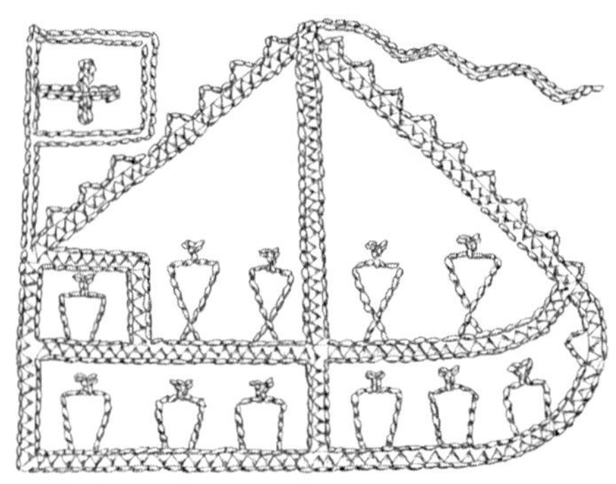

Chapter Fourteen

Undoing Unilateral Multiculturalism

If Canada already has a Multiculturalism Act, why do we need to return to the Covenant Chain–Two Row tradition? Don't they do similar things – recognize the differences among us while still keeping our arms linked to each other?

When the federal government was introducing the policy of multiculturalism in Parliament back in 1971, Pierre Trudeau would commonly assert that "although there are two official languages, there is no official culture." It's a catchy statement, but we know that it is not as easy to detach culture from language as he suggested.

Canada eventually passed its Multiculturalism Act in 1988. The act opens with a preamble that presents a set of "Whereas" clauses listing conditions and precedents from the 1982 Constitution that this particular piece of legislation must respect and enact. The first four of these are:

> WHEREAS the Constitution of Canada provides that every individual is equal before and under the law and has the right to the equal protection and benefit of the law without discrimination . . . ;
>
> AND WHEREAS the Constitution of Canada recognizes the importance of preserving and enhancing the multicultural heritage of Canadians;

> AND WHEREAS the Constitution of Canada recognizes rights of the aboriginal peoples of Canada;
>
> AND WHEREAS the Constitution of Canada and the Official Languages Act provide that English and French are the official languages of Canada and neither abrogates nor derogates from any rights or privileges acquired or enjoyed with respect to any other language . . .

In these few opening lines of the preamble we encounter a tangle of mutually conflicting and limiting assertions. We see a commitment to "protection" – not the Royal Proclamation's reciprocal protection of the Crown's own security gained by linking arms with those "with whom We are connected," but of disconnected individuals' rights "before and under" the law. So the "multicultural heritage" being preserved and enhanced in the second Whereas clause is that of the individuals mentioned in the first one. But, of course, no one possesses a "culture" individually. Indeed, when we think of the "culture" or "cultures" represented by the Covenant Chain–Two Row tradition, it's all about linking arms between explicitly different cultural *groups* that was meant to accomplish mutual protection, to achieve "perseveration," or even "enhancement."

Perhaps that collective idea of culture is set to the side by item number three, the Constitution's recognition of the particular "rights of the aboriginal peoples of Canada," which are distinct from the rights of the individuals named in item one. The Aboriginal rights that are distinguished from other people's *individual* rights put Indigenous collective ways of doing things, such as *Tehontatenentshonteronhtáhkwa*, in a kind of parenthesis, a different category, a culture not in dialogue with the other cultures that make up *multiculturalism*. The other cultures of multiculturalism are not collectives with rights but individuals with rights. I'm guessing that this is why, to go back to Sections 25 and 35 in the Constitution, they are referred to as "aboriginal and treaty rights," not "individual rights." But, as many have observed before me, individual rights is a concept unfamiliar to Haudenosaunee treaty-making.[1] Indigenous traditions such as the Linked Arms treaty tradition represent collective, reciprocal care for the purpose of mutual collective protection, and multiculturalism is not an offer of mutual protection. Instead, it's a unilateral promise by Canada to preserve and enhance individuals' multicultural heritage.

The different cultures' worldviews about "rights" evident in the gap between Whereas one and Whereas three grow even wider in another gap that becomes clear in Whereas four, the reminder that "English and French are the official languages of Canada."

Let's think about this statement for a minute. Why are English and French Canada's official languages? Well, because of the Official Languages Act (1969), whose precedents trace back to the Quebec Act (1774), when Canada's British colonial administration granted French-speaking people in Lower Canada (downriver on the St. Lawrence) the right to conduct official business in their own language (French), religion (Catholicism) and legal system (civil, rather than common, law). The story commonly told in Canada is that this compromise, aimed to keep francophones from joining the emerging revolutionary rebels in the thirteen colonies, established Canada as a nation with two founding Peoples, two charter groups. So here we do have an idea of collective rights – and the two collectives are anglophones and francophones.

But this version of history pretends that Sir William Johnson, who died in 1774, the year the Quebec Act was passed, had never existed. The story of two founding nations (and languages) makes it as if he, as a two-nation, two-language person, had not worked so hard in the 1760s to protect the Crown's security in America by protecting Indigenous Peoples' lands and ways of life from being overrun by British colonial land aggression. As if he had never toured busily from Albany to Philadelphia to Detroit to Niagara, sending his deputies farther afield to North Carolina or Nova Scotia, to extend the Covenant Chain between the British Crown and every Indigenous nation with whom he could build an alliance from the Cherokee in the south to the Anishinaabeg in the west to the Wabanaki Confederacy in the northeast. As if he had never learned how to do this official, agreement-making work in fluent *Kanyen'kéha*, which meant that he attempted to translate concepts like *rights* and *protection* in the contact zone between Mohawk and English worldviews.

The two official languages version of Canadian history also hides the fact that Sir William Johnson set the precedent for the Quebec Act's guarantee of French language and Catholic religious rights not first with French Canadians, but with *Kanyen'kehá:ka* Mohawks. As British forces converged upon Montreal in August 1760, Johnson met with representatives from the Mohawk settlements of Oswegatchie, Kahnawà:ke and Akwesasne to make treaty with the "praying Indians" there who had converted to Catholicism and allied themselves to New France. During the past fifteen years, he had followed previous commissioners from Albany, who had been meeting with the St. Lawrence Mohawks ever since 1725 to renew their alliance with the British.[2] On his way to Montreal for the surrender of New France, therefore, he stopped at their settlements to assure the relationship. In return for a promise of non-intervention in the British advance upon Montreal, Johnson guaranteed these Mohawk communities "that there would be no reprisals for past actions on behalf of the French, for freedom to practise the Catholic religion, for the protection of all rights and privileges enjoyed during the French regime and for the guaranty of the integrity of Indigenous lands and property by the Crown."[3] These rights would have included the right to continue to keep their own culture, beliefs and laws as laid out in the Two Row version of the agreement and therefore to speak *Kanyen'kéha*. So the precedent for the Official Languages Act identifying French and English as Canada's recognized languages, usually traced back to the Quebec Act, actually has further precedents in the renewal of the Covenant Chain with the Mohawks of Oswegatchie and Kahnawà:ke in 1760.

English, French and the Abrogation of *Kanyen'kéha*

The point is that it's not possible to name English and French as Canada's official languages without abrogating and derogating from *Kanyen'kéha* and the other languages in which Canada negotiated its true multicultural, inter-national origins. Far from preserving and enhancing Canadian multiculturalism, the official endorsement of two official languages expunges from Canadian multicultural history the Indigenous language-cultures in which our founding agreements were actually worked out.

To me, Canada's designation of two official languages deploys the European "law of nations" in the domain of speech. It removes Indigenous Peoples from charter group status, from founding language status, and then divides language in which Canada is constituted between the remaining European powers.

The resulting losses to our understanding of *multi*culturalism are profound. Take the simple example of pronouns that I gave earlier from my introductory class in Mohawk language. Think of what a difference it would make to Canadians' perceptions of multiculturalism if we had dual and plural, inclusive and exclusive pronouns in English or French. Rather than stumbling about with our undifferentiated, paternalistic understanding of "we," we could distinguish between *kinds* of "we," different kinds of collective inclusion. If we had the dual inclusive *teni-* ("you and I"), and the plural inclusive *tewa-* ("you and I and some other persons"), let alone the dual exclusive *iakeni-* ("we two and not the person addressed"), plus the plural exclusive *iakwa-* ("we three or more without the person addressed"), we might not assume the all-absorbing "we" of English or "nous" of French, that readily speaks for others as if they were already assimilated into *our* first-person collective. We would have, baked into our way of thinking, the understanding that "we" is always a matter of linked arms between differentiated Peoples.

And this is just one example from my beginner's lessons about *Kanyen'kéha* pronouns. Think of how rich our alternative understandings would be if fluent speakers could provide their language's understandings of *multi cultures.*

This is why multiculturalism, as officially formulated in Canada, needs guidance from the Covenant Chain–Two Row way of conducting matters between Peoples. Canada's current version of multiculturalism disempowers and empties the "cultures" that it supposedly preserves and enhances; it engages them as deprived of their own authority, their own linguistic thought-worlds, as drained of what the *rotiyaneshon* in Jake Thomas's oration of the agreement called their "culture, beliefs, and laws." Multiculturalism could have opened a clearing in the woods, a potential space for ethical encounter between different cultures. Unfortunately, it was saturated with such a powerfully unilateral worldview that the very possibility of a substantial encounter with difference was neutralized before it could start.

Distracted by the mythic precedent of having been founded by two white founding nations and by their set of European linguistic, religious, legal and political traditions, official Canadian multiculturalism tried to contain and manage growing pluralism by shoehorning multiple cultures under the jurisdiction of that bilingual tradition, and by doing so it overlooked the much more profound precedents for living with different laws and authorities found in the Covenant Chain–Two Row treaty tradition. It culturalized the encounter and thereby turned the potential ethical space of encounter into a fairground of tents purveying samosas, belly dancing, dream catchers or fado music.

But there is another domain within which to consider these matters, for popular Canadian understandings of multiculturalism have fallen behind remarkable developments in the domain of constitutional law since the 1980s. As legal scholars such as James Sa'ke'j Youngblood Henderson, Kayanesenh Paul Williams, James Tully and John Borrows have separately observed, Canada's Constitution does not derive its authority purely from British and French law, nor does it flow from the ultimate sovereignty of the Crown, but from the *encounter* of these legal regimes with already-existing Indigenous ones.

Against many Canadians' view that Indigenous Peoples have "special concessions" *from* the Crown because of their various treaties, the Canadian Constitution acknowledges that Indigenous Peoples have sui generis rights – that is, they are unique and original. As the Supreme Court explained in *Van der Peet* (1996), Aboriginal rights had to be included in the Constitution "because of one simple fact: when Europeans arrived in North America, Aboriginal peoples were already here, living in communities on the land, and participating in distinctive cultures, as they had done for centuries. It is this fact . . . which mandates their special legal, and now constitutional, status."[4] "Properly understood," Henderson goes on to explain, "Aboriginal sovereignty is the source of all law in Canada. It flips over the colonial concept that all power derives from the imperial Crown or imperial Parliament, and it creates a distinct way of looking at the patriated constitution of Canada and the divisions of powers."[5] Basically, I understand this to be the obvious realization that the only way the Crown could legitimize any authority it gained in North America is through the covenants it made with the nations that were already here and their legal systems.

And the whole argument of this book is that one of the first ones the Crown encountered was that of the Haudenosaunee, who taught them how to make peaceful agreements by means of *Tehontatenentshonteron-htáhkwa* and *Tékeni Teyohà:te*.

Henderson observed in 2014 that in the years since the Constitution was patriated in 1982, there had already been by that date over forty court cases investigating what is meant by the Constitution's use of terms such as "aboriginal rights," "treaty rights" or "land claims agreements" and what these terms mean for the development of what he calls "a truly Canadian legal system based on symbiotic constitutionalism and legal and epistemic plurality. That is, [the Canadian court system] has had to develop innovative principles of adjudication that seek a convergence of Aboriginal and Eurocentric legal traditions."[6] This convergence is a far cry from multiculturalist "preservation and enhancement" of Indigenous culture, from attendance at powwows to the retailing of moccasins and beadwork. It demands a serious recalibration of the legal regimes that govern Canada by means of what Henderson calls a "trans-systemic" and John Borrows calls a "multi-juridical" dialogue between Indigenous law and Crown-derived Canadian law that would open up the necessary ethical space within which we could actually parse out and identify a dialogue of sovereignties that form the legal grounds for a truly *Canadian* constitution.[7]

Essentially, rather than putting "aboriginal rights" in parenthesis in the preamble to the Multiculturalism Act, reviewing the original Covenant Chain would engage all parties in a truly multicultural way of thinking that could "preserve and enhance" cultures that have been disempowered in Canada.

Toward a Two Row Reinterpretation of the *Culture* in *Multiculturalism*

An Anishinaabe descendent of some of the first People to develop wampum relationships with the Haudenosaunee, John Borrows recognizes that there are many challenges to realizing a multi-juridical legal system in Canada – one that goes beyond English common law and French civil law. Primary among them is Canadian society's inability or unwillingness to understand the larger concepts and worldviews out of which Indigenous laws have grown. For example, the effort to realize the Aboriginal rights guaranteed in Section 35, Borrows observes, cannot succeed without a stronger, widespread understanding of Indigenous legal principles or precedents. In the absence of this understanding, he says, "the Supreme Court of Canada has taken to translating Indigenous perspectives and practices into common law rights." In other words, Indigenous legal concepts are unilaterality transformed into common law understandings. The translation is one-way. "Making common law the ultimate measure of ancient Indigenous traditions," he continues, "virtually ensures that non-Aboriginal cultural aspirations will predominate within section 35."[8]

Borrows provides various examples of how Indigenous legal principles get crushed when they are forced to fit into English common law. For instance, he cites the case known as *Jack and Charlie v. The Queen* (1985), in which two Salish men were accused of killing a deer out of season. They claimed the Canadian Charter's guarantee of freedom of religion, explaining that they killed the deer in order to burn the meat in a ceremony to nourish the spirit of a recently deceased community member. The court didn't understand the symbolic importance of the community ritual, suggesting that the ritual burning could have used frozen deer meat, and not seeing the ceremonial significance of the hunt itself and of the community's participation in preparing the deer – skinning the hide, removing intestines, preserving bone and brains for tanning, sectioning venison – as necessary to the nourishment offered to the deceased person.[9] Among other things, it's an example of how culture contains law, and how law informs culture.

A case like this reminds us of the necessity of Two Row alertness to the cross-cultural process of interpretation that will be required if Section 35 can ever be anything more than lip service. It reminds us of the challenging gift we have inherited from Canada's Indigenous-French-and-British constitution. Our legal and political system emerged from the early negotiations between already existing law systems; it is not a single, nor even a bilingual or bicultural system, but a multicultural, multi-juridical one. In order to enact our polysystemic constitution, in order to live it out in reality, more and more of us Canadians need to be able to think in multiple systems. And to do this, we need to know enough about one another's culture, beliefs and laws in order to live in mutual respect and understanding. This mutual knowledge is central to the principle of respect that happens when we enter the Clearing at the Edge of the Woods. This kind of substantive respect is the multiculturalism that needs preserving and enhancing.

In a different example of Indigenous culture at work in law, Borrows describes a community consultation that took place among the people of his home community Neyaashiinigmiing, the Chippewas of Nawash on Cape Croker reserve. The powwow the Anishinabek community hosted each August had grown so large that they considered moving it to a larger treeless area known as the prairie. But to get people and equipment there would require building a road across an alvar, a dolomite plain of rock that spreads along the ground surface like pavement and is among the oldest exposed stone in Ontario, being more than 440 million years old. "For many Anishinabek, the alvar is a storyteller who recounts the time when the land was younger and was covered by shallow tropical seas," Borrows writes. It "is also home to spiritually significant 'spirit trails' that wend their way through the area."[10]

Because of the deep significance of the alvar, a broad community consultation was held over whether or not to build the road to the proposed powwow site. Observations were solicited from scientists, elders, lawyers, grandmothers, artists, medicine people, band councillors and community employees. Eventually, the community decided that the alvar should not host the roadway to the annual powwow. "This brief review of Anishinabek law" through community decision-making, Borrows explains, "demonstrates that Anishinabek beliefs concerning the Earth as a living being can be legally recognized and affirmed. It also shows how Anishinabek law can lead to land being accorded political citizenship with its other close relations. Attentiveness to the land's character and sacred power gives the Earth an important place within this jurisprudential system."[11]

Borrows's story does not separate legal decisions from cultural beliefs, nor these beliefs from human relationships with the more-than-human beings of the environment. It negotiates the "political citizenship" of the alvar in the context of what many Canadians would consider a cultural festival – the form of pan-Indian cultural gathering that has become widespread particularly since the twentieth century and known as a powwow.

The Cape Croker community's ruling in protection of the alvar flies in the face of English common law, which is fundamentally premised on the *cultural* belief that land is not animate, is not capable of political citizenship and does not convey "stories." The community's ruling operates on principles very different from John Locke's influential formulations, in *Two Treatises of Government* (1689), building on the earlier mentioned Thomas Hobbes's formulations about how civil authority emerges from reasonable agreements among people about the transfer of inanimate property. What makes anything into property, Locke explained, is human labour. A person's right to an oak tree's acorns corresponds to how many acorns he can gather, just as a person's right to fence off land as his own corresponds to how many acres he can cultivate and reap. For Locke, human labour, the cultivation of acorns or planting of corn, constitutes improvement of the land, and this improvement generates the right to its resources, whether that be water derived from digging a well or diamonds dug from under the earth. It is the investment of labour that makes wine, bread or silk worth more than water, acorns or skins. And it is the investment of labour that makes fenced and farmed fields in England worth more than the "waste" lands of America. "There cannot be a clearer demonstration," writes Locke, of the truth of these ideas "than several nations of the Americans [i.e., Indigenous Peoples], who are rich in land and poor in all the comforts of life; whom Nature, having furnished as liberally as any other people with the materials of plenty – i.e., a fruitful soil, apt to produce in abundance what might serve for food, raiment, and delight; yet, for want of improving it by labour, have not one hundredth part of the conveniencies we enjoy, and a king of a large and fruitful territory there feeds, lodges, and is clad worse than a day labourer in England."[12] Remember that Locke had never been to the Americas, and he was relying on reports brought back by European travellers. He must not have heard of the thousands of bushels of corn stored by Senecas at Ganondagan, of the fine beaded clothing of the people Cartier had met on the St. Lawrence River, the copper implements traded from Central America to the city of Cahokia near the site of modern day St. Louis. Statements like his reveal the basic and widespread ignorance of Indigenous culture, beliefs and laws and how it led to the common law tradition's unilateral suppression of them.

For the Hobbes-to-Locke line of thinking, and for those of us who inherited their legacy, land has no agency, no sentience or spirit. It is inert and can only come into productivity when humans invest their labour into it. All of these are *cultural* beliefs, ways humans organize their interaction with the world around them. According to what we might call Lockean culture, land has no memory. It is not a storyteller. Given this founding premise, Indigenous Peoples' recognition of what Borrows calls the alvar's "political citizenship" can only seem like naïveté about the necessity of producing property out of nature's commons. Any decision that seems to refuse an "improvement" – such as a road across the alvar – can only be the logic of people bent on living lives of poverty and self-denial. It can only be seen as "waste" – as land and opportunity wasted. Considering how the community's recognition of the alvar's sacred status pre-empted profits the Cape Croker council might have collected if the powwow had been held on the prairie, it's not hard to see why Borrows says "the Earth's agency potentially threatens the core of North American economic organization in the twenty-first century."[13] Because it lacks the concept of "Earth as a living being [that] can be legally recognized and affirmed," Industrial Growth Society cannot question the priority of unrelenting "improvement," which means that the Cape Croker community's decision not to use the alvar appears incomprehensible.

This contrast between the culture, beliefs and laws of Anishinabek tradition and that of English common law, however, need not remain a matter of eternal bewilderment. In fact, we are slowly awakening, even in the Western sailing ship, to the harm our culture's unquestioned idea of "improvement" has had and is having on the Earth itself. We have been alerted by new phenomena such as the "continent" of single-use plastics floating in the Pacific Ocean and appearing as an eighty-eight-pound block of calcified plastic in the belly of a dead whale in the Philippines – not the first whale to have been found with such a block in its digestive system.[14] We have been alerted by repeated warnings from scientists about the increasing dangers of violent weather events because of global climate change. We have been alerted by conundrums over what to do about nuclear plant meltdowns, the toxic waste of tailings ponds and industrial slag, the rapid decline of songbirds, monarch butterflies or bees.

Faced with these looming disasters, many Canadians are losing confidence in a legal culture based on the production of property rights through never-ending "improvement" of nature. What happens when an improvement in one domain becomes a hazard in another? The logging of "wasteland" forests to make paper products contributes to increased airborne carbon and steadily climbing global temperatures. The durable elements of those plastic bottles and bags are floating, not just in the Pacific or the bellies of whales, but as microplastics in our own bloodstream. How can such a culture apportion responsibility for the five to thirteen million metric tons of plastic waste that find their way into the earth's oceans each year? Without reference to a different juridical culture, a different concept of "improvement," how can we ensure a self-sustaining "commons" – the common air we breathe, the common water we drink?

Borrows's examples of the alvar and the *Jack and Charlie* case help us English and French speakers see how multiculturalism, as currently enacted in Canada, has been gutted of its potential. A multiculturalism that re-engaged its Indigenous precedents would involve a radical shift that does not try to separate language from culture, nor culture from nature. This multisystem *culture* would be a true, or holistic, *multi*culturalism. It is one where, to adapt from the federal government's website on "Canadian Identity and Society," "all citizens," whether human or not, "keep their identities, take pride in their ancestry and have a sense of belonging."

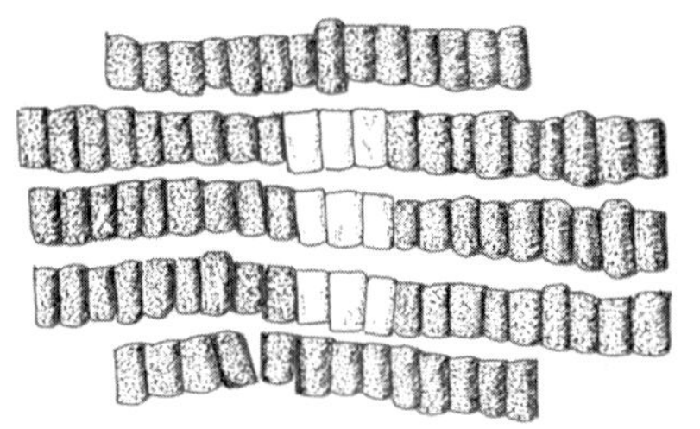

Part IV

Covenant Chain–Two Row Ecologies

In one fascinating sequence of the Haudenosaunee Creation Story, Thawískaron ("Icy Crystal," likened to "Flint") smells a tantalizing scent, something oily sizzling over a fire and wafting from the bark lodge of his twin brother, Tharonhyawá:kon ("Earth Holder" or "Earth Grasper," "He Holds the Heavens"). He hurries through the woods tracing the aroma, until he stoops in the doorway and sees his brother roasting an ear of corn over the fire. Near his brother's lodge, he notices all kinds of things he has never seen before, such as the beautiful flowering shrub growing right beside the hand he leans upon his brother's doorjamb.[1]

"What's that?" he asks. "What are you doing?"

"I'm creating foods," Tharonhyawá:kon explains. "That bright yellow plant over there is sunflower. I started with the medicine red willow, then strawberry, thimbleberry (mallow), mulberry, and huckleberry, and that big fruit, apple. The thing I'm roasting here is corn."

"It smells delicious," says Thawískaron, "and I'm starving. Can I have some?"

"Soon," his brother replies. "It's too new. It needs time to reproduce itself. Pretty soon there will be lots for everyone. Eventually, so much that it will feed the human beings I plan to create one of these days."

"But I'm hungry *now*," says Thawískaron. Thawískaron is always edgy, like the flint of which his tongue and the crest on his head are made. He's always in a hurry. He's usually irritated by his brother's patient way of doing things.

He's always been that way. Even when they were about to be born, Thawískaron couldn't wait to slip down his mother's birth canal as Tharonhyawá:kon had done. He was in such a hurry, he cut his way out of her armpit, and killed his mother in the process. Then he avoided the blame by convincing his grandmother that his gentle, careful brother, Tharonhyawá:kon, had caused their mother's death. Ever since, Grandmother has preferred Flint, the restless twin, and left Earth Holder to look after himself. She feeds her favourite, makes him a bow and set of arrows, urges him not to tell Tharonhyawá:kon.

Angry at having to wait for a taste of corn, Thawískaron stomps off in a huff, but he comes back when he smells that delicious aroma again. He can't keep himself away. Again he asks if he can have some, and this time Tharonhyawá:kon gives him a couple of kernels, a berry or two, a couple of apples – a little taste from the plenitude he is creating to share with their grandmother. But he reminds his brother that these foods are still young and vulnerable. They need to be protected so they have time to propagate themselves, to live their lives, to reproduce until there's lots for everyone in the years to come.

Not long after this, Thawískaron and his grandmother notice new animals moving about the woods in which they live on Turtle's back: bluebirds, robins and pine martens; then deer, moose and buffalo; and after that porcupine, wild turkey, raccoon and beaver. He goes over to his brother's place and asks, "Where are all these creatures coming from? What material did you use to make them?"

"From earth," Tharonhyawá:kon says. "The earth is alive. It has life in it. So I made them from earth. Each living thing arises from the life within the earth – but they don't live forever. Eventually, each creature – plant, animal, human – will return again to earth."

Seeing his brother's game animals running tantalizingly through the woods, Thawískaron and his grandmother come up with an idea. He herds all the animals into a cave, and he rolls a big boulder over the mouth. "Now I have everything under control," he says to himself. "My grandmother and I will have meat whenever we need it." Grandmother advises him not to say anything about this to Tharonhyawá:kon. It's their exclusive secret, their private supply.

Pretty soon, though, Tharonhyawá:kon notices that he's not seeing any of the animals he had made. He goes to see a strange man he had talked with earlier, the one who lives in a lodge under the water. In that prior visit, this man had told him to keep an eye on his grandmother, since she was not dealing fairly with him. This time, the man tells him to keep an eye on his brother too. From the bushes he therefore watches Thawískaron go to his cave, roll aside the boulder and emerge with a porcupine, which he takes home to his grandmother.

At this, Earth Holder goes to the cave and frees the captive animals. "You're made to run freely," he tells them. "And humans are supposed to exert themselves by hunting if they need your bodies for food. You need to be free and wild. I made the various plants and shrubs and fruit in the same way as you: just as they need to eat and grow and propagate themselves, so do you. You can't do that in a cave."

But he doesn't do what I'd be tempted to do – go over to Grandmother and Thawískaron's lodge and give them a well-deserved dressing down. He's already told them a few times: these new creations are vulnerable, they need time to establish themselves. If you pen them in or eat them all, they won't thrive and become abundant, and then where will we all be?

Instead, he shows his family members a better way. He chases one animal, shoots it with an arrow and asks it to run and fall by his grandmother's lodge. I can't tell from Tuscarora ethnologist J.N.B. Hewitt's translation of Gibson's story about the timing between each one, but he does this with a deer, then a raccoon, a buffalo, a bear, a moose and a wild duck. One at a time – maybe he does this when he thinks his grandmother and brother will be in need of another meal? – he shoots an animal and instructs each one to run to his "dear grandmother's" lodge to die. Grandmother is amazed at this provision. But Flint knows what's going on. He recognizes the arrow in each meal as that of his brother. But he says nothing.

Earth Holder doesn't just send his family food, however: he then goes over to Grandmother's lodge, and he dresses, quarters and skins the animals he had sent over. It takes work. He even makes Grandmother a bed out of the skins, so she has soft blankets to keep her warm on chilly nights. He respects the animals who gave themselves by exerting himself, and using everything he can, whether meat, bones or hide, to make gifts for his ungrateful family members.

All the while, he says to himself, "Pretty soon the human beings I make from earth will be born and reproduce themselves. And their minds shall be continually consoled by the things which the earth shall continue to contain."

Seeing Tharonhyawá:kon liberate the animals from his cave and then supply him and his grandmother with the food they need, Thawískaron decides that he should change his ways. He tries to do things like his brother. He takes the living earth and tries to fashion his own new creatures. But something of his spiky, irascible nature appears in everything he makes. When he tries to copy his brother's pigeon, it comes out with teeth instead of a beak, the fur of a bat instead of feathers of a bird. When he tries to match his brother's sunflower, it comes out thorny, a thistle.

Seeing these scary, sharp-teethed and spiny creations of his brother, Tharonhyawá:kon realizes how true the man at the lodge's advice had been about the need to protect the world he was making from his brother and his fanged and flinty ways. So he divides the island on which they live by placing a body of water between the two dwellings, and he situates his lodge on the far side of its swift-flowing current.

Whereas he and his twin had been joined in the womb and, after their birth, they had shared the land together, now he institutes a division, a boundary between his brother and grandmother's world and his. You could say it's a precedent for introducing *Tékeni Teyohà:te*, the separate paths, to address tensions that were growing within *Tehontatenentshonteronhtáhkwa*, the arms linking them as family. The brothers continue to share the ongoing work of creation, but they now do so from their homes on the two sides of the river. Earth Holder keeps needing to find solutions for the challenges raised by Flint's restless, sharp-edged vigour. The world we know emerges from balancing their two forms of creative energy.

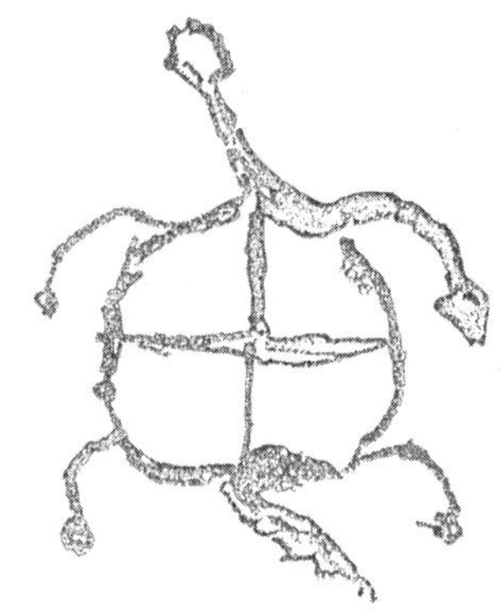

Chapter Fifteen

The Family of Earth

This earth is alive, be it known, so therefrom I took up earth by which I made all the things I have planted and I have finished living bodies, so that is the reason all they are severally alive and that in their bodies severally they will die, that earth they will become again.
– Tharonhyawá:kon in John Arthur Gibson's oration of the Creation Story, Grand River, 1900

You came out of the Ground in a Country that lies beyond the Seas, there you may have a just Claim, but here you must allow us to be your elder Brethren, and the Lands to belong to us long before you knew any thing of them.
– Canesatego's oration of the Covenant Chain–Two Row Wampum, Lancaster, Pennsylvania, June 26, 1744

The whiteman said, "What symbol will you go by?"

The Onkwehonweh replied, "When the Creator made Mother Earth, [humans were] created to walk upon the Earth to enjoy all nature's fruits, saying that no one will claim Mother Earth except rising faces which are about to be born."
– Jake Thomas's oration of the Covenant Chain–Two Row Wampum, Grand River, 1988

The agreement to link arms is an agreement to share in peace the living earth. It's an agreement to make family. The people who make such an agreement emerge, themselves, out of the earth, who mothered them into being and who continues to nurture them every day. Their only chance of living in peace with one another depends upon living in peace with the living earth that keeps giving them – giving everything – life, just as Tharonhyawá:kon had said. Although humans were meant to enjoy all of nature's fruits, "no one will claim Mother Earth except rising faces which are about to be born." I understand this to mean that the participants in and beneficiaries of the agreement, then, the ones who will thrive in the future, are pictured as seeds in the dark womb of earth, as embryonic life embedded in the cycles of nature – the sun that warms the earth and generates days and seasons; the water that seeps down to the waiting seeds, soaking and quickening the tendrils of roots; the solar-powered photosynthesis that energizes chlorophyll every spring. These kernels in the earth, these future generations, are seen as having faces, distinct features, unique personhood.

Reflecting on the ideas that grew into the practice of linking arms, *Tehontatenentshonteronhtáhkwa*, from its origins in the Creation Story, Amber Meadow Adams puts it this way: "We hold Earth first. How we hold her, and how she, in turn, holds us, is the blood that runs through every treaty, every policy, and every law. We can't talk about what they mean and how we use them today without talking about . . . each brother, or family, or nation, or alliance and the kind of relationship each has grown with yethi'nihstenha [Mother Earth]."[1] These are norms in Haudenosaunee ways of making agreements that arise from the ground itself.[2] The People knew any agreements they made with other humans would need to benefit the "rising faces which are about to be born," to submit to and cooperate with nature's way of being, her laws and requirements.

This is the potential that lies in "aboriginal and treaty rights" appearing in the Canadian constitution: it's an opening for Canadians to link our ways of doing things back to the original instructions Haudenosaunee People received about how to live with good minds in the ecosystems that nurtured them.

Long before the Great Law of Peace, the story of creation showed that peace is not a humans-only thing. Any peace negotiated between people must also seek the peace of all things. Peace between the twin brothers required the orderly arrangement of separate spheres so that the beings they created could live in peace. It required the protection of each living being's chances of living and reproducing itself so that future generations could have the sustenance they needed to live. Later in the story, after Creator had returned to sky world, it took a young man to observe that the plants and animals lived orderly peaceful lives by living in families, each with its own duties, and the people likewise organized themselves in clans and families with their particular duties and responsibilities. As Seneca Elder Henry Lickers puts it, "We believed that, by observing the natural laws of the Earth, we would be able to learn the right way to live. As we studied the environment, we came to believe that we could achieve a state in which we could understand the instructions of the Creator."[3] The quieting effect of the Good Mind came from putting things in order, from careful observation of the world's various beings and their various functions, from aligning one's heart and mind with the family of beings that makes up the natural order, aligning oneself with Mother Earth.

Earth as Family from Francis to Fernando, Medieval to Modern

Thinking of nature in terms of personhood is not easy for twenty-first-century people. Calling earth "Mother," her womb of seeds about to be born, can sound to modern ears like sentimentalism – a hippie, flower-power, hopeless idealism that industrialized culture grew out of. But the idea of relating to other beings of nature as family members is not just an Indigenous one; it's got deep roots in European culture too. The early French, Dutch and English traders who met the Haudenosaunee in the sixteenth and seventeenth centuries, for instance, could have known St. Francis's much-loved "Canticle of the Creatures" composed in 1225–1226. In the Canticle, Francis famously refers to the earth as his mother and to the sun and moon as his brother and sister:

Most High, all-powerful, good Lord,
Yours are the praises, the glory, and the honour, and all blessing.

To You alone, Most High, do they belong,
and no human is worthy to mention Your name.

Praised be You, my Lord, with all Your creatures,
especially Sir Brother Sun,
Who is the day and through whom You give us light.

And he is beautiful and radiant with great splendour;
and bears a likeness of You, Most High One.

Praised be You, my Lord, through Sister Moon and the stars,
in heaven You formed them clear and precious and beautiful.

Praised be You, my Lord, through Brother Wind,
and through the air, cloudy and serene, and every kind of weather,
through whom You give sustenance to Your creatures.

Praised be You, my Lord, through Sister Water,
who is very useful and humble and precious and chaste.

Praised be You, my Lord, through Brother Fire,
through whom You light the night,
and he is beautiful and playful and robust and strong.

Praised be You, my Lord, through our Sister Mother Earth,
who sustains and governs us,
and who produces various fruit with coloured flowers and herbs.

Praised be You, my Lord, through those who give pardon for Your
love, and bear infirmity and tribulation.

Blessed are those who endure in peace
for by You, Most High, shall they be crowned.

Praised be You, my Lord, through our Sister Bodily Death,
from whom no one living can escape.

Woe to those who die in mortal sin.
Blessed are those whom death will find in Your most holy will,
for the second death shall do them no harm.

Praise and bless my Lord and give Him thanks
and serve Him with great humility.

This is not the place for me to go into a lengthy theological disputation about how Francis's understanding of creation was part of his overall challenge to the crusading, imperial Christianity of his times. What we can simply observe here is that his descriptions of the elements of nature as family members – Sir Brother Sun, Sister Moon, Brother Wind, Sister Water, Brother Fire, Sister Mother Earth and even Sister Bodily Death – sound somewhat like the *Ohén:ton Karihwatéhkwen*, the Thanksgiving Address spoken at the beginning of Haudenosaunee meetings. Both recognize and praise the various elements of earth as participants in the cycle of more-than-human life. And his Canticle was not only widely understandable to his thirteenth-century followers, but it also remains a major component in St. Francis's ongoing popularity today. His understanding of himself as a member of the family of earthly creatures explains why Catholics continue to think of him as the patron saint of environmentalism.

But it is also the case that St. Francis has often been infantilized for this belief. His childlike innocence, giving sermons to the birds and such, has been seen by many in Euro-American culture as endearing, but hopelessly naive – meaning unscientific and irredeemably "medieval." Francis can easily stand in for Europe's erstwhile innocence, long surpassed by its modern complexity and sophistication. "Today someone read me St. Francis of Assisi," wrote Portuguese poet Fernando Pessoa in 1917:

I listened and couldn't believe my ears.
How could a man who was so fond of things
Never have looked at them or understood what they were?

Why call water my sister if water isn't my sister?
To feel it better?
I feel it better by drinking it than by calling it something –
Sister, or mother, or daughter.
Water is beautiful because it's water.
If I call it my sister,
I can see, even as I call it that, that it's not my sister
And it's best to call it water, since that's what it is,
Or better yet, not to call it anything
But to drink it, to feel it on my wrists, and to look at it
Without any names.[4]

Fernando Pessoa (1888–1935) lived at the high-water mark of European modernity, and he's a very tricky figure to get hold of, because he kept composing personae for himself as a writer. So it's not always easy to tell what views he himself held and which he invented for the speakers in his various poems. In this, Pessoa typifies a kind of hypermodernity. In his many personae, he captures modernity's awareness of the many conflicting views and experiences that make up cosmopolitan, urban society, yet he also exemplifies its hyperindividualism. He could convey different views convincingly, and he could do this all by himself.

The other thing that makes Pessoa hypermodern is that he and his personae convey a massive confidence in modern "progress." His was a period in Europe and America when people expressed remarkable trust in the ability of enlightened people to smooth out life's difficulties and nature's challenges through human ingenuity – whether through smart technology, well-oiled mechanisms of governance or sophisticated social and economic arrangements. Pessoa was part of that first generation of Europeans for whom hot water ran over his hands from a tap and a sewer washed away the dirt. He died in 1935, just when fascism was arriving in Europe and the Dictator Salazar's regime in Portugal would reveal how the grand belief in modern progress could give rise as easily to genocide and gas chambers as it could to the development of indoor plumbing or vehicle airbags.

For high modernists like Pessoa, calling water your "sister" only confused things. You don't drink your sister. You don't bathe in your sister. You don't float canoes or sailing ships on your sister. Confidence in modernity, which somehow survived fascism and the Second World War and the nuclear bombings of Hiroshima and Nagasaki – let alone the spread of DDT around the world – is all about ridding the mind and society of these obfuscating ideas, these anthropomorphic metaphors, and getting on with reality, clear and simple.

Modernist logic appeals to many of us because it seems practical and direct. Water is water. It's a thing. A noun. It feels good on your wrist when you're washing your hands. It quenches your thirst. In fact, if you think of water as family, as active and alive, you may hesitate to use it to wash your hands or to take a drink. And then where would we be? Not heading toward progress.

Pessoa's literalism, if we want to call it that, is suspicious of the distortion that happens when we lose the hard certainty of matter, of things as positive facts. This positivist way of thinking gets nervous when nouns get overactive. When they act like verbs, and one thing moves with or transforms into another thing. When non-human things act like humans, and we forget that they are different from us. Pessoa writes:

> If sometimes I say that flowers smile
> And if I should say that rivers sing,
> It's not because I think that there are smiles in flowers
> And songs in the rivers' flowing . . .
> It's so I can help misguided men
> Feel the truly real existence of flowers and rivers.
>
> Since I write for them to read me, I sometimes stoop
> To the stupidity of their senses . . .
> It isn't right, but I excuse myself,
> Because I've only taken on this role, as interpreter of Nature,

> Because there are men who don't grasp its language,
> Which is no language at all.[5]

Pessoa is smarter than the people he writes to, the weak-minded ones who anthropomorphize the world, who need to pretend that everything must be humanlike for people to understand it, let alone sympathize with it. His poems warn us that personifying natural things like flowers and water can be a sloppy-minded egocentrism: where we demand that they be translated into our terms, that they smile and sing, in order for us to notice them and see their value.

But it doesn't take much imagination to see how this equation can work the other way around too – if you don't think of having some kind of relationship with water – maybe not as a family member, but at least as a living being that feeds and nurtures you and that you must therefore care for – then it's much easier for the objectified properties of water (its cool feeling on your skin, its ability to quench your thirst, its capacity to rinse away dirt) to become services or commodities. Water becomes a thing among things.

If water is purely an inanimate, inert object, then it's easier to put it in a plastic bottle and sell it. We can run it in pipes into buildings and charge people for it. We can privatize it. We can block its natural flow down a river and contain it in lake-sized reservoirs, like Thawískaron did with his cave of animals. We can force it through channels or pipes over turbines to create electricity. We can pump it up towers and run it through plastic or copper tubes to our kitchen sinks and our toilets. Once we construct massive drainage pipes taller than two- and three-storey buildings under our cities to deal with sewage and what we have come to call "waste" water, we feel less and less responsible to the cool water running out of our taps and over our wrists.

And I haven't even approached the whole legal apparatus of "water rights," whereby fracking companies, for example, can buy the rights to the water everywhere – from well water to rivers and lakes – so that they can pump trillions of litres into the ground to flush out natural gas that we can pipe away to heat our homes and piped-in water. Not to mention the questions about what will happen to the oily, gassy effluent that then needs to be held in tailings ponds until we can figure out how to remove the toxicity.

The rejection of water as a sister is necessary to treating it with this kind of detachment, and treating it with detachment is necessary to all these practical functions. But what do we do now, in late-modernity, now that we have seen what a century and a half of flushing billions of toilets into our watersheds is doing, not just to water lilies and fish, but to our own future?

Yethi'nihstenha Onhwentsyakekha'

"*Yethi'* [she to us] + *nihsten* [strength, capacity, even harshness] + *ha* [living now] *Onhwentsya* [earth] + *kek* [on it] + *ha'* [here present]): 'she to us is exerting her capacity and strength to keep us living now.'"[6]

Maybe, the problem lies not in calling water our "sister." The problem isn't in thinking of the beings of nature as family, but in our English-language concept of "family" itself. Maybe the problem is in the anthropocentric idea that family is always and only human. That it's a thing, a noun, that applies first and best to humans.

In Haudenosaunee languages, it's a verb. Not a metaphor, where one *thing* stands in for another, but a verb. The words for family members are actions, not titles. Lots of beings do the birthing and nurturing acts of mothering. Animals and birds, obviously. And plants, too, and water, not to mention the cells of which it's made.

In "For Our Mother Earth, Iethi'nistenha Onhwenstia," the chapter she contributed to the Haudenosaunee Environmental Task Force's book *The Words That Come Before All Else: Environmental Philosophies of the Haudenosaunee*, the late Kawennotakie Salli Benedict (Akwesasne *Kanyen'kehá:ka*, Mohawk) writes about how *Kanyen'kéha* language conveys a concept of motherhood different from how we usually understand the term in English: "In Mohawk culture," she says, "the word for [my] Mother is Akennistena. It is also the special word of respect that we use when referring to our Mother's sisters or our aunts. We use this special word of respect as part of a special cultural support mechanism. The child and the child's Mother acknowledge that there is support of other 'Mothers,' if the biological mother should die."[7] This explanation accords with Tyendinaga Mohawk David Kanatawakhon Maracle's discussion of the words for "mother" and "aunt" in his *Karoron Ne Owennahshonha: Mohawk Language Thematic Dictionary* (2001), where his English orthography is slightly different for the same idea:

> Mother **Ihsta'a [Ihs-tá:-'ah]**
> This term is similar to that given for 'aunt' as it is based on the matrilineal tradition that a woman's sisters were also considered to be mother to her children. There is the variation **Ihstenha** used by some speakers to differentiate between the biological mother and her sisters.

Maracle's *Dictionary* goes on to the pronominal prefixes, such as *Ake'nihstenha* or *Ako'nistenha* that we translate into English as "my mother" or "her mother." To this pronominal list he adds, "The term '**Yethni'nihstenha**' is often used in place of '**Onkwa'nihstenha**' [our mother] in situations of ceremonial reference of importance, such as in the designation '**Yethi'nihstenha Onhwentsyakekha**' [Yet-hi'-nihs-tén-ha' On-hwentsya-kék-ha'] '*our mother earth*' (literally: 'she is to us mother the earth')."[8] This brief tracing of *Kanyen'kéha* words for motherhood helps us see how the idea of "mother" conveyed in Mohawk language extends the basic actions of mothering, of nurturing and sustaining life, from biological mothering to the circle of aunties' mothering to the circle of creation's mothering. "Mother," "sister," "brother" are verbs, things humans and more-than-humans do. They aren't strictly, or only, gender identities. These are verbs, actions, not essences or fixed identities.

Benedict goes on to explain how this activity of mothering operated in her own family:

"My Grandmother, Kahentineshon, was orphaned when she was just a baby. She was taken in by her mother's sister Kaiatahente. Kaiatahente raised several other nieces and nephews who lost their parents, when they passed away prematurely. She raised seven in all. My grandmother Kahentineshon was raised with Kiohontasen, whom she called sister. She was actually my grandmother's first cousin, who also was cared for by

Kaiatahente."[9] Benedict does not dwell on the devastating grief and loss submerged in her quick story of aunties raising orphaned children and nieces together as siblings; she doesn't comment on what happened to their missing biological mothers.

Instead, Benedict focuses on the mothering by sisters and aunties who constituted what she calls a "cultural support mechanism." "Was taken in," "raised," "was cared for" – these are Benedict's English words for *Ihsta'a/Istenha* actions of mothering/aunt-ing. One is a mother by doing the action of mothering, not just by the fact of having given birth, but by the ongoing activity of mothering. The one who mothers us is our mother; the one who does the actions of sistering, beyond the biological linkage, is our sister. Same with "brother," or "father," or "uncle." And this action-oriented idea of relation does not stop at the borderline of humanness. Water does watering, earth does the uplifting, rooting, supporting actions of grounding everything – *Yethi'nihstenha*: "she to us exerts her capacity and strength to keep us living now."

As such, Earth does the everyday earth-work of mothering our human and more-than-human lives.

Salli Benedict tells of how the great aunt she grew up calling her grandmother, Kiohontasen, was renowned for her skill in making baskets from black ash splints and sweetgrass. She participated actively in the circle of motherhood that passed on these skills to Benedict's mother. She says, "Kiohontasen taught my mother [Florence] plant medicines and their uses, our relationship with the earth and the elements of Creation, how to give proper Thanksgiving to the Creator, how to till the earth, how to prepare fish, how to store and save food for the winter, how to collect food from the earth, and great knowledge about the environment within Akwesasne. This is all Mother's knowledge that is passed from a mother to her children."[10] "Taught," "give proper Thanksgiving," "till the earth," "prepare fish," "store and save food," "collect food," "passed from a mother to her children" – *ista'ah, istenha, Yethi'nihstenha*. The person who does this is mothering.

Later in life, Kiohontasen would get a ride from her "son," Benedict's father, Ernie, whom she adopted and mothered, to a place where sweetgrass grew downstream from where he worked as an electrician at Alcoa, the aluminum smelter in Massena, New York, upstream and upwind from Akwesasne. She'd pick sweetgrass all day while he was at work and then take the vanilla-and-honey-scented bundles she had collected home when he picked her up again at the end of his shift.

She used sweetgrass in her basket weaving. Like many basket makers, she would hold its stems in her mouth as she worked. The scented stems of the grass blended with her saliva. Benedict says that her great-aunt/grandmother was remarkably health-conscious, harvesting and eating only foods supplied by Mother Earth all her life, so the family was shocked when she died of stomach cancer – of all the kinds of cancer! – at age eighty.

Well, she was eighty, after all. So maybe it was just bad luck. Who knows whence cancer comes?

Several years later, however, the family came upon Alcoa conducting a massive earth removal project in the fields where Kiohontasen used to pick sweetgrass. Acres of soil were being carried away in trucks. The earth of the picking place had been contaminated by toxins from the aluminum plant, and the corporation had been ordered to remove the hazard.[11]

Here, Benedict's story takes a turn, swerving into a story of how the web of relationships gets twisted. The land Kiohontasen trusted as *Yethi'nihstenha* had been poisoned, and it had fed the poison to her. Alcoa's demonstrated belief that the land is not your mother, supported by a legal system of land ownership that assumes land does not constitute the circle of mothering that sustains you, enabled the corporation and its industrial cousins in the region, General Motors and Reynolds Metals, to consider it a thing, an inanimate service site, where toxic chemicals could be discharged without harming their family's health and welfare.

Or, perhaps it might harm Kiohontasen's family, but because Alcoa didn't share the same mother as she did, that would be their own tough luck.

If pressed, the corporation's lawyers could demand absolute proof that the toxins their factory spewed into the air and watershed, which then rained down onto the sweetgrass fields, were definitely what killed her. They could separate the corporation from its behaviours, and its behaviours from the consequences upon the mothering capacities of earth. Furthermore, they could also defend Alcoa's activities in the neighbourhood by pointing out how they *did* nurture and sustain Akwesasne residents by giving them jobs: don't forget that Kiohontasen's adopted son had been employed there as an electrician. This is the most common way that Industrial Growth Society translates nurturance and care from the world of intimate, sustaining, interpersonal actions into objective, countable economic facts. It's all very well, we think, to consider the earth as your mother when you're a child, but eventually you have to grow up and smell the coffee, toughen up and get a job. Realize that it's sweet to give your kids a hug at bedtime, but if you really want to show them your love, bring them home a paycheque.

Understanding our relations with earth as familial, as intimate actions of support, troubles our ability to extract paycheques from it. Smelting aluminum, for example, requires mining the earth for bauxite, which is then processed by means of electrolysis whereby a direct current is passed through a solution of alumina dissolved in molten *cryolite*, or sodium aluminum fluoride, to separate out the pure aluminum.

If you want to have lightweight eavestroughs, airplanes or lawn furniture, you need to scale up factories, workers, shipping piers, train cars filled with bauxite, trillions of kilowatts of electricity, fluoride, robots and heavy machinery. You need these things if you want to deploy this amazing metal that oxidizes quickly when it touches the air, protecting it from rust.

Aluminum smelting emits into the air perfluorocarbons (PFCs), polycyclic aromatic hydrocarbon (PAH), fluoride, sulfur dioxide (SO_2) and carbon dioxide (CO_2). Difficult, polysyllabic words to say, even more difficult to breathe.

In his chapter in *The Words That Come Before All Else*, Les Benedict writes:

> The smelter has released tons of fluoride each year into the local environment. The emissions, containing fluoride, have affected plants, animals, and humans . . . The emissions, deposited on grasses, have harmed cattle, bees, and wildlife. The people of Akwesasne, who once relied on home

> gardens for food, have stopped using their gardens, in fear of ingesting fluoride . . . The impact of the smelter has affected several generations and severely limited Akwesasne in being able to maintain self-sufficiency and quality of life.[12]

In the early 1980s, the New York State Department of Environmental Conservation found that PCBs had been found in the groundwater under the former site of the General Motors property, and later in private wells on the St. Regis Mohawk reservation. They found PCBs in fish and animals, and there were concerns in the community about high numbers of miscarriages and birth defects.

Around that time, another contributor to the Haudenosaunee Environmental Task Force's book, Tekatsi'tsiah:khwa Katsi Cook (Wolf Clan), began studying the relation between mothers' and babies' health and that of *Yethi'nihstenha*. She founded the Mother's Milk Project, bringing together *Kanyen'kehàka* understandings of mothering with Western medical and environmental research to improve both earth's and people's life chances in this very contaminated area. In a much-cited speech, Katsi Cook summarizes the findings of her many years of research. "Women are the first environment," she says. "In pregnancy, our bodies sustain life. At the breast of women, the generations are nourished. In this way, we as women are Earth."[13]

She's not anthropomorphizing, not speaking metaphor. You might say she's putting motherhood back in its natural environment, the action of mothering back in the body where it lives.

Once you trace something as literal as moving toxins, the dividing line between the body of a baby's mother and the body of Mother Earth gets very thin indeed, if it exists at all. If mothering is the action that nourishes you, if your mothering happens within a set of holistic cultural practices that nourishes you, that mothers you, then it's a particular kind of self-harm, self-isolation, that rejects water as mother or sister, water as my family. In a 2018 interview, Cook says, "You are a part of nature no matter how much concrete and plastic surround you. This was one of the painful parts of my midwifery practice in my own community, finding that our proximity to an EPA [Environmental

Protection Agency disaster relief] Superfund site meant that PCBs are now in our bodies, in our mothers' breast milk. When one of our babies is born, the cord blood has over 200 industrial chemicals in it."[14] What we put in Mother Earth, what we sluice into Sister Water, circulates in our children's umbilicus. It's how we mother our babies, the faces about to be born.

As a result of investigations into the environmental impacts of aluminum smelting in the Akwesasne region carried out by people like Katsi Cook, the EPA announced a $20 million reparative settlement in 2013 to be paid by Alcoa and the former Reynolds Metals Company to the Mohawks of St. Regis for habitat, wildlife and cultural restoration.[15]

This payment is not a magic bullet. It's a purifying drop in a contaminated bucket. The toxins are still in the water, in the land, in the body of earth. To this day there is a no-fishing advisory in the region. The people have been separated from the life of the rivers.

In fact, the rivers themselves have been made into dividing lines. The fact that the Mohawks of Akwesasne have river borders running through their familial territory has meant that parts of the reserve are in New York State, parts in Ontario and parts in Quebec – which means different laws and governing bodies divide jurisdiction among the same family of people, let alone family of earth. The result has been toxicity not just in the rivers or the land, but in the residents' minds. There have been extreme tensions in Akwesasne over the arming of border patrols; over the right of Mohawk People to carry goods across the borders, within their own territory and between different provincial and state law systems and tax regimes; over whether local employment and income should or should not be boosted by casino gambling and who should then provide security and law enforcement. Over whether and who to sue for the damage that has been done to *Yethi'nihstenha*.

Note, too, that the General Motors plant is no longer running, which means that the paycheques for local workers are no longer coming. The families still need nurturing and support, but a number of the industries that spread toxins over Mother Earth have now left, and left her ability to provide for them compromised, to say the least.

The state of Mother Earth reminds us that colonialism is a structure, not an event. It has restructured families and made it very difficult to return them to a healthy state.

Indeed, Salli Benedict is herself no longer alive to tell this part of the story. She died in 2011 at age fifty-seven after waging what a tribal council statement called "a heroic and courageous battle."[16] One of her mourners posted a condolence at the obituary website: "We must know by now how the fluoride emissions in the air is affecting all of us and how this problem will remain in the public air for a long time . . . As an alumni of St. Lawrence University, I ask them to restart the Flouride Network and bring to justice the polluters."[17]

Recall Salli's quick reference to her *ihstenha* Kaiatahente who raised seven nieces and nephews who had lost their parents, when they passed away prematurely. And then her family lost her great-aunt Kiohontasen, whose adopted son drove her over to the toxic sweetgrass meadow. Now Salli is gone too.

So much grief, so many losses in the cultural system of support.

I never knew Salli Benedict or her family. I don't live in Akwesasne or in the neighbourhood. But because she was raised in a strong family that knew her language's understanding of what mothering is, because she and others in her family and neighbourhood wrote about it, she reminded anyone who reads her work that hers is a story about family. All of our stories on Earth are about family. Literally.

It's the law. Maybe not the state or provincial law. But it's the law of water, earth, air, fire.[18]

Salli Benedict and her family worked over multiple generations to address these concerns, to repair the divisions, the harm to the family of people, the family of earth. "It is a testament to her hard work and commitment that our community's land claims are being negotiated with the government of Canada," said Mohawk Council of Akwesasne Grand Chief Kanentakeron Mike Mitchell. "As a result, we wanted so much for her to be with us on the final leg of this journey. She was so much a part of negotiations, and she will still be with us in spirit. We will continue to work just as hard as if she was still by our side encouraging us all on."[19]

Learning Who Our Relatives Are

In his opening chapter to *The Words That Come Before All Else*, Kayanesenh Paul Williams writes, "We will spend our lifetimes continually learning who our relatives are and learning to give them the proper thanks."[20] Stories like that of Kiohontasen's family are accumulating throughout Industrial Growth Societies around the world – from the toxic properties of abandoned plastics floating around the world's oceans and mercury leaking downstream from mining and lumber operations in both remote and urban locations to the runaway forest and bushfires spreading around the world. These are all stories of denied intimacy, of disrespect, of rejected reciprocity with our non-human and human neighbours.

Why call water your sister, if she's not your sister? Pessoa may not have foreseen how the system that ran the water to his kitchen tap in Portugal could eventually run PCBs into his own bloodstream (the industrialized Tagus River, running through Lisbon, is hardly crystal clear), but it is within the scope of our lifetimes to learn who our relatives are.

The image of linking arms arises from an appreciation of more-than-human motherhood conveyed in the story of Earth's creation. As Amber Meadow Adams explains, the

> *Tehontatenentshonteronhtáhkwa* agreement starts in the story of Earth's creation. The first link the end of an arm forms is with the as-yet-to-be Earth: a young woman, refugee from another world, uses fingertips, hands, elbows, and shoulders to shape the raw materials she carries, and those she is given, into a dwelling place, then a biome, then a whole planet. The primary link, or relationship, in *Tehontatenentshonteronhtáhkwa* is with *yethi'nihstenha tsi yonhwentsyake*, our mother the Earth. The next clearest example the story presents of the many other kinds of relationships represented by joined arms comes when the daughter of the refugee from the world above becomes pregnant with twin boys.[21]

Linking arms is about making earth family, building relations, even if the paths may be different among those who share the river, who share the Mothering Earth.

After all she has learned about the harm to mothers both human and environmental in her community, Katsi Cook says, "Rather than mourning this fact as a source of continuing oppression or depression of how we as human beings continue to violate the original instructions that come with living on the planet, instead I took it as a quest – a quest that each one of us has to pursue in our own lives: How to return to an honorable relationship with the environment that sustains us?"[22]

In *The Words That Come Before All Else*, James W. Ransom (Akwesasne Mohawk, Wolf clan) notes how Haudenosaunee communities and ways of life were disregarded in the rush to build hydroelectric plants from the 1930s onward, not just at Akwesasne, but when the Lewiston Reservoir expropriated Tuscarora lands near Niagara, and the Kinzua Dam flooded Seneca territory in northeastern Pennsylvania. As these various projects came up for relicensing in the 1990s, Ransom reports that the Haudenosaunee Task Force knew that Two Row understandings of the unique concerns of canoe and ship communities would not be given due consideration. The authorities from the State of New York indicated an interest in consulting with the Mohawks of Akwesasne, but the Task Force members could see that Haudenosaunee understandings of the familial relations that constituted each of these environments would be considered just one of several stakeholders' views in any consultation process, and that the dysfunctional understanding of family held by the majority of "partners" would predominate once again. You can't enter into a true consultation about environmental degradation if three-quarters of the people involved think water is a dead thing, a "resource" or a "property."

The Task Force therefore insisted, says Ransom, that "we must participate in a manner that is respectful of the canoe, that is based on helping each other as was intended by the Two-Row Wampum Belt. The focus must be on our common interest, the St. Lawrence River, which is part of the river of life, and not on the ship."[23] "Let's not focus so much on the ship with its goods and cargo," say the People of the canoe. "Let's focus on the river."

"As long as the sun shines upon this earth," the *rotiyaneshon* had said, "as long as the water still flows, and as long as the grass grows green at a certain time of the year."

The flow of water in the river is central to the linking of arms, to the Two Row agreement. It is a life source on which both signatories depend. As Ransom puts it, it is our – everyone's – common interest.

As the gap between St. Francis's espousal of nature's beings as sisters and Pessoa's denial of them indicates, the parties meeting at the river may have very different understandings of what constitutes family. These differences can distort our relationships, causing tensions between our cultures, and they can also cause conflict with the river itself. But the meeting at the edge of the woods, the decision to pull our various watercraft onto the riverbank and the determination to put ourselves in a good mind, to build respect and unity, and therefore establish peaceful relationships, can still happen.

Who knows? Maybe aunties, sisters, mothers and grandmothers and wampum diplomats, EPA officers, members of the Haudenosaunee Environmental Task Force, as well as provincial and state negotiators can build a better relationship with the Earth that Mothers us all, a cultural system of support for new children growing up in the very place where toxicity was heedlessly rained down on everybody, regardless of parentage, whether Mohawk, Ontarian, pickerel, New Yorker, black ash, Quebecoise, sturgeon or sweetgrass. Maybe water in the river will flow more freely once again, maybe she can act more like a sister, an auntie, a mother to anyone, relieved of her toxic burden, regardless of what kind of craft they float upon her.

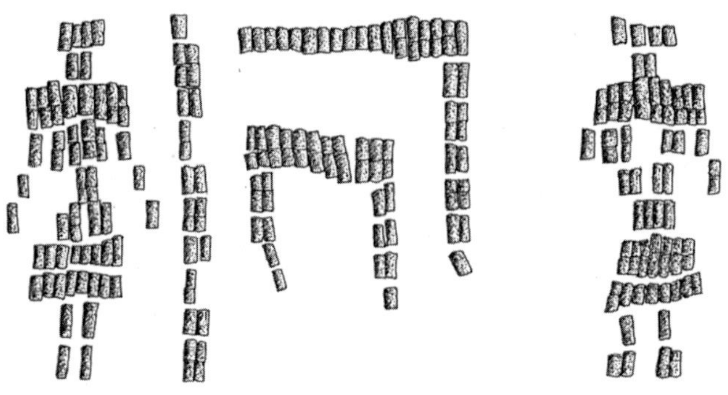

Chapter Sixteen

Divided Home

economy (n.): 1530s, "household management," from Latin *oeconomia*. . . , from Greek *oikonomia* "household management, thrift," from *oikonomos* "manager, steward," from *oikos* "house, abode, dwelling" (cognate with Latin *vicus* "district," *vicinus* "near;" Old English *wic* "dwelling, village," from PIE [Proto-Indo-European] root **weik-* (1) "clan") + *nomos* "managing," from *nemein* "manage" (from PIE root **nem-* "assign, allot; take"). Meaning "frugality, judicious use of resources" is from 1660s. The sense of "wealth and resources of a country" (short for political economy) is from 1650s.

ecology (n.): 1873, *oecology*, "branch of science dealing with the relationship of living things to their environments," coined in German by German zoologist Ernst Haeckel as ***Ökologie***, from Greek *oikos* "house, dwelling place, habitation" (from PIE root **weik-* (1) "clan") + *-logia* "study of" (see *-logy*). In use with reference to anti-pollution activities from 1960s.
– *Online Etymological Dictionary*

One reason so many of us in the twenty-first century feel that nature is not our family, that water is not our sister, may be that we were raised in a divided home. It's possible to say that, since the rise of Industrial Growth Society in the eighteenth and nineteenth centuries, what had been one home got divided into separate, conflicting allegiances: into "economy," meaning "household management or thrift," on the one hand, and "ecology," "the relationship of living things to their environments," on the other. Only later in the nineteenth century, when we European language speakers belatedly began to realize what had happened and began to study the gap between them, did we think we needed the word "ecology" to describe something distinct from "economy." Before that, it was all one "oikos," all one home. But ever since, like children from a household in conflict, we are asked to give our devotion to just one of our antagonized parents: frugal finance or nurturing earth. The relatively recent idea of household economy, then – what many of us studied in school as "Home Ec" – has been presented to us as what we could wrest from nature, what we could secure for ourselves out of the relationship of living things.

Like the game animals trapped in the cave by Thawískaron.

You see it all the time: not long ago the newspaper reported on the Ontario government's proposal to double logging volumes in the province over the next decade from fifteen million cubic metres to thirty million cubic metres in order to "create more jobs and revitalize the industry."[1] This, in the midst of widespread concern over climate change and repeated evidence that mature trees are among the most effective ways to reduce airborne carbon and replace it with oxygen. We are regularly told we must choose between more jobs, on one hand, or better air, on the other. It seems economy and ecology are always forced into competition with each other.

In the same day's paper, there was also a piece reporting that the Trans Mountain pipeline project had cleared a legal hurdle when the Federal Court of Appeals ruled that Ottawa had adequately consulted with Indigenous communities (that is, with Ottawa-financed band councils) along the line's route. This project, which was completed in May 2024, has boosted the shipping of Alberta crude oil from 300,000 to 890,000 barrels a day between Edmonton and Vancouver, thus opening the way to new Pacific markets for petroleum from the tar sands. The debates over pipelines to export Alberta crude was one of the stickiest challenges faced by Prime Minister Justin Trudeau's government. Here's how a September 30, 2016, editorial in the *Globe and Mail* put it back when his government was in its first year:

> Canada is blessed with an abundance of oil and gas, the jobs that go with it, and the potential for hundreds of billions of dollars in investment to extract, upgrade and move these resources. But Canada is also committed to dramatically lowering its greenhouse-gas output, and its use of carbon-based fuels like oil and gas, as part of the fight against global warming. Figuring out how to strike a balance between the two, so as to achieve the greatest environmental improvement at the lowest possible economic cost, is the most important, complex and politically fraught issue on Ottawa's plate.[2]

As this editorial put it, environmental improvement seems only to come at an economic cost; because ecology and economy are understood to be in bitter conflict, any love we show to the first has to be taken from the latter.

It's a divided home that arises from a divided mind.

Yes, Canadians may admit that the tar sands are the single largest producer of greenhouse gas emissions in the country, with the result that Canada produces more of these emissions per person than any other G20 country,[3] but we consider these the necessary costs Mother Earth must pay so we can maintain the household economies of thousands of Canadians, not just those who work in the fossil fuels sector, but all of us who keep our gas furnaces burning through the winter. It's a simple equation: what you give to one has to come from the other.

But as our Haudenosaunee allies, our elder brothers in this land have long known, it's the same home; it's the same household and clan, the same *oikos*.

Essentially, Eco cannot pay indefinitely for Eco without bankrupting itself. As anybody who's lived through a breakup knows, parting ways doesn't erase the interwoven nature of the former household. Someone still needs to pick up the kids from school. The family's bank accounts may have been separated, but the lawyer's fees are still deducted from both. Likewise, it's nigh on impossible to escape either of these two ecosystems: the harvesting of trees and burning of fossil fuels are deducted from your air quality whether you vote Conservative, Liberal, NDP or Green.

Tehontatenentshonteronhtáhkwa, the Agreement to Link Arms, is about making family. About making common cause between our different ways of doing things, as we share the river of life. It's one river, one watershed, one household. You may bust up the closeness, pretend the other members don't matter, but this doesn't end the relationship. It just turns a mutually nurturing relationship into a hostile one. The interdependencies outlive our illusions of independence. We may not act like it, but we're all still sharing the same home. This is the real law – the law of how things work. But also the law of how we are constituted as people in the world. It's a reminder of our primary *constitutive relationship*, a reminder that our arms are already linked.

In our present economy, everyone who loves a hot shower in the morning, like I do, is contributing to the petro-economy, which is the petro-ecology, whether we like it or not. Even if you go old school and heat your bathwater in an iron kettle over a woodfire, you're still burning trees, releasing carbon and heating the atmosphere. We speak about living "off the grid," but things like solar panels are made of silicons that have to be dug out of the earth. It's almost impossible to create an absolutely pristine place, some righteous pinnacle, a person can escape to from which to judge and condemn the members of their rejected household.

It is a short-term delusion to think that the web of relationships that constitutes an economy can be extricated from the web of relationships that constitutes ecology. This is the same self-alienating delusion that insists that water is not my sister, the Earth is not my Mother, the beings around me are not my family.

The Story of Division

It matters what story you tell, what story you've been taught, what story you keep telling yourself about how to live in the world.

The Western mind-habit of division, the tendency to separate and subdivide, to understand ourselves and our world by compartmentalization, is a home-breaker. Nature versus nurture; nature versus culture; sacred versus secular; animal versus plant versus mineral; church versus state; art versus science; myth versus law; sailing ship versus canoe. Many hear the two paths teaching of the *Tékeni Teyohà:te* through the Western ears of division – focusing on the non-intersecting paths of the two separate vessels. When we do, we forget that the agreement is about how to Link Arms, by means of the three rows of white beads – *skén:nen, kentèn:ron* and *ka'nikonhriyó'tshera't* – the links of the silver chain, the peace, friendship and good-minded respect that connect the two brothers in *Tehontatenentshonteronhtáhkwa*.

By contrast, the Enlightenment's theory of mind-division, René Descartes' famous *Cogito, ergo sum* "I think, therefore I am," imagines the individual human being as separate or distinct from all other beings on the basis of conscious thought. It places division or distinction-by-separation at the core of human self-definition. European-descended individuals like me have come to know ourselves and the world by isolating ourselves from (and usually above) other beings around us, by observing family resemblances and then subdividing them in a competing taxonomic order: kingdom, phylum, class, order, family, genus and species.

A hierarchy of nouns. We inheritors of the Greek and Latin family of languages tend to think in nouns, categories, distinguishable objects. For us, it really helps to keep things clear if they don't move, if the things we know aren't mobile, interactive verbs.

We may be from the same general family as other living beings, but our genus and our species subdivide the laws of equity, make loopholes in the rules of interdependent family responsibility. And the subdivisions naturalize the story of endless competition. Whether in the domain of biology, entertainment or politics, we twenty-first-century Canadians seem to view things this way – it's always a contest between players competing for limited rewards. Divide everyone into groups, give them different uniforms to wear to keep them distinct and have them vie for just one trophy: winner takes all. Ultimately, there's only one survivor. Whether you watch it on the *National Geographic* channel, on TSN or CNN, *Wheel of Fortune* or *Survivor*, you gather all the contestants on one stage or playing field, divide them into teams, and they compete with one another for the million-dollar prize. Each time the competitors meet, one gets eliminated. Vote one contestant off the island until there's only one left.

It seems so normal and apparently natural, we hardly see it, until we consider stories like the Haudenosaunee one about Tharonhyawá:kon. How, although he put the river between his house and that of his brother, he didn't vote Thawískaron off the island. The Earth Holder thought differently. He shared the *acts* of creation with his brother, even though they had such different ways of going about it. This left him vulnerable to his brother's split-mind, the way he mixed creativity with destruction. Tharonhyawá:kon was not passive before his brother's aggression, but acted to save the biodiversity that had been trapped in Thawískaron's cave, and when the rivalry between their ways of doing things got so intense that it required him to force his brother and his creepy, dangerous creatures into the nighttime world underground, he knew that even this division of territories was part of a balance, one necessary to the cycle of death and decay that creates the humus out of which life itself grows.

Creation, creativity, is not a zero-sum game.[4]

Recently, botanists have come to learn more about the mycorrhizal networks of fungi that interact with the root systems of plants deep in Thawískaron's dark, underground world. Plants provide the fungi with sugars that are produced through photosynthesis while the fungi get nutrients and water from the soil and pass them on to the plants. These botanists have learned that mycorrhiza fungi can also protect the plants from pathogens that can cause disease, and even break down toxins such as petrochemicals in contaminated earth.[5]

But until these late realizations, everything has been explained to us in Industrial Growth Society as a competition for scarce resources. We lose sight of the reality that we share the same *oikos* and *weik*, the same household and clan. We may support the Liberals or Conservatives, but they govern the same home, the same community; Maple Leafs, Flames or Canadiens, it's the same game. "When I questioned my grandfather about the concept of the Family of the Earth," explains Elder Henry Lickers in the closing chapter of *The Words That Come Before All Else: Environmental Philosophies of the Haudenosaunee*,

> I wanted to know if all animals, even spiders, were part of my family, my brothers or sisters. He told me that all things in Creation were part of my family, animals, plants, sky, moon, Earth, and rocks. He said that we were not the older brothers of Creation, but the younger brothers. We, like how young brothers sometimes do, did not know how to act in Creation, but by observing the rest of Creation, we would learn the natural laws and how to act. As younger brothers of Creation, we were dependent on the rest of our family for our existence.[6]

You cannot become the sole survivor by voting any of these family members off the island, since we are all interdependent. They are our elder brothers or sisters; they teach us how to act. As Joe Sheridan and Dan Longboat – Roronhiakewen (He Clears the Sky) point out, we learn a practical, realistic imagination from them.[7] One way to act is to know how dangerous spider venom can be and to keep one's respectful distance. That respect also recognizes the role venomous spiders play in keeping the balance of our eco-home, so we know enough not to simply wipe them out with DDT. The rules that govern the lives of spiders, plants, sky and rocks govern our human lives too. There is no separation of the laws of economy from the laws of ecology. You can't deduct jobs and salaries from *Yethi'nihstenha*'s bank account without deducting them from your own nest egg.

It's not hard to see how the story of competition between opponents has been made to seem natural to us, because everyone, every being, must consume to live. Whether human, animal or plant, everyone consumes the lives of others. The roots absorb the earth's nutrients to grow the leaves that insects and animals eat. We too eat plants and animals, and we all in turn are eventually consumed back into the soil ourselves, which feeds a new generation of plant roots. Seen through the win-lose lens of division, of nouns consuming nouns, the laws of nature are made to seem like one huge competition between creatures who must do violence to one another to acquire scarce resources. As evolutionary science was explained to many of us, the world added up to the "survival of the fittest" – a bloody fight to the death between winners or losers, hunters and hunted. We didn't realize, many of us, how peculiar and limited a story about the world this was, a way of seeing things, that still runs through everything from the FIFA World Cup of Soccer to the A's and B's on school report cards.

The whole storyline depends upon the motivating fear of scarcity – why would the two teams exert such energy, such violence against one another, if there were plenty to go around, if both teams could win first place, if they delighted in each others' success? There has to be only one trophy, only a little bit of moisture left in the water hole, to generate the excitement, the tense situation, in which the two sides will gore each other to death so one side can survive. This tension makes the energy of a compelling story. That's why you send the film crew to the water hole to catch the moment of the kill, not some quiet pasture where all the animals do is chew their cud.

The climate is heating up. There's an emergency coming: flooding, famine, a general breakdown. You'd better stockpile all the supplies you need. Better yet, if you're super-rich, rent a rocket to fly to Mars, and survive in a bunker with your own oxygen tank.

Or another version: there are freeloaders at the border, time to build a wall or fence along the border to keep them out.

The storyline of scarcity, of competition for scarce resources, evaporates the sense of common cause and sharing, of conscience, ethics, responsibility. Of the Linked Arms, of the Covenant required if we (plural, inclusive) are to share the same longhouse, the same *oikos*.

By contrast, "The concept of responsibility is central to the beliefs of the Haudenosaunee," Henry Lickers explains.

> So each animal, plant, and rock in the universe has a purpose and instructions from the Creator of all things and is striving to carry out their responsibilities. Our successes lead to the generation of happiness, while our failures lead to sadness. Whenever we are able to live in balance and harmony with each other and the environment, we create beauty and happiness. Ugliness and sadness [are] created by strife and imbalance. Our responsibility to the Creator is to live in harmony and thereby generate more beauty. As Haudenosaunee, we have always striven for harmony and through this, add to the beauty of Creation.[8]

The story of ecology and economy being in a battle for resources became possible once Western culture separated balance and harmony, responsibility and an intuitive sense of justice from hierarchically imposed rules of law and order. It became possible once we children of the supposed Enlightenment were able to assure ourselves, as we voted some competitor off the island, that we need not feel badly for the loser – because it's just how nature works, "it's only business." Once we had trained ourselves to this strange kind of detachment – the idea that if I can find a loophole in nature's laws, I can hoard all the game animals in a cave for me and my family alone without eventually cutting off my own future supply. The idea that if I can find a gap in the law to excuse me from paying taxes, I need feel no moral quandaries about not contributing to garbage pickup, healthcare or carbon reduction. Anybody would do it, if they could find the same loophole. If they could sneak their money to an offshore tax haven, they would do it too.

Having separated what Henry Lickers calls nature's laws from national laws, we can steal forests or water or coal from Earth's storehouse and say, "it's only business." Regardless of what our conscience says, our legal system allows it. Human laws, organized by "sovereign" nation-states, take precedence over natural laws that are necessary to ecological balance. In contrast to fundamental assumptions of anthropocentric concepts of law, Lickers reminds us that Haudenosaunee teachings

> believe, not in the equality of all people, but in the equality of all of Creation. The animals, plants, rocks, and elements have as much right to

> exist as people do. We believed that, by observing the natural laws of the Earth, we would be able to learn the right way to live. As we studied the environment, we came to believe that we could achieve a state in which we could understand the instructions of the Creator. We called this state the "Good Mind." In this state of the "Good Mind," the proper way to act, feel, and live became obvious to the people and the individuals.[9]

Lickers' words take us back to Tharonhyawá:kon telling Thawískaron and their grandmother that they can enjoy only a small taste of the corn and a bite from one apple until these plants have had time to grow and reproduce. Then there will be plenty for all. His house rules simply observe the laws of plant growth and reproduction. A good mind doesn't hoard abundance in a private cave, doesn't create scarcity for others. It doesn't do so because it understands symbiosis: my life depends upon their lives. If I want to eat corn or rabbit, their families have to thrive. My economy grows with the health of their ecology – *our* shared *eco*. So, a good mind ensures the health of the lives on which it depends. And, when it does consume them, it receives their lives not as rights but as gifts. There will be abundance, if we live observing the natural laws of the Earth.

These principles for good living are simply house rules for how to provide for one's own future, while providing for the future of others within the family of earth.

It's not a competition. It's an *oikos*.

Gift *Oikos*, Commodity *Oikos*

These principles, or house rules, emerge from the world of *Yethi'nihstenha*'s gift *oikos* or homeland, rather than from the misleading storyline of a commodity economy, a homeland founded on competition. But the gift or cooperative way of interacting with the world around us has become so unfamiliar to most of us in Western culture that it will take me a little while to explain – and it's a new way of thinking for me too, so I can only sketch out how much of it I'm coming to understand.

I've spoken earlier of Thomas Hobbes's and John Locke's concept of the "state of nature." For these Enlightenment thinkers, "nature" is a state of chaotic violence from which humans protect themselves by producing order: for Hobbes, humans create political and economic order by giving power over life and death to a dread sovereign, whose absolute authority keeps unpredictable violence at bay. For him, you at least know where you're at with sovereign violence, whereas you would live in never-ending fear if violence can come from anywhere. For Locke, the rationale for social order gets refined as humans submit nature to cultivation: by improving random or disorganized nature through the work of sowing and harvesting, fencing and surveying, humans establish rights to the fruits of their toil. Civilized as opposed to barbaric society emerges, according to Locke, when humans invent orderly arrangements for how they exchange these property rights.

Haudenosaunee thinking, by contrast, does not see nature as that chaotic state of unpredictable, violent threat. As Tharonhyawá:kon said during his work of creation, "human beings will be born here on this earth, and . . . *their minds shall be continually consoled* by the things which the earth shall continue to contain."[10] Toward the end of his recitation of the Creation Story, John Arthur Gibson tells of how the twins Tharonhyawá:kon and Thawískaron eventually complete the cycles of creation in which they have both engaged, and they depart from the earth to return to the Sky World from which their grandmother descended. But the humans the Earth Holder had created keep forgetting their instructions. They neglect to perform the ceremonies, such as the *Ohén:ton Karihwatéhkwen*, the words of Thanksgiving, the Words Before All Else, that align their hearts and minds with the natural laws of earth. So Tharonhyawá:kon has to return, several times, to remind humans how to fit themselves into the orderly world he and his irascible brother had fashioned.

On the third of these visits, the gentle-minded Creator gives some specific examples of how humans are to interact, for example, with plants. Some of these plants have duties to provide medicine, others food. Having assembled the people, Tharonhyawá:kon holds up each plant, one at a time, and describes its uses and qualities – its duties and responsibilities. He asks people to remember each one's name and gives them time to ask questions about each plant. After reviewing several plants, he notes that only a few people remember their names and medicinal functions, so he designates these people as medicine people, the healers. Their gift for remembering the powers of plants gives them duties and responsibilities. When someone falls ill, therefore, they must bring tobacco to ask for the medicine person's help. That person will then take the tobacco, go to the right plant and say (in the translation Hewitt meant to sound biblical): "'Thou here art selected in that one has put dependence on thee, that thou shouldst aid the ill person whose body lies supine yonder, a human being.' Now, at that time, one will name the person, and one will say, 'Here, then, is the thank-offering that one makes, that we should aid that one.'"[11] And the person will leave tobacco for the plant, and then also importune Creator on behalf of the sick person.

In Earth Holder's world, each being has been given its particular life force or energy and its attendant duty. That duty enhances the lives of others, like mycorrhiza transferring sugars to fungi and nutrients to plant roots. Each plant provides its unique medicine, which calls forth thanks from the medicine maker who collects it. One plant, the original tobacco, has the power to enhance communication. Its fragrant smoke, Tharonhyawá:kon tells the people, has the power to lift people's hopes and prayers to where he is in the Sky World. When communicating with medicine plants, then, tobacco should be left as a gift to express thanks to the medicine plant's generosity. Each medicine collector, in turn, offers their particular gift, their understanding of the medicinal powers of plants, to those who are sick, who, in turn, burn tobacco and offer thanks as well. Each being's gift is their responsibility or duty circulated in the economy of medicine, the ecosystem of healing.

This is a truly *universal* healthcare system. It includes the plants on which the whole system depends, not just the humans.

And the whole thing is free. Even though it's an economy: a system of household management that asks each being to exercise their gifts to make health throughout the community. The "payment," a kind of currency or honorarium that indicates trust or belief in the effect or power of each gift, is tobacco, a token of gratitude that trusts in the coming gift of healing.

After teaching the people about medicine plants, Tharonhyawá:kon then speaks about how to relate to the Three Sisters – corn, beans and squash. He instructs the people to perform the Great Feather Dance when they plant these three during the season when the soil warms up, and they are to offer thanks as they do so to each other as well as to him. These three food plants famously support one another, with beans feeding nitrogen to the roots of their sisters, corn and squash; squash's prickly leaves protecting the stems and keeping moisture near the roots of her sisters, corn and beans; and corn providing vertical height for the beans to climb upon so flowers and fruits can ripen in the sun.

In her chapter in *The Words That Come Before All Else*, Brenda LaFrance, a long-serving member on the Mohawk Council of Akwesasne, points out how this cooperation is given, likewise, to the humans that consume the Three Sisters. "The sisters provide essential proteins, vitamins, and minerals," she writes. "The Corn Sister, when washed with ashes, provides calcium enriched food. The Bean Sister provides protein from a vegetable source. The Squash Sister provides natural sugars . . . The Three Sisters are our medicine."[12]

This interaction and interdependency is the true state of nature. Not chaos and violence, as Hobbes and Locke asserted, not unpredictable tooth and claw, but mutual dependency and cooperation. It's not hard to see why Tharonhyawá:kon says that human beings' "*minds shall be continually consoled* by the things which the earth shall continue to contain." This is why Brenda LaFrance writes that "we can learn a great lesson from the Three Sisters – to support each other, to share our space, to protect each other from harm, and to give what we have so that others may live and flourish."[13]

No wonder, then, that when the first of the three (beans) bears fruit, Tharonhyawá:kon instructs the people to choose someone from among themselves to offer the Thanksgiving Address that he had taught them. It's why he instructs them to review the blessings they have received, to perform the Great Feather Dance and to share the beans equally among themselves, to be happy in what is repeatedly provided for them. They are to do the same when corn and then squash ripen later in the year. And this instruction expands to other harvested plants: "When you shall again see all kinds of things, who are Sisters, one to another, upon whom you live, at that place, verily, where the ceremony is marked wherein you shall collect for yourselves the Grand Food. Now, at that place and time, the great rejoicing of the Four Ceremonies shall be performed."[14] As Rick Hill said in a comment on this passage, after the Creator's work itself, "Gratitude is the second force behind the Haudenosaunee economy. Properly applied, it encourages the seeds to fulfill their destiny in fine fashion, combined with the earth, sun, rain, moon, stars and their own spiritual energy, to ripen and produce offsprings that are both a food, and a seed of hope that it will all happen again next season."[15]

By being themselves, by following the instructions they were given, each of the food and medicine plants feed and nurture one another. They are family, sisters to one another. The same is true of the animal Peoples, who depend on the lives of these plants, and who in turn become the food of others, including the plants such as the Three Sisters who, according to one version of the story, grew from the grave mound of the twins' mother. Sisters, then, in a manner of speaking, of the Creator Twins.

The same story of consumption, therefore, can be understood as a story of gifts, which we cultivate by offering thanks, or we can understand it as a story of brutal competition. How we think about it makes it so. Remembering the ceremonies is a way to remind ourselves and each other that peace and happiness come from participating in the cycle as beneficiaries of gifts, not as competitors over ownership or control.

Tyendinaga Mohawk herbalist Suzanne Brant Katsi'tsiarihshion is one of those kinds of people who, like the people in the story about Tharonhyawá:kon teaching the people about plants, has demonstrated aptitude for medicinal knowledge. It's worth quoting at length from her chapter on "The Medicine Plants" in *The Words That Come Before All Else* because she shows how powerfully the way we think about nature's gifts shapes the gifts themselves – and their ability to continue in the cycle as gifts:

> In our way, nobody "owns" the medicines. Nobody "owns" the knowledge of them, either. Our people have kept and shared the knowledge of the

> plants. We have not tried to make the knowledge our property. While we acknowledge that there should be a reward for hard work and research, it troubles us that "patents" are being registered for knowledge that comes from us, and that we shared.
>
> We believe that most medicines are best in their natural state. Pharmaceutical companies often view the plants differently: they try to identify the "active ingredient" and isolate it. Often, they go beyond extracting it to trying to create it synthetically, without even using the plant at all . . . The medicine plants were intended to be used whole, as they were created. There is another side-effect of synthetic medicines: the plants themselves, and the places that they grow, become unnecessary . . .
>
> Our elders always talk about the earth being our mother, a mother who will provide us with all things we need to be her healthy children. The medicines continue to take what they need from our mother, to provide us with what we need, in the hope that we will use them. The medicines are continuing to do their job and to follow their original instructions from the Creator. We are all a reflection of our Mother Earth and as our mother becomes more and more polluted, so do the plants, animals, insects, berries, birds, trees, and people. If we want to become well, we must heal our mother.[16]

If we want to become well, we must heal our Mother the Earth, who nurtures the lives of plants, who in turn heal us. It's a cycle of gifts, a *gift ecology*, rather than a *property-and-patents economy*.

I was not raised with these ideas, these ways of understanding myself, my family, my household, in the world. Neither were most of us who were raised in Industrial Growth Society.

But trying to wrap my mind around these different understandings of the living earth is helping me understand why treaties have been understood so differently by people of the commodity economy as compared to people of the gift ecology. The key word in Canadian legal understandings of treaties is the word "extinguish": in making treaty agreements with the Crown, Canadian courts insist that Indigenous Peoples *extinguished* their rights to the land – meaning that they gave up any say over how it would be used or treated. Understanding land as an inanimate resource or commodity in the tradition of John Locke makes it possible to consider that Indigenous land was "sold" or "traded" to the Crown for certain negotiated items such as education, healthcare or annuities.[17]

This idea completely misses the understanding that people live by means of a cycle of gifts, one in which exchanges of duties and gifts – the responsibilities for recycling those gifts – are never-ending.[18]

Our Western idea of buying and selling assumes the end, rather than continuance, of relationship. When I pay you for a house or a bicycle, it's now mine. Because I paid, because we made a deal, I don't owe you thanks. I don't need to come over to your house a week or a year later to say how much I'm enjoying the view or riding around. I paid you. I never need to speak to you again, if I don't want to. Everything is fair and square. In this sense, our covenant to enter into an agreement to do business ends, is extinguished, by the receipt of payment.

Likewise, we Canadians tend to think each isolated treaty transaction terminated a First Peoples' relationship to land. We think in terms of competing interests, rivalries, not of ongoing symbiosis. We don't think Three Sisters. We think there's a timeline with an end to the Agreement to Link Arms.

In my region, this permanently divided way of thinking remains at the centre of the conflict over the Douglas Creek Estates and 1492 Land Back Lane. Canadian residents and developers in and around Caledonia refer to the "General Surrenders" of Six Nations land in the 1840s as evidence that the Confederacy chiefs terminated their relationship with that land, regardless of the expressed intention of the Haldimand Proclamation to ensure the Haudenosaunee a place that they and their children were to enjoy forever. Extinguishment, in our legal system, insists that Indigenous Peoples gave up any relationship or responsibility to this land, and settlers gained the right to do what we wanted with it. The land itself was not a party to the agreement; it was an object to be exchanged, not a participant with duties and responsibilities within the relationships being worked out.

Understood from the perspective of gift-ecology thinking, however, the treaties did not extinguish Indigenous responsibilities for the land, nor did these agreements terminate the relationship between the "buyers" and the "sellers." The Covenant Chain–Two Row treaty tradition established the English phrasing that has been repeated in British and Canadian records of treaty after treaty across the continent from the seventeenth to the twentieth centuries, insisting over and over again, with People after People, that the accord was meant to last "as long as the sun shines upon this earth, as long as the water still flows, and as long as the grass grows green at a certain time of the year, that is how long our agreement will stand." These treaty agreements established relationships with mutual responsibilities, and the land itself was a central party – a being whose duties and responsibilities needed to be respected – in the terms of the agreement.

My point here: Reorienting our understanding of economy from the management of resources to an ecology of gifts might become a way to restore our divided home. This reorientation involves a change of mind and heart, a change of spirit. "It is human perception," Potawatomi ethno-botanist Robin Wall Kimmerer says, "that makes the world into a gift." Later she says, "Scarcity and plenty are as much qualities of the mind and spirit as they are of the economy. Gratitude plants the seed for abundance."[19]

Conservationists operating within the scarcity mindset of the commodity economy, for example, agitate for the removal of humans as the best way to protect threatened ecosystems. In order to protect a forest or a species, build a fence around it, declare it off-limits to humans so that its few threatened survivors can repopulate themselves. It's true that sometimes the only way for Tharonhyawá:kon to ensure the future gifts of corn or apples is to keep Grandmother and Thawískaron from eating them all before they have a chance to reproduce. But not always. Later, once these food plants have established themselves, the Earth Holder holds up plant after plant to instruct humans how to harvest them and make use of their powers, their gifts. The gift of plants requires the exercise of corresponding gifts from humans – an investment of learning to respect the properties of plants and then of informed labour – cultivation, harvesting, collecting seeds and protecting future generations – in order for the plants to flourish.

Kimmerer provides numerous instances of how humans, when they don't see themselves as forced to choose economy over ecology, become necessary rather than dangerous to the regeneration of the lives around them. In an essay on black ash basket-making, for example, Kimmerer describes how Haudenosaunee basket weavers such as the Akwesasne basket makers – of which Salli Benedict's circle of grandmothers, aunties and mother had been members – approached her lab with the question of whether their harvesting of black ash might reduce the numbers of ash trees in their region over time. To ask such a question in the first place indicates that the basket makers understood their own livelihood to be interdependent with the lives of the trees. They did not curtail their economic analysis to an artificial timeline – so many baskets to be extracted before the "resource" was depleted, before they would have to move house and home to a new region where black ash grows. Taking up the question, Kimmerer and one of her graduate students conducted a study of black ash in upstate New York. They found that, despite the threat of emerald ash borer to the health of ash trees throughout the region, black ash remained in good numbers in two places: where Dutch elm disease had removed elms as competitors and near communities of basket makers. Speaking of this situation, Rick Hill writes that in 1977:

> I was helping to make a film on Akwesasne Mohawk basketmaker Mary Adams. She explained that she has been making baskets all her life, it was her economy. However, the men who helped her harvest the ash trees and pound the logs to make the splints she used, had to go further and further away in order to find trees to harvest. The competition for basketmaking income, almost wiped out the black ash trees at Akwesasne. The Akwesasne Environment Office under Henry Lickers did a study of the trees left and determined that they needed to have an aggressive ash tree protection and seeding program. The Akwesasne Task Force on the Environment developed the ash tree program that has produced the local trees. But a good ash tree can take 40–50 years to grow, so it is a long-term project for sure.[20]

Thirty-six years later, Kimmerer concludes, "Black ash and basket makers are partners in a symbiosis between harvesters and harvested:

ash relies on the people as the people rely on ash."[21] These are practices that arise from an integration of economy and ecology, from a worldview that looks down the length of at least seven generations, from a different mind and heart.

The Gift Is Linking Arms

The same laws govern economy that govern ecology, because it's the same house. No living thing can avoid the relation of consumption. All beings consume the lives of those around them in order to live. And – here is the attendant truth – all beings must inevitably give their lives to be consumed: this law of reciprocity is as true of soil pH as it is of billionaires. And it is true at every scale, from hunter-gatherer societies to hyperindustrialized ones. There are no loopholes in this law, no tax shelters or unpaid dues.

Oftentimes, it can seem that the best way to restore a healthy and balanced ecology would be to remove humans, its biggest consumer. Just as park wardens might restore a river valley's last few aspens by trapping and removing the beavers who cut them down, we might think the best way to restore ecosystem health is to remove the humans. But Tharonhyawá:kon's instructions to this brother about the first corn and first berries, let alone to the people about collecting medicines, remind us that humans can contribute to, rather than detract from, the lives that compose their neighbourhood. Whereas the first student in Kimmerer's lab had studied the health of black ash trees near basket-making communities, another of her students revealed very similar findings with sweetgrass, which was more abundant where it was harvested respectfully by Indigenous neighbours than where it was left alone. The thinning of its growth, whether by being pulled up by the roots or being cut off close to the ground, seemed to stimulate its health and vitality.

These guidelines, these rules of a gift ecology, apply as readily to economies of scale as they do to the intimate harvests of plants. "Taking coal buried deep in the earth," Kimmerer explains, involves "irreparable damage [and] violates every precept of the code. By no stretch of the imagination is coal 'given' to us. We have to wound the land and water to gouge it from Mother Earth." By contrast,

> The wind blows every day, every day the sun shines, every day the waves roll against the shore, and the earth is warm below us. We can understand these renewable sources of energy as given to us, since they are the sources that have powered life on the planet for as long as there has been a planet. We need not destroy the earth to make use of them. Solar, wind, geothermal, and tidal energy – the so-called 'clean energy' harvests – when they are wisely used seem to me to be consistent with the ancient rules of the Honorable Harvest.[22]

Sotsisowah John Mohawk called these sources of energy "technologies of liberation": "Given the impending world crisis in the areas of food and energy," he wrote way back in 1977, the same year Rick Hill was making the film on Mary Adams's basket making, "a comprehensive strategy for survival will include a conception of liberation technologies that free peoples from dependency on economies that are controlled by external interests."[23] His examples were water wheels, solar collectors, biomass plants, woodlots, underground home construction and more.

To develop technologies of liberation, Mohawk declared, we'll need a different mindset, a different story about ourselves in the world, than the one most of us educated in Western culture have been taught all our lives. Echoing the radical Latin American theologians of his times, Mohawk called this story a "liberation theology," which he defined this way:

> Liberation theologies are belief systems that challenge the assumption, widely held in the West, that the Earth is simply a commodity that can be exploited thoughtlessly by humans for the purpose of material acquisition within an ever-expanding economic framework . . . It will be obvious to many non-Western peoples that it is the renewable quality of Earth's ecosystems that makes life possible for human beings on this planet, and that if anything is sacred, if anything determines both the quality and future possibility of life for our species on this planet, it is that renewable quality

of life . . . call it a philosophy or cosmology if you will, but we believe it to be a theology . . . that arises out of our culture and is the product of the Natural World.[24]

This way of understanding ourselves in the world sees through the ruse of dividing up into two teams, limiting the rewards to one trophy that can be won by only one team and cranking up the competitive urgency. I like to watch sports on TV as much as anybody else. I enjoy the tension, the unforeseen matters of chance, the breathtaking agility, strength or endurance of the players, that make a game exciting. But it's a game. Some say humans invented sports so as to absorb these energies and tensions instead of going to war. And the habit of making everything into a competition can destroy the prize itself. Gather excellent chefs on a sound stage kitchen, limit their ingredients and artificially constrain the amount of time they are allowed: you may create excitement, but the food will not taste as good as if they had all the ingredients they need and time to correct their seasoning.

But there are other kinds of games. The Haudenosaunee say games like lacrosse and the bowl game were given to them by the Creator. Let's take the bowl game, which is played, in Rick Hill's account, in order to re-enact the Creation and to reassign duties between the clans. Coloured seeds are used as counters, and the teams are literally playing for the future of food. Some refer to it as the Great Sacred Gamble. Sometimes your clan wins; sometimes they don't. No matter who wins, the other side makes sure that things continue – you could say it is a way of distributing and resorting the seeds, the gene pool of the food plants. It is a competition, but one in which the teams together depend on the toss of the dice, to redistribute the seeds and thus spread the "rising faces which are about to be born."[25]

It's becoming crucial for us humans to realize the delusion of the divided home – the idea that economy can be extracted from ecology without harming itself. It's important to understand it's the story we tell ourselves that screwed up the home we live in. We could improve our good minds if we stopped confusing ourselves with enticing rivalries, sensational scandals or fierce competitions over artificially heightened scarcity. It would be good to acknowledge the realities of what we were given in the home we were born into and think about the best way to carry out our responsibilities so as to support future lives. If we received bitterness and harm from our screwed-up home, how do we do something better than pass on the hurt? And what about the gifts conveyed in every situation – from air to breathe to the unasked-for, undeserved kindness of sky or grass? Every web of life contains gifts requiring appropriate responses – basic, mature response-ability. "When the Creator made Mother Earth," said Jake Thomas in his 1988 oration of the Two Row Wampum agreement, humans were "created to walk upon the Earth to enjoy all nature's fruits, saying that no one will claim Mother Earth except rising faces which are about to be born." Each *oikos*, each bioregional home, requires us to think about how to participate respectfully, how to walk upon the Earth and enjoy nature's fruits, what to give back, how to nurture the lives that have been given and are continuing to be given to us, how to ensure these gifts are passed on to the rising faces that are about to be born into our same household. This isn't a Haudenosaunee thing; it's not something the ones who formulated the *Tehontatenentshonteronhtáhkwa* can do on their own. It has to become *our* thing: learning to reintegrate our house, to Link Arms with the earth. To make the house stronger for those future generations who will then do their best to plant the seeds for the next generation.

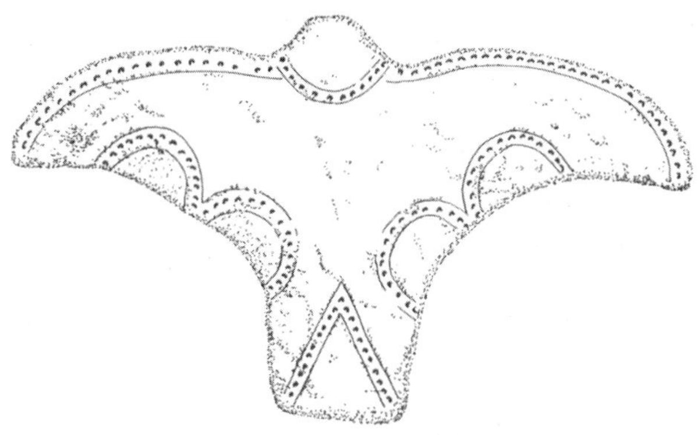

Chapter Seventeen

Awe and Respect

> Another duty [of the Thunderers] is to [confine] the spirits which at one time roamed our Mother Earth and preyed viciously upon the people. The Creator placed these spirits beneath the ground. The Thunderers were given the duty of striking the ground where these spirits attempted to come close to the surface of the earth. The Thunderers are regretful that sometimes a person is struck . . .
> – Jack Jacobs, Akwesasne Mohawk, "The Thunderers," *The Words That Come Before All Else*

> The fear of the Lord is the beginning of wisdom; all those who practice it have a good understanding.
> – Psalm 111:10

You could say that modernity is premised on overcoming and dispensing with the crippling fears and superstitions that made humans afraid of what they didn't know – of evil spirits or dark terrors beyond their immediate understanding. Modern people turned instead to reason, logic and the scientific method to isolate mysterious phenomena so that, shorn of their terrifying inscrutability, they could be studied and explained. By so doing, curious minds could face and overcome irrational panic and the fight-or-flight instincts that ruled what Hobbes called the violent and chaotic "state of nature."

You could say that we modern humans try to protect ourselves from the vulnerability and exposure we might experience in the clearing at the edge of the woods – the edge of what we know.

This is the precise site where Ayonwátha's wampum emerged in Haudenosaunee civilization as a step-by-step, bead-by-bead way to calm troubled minds and make rational communication – to reduce grief, fear, the impulse for violence. Set against the context of brutality, chaos and treachery, the Peacemaker, Jigonsaseh, Ayonwátha and the other leaders instituted Haudenosaunee modernity by prizing reason and good-mindedness as defences against the threats of terror and violence.

Modernity's Fear of the Edge of the Woods

Both Western and Haudenosaunee societies appealed to reason, therefore, as a way to address the anxiety and fear that occurs at the edge of the known or familiar. Yet I believe they understood this mental disturbance in very different ways. One of the biggest differences between European and Haudenosaunee approaches to reason or good-mindedness is that, from the Edenic fall from Paradise to Tennyson's infamous "nature red in tooth and claw" or Hobbes's violent "state of nature," the former considered nature non-rational and chaotic and therefore tended to try to protect human society from its anarchy by extracting humans from the web of bioregional life, while the latter perceived nature as orderly, good and rational, and therefore the source of civilization. Europeans tend to see civilization, culture, society as what humans have made by vanquishing nature, while Haudenosaunee see nature as the first culture, the origin and model for civilization or society. Because of this difference, Enlightenment images of the "good" aimed to transcend nature and the physical world, whether by religion or technology, while Haudenosaunee concepts of reason and peaceful living were sought *within* creation, in the cycles, energies and interactions of the earth. For Indigenous cultures such as the Haudenosaunee, the manifold beings of nature hold the ultimate powers, of life and death. As such they must be feared – that is, deeply and profoundly respected.[1] It makes sense, it's reasonable, to hold them in reverential esteem, in awe.

This, for example, is the function of the Thunderers in the Haudenosaunee Creation Story, who are frightening, to be sure, but who function as grandfathers who use their terrifying voices and bolts of lightning to protect the world from even larger, unseen dangers. At the end of their long rivalry, after Tharonhyawá:kon had overcome his restless brother Thawískaron and managed to push his predatory creatures into the underworld, the kind-hearted Creator brother says he will call the Thunderers, *Hadiweñnodad̨ie's* in Onondaga, to direct the rains to wash the earth and to keep Flint's vicious animals in check, so that they don't destroy the humans and other animals. In his chapter on "The Thunderers" in *The Words That Come Before All Else,* Jack Jacobs explains:

> One duty of the Thunderers is to continue to make fresh water or bring the rain, which replenishes or renews the water supply . . . Another duty is to water what the Creator has planted on our Mother Earth, so that these plants and the gardens of the people can grow well . . . Another duty is to keep the spirits, which at one time roamed our Mother Earth and preyed viciously upon the people. The Creator placed these spirits beneath the ground. The Thunderers were given the duty of striking the ground where these spirits attempted to come close to the surface of the earth. The Thunderers are regretful that sometimes a person is struck, for these spirits try to seek cover by hiding under people as they rise to the surface of the earth.[2]

I recall a conversation with Rick Monture, Mohawk Turtle Clan professor at McMaster University, saying that he's heard older people say that this is why they are so distrustful of oil extraction and the fracking of gas. The ancient monsters, like dinosaurs, who preyed upon early humans have been pressed underground for thousands of years. Their angry and fiery spirits now are being unearthed as fossil fuels, which are now being heedlessly piped in, with their toxic energies and fiery effects, to where people live. Humans are not respecting the lesson of the Thunderers, who see this danger and do their best to keep these dangerous creatures under the ground.

The earth is alive, Creator had said. That life force is of many kinds and energies, and the first rule for living peacefully with those energies is to respect them, to hold them in a certain amount of awe. A concept of the spirit within all things requires a ceremonial approach, a mixture of thanksgiving and propitiation, even of awe, with which we humans approach other lives and other beings, understanding that those beings may have positive or negative energies within them, and we need to mitigate the dangerous ones and enhance the beneficial ones. Essentially, this approach constitutes the attitudinal and ceremonial awareness that prepares humans to enter into the reciprocal relations outlined by Tharonhyawá:kon when he instructed medicine people to leave tobacco for the plants they harvested or when he asked the game animals to give their lives so that his brother and grandmother could eat.

This kind of respect is at the core of the original instructions.

If there remain any vestiges of this posture of awe-filled respect in mainstream Western thinking, it's likely to be associated with religious traditions. Take, for example, the passage from Jewish scripture quoted at the head of this chapter: "The fear of the Lord is the beginning of wisdom." For many post-Enlightenment people, concepts like the "fear of the Lord" reveal the regressive mindset of religion. Is not fear the opposite of good-mindedness, of anything we might consider to be wisdom? For many among us, this idea encapsulates how religion imprisons human potential and liberty by mongering fear. "The fear of the Lord is the beginning of knowledge" (Proverbs 1:7), we read in the Jewish scriptures; "Fear God and keep his commandments, for this is the whole duty of man" (Ecclesiastes 12:13).[3] And, in case we assume that injunctions to "fear the Lord" may be isolated to Jewish religion, we should recall that the Christian scriptures insist that we should "work out [our] own salvation with fear and trembling" (Philippians 2:13). Likewise, the Qur'an uses the Arabic word "taqwa" (fear of God, a word repeated over two hundred times in the Qur'an) to insist that "indeed, God is with those who fear Him and those who do good" (Quran 16:128). Like the Christian scriptures, the Qur'an attaches salvation to fear of Allah – "whoever fears God – He will pardon him his sins and grant him a great reward" (Quran 65:5).

For the most part, the modern rejection of fear as a human or social good has tended to dismiss these kinds of religious injunctions. For there are many good reasons to reject or overcome fear: from the person trapped in an abusive household to those too intimidated to speak truth to power, we know that finding the courage to face and reject the self-constraints of fear are essential to realizing a person or society's creative potential. Indeed, human-generated fear is usually a strategy of control: whether a threat of violence by state police, a terrorist cell, an abusive spouse or a back-alley mugger, the intent is to commandeer the victim's freedom. Whether dictators or terrorists, you could say they use exceptional violence – Hobbes's unregulated "state of nature," where people live in "continual fear, and danger of violent death"[4] – to gain control. By contrast, modern "civilization" is built around regulating nature and human society so as to reduce the terror of living in constant fear.

I have no desire to suggest that people should somehow return to living in an unregulated state of fear. That would be arguing to live under the terrifying thumb of Atotáhrho before he had the snakes combed out of his hair. But something has been lost in modernity's total rejection of fear – and that is a healthy amount of what we might call *awe*, something more closely resembling a reverential respect, mixed with wonder and some fear, as well as a practical awareness of the consequences of ignoring the powers and energies of other beings who live beyond our ken, beyond our control.[5] Rather than living in a disenchanted, devitalized world where all non-human beings are "things," a series of manipulable objects, truly self-actualized humans retain a reasonable awe or even fear of the powers and dynamics that exceed our current knowledge and understanding.

One way to understand how there could be any wisdom in awe or "the fear of the Lord," then, is to understand this kind of fearful wonder as a respect for the inviolable otherness, the sheer difference and inner vitality, of other beings. This experience is encapsulated in the vulnerability you feel at the edge of the woods.

This is my understanding of what is evoked in three central concepts at the heart of the Covenant Chain–Two Row Wampum: *ka'nikonhriyó'tshera't* ("the Good Mind," which includes wisdom, flexibility, magnanimity and self-discipline, as well as discernment, pragmatism, kindness and wit) can only grow out of a certain amount of mutual knowledge and respect, which builds friendship between different beings so they can enjoy *ka'shatsténhsera* ("power, the ability to act," including capacity of body, mind or spirit, as well as ruggedness, toughness and durability), and the result is *skén:nen* ("peace," but also the physical health, emotional wellness, social cohesion, ecological balance and spiritual fulfilment or harmony within a multidimensional thriving world).[6] Lack of respect, the inability to feel awe at the sacred and particular powers of other beings makes us heavy-booted egotists trampling tender shoots and tendrils in our own garden. This self-absorbed obliviousness can be witnessed throughout Industrial Growth Society from Alcoa's poisoning of water, air and land around Akwesasne to basic, everyday naïveté about respecting the life forces of the natural world. The newspapers where I live, in Hamilton, Ontario, frequently publish stories of hikers needing rope rescue after having fallen from the cliffs around waterfalls where they were trying to take selfies in their flip-flops on the slippery rocks. This last week, CBC News carried the story of a firefighter who was seriously injured as he and his crew were trying to rescue a group of hikers who had climbed over the safety fences at Albion Falls and trapped themselves on a precarious ledge.

A little dose of fear is the beginning of wisdom.

It's good to have a practical sense that some things are sacred, not so much in the sense of being secret or mysterious, but of being inviolable. We should not mess with them. Sometimes, this awareness is so basic that it's embarrassing to have to say it out loud. Earlier, I quoted Onondaga faithkeeper Oren Lyons about how the laws of nature are absolute and uncompromising. If you go hunting improperly dressed for the cold, you will freeze to death. If you swing your steel golf club out on the fairway during a thunderstorm, you risk the wrath of lightning. If you don't eat, if you don't drink, you'll die. The same is true for dogs or humans. This is why government laws need to accord with nature's laws, which will prevail every time.[7] Lyons insists that an awareness of things being sacred need not be super-mystical or religious, and they are not opposed to the attentive, scientific work of studying everyday things. Indeed, the more you understand winter weather, how ice crystals form, where the water sources are or how slippery mossy rocks can be, the better you will be able to navigate the inviolable natural law. This law is, in part, about the limits to human exceptionalism, to human ambitions to transcend nature's laws and avoid mortality. If you dump PCBs into the water that you, your neighbours and the deer drink, you will all die. Irrational faith in magical technological solutions – in instant ways to clean up those PCBs and to be absolved from dumping them there in the first place – will not save your drinking water, let alone your soul.

A renewed perception of the sacred – by which I mean that which demands ultimate respect or reverence – within the vital web that constitutes earth is not restricted to Indigenous philosophies alone. More and more eco-conscious members of Western culture are realizing, belatedly, the necessity of this kind of healthy fear, this life-giving awe. "Every being has its own interior, its self, its mystery, its numinous aspect," wrote Fordham University environmental philosopher Thomas Berry in *Dream of the Earth*.

> To deprive any being of this sacred quality is to disrupt the larger order of the universe. Reverence will be total or it will not be at all. The universe does not come to us in pieces any more than a human individual stands before us with some part of its being. Preservation of this feeling for reality in its depths has been considerably upset in these past two centuries of scientific analysis and technological manipulation of the earth and its energies. During this period, the human mind lived in the narrowest bonds that it has ever experienced. The vast mythic, visionary, symbolic world with its all-pervasive numinous qualities was lost. Because of this loss, we made our terrifying assault upon the earth with an irrationality that is stunning in enormity, while we were being assured that this was the way to a better, more humane, more reasonable world.[8]

Berry, who died in 2009, was a Catholic priest of the Passionate Order. He criticized his own Christian religion, along with other Western religions, as well as science and technology, for contributing to the destruction of our planetary home by trying to liberate human aspiration from the web of earthly interdependencies. Essentially, he wrote, Western religions and techno-science aspire to *transcend* the earth, to escape what Oren Lyons calls the natural law. Calling himself a "geologian" rather than a "theologian," Thomas Berry lamented that "unfortunately Western religious traditions have been so occupied with redemptive healing of a flawed world that they tend to ignore creation as it is experienced in our times. Consequently, one of the basic difficulties of the modern West is its division into a secular scientific community, which is concerned with creative energies, and a religious community, which is concerned with redemptive energies."[9] Both, he suggested, are so mesmerized by a vision of humans-only upward "progress" that they can only view the web of living things down below as resources to fuel that airborne fantasy. I know it seems strange to consider this kind of transcendent habit as "narrow thinking," but its unquestioned belief in progressive improvement, of ultimate liberty from the limitations of life on earth generated either by technological or religious redemption, has blinkered us to the real complex of interdependencies in which we live.

How Fear of Human Law Overwhelms Respect for Natural Law

Political life in the city of Hamilton was rocked in the past few years by City Hall's suppression of information about a leak of untreated sewage and storm-drain water into Chedoke Creek in a fiasco that has come to be known as "Sewergate." Hamilton is geologically divided between the lower part of the city that stretches along Hamilton Harbour at the western tip of Lake Ontario and the upper part of the city above the Niagara Escarpment that runs like a curved and jagged three-hundred-foot-high wall between the two parts. The city grew gradually from its first buildings scattered along the shoreline below the cliff faces in the late eighteenth century and then mushroomed into suburbs above the escarpment in the mid-twentieth century. Accordingly, the infrastructure above the wall is new compared to that below.

Whereas the system of pipes that drains water from streets and parking lots above the rockface is separate from the system that drains away sewage from homes and businesses, the pipes under the streets and neighbourhoods below the escarpment were laid before anyone had thought of separating sewage from street runoff. What this means is that when there's a big rainstorm and the pipes below the escarpment can't drain the system quickly enough, sewage combined with storm drain water has had to be flushed into the creeks and marshes of the watershed. Combined with the effluent and toxic runoff from over a hundred years of steel-making in the city, this contamination has accrued in the watershed until Hamilton was listed in 1987 as a "major site of concern" in the Great Lakes Water Quality Agreement between Canada and the United States.

In recent years, therefore, the City of Hamilton has been trying to address this problem by installing massive underground holding tanks called Combined Sewer Overflow tanks in low-lying areas below the escarpment. To my knowledge, by 2021 the City had constructed and buried fourteen of these CSO tanks throughout the lower neighbourhoods. The idea is that these hockey-arena-sized tanks can store the water from a storm until dry days, when it can be gradually pumped down to the Woodward Avenue Treatment Plant for cleaning.

That is, if everything works as planned.

The technical glitch that sparked "Sewergate" came to public attention when the *Hamilton Spectator* revealed in November 2019 that the Cathedral Park CSO tank between King and Main Streets, with a capacity to hold seventy-five million litres of stormwater runoff, had been leaking into nearby Chedoke Creek for four years. The problem was a literal sewer gate. One of the tank's massive steel doors had been stuck open a few inches and, over those four years, an estimated twenty-four billion litres of contaminated water, mixing street runoff with sewage from the CSO, had leaked into the creek and from there into the fragile ecology of the marsh known as Cootes Paradise. The door is controlled electronically, so inspectors occasionally checked cameras, but no one actually went down into the foul-smelling tank to see how tightly the bottom of the huge door met the floor. Our city's trust in technology let us down.

The leak is terrible news indeed, but on its own, it was not what caused the biggest outrage among city residents.

The cause of the outrage is that City Council had known about the leak for eleven months – since at least January of that year – and that, not once, but twice the council had voted to keep the leak secret from the public. Councillors who were embarrassed when the story was published claimed that they had been advised by their lawyers not to inform the public so as to avoid legal reprisals.

Essentially, you could say that fear of human lawsuits overwhelmed respect for natural law, so our political representatives voted to keep the violation of the watershed "secret."

The point, however, is that, seen from another perspective, it never was and never had been a secret. Evidence of the constant pollution of the creek was everywhere. The beings of nature were speaking loudly.

As far back as November 14, 2015, Indigenous Hamilton women "water walkers" Kristen Villebrun and Wendy Bush had begun holding a floating protest on a raft in Hamilton Harbour where they called attention to what the waves revealed: needles, feces, plastics, consumer detritus piling up on the shore. When Ward 1 Councillor Aidan Johnson visited the protestors and viewed what they showed him on the shoreline, he said, "It looks to me like there are layers of debris. There's like an archeological phenomenon going on of layers."[10] You just have to look at what nature's layers reveal.

Two and a half years later, another Hamilton resident, John Boddy, troubled by the stench wafting off Chedoke Creek, called the Ministry of Environment, Conservation and Parks. After coming down to the creek and smelling it too, the MoE began tests of what was in the water. Around the same time, in 2018, my friend John Terpstra published *Daylighting Chedoke*, a book in which he traced the human history of the creek, and especially how it grew more and more polluted as it became increasingly channelized since the 1960s in underground storm drains above the escarpment. Later, in July of that year, Public Health Ontario informed the province that they had found E. coli levels of 3.4 million bacterial units per 100 millilitres of water. These results were confirmed by further tests conducted by the city, the province and the Hamilton Conservation Authority, until the city vacuum-cleaned the creek for two weeks, removing 242,000 litres of "floatables" out of the creek.

None of these signs were secret.[11]

Throughout these years, Tys Theysmeyer, the Head of Natural Areas at the Royal Botanical Gardens, and his staff had been working valiantly to restore the health of Cootes Paradise. I once heard Tys say in a public talk that half the fish of western Lake Ontario are born in Cootes. Water health in the marsh is crucial to the ecology of the entire region. The RBG has made effort upon effort to protect and restore Cootes, from building a fish weir back in the 1980s to keep Eurasian carp from digging up the silt at the bottom of the marsh so native plants can grow and oxygenate the water to replanting acres of marsh with cattails, lily pads and other restorative plants. They had seen good results: bald eagles have been raising young for the first time in fifty years in Cootes Paradise, evidence that the contaminants in the water have been reduced enough for them to successfully hatch eggs once again. But there were also failures. RBG staff had noticed die-off among the new water lilies, for example, in the summer of 2018, and Tys and his colleagues, such as Chris McLaughlin, Executive Director of the Bay Area Restoration Council, were trying to determine where the pollution was coming from. They had already identified Chedoke Creek as a major problem. So the secret was not a secret.

The whole sewergate incident demonstrates a distortion of awe and respect by fear of fellow humans. We try to keep our eco-sins "secret" so as to avoid the judgments of other people. And because the fear of other humans preoccupies us, takes up the forefront of our anxious attention, we seem naively unaware of the ultimate judgment hanging over us.

If we dump used band-aids or condoms into our toilets; if we flush antibiotics, antidepressants or goldfish down into the CSO holding tanks, these will mix there with feces, excessive quantities of nitrogen and E. coli. And if we aren't worried about the increasing number of major "rain events" we have been experiencing in this region each year, and if we don't hire enough inspectors to check the gates in our Combined Sewer Overflow tanks, we will soon have watersheds filled with undrinkable water flushed out of our own sewage systems that will sicken humans, plants and animals alike.

This is no secret. As everyone from residents like Kristen Villebrun, Wendy Bush and John Boddy to public institutions like Public Health and the Royal Botanical Gardens knows, a healthy fear of the consequences is our only protection against nature's non-negotiable rules. It doesn't take rocket science to see this.

Buried somewhere in City Council's effort to keep the sewage leak secret is a residual but misguided "fear of the Lord." It's not a religious terror of the Almighty, but there's a shame, an anxiety about being caught out, of not attending to our responsibilities in the natural world, of hoping we can transcend its rules. Until it says differently.

The fear of the Lord, which I am borrowing from Western religion's old language for awe and respect for the powers of creation on which our lives depend, is the beginning of wisdom – the beginning of environmental ethics. This is a fear that sees beyond the fear of social conventions or even of current human laws, especially ones premised on a dead or inanimate natural world. This is the kind of reverence we accord to the Thunderers, whose lightning awakens the hairs on the back of our necks – and keeps the monsters underground. Whether ceremonies of planting trees to sequester carbon and reverse global warming, community organizing to counter corporations' proposals to pave over wetlands, ceremonies to purify the water after sewergate or communal gatherings to resist the building of new pipelines, these are ways we formally express awe and even fear of the consequences of flouting nature's laws. It's how we link arms to make harmony with powers that are bigger than ourselves.

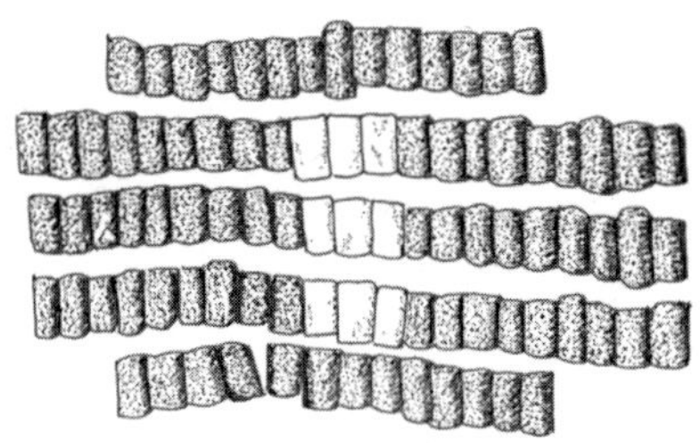

Chapter Eighteen

Dish With One Spoon–Land Back

> Decolonization means giving the land back so that Indigenous people can live in good relations. . . . Thus, the work of decolonization is the work of restoring our relations.
> – Joseph M. Pierce, "A Manifesto for Speculative Relations"[1]

So what do we Canadians *do* about restoring our Covenant Chain–Two Row agreement to share the river of life in peace with linked arms and clear minds? How will we rebuild broken relationships with land, with the Indigenous Peoples who have been its denizens and guardians for centuries? How will we renew our alliances with and within the biomes on which we depend?

How do Canadians reconnect with the family of earth – our Sister Water; Grandmother Moon; Elder Brother Sun; plant, mineral and animal neighbours? How do we open ourselves to the awe and respect that can enable us to live interdependently within the ecosystem that is our family? How do we do something more than generate a report or launch an inquiry?

I wrote the first draft of this chapter in the wake of media reports that ground-penetrating radar had detected the remains of close to a thousand children buried in unmarked graves at the Kamloops and Cowessess Residential Schools. The subsequent outpouring of grief and rage across the country was heartfelt and moving, but this revelation should not have been "news." Anyone who has listened to survivors or their descendants knows there are unmarked graves surrounding most residential schools. Within weeks of this news story, investigations at other residential schools across the country were initiated that will undoubtedly reveal many more hidden gravesites.

"Survivors tell us there are children buried out here," said our guide when we stepped outside the kitchen at the back of the Mush Hole (also known as the Mohawk Institute in Brantford, Ontario). I had joined a tour of twenty-five people back in 2015. We stared at the cluster of trees and shorn grass covering the ground where the children once laboured in what had been the school's apple orchard and garden. She said that, while the fresh lettuce, carrots and potatoes the children tended got wagoned off to market, they themselves returned each day to the dining hall where they faced the endless bowls of mush that gave the school its unofficial name. "The school authorities didn't want people to know how many children were sick and dying," she said, "so they just buried them quietly. Digging tools like pickaxes, shovels and wheelbarrows were being used out here all the time anyway, so citizens of Brantford would hardly notice."

We in the tour group shaded our eyes from the sun as she spoke. The blue sky was filled with birdsong. The uncut grass beyond the trees waved in the breeze. Someone in our group took out a Kleenex and blew their nose.

This is the earth on which we walk every day.

The Mohawk Institute stands on a tiny piece of Six Nations land surrounded by the municipality of Brantford. As I've noted earlier in this book, Six Nations has less than 5 percent of the land set aside for them in the 1784 Haldimand Proclamation. The money they had raised from early land leases and sales, and then set aside in trust funds "managed" (!) by the British and then Canadian governments to provide for Six Nations' future, was mismanaged and stolen. Despite Indian agents like William Claus and Samuel Jarvis being charged with fraud over missing funds and lands, no one ever went to jail, nor were money or lands returned.[2] The Confederacy Chiefs had to request allocations from their own trust fund to operate their nation. The local Indian agent in Brantford or the superintendent in Ottawa made the final determination on how Six Nations trust funds were to be spent. The resulting impoverishment has generated many problems, from a dependency on Ottawa-funded schooling to the out-migration of people looking for work and the strain on family units, as well as high rates of children adopted out to white families. The capacity of leaders on the Grand River territory to address these challenges has been undermined by political divisions introduced by the Canadian government's withdrawal of recognition from the traditional Confederacy Council and imposition of the band (or "elected") council in 1924. These divisions continue to trouble Haudenosaunee decision-making right up to this day, so that developers like Foxgate Developments Inc., for example, claim that they paid for the approval of band council before they began laying out the streets and underground drain systems at the site they call McKenzie Meadows, now occupied by Haudenosaunee land defenders and renamed 1492 Land Back Lane. We have fallen a long way away from the three links of the agreement that bound newcomers and the Haudenosaunee in respect, trust and friendship.

How do we restore the Linked Arms? How do we rebuild peace on the river of life? How could we rebuild respect, or trust?

I must confess that the complexity of the question – with millions of non-Haudenosaunee having occupied the lands identified in the Haldimand Proclamation and the privatization of these Haudenosaunee lands consistently approved in Canadian courts since the 1830s and 1840s – makes any process for rectifying the injustice and returning the land boggle the mind. Any fair-minded look at the sordid history of the Haldimand Tract would agree that the 1784 initiative to set aside land for Haudenosaunee allies in compensation for what they had lost in upstate New York has been betrayed and that the Haldimand lands that were not legally leased and properly paid for should be returned to the Haudenosaunee.

But just because the problem is complex doesn't mean nothing can be done. As the unresolved standoffs at Douglas Creek Estates and

McKenzie Meadows indicate, years of deflection and avoidance have not made the underlying question evaporate. Indeed, in 2021 members of the Confederacy Council announced a moratorium on any further development throughout the Haldimand Tract without their approval.[3] The injustice still cries out, and the suppressed violence resurfaces in ground-penetrating radar, truth and reconciliation inquiries, court injunctions, arrests, scuffles in the streets and police raids – not to mention poverty, lack of clean drinking water and long-festering resentment of betrayal in the hearts and minds of their long-standing treaty partner.

When things get overwhelming and confusing, the story of Ayonwátha's invention of wampum reminds us to look as steadily as we can through the confusing maelstrom and to regain a good, clear mind by focusing on the beads, one at a time, to retrace a consistent flow of thought by focusing on one physical, basic thing at a time. In the present instance, for example, we could follow the Haudenosaunee practice that Salli Benedict demonstrated, above, of keeping our eyes on *Yethi'nihstenha*, Mother Earth, the land. We can try to sort through the welter by focusing on one thing, starting with the ground that holds us up, the Earth. What actually happens to land throughout the vagaries of settler colonial society's interactions with Indigenous Peoples?

Yellowknives Dene scholar Glen Coulthard observes that in the very period when a "politics of recognition" means governments reluctantly acknowledge things like the attempted genocide of residential schools, Indigenous rights to self-government or the duty to consult with Indigenous Peoples before putting industrial shovels in the ground, more and more land continues to be removed from Indigenous jurisdiction. *Recognition*, says Coulthard, has become a political distraction that masks ongoing removal of Indigenous relations with land. For this reason, Eve Tuck (Unangax̂) and K. Wayne Yang write that decolonization cannot be treated as a metaphor. It's true that we collectively – Indigenous and non-Indigenous people alike – need to decolonize our minds, our language and our ways of thinking, but if "decolonization" remains abstract rhetoric, if it becomes a metaphor we use for any kind of effort to address injustice, and no land is ever returned to Indigenous jurisdiction, then decolonization becomes an empty signifier. I observed this emptying happening earlier when the Hawthorn Report of 1967 suggested that "decolonization" would occur when Indigenous people "accommodate themselves to the requirements of an impersonal, bureaucratic, technological society." Hawthorn's hollowed-out "decolonization" turns into its opposite, requiring Indigenous Peoples' complete capitulation to Industrial Growth Society. According to this line of thinking, *Yethi'nihstenha* – "she to us exerts her capacity and strength to keep us living now" – is turned into an inanimate object, open to extraction. Her children and dependants are completely absorbed into the colonial machine.

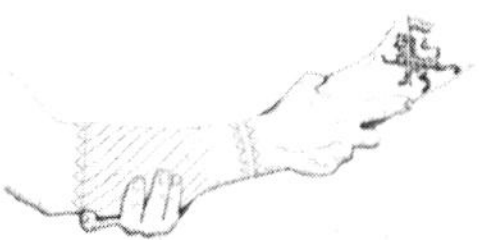

Land Back

As Indigenous leaders and thinkers have been saying for years, then, Indigenous culture, beliefs and laws need to be restored in strength to keep the rogue and misguided Canadian ship from permanently destroying the river on which we all depend. Two things need to happen if the river of life is to sustain us all into the future. First, Indigenous land and waterways literally need to be returned to Indigenous jurisdiction, and second, we non-Indigenous people need to learn the rules for how to live sustainably from our elder brothers with whom we Linked Arms when our ancestors first arrived in these lands. In short, this second element requires Indigenous governance in Canadian affairs, what some are calling "*governance back*."[4] That is to say, the expansion of Indigenous jurisdiction needs to reshape more generally how we conduct affairs throughout Canada.

"You came out of the Ground in a Country that lies beyond the Seas," Canesatego reminded the British governors back in 1744, "there you may have a just Claim, but here you must allow us to be your elder Brethren, and the Lands to belong to us long before you knew any thing of them." There's so much we newcomers still don't know about them. There's still so much to learn.

I know the initiatives outlined here and the subsequent chapter may seem radical to some, but, in fact, they are *conservative* in the original sense of the word: they would constitute a collective return to the original instructions given to the Peoples who came out of this ground, a return to Canada's founding norms, its initial constitutional precedents, and they would conserve and protect the basis of our future as a way of life.[5] The first – literal return of land – constitutes a basic fulfilment of the *Tékeni Teyohà:te* agreement to keep one's culture, beliefs and laws in one's own canoe – that is, it would restore the vessel Indigenous Peoples need to maintain their way of life. Taking our lead from the original division of territories in the Creation Story, we would see the wisdom of protecting Tharonhyawá:kon's part of the island from Thawískaron's predatory creatures. It is undeniable that the philosophies and practices of the Ship have caused grave harm to our Mother, and that the values, beliefs and traditions of the Canoe might be the only way to undo that harm.

And second – Canadians learning to live by the rules laid out in their Haudenosaunee elder brothers' original instructions – would help us learn how to rebalance and restore our primary relationships in such a way as to ensure the peace and health of the river – of *Yethi'nihstenha*, the ecosystem that mothers us, what Salli Benedict called the cultural system of support, on which we all depend. Rick Hill explains, "Indigenous jurisdiction is driven by the fact that nature, our Mother, sets the ground rules. Humans are not 'stewards' of the land, meaning we are not in charge of the land, or in charge of its regeneration. The earth is a living network of reciprocal relationships and has its own spiritual energy to make things right. The earth is self-regulating, so Indigenous jurisdiction consists of social rules and protocols meant to help us remain in harmony with the earth's rules."[6]

By contrast, what we have had in Canada ever since it was officially constituted in 1867 is Dominion given over to corporate extraction – from Sir John A. Macdonald's Canadian Pacific Railway to Justin Trudeau's Trans Mountain pipeline.

To cite a recent example, since 2018 Mi'kmaq protestors have been fighting the Alton Gas Company's bid to frack gas out of the ground by pumping enormous quantities of water into underground caverns, which will, in turn, sluice high levels of saline into the Mi'kmaq fishing grounds on the Shubenacadie River. Hearing that Alton Gas had received a court injunction to remove protestors from the site, one of the

Mi'kmaq observed, "Canada is not a nation. Canada is a corporation."[7]

What a situation like this points out is that, ever since its official founding in 1867, Canada has replaced the *Tehontatenentshonteronhtáhkwa* with a tacit agreement to link arms with the captains of Industrial Growth Society. Without any official rejection of the Covenant Chain, in behaviour and action Canada has made its primary alliance with corporate extraction. This distorted covenant has so compromised the health of the rivers and the ecosystems that we are in desperate need of a new – but actually old – set of ground rules, that could come through renewing our relationship with *Yethi'nihstenha* and the Peoples who have retained their allegiance to her cultural system of support. We need to pull on the old Covenant Chain to alert our partners to our need for help, to learn what solutions to our predicament can be suggested by our allies from the "culture, beliefs, and laws" of the canoe.[8]

Many Canadians will fear this rebalancing, afraid that turning land back to Indigenous jurisdiction and returning to our primary alliance with Peoples who follow the original instructions will jeopardize our future livelihoods. But I ask those who harbour these fears: What alternatives are there? Time after time, we have seen the shaping of federal and provincial policies to privilege the agents of industrial extraction, jeopardizing our collective futures, through any number of government-approved and government-protected activities, from clear-cutting globally crucial forests that provide carbon sequestration and oxygen replenishment, to strip-mining or urbanizing arable land, to flushing clean water through oil-rich shale into toxic tailings ponds and spewing PCBs or carcinogenic particulate matter into the air we breathe and the water we drink. So you have to ask: How has the current alliance between government and industrialized growth economies been working for us so far? If it has provided livelihoods, even remarkable wealth, for some Canadians over the past century, what about those it has not benefitted, let alone the ones who hope to live in the future? Will the same system of shareholder-required profits produce companies that can restore the river in ways that can provide for the next seven generations?

In an online webinar on "Land Governance: Towards a More Just Future" hosted by the David Suzuki Foundation on May 20, 2021, one of the panellists, Doug White (Kwulasultun), a lawyer who is former Chief of the Snuneymuxw First Nation in Nanaimo and Chair of the BC First Nations Justice Council, offered the view that the Land Back movement is not meant just to benefit Indigenous Peoples, it is a positive step for *all* Canadians. If we wish to ensure land will still be willing and able to sustain the lives of future generations, if we want climate justice that constitutes justice for all, he suggested, we need a different set of guiding principles, a different way of proceeding. Indigenous self-determination, he explained, is not a threat to Canadians, but an active concern *for* Canadians. Indigenous jurisdiction over traditional lands is about mutual well-being, he said, a concrete instance of "unconditional love" (his words) about "how you [Canadians] are doing." That is to say, Indigenous laws about ensuring the health and well-being of the land's interlocking set of ecosystems can guide Canadians back on track to caring for ourselves, let alone each other, for protecting and providing for our own future, not just Indigenous Peoples'.

We are back to the question of *protection* at the heart of our Agreement to Link Arms that goes back to the Royal Proclamation and beyond to the 1701 Treaty of Albany: Who is protecting who and from what? We are at a point now, White said, where Canada has to evolve into a new kind of federalism premised on the Two Row Wampum. Here he echoed the words of another panellist, Grand River Mohawk law professor and past president of the Native Women's Association of Canada Beverley Jacobs, who emphasized the principles of reciprocity and responsibility conveyed in the Covenant Chain–Two Row relation.[9] The priority, she explained, is not rights, but a mutually concerned relationship that builds from Indigenous understandings of law built upon ecological principles of healthy autonomy, ongoing and future interdependency, and sharing. Our collective responsibility, Doug White added, is to ensure land relations for future generations. "These changes won't happen," he said, "until the people of Canada demand them."

Aimée Craft, the Anishinaabe host for the webinar, agreed. She observed that there are many different perspectives on what Land Back could look like. To her mind, it's not about drawing conflictual lines between Canadians and Indigenous Peoples. Rather, it's about working within our own spheres of activity toward a common goal. To do that, however, she suggested that Indigenous Peoples don't want a "seat at the table" in Ottawa or at any provincial legislature. They don't need to be "consulted" within a system of decision-making that is completely stacked in favour of a government-supported extraction economy. Instead, she echoed the invitation she keeps hearing from her elders: "come to our house," take a seat at a table governed by Indigenous laws and values.

This is how I understand John Borrows's call, in his book tellingly entitled *Recovering Canada*, for "Indigenous control of Canadian affairs." Borrows adapts this wording from Harold Cardinal's famous call for "Aboriginal control of Aboriginal affairs" in *The Unjust Society* (1969). Borrows notes that while Cardinal's phrasing was a powerful way to resist Trudeau Senior's effort to wipe out Aboriginal and treaty rights in the 1969 White Paper, it restricts Indigenous law and influence to the tiny bits of land remaining on reserves. It hampers Indigenous Peoples' ability to exercise their responsibilities under Indigenous laws to their traditional territories – which extend far beyond the boundaries of any reserve.

What watershed is limited to the size of a reserve?

In my region, for example, "Aboriginal control of Aboriginal affairs" makes it impossible for Six Nations People to ensure the health of the Grand River, where the world's biggest producer of bottled water, Nestle, had until recently a plant in Aberfoyle, Ontario, that pumped 3.6 million litres of water a day out of the river's watershed.[10] This, despite government's fiduciary "duty to accommodate and consult" First Nations and to make sure other parties do the same when extracting any natural resource from Indigenous land. Meanwhile, despite the recent building of a new water treatment plant at Six Nations in the same watershed, 91 percent of the people living on the Grand River Territory are not connected to the reserve's water treatment plant and must either boil their water or buy it in bottles from companies like Nestle.[11] We've seen this kind of cruel irony happen in Canada hundreds if not thousands of times before. Any understanding of what Borrows calls the "citizenship" of the land or the ecosystem, what the original formulators of the Covenant Chain–Two Row protocol called the "river of life," is consistently denied by the culture, beliefs and laws of Canada. This is why we need Indigenous ways of doing things to reshape Canadian affairs. We need Indigenous "laws," by which I mean Indigenous understandings of the rights of the watershed, Indigenous social rules and protocols meant to keep us in harmony with the Earth's rules, the "house rules" of living within nature's regulations, to rewrite the Canadian and Ontarian laws that allow a private corporation to endanger the health of the river of life for the benefits of its faraway shareholders and then to charge local Indigenous Peoples for potable water derived from their own watershed.

"To preserve and extend our participation with the land, and our association with those who now live on it," Borrows wrote almost twenty years ago,

> it is time to talk of Aboriginal control of Canadian affairs. Various sites of power in Canada must be permeated with Aboriginal people, institutions, and ideologies. . . . Aboriginal people must work individually and as groups beyond their communities to enlarge and increase their influence over matters that are important to them. We need an Aboriginal prime minister, Supreme Court judge, and numerous Indigenous CEOs . . . They should be joined by Indian scientists, doctors, lawyers, and educators; by Aboriginal union leaders, social activists, and conservative thinkers. We need these people to incorporate Indigenous ideologies and perspectives into their actions, including ideas about the federalism we should enjoy with the earth.[12]

Federalism *with* the Earth

Speaking directly about the Two Row Wampum, Borrows observes that Harold Cardinal's 1960s manifesto of "Aboriginal control of Aboriginal affairs" emphasized the separation of the two purple rows. The urgencies of the present show us how that 1960s manifesto failed to consider the original meaning of the white beads of the river of life that the two rows share. "The ecology of contemporary politics teaches us that the rivers on which we sail our ships of state share the same waters," Borrows continues. "There is no river or boat that is not linked in a fundamental way to the others; that is, there is no land or government in the world today that is not connected to and influenced by others. This is one reason for developing a narrative of Aboriginal citizenship that speaks more strongly to relationships that exist beyond 'Aboriginal affairs.'"[13] The *Tékeni Teyohà:te*'s white beads of *skén:nen* (peace, clarity), *kentèn:ron* (friendship) and *ka'nikonhriyó'tsherа't* (good mind) make up the three rows that connect the two purple ones on the river of life. These three rows remind us of the primacy of respect, trust and friendship for the relationship to work. Given the interdependencies of the political, legal and biotic ecosystems that we are finally, if reluctantly, awakening to in Canada, I think John Borrows is right: *we all* need Indigenous (as opposed to corporate shareholders') governance of Canadian affairs.

After all, who would we rather have making the decisions about how to deal with the ecosystem of any particular place – Alton Gas's and Nestle's shareholders, who are spread around the globe and have never seen, will likely never see, where the gas and water is extracted from? Or would we prefer these decisions be made by People who have lived in the locale so long that the balance of relationships between the living things of that biome have shaped the very clans, languages, economies and laws that the People use to identify themselves and their kin? "Surely this is better," writes John Ralston Saul, "than commodities companies coming in for a decade or two, sucking out whatever wealth there is, then walking away leaving the locals to pick up the broken pieces. Surely what most of us . . . need are people who want to live in the [region] and have an indigenous philosophy of how to care for it."[14]

This polishing of the Chain or rebalancing of the Two Rows requires more than a seat at the same old table in Ottawa. It demands a true repositioning of where the dialogue between partners takes place and whose culture, beliefs and laws give it shape and meaning. This is why Aimée Craft evoked the elders' invitation to "come to our house." Which house? Well, in this book, we're talking about "Those Who Are Building the House," a house that was meant to extend its rafters to those who wished to live in the way of peace. In each region of Canada, there is a house where the local elders meet. Each house operates by its house rules. Coming to each house means learning and being governed by the rules of each culture and ecosystem.

These house rules have been discussed, negotiated and summarized by Indigenous Peoples across Canada for years. They have been laid out in extensive detail in report after commission after court case after consultation from 1967 to the present (not to mention delegations that extend back to British and French colonial times). So I have no "new" solutions or approaches to suggest here. They have all been said, many times over, by Indigenous leaders before. But I think it's important for Canadians like me to add my voice to theirs.

"Actual Land Needs to Be Returned to Indigenous Jurisdiction"

"First, actual land needs to be returned to Indigenous jurisdiction." As RCAP pointed out twenty-five years ago: "Aboriginal claims are not entreaties against the Crown's superior underlying title . . . Aboriginal rights do not exist by virtue of Crown title; they exist notwithstanding Crown title. They are recognized by section 35 of the Constitution Act, 1982."[15] The restoration of Aboriginal title to the majority of Canadian land is not as impossible as many might think.

Saulteaux scholar Johannah Bird recently pointed out to me that 89 percent of Canada's territory is currently designated "Crown land." Eighty-nine percent! As RCAP reminds us, "Crown land" is a legal chimera. If not redesignated as "Indigenous land," then this land should at least be redesignated as "*Sewatokwa'tshera't* (Dish With One Spoon) land" – land as a dish or bowl of provision that the Peacemaker had indicated rivalling nations could share in peace, with a "spoon" and no "knife," so that blood would not be shed, and with a commitment to protecting and preserving the ecosystem within that dish. Famously, the Haudenosaunee and Anishinaabe exchanged a Dish With One Spoon Wampum Belt with one another as part of their Covenant to

Link Arms.[16] Crown land as Dish With One Spoon land would refer, first, to the primary and eternally binding relationship between land and humans to sustain one another. Second, it would require people to make peace with each other so as to share the gifts of the land equally and without violence. If the idea of "Crown land" derives from the Royal Proclamation's innovation within British law to "protect" land as a kind of commons within which its Indigenous allies could sustain themselves, and not exclusively from the pre-1215 English notion of lands, set aside like King's Forests, for the exclusive and arbitrary use of the king that generated Magna Carta's restriction of the king's powers, Dish With One Spoon lands would also function as a commons, protected by Indigenous Peoples and their laws. Given the disrespect that has polluted the common dish, especially during the 150 years of Canada's existence, future decisions about human incursions upon Dish With One Spoon land would need to be governed by Indigenous rules and norms and not by the groundless values of Industrial Growth Society that have brought us to the current dangerous moment.

The result would be that Crown land would no longer be approached, as it has been repeatedly, with the sharp knives of extraction, as a resource frontier brokered by the government.[17] As Dish With One Spoon land, the land itself would feature as the primary guarantor and beneficiary of the "culture, beliefs, and laws" that guide how we live within it, its laws set and guided by local Indigenous protocols whose role is to guard and provide for the faces rising to be born for the next seven generations. This redesignation of Crown land would focus more on *responsibility* to land than ownership (or leased) *rights* to it, a redesignation already anticipated in laws about public land such as the 2006 Ontario law on the disposition of land – PL 4.09.01, which stipulates under 3.2 (B):

> When public land is required by the federal government or one of its departments, or any provincial ministry, the land itself is not transferred. What is transferred is the responsibility to manage the lands on behalf of Her Majesty the Queen (HMQ). This is accomplished by an Order in Council or a Minister's Order which transfers management of the land either from HMQ in right of Ontario to HMQ in right of Canada as

represented by a Department or to HMQ in right of Ontario as represented by another Ministry. The Crown does not transfer ownership to itself.[18]

The Crown's original arrangement for lands in North America, the Royal Proclamation, took on the responsibility to protect lands *for* (not from) Indigenous allies, whose own provisions for lands were informed by the land's own requirements for ecological flourishing, which, in turn, fundamentally shaped wampum protocols such as the Dish With One Spoon, itself a precedent for the Covenant Chain–Two Row Wampum treaty tradition.

Not only should Crown lands be returned as Dish With One Spoon lands to Indigenous governance on behalf of us all, but so also should expropriated, privately owned lands be returned to Indigenous jurisdiction, even in regions where settler populations now live in large communities on disputed traditional lands. Even if these returns cannot be made overnight, it doesn't take rocket science to set things in motion for land to be returned without raising non-Indigenous people's fear of being forced from their current properties.[19] Why can the federal and provincial governments not take some of the money they currently spend on defending themselves against Indigenous land claims, and use it to build up a fund to buy back lands as they come up for sale in the Haldimand Tract, to take a local example, and return them to Six Nations' jurisdiction?

On March 30, 2021, APTN News revealed that in the six months between July 2020 and January 2021, the Ontario Provincial Police (OPP) spent $16.3 million to patrol the Haudenosaunee occupation of the McKenzie Meadows housing development in Caledonia, Ontario. The same news agency noted a year later on May 31, 2022, that the cost of policing dropped after the intense first six months so that the cost over the first year came to $21 million. But even at $21 million a year – or less if the intensity of policing continued to drop – for three years since July 2020, multiplication would put the figure somewhere between $40 and $63 million.[20] That money could buy a significant amount of land – and that's just one dispute over Indigenous land in this country!

Several of the flashpoints of conflict over land in the Grand River region have focused on new housing developments like McKenzie

Meadows and Douglas Creek Estates on the edge of Caledonia. Why cannot the various levels of government – the Confederacy chiefs; the band council; and the federal, provincial and municipal governments – negotiate a long-term plan to return lands to Six Nations, and, where that return is not immediately possible, to protect the integrity of the land itself in this area where suburban sprawl threatens to subdivide and pave over some of the best agricultural land in Ontario? The failure to date of Canada's parliamentary and legal system to protect the river of life leads me again to the wisdom there is in Borrows: the best way to "recover Canada" is to seek out Indigenous governance of Canadian affairs.

Chapter Nineteen

Linked Arms–Land Back

My second point about Land Back grows from the first, and it suggests that Indigenous leadership in Canadian affairs necessitates what both the RCAP and TRC proposed – "a 'New Royal Proclamation.'"

Clearly, we Canadians are in similar circumstances to those identified in 1763 when the original Proclamation observed that "great Frauds and Abuses have been committed in the purchasing Lands of the Indians, to the great Prejudice of our Interest, and to the great Dissatisfaction of the said Indians." The "our" in this eighteenth-century statement refers to the royal "we," and, within its monarchial context, this "we" (the king or "Crown") was assumed to protect the "Interest" of the entire kingdom and its populace. In our current parliamentary democracy, this royal "we" has been transferred to the citizenry of Canada and our political representatives. It's not in Canadians' collective "interest" to allow *Ye-thi'nihstenha*, our mother the earth, to be governed by those who continue to countenance and defend frauds and abuses.

For this reason, to return to the language of the Royal Proclamation, "It is just and reasonable, and essential to our Interest and the Security of our [country], that the several Nations or Tribes of Indians, with whom we are connected, and who live under our Protection, should not be molested or disturbed in the Possession of such Parts of our Dominions and Territories as, not having been ceded to, or purchased by Us, are reserved to them as their Hunting Grounds."

The reason twenty-first-century Canadians and Indigenous Peoples need a *new* Royal Proclamation is that the assumption of paternalistic "Protection" – as the original formulators of the Covenant Chain–Two Row agreement foresaw – has meant that, rather than treating those "with whom we are connected" as siblings, as brothers, as family with whom we have joined arms, successive Canadian governments have acted as rogue patriarchs whose cynical deployment of "protection" has masked ongoing frauds and abuses. This has happened even as they passed protective law after protective law, including the Child Protection Act (how have Indigenous children *ever* been protected by Canadian authorities?), the Environmental Protection Act (how did this protection fare when ministers managing the Environment portfolio were approving enormous expansion of the Alberta tar sands?), the Immigration and Refugee Protection Act (from the refusal of Sikhs in 1914 to turning away Jews on the cusp of the Second World War to long lineups for immigrant status today, how often has protection been refused?) and the Navigable Waters Protection Act (was it the navigation of bitumen that was "protected" when this act was revised in 2012 to prepare the way for Trans Mountain pipeline to be built along and across sensitive watercourses from Alberta to BC?). Clearly, the assumption that the Fathers who run Canadian Confederation are somehow "protecting" us and those with whom we are connected, is an old ruse of extractive power in Canada.

Protection, as Tharonhyawá:kon demonstrated, means not capturing animals in a cave for private consumption, but protecting the future lives of plants and animals and rivers – as well as humans – so that they can live and reproduce themselves to supply a future abundance for everyone.

Ground Rules

If we are to survive long term, we need to give the land back, first, to *Yethi'nihstenha* herself, to her rules and practical laws, and, second, to Indigenous governance and ways of proceeding, which were fashioned within the framework of her rules. To do this, we need to align our laws, as Indigenous Peoples have been telling us all along, with earth's laws, with what Onondaga naturopathic doctor Johanne McCarthy calls Mother Earth's house rules, her "ground rules."[1] Western legal systems cannot give the land back to its own ground rules because they are grounded in a foreign and inappropriate set of basic philosophical assumptions about what land is and what its laws are. As Oren Lyons reminded us earlier, "It is important to understand that when a government develops laws to rule the people, it must develop those laws in accordance with the natural law; otherwise, the laws will fail."[2] The PCBs collecting in the rivers and mothers' milk at Akwesasne, the sewage in Hamilton's Chedoke Creek, constitute their own judgment, regardless of what courts or city councils decide. These pollutants are handing out sentences to fish and algae, lake grass and white pines – and to humans. Already people have been forced to move their habitations, businesses, farms and fisheries to other places, out of immediate range of toxified watersheds. There are no loopholes, no exceptions, no pardons, bail nor parole. The true sovereignty of land itself remains non-negotiable.

And it is Indigenous understandings of land as animate, sovereign, reasoning and reasonable that can challenge and reorient the damage caused by the assumptions carried within the Western sailing ship. We need to reassess the culture, beliefs and laws that have steered us so far off course, causing us to smear the living skies, lakes and rivers with deadly chemical sludge. Perhaps, as the extent of our predicament grows upon our awareness, we will reach for our end of the Covenant Chain, asking our disregarded allies of the canoe for their help to address the self-made threat to our own – as well as their – way of life. Perhaps we will begin to ask: What are the laws of this land whose sovereignty we ignored? What, in fact, is land, in the first place? And what is it "for"?

Listening to Indigenous ways of thinking might open us to the sentience of earth, to what Anishinaabe-Haudenosaunee philosopher Vanessa Watts calls "place-thought." "Place-Thought," she explains, "is based upon the premise that land is alive and thinking and that humans and non-humans derive agency through the extensions of these thoughts."[3] Hearkening to the teachings contained in her ancestors' creation stories, of the Sky Woman who fell to earth where sentient waterbirds and animals conferred about how best to sustain her, Watts illustrates by contrast the Western tendency to split off thinking and brain life (epistemology) from being and body life (ontology). She explains that human exceptionalism grew from the idea that humans are the only ones who think, and this delusion has lifted us off of the ground on which we live, leaving us both groundless and ungrounded. In her ancestors' teachings, by contrast, Watts shows how the land's many beings are understood to express intelligence, place-thought:

> Where waters flow and pool, where mountains rise and turn into valleys, all of these become demarcations of who will reside where, how they will live, and how their behaviours toward one another are determined. Scientists refer to this as ecosystems or habitats. However, if we accept the idea that all living things contain spirit, then this extends beyond complex structures within an ecosystem. It means that non–human beings choose how they reside, interact and develop relationships with other non-humans. So, all elements of nature possess agency, and this agency is not limited to innate action or causal relationships.[4]

Understanding place and land as animated with spirit and agency informs civic, political and legal relationships, as Watts goes on to explain, "Thus, habitats and ecosystems are better understood as societies from an Indigenous point of view; meaning that they have ethical structures, inter-species treaties and agreements, and further their ability to interpret, understand and implement. Non-human beings are active members of society. Not only are they active, they also directly influence how humans organize themselves into that society. The very existence of clan systems evidences these many historical agreements between humans and non-humans."[5]

Watts quotes Cree attorney Sharon H. Venne on the implications for Indigenous understandings of sovereignty. Whereas Western concepts of sovereignty conceive of absolute power vested in human institutions (think of Hobbes's monarchial Sovereign), Venne explains, "For us absolute power is in the Creator and the natural order of all living things; not only in human beings . . . Our sovereignty is related to our connections to the earth and is inherent. The idea of a nation did not simply apply to human beings. We call the buffalo or the wolves, the fish, the trees, and all are nations. Each is sovereign, an equal part of the creation, interdependent, interwoven, and all related."[6]

Understanding the earth's own sovereignty demands that we who have usurped the idea of authority and power need to return the land back to itself, to its set of laws, its own requirements and orders. Its *ground* rules.

Because, in the end, ground *rules*.

To reorient the sailing ship's culture, beliefs and laws requires polishing the chain, reanimating the peace, good-mindedness and respect laid out in the Two Row agreement, to reground our norms by learning from our allies in the canoe. In this sense, it is in all of our best interest – Indigenous and non-Indigenous peoples alike – to support the resurgence of Indigenous Peoples' knowledge, culture, science, art and languages, and the lifeways that emerge from them. Colonialism tried to destroy so many of these things, and it succeeded in separating many Indigenous Peoples from the knowledges and values their ancestors had held. Now we need these teachings – all of us do. The renewed ground rules will require us all to foster the conditions in which current generations of Indigenous youth can re-encounter their elders, learn their languages, participate in their ceremonies, spend time in their traditional lands, so that they can reignite the hearths where their traditions have been maintained.

While this reorientation undoubtedly constitutes a major and profound shift in our own Canadian culture, beliefs and laws, it is not impossible to do. As Watts puts it, it simply requires us to listen to and follow the advice of those whose "ears . . . remain open and low to the ground."[7] Essentially, Canadians would be re-Linking our Arms with land-based Indigenous thinking, Indigenous ways of proceeding. "Only if the land decides to stop speaking to us," she writes, "will we enter the world of dislocation where agency is lost and our histories become provocative Indian lore in an ongoing settler mistake."[8] To avoid this dislocation, mainstream society needs a new understanding of the real conditions of our collective existence, that the *eco* of economy is the same *eco* as that of our ecological home. The practical outworkings are not difficult to imagine. Decisions about land should be led by Indigenous Peoples of each region whose responsibility it has been across many generations to ensure the sovereignty of that land.

Land and Governance Back

Common law assumptions in Canada about property need to be reformulated to ensure the responsibilities of people to protect and enable the rights of the land. In land and resource extraction disputes across the country, Indigenous cultural practices that understand the land as Peopled with plant and animal nations who constitute our family, need to determine governance and jurisdiction. This is not impossible to imagine. Ktunaxa nation writer Beverley O'Neil offers an example of how this process actually worked when the Hupačasath First Nation on Vancouver Island joined with Synex Energy Resources, Ucluelet First Nation and the City of Port Alberni to decide how to generate hydroelectricity in their region with minimal environmental impact. Their particular concern was to identify a dam site that would not stop fish from swimming upriver to spawn. According to O'Neil, this process of "free, prior, and informed consent" of local Indigenous communities was not tacked on to an already moving industrial plan. Indigenous norms and ways of proceeding were, she says, where the project started, so that the project's partners looked to the fish and watershed laws of the land to figure out how to produce enough electricity to power six thousand Indigenous and non-Indigenous homes without impeding the yearly cycles of salmon reproduction in their region.[9]

The Hupačasath nation's involvement in this hydro project is an example of the growing number of Impact and Benefit Agreements (IBAs) and Government Resource Revenue Sharing (GRRS) arrangements, whereby corporations and governments establish consultation and resource-revenue-sharing compacts with particular First Nations whose territory is affected by mining, forestry, hydro or oil and gas extraction. *Land Back: A Yellowhead Institute Red Paper* (2019) surveys a whole series of these kinds of partnerships between Indigenous communities and industrial ventures across the country that can, on the one hand, develop reciprocal gift-economy relationships with the land that are guided by Indigenous norms. But, as Hayden King and Riley Yesno warn in their contribution to the *Land Back Red Paper*, they can also, on the other hand, entice or coerce "Indigenous people into development as junior partners in resource management."[10] The incentives can be tempting, even as the stakes can be extremely high. For example, past Alberta premier Jason Kenney established a Crown corporation with a budget of a billion dollars to broker First Nations IBAs with large industries, with the result that at the time of the *Red Paper*'s release in 2019, three First Nation coalitions were seeking to buy the Trans Mountain pipeline from the federal government to transport tar sands oil from Alberta to the Salish Sea. They hoped to dub it the "reconciliation pipeline."[11] The enticements to return to the same old extraction-economy decision-making table can be very attractive. It will take very strong grounding in Indigenous values to keep the land's laws at the forefront of considerations such as these.

But Canadian governments can participate in giving land back in other ways, as well. In July 2019, news media announced that Grégoire Gollin, a developer who had purchased the land that had been the flashpoint of what is commonly referred to as the "Oka Crisis" of 1990, was offering to transfer "the Pines" – the stand of trees Mohawk Warriors had defended from being felled for a proposed golf course – to the Mohawks of Kanesatake.[12] The idea was to conduct this transfer through Environment and Climate Change Canada's Ecological Gifts Program. Gollin would receive a tax credit from Revenue Canada, and Kanesatake would have jurisdiction over the land and trees that have been a political football, not just for the thirty years since the Oka Crisis, but throughout the three hundred years of murky transfers between various sovereignties. This is land King Louis, exercising his "divine right" to land traditionally inhabited by Algonquin and Mohawk Peoples, granted in 1717 to "Christian Mohawks," who were subject to the missionary administration of Sulpician priests. For their part, the Sulpicians turned most of the land into a seigneury, and then sold it to private owners as if it were their own.

Gollin's 2019 proposed transfer was murky too. The Ecological Gifts Program had not been used previously to transfer title to a First Nation, for one thing. For another, Gollin owned other land in the area, and he was also offering to make around 150 hectares available for purchase by the federal government who would then transfer it to Kanesatake. This stoked long-standing anti-Mohawk sentiment among the people of the town of Oka, whose mayor raised the spectre of a proliferation of smoke and cannabis shacks surrounding the town. Within the reserve, people worried about what benefits Gollin was hoping to receive in exchange for his "gift." He had previously sold off land lots bordering on the Pines, and some trees had been cut down in the process. It's not as if his company is known as ecologically progressive. And they wondered if he might receive other benefits, perhaps pieces of ancestral lands, in exchange for this "gift."[13] To date, the land has not been given to Kanesatake, but, in an effort to exert its interests over the Pines, the town of Oka has rezoned it from residential to environmental conservation, which has effectively blocked Gollin's Gifts Program donation. In response, Gollin has sued the municipality of Oka. Reserve Grand Chief Serge Otsi Simon, wanting to free the land from external regulation of any kind, whether of the Ecological Gifts Program or Oka's efforts to rezone the land, is now proposing that the federal government simply pay Gollin for the land and give it back to Kanesatake.[14] Whichever way this long-disputed land can be returned to Indigenous jurisdiction, if the transfer is eventually made, "ownership" of land will have been transferred from a consumer to a gift economy.

There have been some fascinating initiatives along these lines in the city of Hamilton, as well. In 2007, the City of Hamilton completed construction of a four-lane divided highway through the Red Hill Valley, which had been conservation land – Canada's largest urban park at the time – on the east side of the city. This, despite a decades-long battle by Indigenous and environmental groups against it. The Red Hill Creek Parkway had first been proposed in the 1950s, and way back then Six Nations band council (not the traditional Confederacy) had given its approval. But the proposal was stalled by numerous legal challenges over the half-century before the parkway was finally completed.

During the period when the proposed highway faced its fiercest opposition in the 1990s and early 2000s, members of Six Nations had registered numerous concerns over the parkway's incursion on their 1701 Albany (Nanfan) Treaty rights to hunt throughout the region: the presence of burial remains near the site of an Iroquoian village of longhouses, where fifty-six thousand artifacts had been found; other evidence of Indigenous Peoples in the valley ten thousand years ago at the end of the Ice Age; and Haudenosaunee contemporary responsibility to ensure that medicine plants, forests, deer, fish and their ecosystems continue to live in the valley.

In contrast with the consultative process outlined in the Hupačasath First Nation's hydroelectric project mentioned above, the approval and building of the Red Hill Parkway marks the much more common procedure of "consultation after the fact."

To offset the destruction of habitat and cultural heritage that would result from paving over 65 hectares of the 365-hectare valley, relocating seven kilometres of the creek and installing twenty-three stormwater management ponds, plus a 2.8 kilometre combined sewer overflow pipe in the valley, the City of Hamilton approached the Haudenosaunee Confederacy Council – not before the project started, but while it was already building the parkway – to create a Joint Stewardship Board that would protect (what remained of) the ecosystem as well as the cultural significance in the valley.[15] Although this set of agreements emerged in the midst of deep conflict and as a result of gut-wrenching compromises, it is precedent-setting insofar as it is, according to Mohawk scholar Susan Hill, the first set of official agreements made between any kind of

Canadian government (municipalities are incorporated within provincial legislation) and the traditional Confederacy Council since 1924, when the RCMP closed the Confederacy's Council house and Canada withdrew recognition of their power to govern Six Nations.[16]

The Confederacy Council's website indicates that "the intent of the [Red Hill] agreements was to foster long-term relationships and to create a plan for the Valley that reflects the best thinking of both peoples." Very diplomatically, it doesn't say that these long-term relationships traced back to *Tehontatenentshonteronhtáhkwa*, which had been ignored in the lead-up to building the parkway. Instead, it looks to the future and how to work cooperatively toward what ecological health can be salvaged after the highway was run through the valley. The Joint Stewardship Board is comprised of equal representatives from the City of Hamilton and the Haudenosaunee to ensure cooperation over long-term environmental plans for the Red Hill Valley. These long-term plans are shaped by a series of agreements between the City and the Confederacy guided by a General Agreement (November 17, 2003) and a whole series of specific agreements:

- Facilitated Negotiations (September 19, 2003)
- Respect for and Protection of Human Burials in the Red Hill Creek Valley and Assurances Concerning Archaeological Work in the Red Hill Creek Valley (October 22, 2003)
- Hunting, Fishing, Trapping and Gathering (November 17, 2003)
- The structure and function of the Joint Stewardship Board (December 18, 2003, ratified in 2005)
- Medicine Plants and Other Significant Plants (December 18, 2003)
- Economic Opportunities in the Red Hill Valley (January 9, 2004)
- Respecting the Human Heritage of the Red Hill Valley (January 9, 2004)

These agreements were ratified in the fall of 2007, after the parkway was completed, symbolic trees were planted and the Haudenosaunee presented the Mayor of Hamilton with "the Fire of the Valley" wampum composed of three strings of white wampum, representing peace, respect and friendship. Alluding to the ceremonial terms of the Covenant

Chain–Two Row treaty tradition, the Joint Stewardship Board's website explains that "this new 'fire' represents the values of the council fire; a place and time of bringing minds together for the benefit of future generations; to assure that they have a healthy place in which to live . . . These three foundational teachings are the commitment that the Haudenosaunee Confederacy Chiefs Council and the City of Hamilton have made to the Red Hill Valley."[17] The wampum reminds us that the agreements here, summarized in the three strings of wampum "three words," are about developing a new commitment *to the valley itself*.[18]

In the years since 2003–2004 when the first of these agreements were made, the Joint Stewardship Board has carried out environmental monitoring, species-at-risk assessments, planted two hundred thousand tree seedlings to replace the thousands felled (the exact number is debated) to build the highway, removed invasive species and replaced them with Indigenous plantings, conducted deer population surveys with the help of the Haudenosaunee Wildlife and Habitat Authority, engaged elders from Six Nations to conduct inventories of medicinal plants such as sweet fern and sassafras in the valley in order to protect and recover them. They also provided lists of these plants in Haudenosaunee languages as well as English. The Red Hill Creek had been channelized back in the 1950s and 1960s, long before the building of the highway and before people realized how much harm channelization causes in watersheds, so the City agreed to take advantage of the disturbance of road construction to rethink plans for stream crossing and flood control. As a result, it developed a natural, meandering channel design to create better fish habitat. This design included twenty-three stormwater ponds to help filter stormwater before it is discharged into the creek, improving water quality.

The City contracted Kayanase, a Haudenosaunee-owned plant and seed nursery forty minutes' drive away on the Six Nations reserve, to lead the renaturalization (as far as possible, with a highway roaring overhead) of the valley. This nursery takes a holistic approach to restoration based on Western science and Indigenous Knowledge, involving the collection, processing and propagation of native seeds and the planting and monitoring of native plants. Kayanase led the planting of trees, shrubs and herbaceous plants during the restoration of the Red Hill Valley, and in the process it coordinated with federal internship programs to mentor Indigenous youth in environmental botany and more general ecosystem recovery. Meagan Hamilton, a *Kanyen'kehàka* woman carrying out studies for her master's degree at the time, said, "Restoration of biodiversity goes hand in hand with cultural restoration . . . There's an equivalency between building our capacity to restore land with native plants and building our cultural capacity to restore our identity."[19]

I need to be clear that the work of the Joint Stewardship Board is far from ideal. Its restorative work took place within a deeply flawed process of "consultation" and "joint stewardship." And there are still many challenges facing the Red Hill Valley – the deer population, hemmed in by urban development on all sides of the valley, grows in unsustainable ways; baby trees cannot match mature trees for oxygen production or carbon sequestration, so it will be years before the two hundred thousand new trees will do the ecosystem work that had been carried out by the thousands that were decimated during parkway construction. The Joint Stewardship Board finds itself divided between the never-ending pressures of urban expansion and protection of the cultural and natural habitat; their entire existence depends on the vagaries of city budgets, and, as the *Kanyen'kehàka* past director of the board, Dr. Sheri Longboat, says, the different worldviews between City and Haudenosaunee members makes cross-cultural agreement difficult.[20] To say the least. It's no small thing for Canadians to understand land as a living being who gives us the gifts we need to stay alive, while city and provincial laws tend to treat the land as John Locke did: as inanimate property that can be "improved" by being turned to human uses.

In June 2022, the Red Hill Parkway and Joint Stewardship Board were back in the news. With Hamilton's population expected to grow by another third by 2050 and with the provincial government's recent dedication of billions of dollars to support the development of electric vehicles at Oakville's Ford plant and e-vehicle batteries at Windsor's Stellantis factory, some Hamilton City Councillors proposed that the Red Hill Parkway could be expanded with more lanes to meet future traffic needs. Electric vehicles, their thinking goes, would reduce environmental impact and make a bigger highway harmless. It was news to the Joint Stewardship Board that studies have been conducted since 2015 to see if expansion is feasible. Without, of course, consulting the Haudenosaunee members of the Stewardship Board. Once the idea of expansion was public, however, City Council assured the Stewardship Board that any such plans would need to be passed by them first.

These are the ongoing struggles of reciprocal relationship. The habits of unilateral decision-making are long-ingrained.[21] An example of how ingrained occurred here in Hamilton in July 2024. City Council voted down a proposal put forward by Councillor Cameron Kroetsch in consultation from the Circle of Beads, an urban Indigenous group co-chaired by NaWalka Geeshy Meegwun, to study the conditions that would need to be met to establish a voting position for an Indigenous councillor on City Council. The idea would for Indigenous perspectives to inform the City's decision-making. The proposal was not to *establish* the position, but just *to study the conditions that would need to be worked out* in order to establish it. But even the will to study such a matter was narrowly defeated by an 8 to 7 vote on council.[22] The habits of non-consultative governance are the status quo in Canada, and they do not change easily. My sense, however, is that with court decisions such as the aforementioned *R. v. Williams* and *R. v. Monture and White*, both occurring in 2023 and referring to the Covenant Chain–Two Row Wampum principles of mutual consultation and autonomous spheres of responsibility, we will see more movements toward this kind of mutual consultation over governance and domains of responsibility.

In the meantime, the ongoing existence of the Joint Stewardship Board is an example of the potential to implement the principles of the Covenant Chain–Two Row tradition in the twenty-first century. While the Ministry of Transportation of Ontario and the City of Hamilton maintain official jurisdiction over the region, so official title to the land remains unchanged, Indigenous norms and ways of proceeding continue to insist upon a governing role in shaping our region's collective commitment to the health and vitality of the valley itself.[23] It constitutes a potential example of how Indigenous and Canadian authorities can look to Indigenous guidance on how to give the land back to itself, to its own laws for how things work. The City government operates by its own culture, beliefs and laws, even as it expects the Haudenosaunee government to operate by its own culture, beliefs and laws. Indeed, that's why it needs the Confederacy Council to act as its Covenant Chain–Two Row ally. The band council, by contrast, is tied to the culture, beliefs and laws of the sailing ship that formed it and laid out its rules of procedure in the first place. So compared to the traditional Confederacy, it is forever hamstrung from bringing an authentic Haudenosaunee understanding to the partnership.

As the traffic snarls overhead on the raised overpasses, Indigenous and non-Indigenous schoolchildren gather in the shade of maples at the Bear Meeting place in the valley below to learn about the healing powers of sassafras, the Thanksgiving Address and white pine. The valley they meet in is too compromised to be paradise, but paradise is not an Indigenous concept – nor an ecological one – anyway. Instead, the Red Hill Creek Valley remains an urban site where the City and the Confederacy have committed to working out how to exercise our linked responsibilities to the creek and the land, to Hamilton's growing population, to the myriad beings that make it what it is.

The Joint Stewardship Board represents one instance of Linked Arm allies working out how to exercise their distinct responsibilities: to the damaged ecosystem of the valley itself, to the people of Hamilton, to the Six Nations and Mississaugas of the Credit, to the ancestors whose remains are buried in the earth alongside the faces – human and more-than-human – who are rising to be born from that earth. It doesn't take extraordinary genius to figure out how to do this, but that's because the ways to conduct matters like these were laid out in Haudenosaunee thinking long ago.

We can find guidance in the Covenant Chain–Two Row's principles for developing the kind of good-mindedness that can build strength in unity among us so that we can sail down a healthy river of life together.

Part V

Conclusion

Can We Restore the Linked Arms?

Thereupon [the Peacemaker] said, "Now, moreover, I decree that you chiefs of the Five Nations, that is to say, the Mohawk and the Oneida and the Cayuga and the Seneca and the Onondaga, who have the Good Message and the Power and the Peace and the Great Law, this is what I decree: do not ever disagree, thus there shall always be unanimity! It will be like a single person; you will have one body, and one head, and one heart, which means that as it became one family, when we unified, creating relatedness and kindness, each person will now be kind to one and all. Moreover, we have completed all matters that follow in the family through the generations, and these shall last as long as the earth exists, and as long as they are going to grow, the grasses and also the various weeds, and as long as the shrubs keep growing wild . . . the trees, all kinds of trees; and as long as springs emerge the water of the rivers will keep flowing, also the large rivers and the various lakes; and as long as the sun keeps rising and setting and the moon keeps up its phases, and in the sky the stars do the same, and the wind is stirring on

> the land, and heavenly bodies continue to provide light by day and by night; thus, it shall last the task we are completing, the Great Law, and these two will cooperate, the earthly land and the other one, the heavenly land."
> – John Arthur Gibson, *Concerning the League*

When the People Who Are Building the Longhouse formed their Confederacy, the Peacemaker and his friends established the circle of fifty chiefs whose joined hands would protect *Ohnehta'ko:wa*, the Great White Pine, in their midst. In order to ensure the end of violence, the Peacemaker had lifted the tree from the earth and the confederating nations had thrown their weapons into the hole where it had been. He then replanted the Tree of Peace, and said that people from all over the earth, from east, south, west or north, could follow the four white roots to join those who had banded together to create the Confederacy of Peace. Ever since, wampum keepers have maintained the Circle Wampum, which they use to remind the People from generation to generation of their need for unity among the chiefs on which the Confederacy relies.

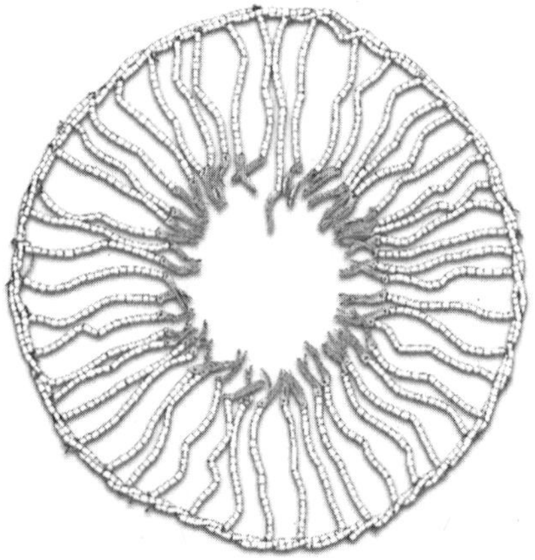

Circle Wampum, Rotinonshón:ni Teiotiokwaonháston, Mohawk language, meaning "It circles the people." (Image and photo by Raymond R. Skye, Tuscarora artist, Six Nations of the Grand River Territory)

The Peacemaker also told everyone that the culture of peace and harmony within that circle would need vigilance, because he foresaw troubles ahead. Sakokweniónkwas Tom Porter speaks of having been asked by the Confederacy chiefs to translate their ten-day-long oral recitations of the Great Law from *Kanyen'kéha* to English several times, and from this familiarity he has produced what he calls a reader's digest of it in his book, *And Grandma Said . . . Iroquois Teachings as Passed Down Through the Oral Tradition.*[1] I quote the Peacemaker's warnings at length from Porter's version:

"But you must hold tightly in there. For inside of that circle are your people, your territory, your clans, your language. Everything that you have is in there and is protected by the fifty leaders . . .

"But I want you to know that in the coming years, there will be a people coming here that you've never seen before. And they will carry an axe with them. And they will sneak under the arms of the leaders that are in the circle surrounding the tree, when they are not looking or paying attention. And they will come in there, trying not to be seen, and they will try to destroy the Tree of Peace. And they will take the axe and they will hack the roots, the four roots, because they want the tree and what it stands for to fall. They want to kill it . . .

"When that has been done, the tree will begin to die, because it'll be getting no more nourishment from its roots in Mother Earth. When it dies, it will begin to fall, and all that it stands for will begin to fall. But because those fifty leaders are holding hands together around it, it will fall on their clasped arms. And therefore it won't hit the ground. But it will hit a blow to them, because it's so big and heavy. And now they must hold it on their arms, whereas before it was upright. . . .

"And for many generations, those leaders will struggle to hold the tree from hitting the ground. And the time will come when there's almost nobody left, except those leaders holding hands. And now, after so many years, they're just trembling from the weight of it, because they're losing the power to hold such a heavy thing by themselves . . .

"But when those people, like culprits, run away from chopping the tree's roots, when they run away from their evil deed, they'll know it's evil, what they did. They will run to escape any consequences . . .

"But one day the supernatural will come. And those people will hemorrhage from their eyes. They'll hemorrhage from noses, their mouths, their ears, and their bottom parts will hemorrhage. And they won't go far, and they will drop. And they will die, for what they have done." . . .

And that leaves the leaders [Tom Porter explains] having to hold up this very heavy thing, all by themselves. No help. So that means that the people are in disarray. The Chiefs have got no more people . . . The rest of us weren't there by their side. We weren't there with them through thick and thin. And they did this, all this time.

> And so we blame a lot of stuff on them. And sometimes we get mad at them, because we think they're not right. But they didn't have much time to do anything else except strain all these years, under tremendous ridicule, under tremendous suppression, oppression not just by society but even from *our* people . . .
>
> And it says in our prophecies, "And so there will come a time when they will tremble and they will come to the last fiber of their strength to keep this tree from falling. And it's already fallen, it's just that they're holding it from falling on the *ground*. And just as they're ready to let go, and the tree begins to fall the rest of the way to the ground, you will notice from the north and the east and the south and the west, our great-grandchildren will come running, the girls and the boys . . . And by the hundreds of them, they will grab the tree for the last time. And they will push it back upright *one more time*."[2]

Maybe the chiefs weren't alert to the people who brought axes because they trusted them. The Peacemaker had said that anyone could follow the white roots to the Tree of Peace from any of the four directions, including people they had never seen before. Perhaps the ones who arrived in sailing ships from the south up the Hudson River appeared different from the ones who had arrived from the northeast on the St. Lawrence, with their muskets, soldiers and scurvy. Whereas the French attacked the Haudenosaunee circle of chiefs outright, the Dutch merchants came with axe heads and other useful implements, from copper kettles and iron nails to muskets. These items enabled the Confederacy to expand its trading capacity and power throughout the region. Through the Covenant Chain–Two Row system of agreements, the chiefs joined hands with these newcomers, extending the Great Peace by means of cooperation, commerce and military alliance. Later on, they gave British newcomers like William Johnson land to live on and to build estates among them. They made family with them. Their people intermarried with the newcomers, and the blended families grew up within the Circle of Linked Arms.

Perhaps trade and intimacy with these peaceable newcomers distracted the chiefs from seeing the danger carried in the mindset that guided the merchant ship. Despite their friendly approach, for example, the newcomers did not understand Earth to be a living being, let alone their Mother. Rather, they considered her to be an inert object needing improvement. The idea of improvement transformed living beings into trade goods and property. The iron axes made swift work of chopping down the great white pines of the northeast, which axemen needed for ship masts in the Royal Navy. Iron pickaxes and ploughs enabled them to dig out the roots, a task that used to take years with stone tools or fire. The holds of the newcomers' ships brought seeds for new grains, vegetables and fruits the Haudenosaunee had never before seen. They also brought enslaved Africans. The seeds grew quickly and, with the extra labour of human chattel, the fields of crops spread so widely there soon remained only a few fringes of woods around the farms. It was hard to remember the danger that used to lurk at the edge of the woods, outside the circle of chiefs. The ways of the newcomers wound themselves into the ways of the Haudenosaunee, so that Joseph Brant, for example, followed the lead of Sir William Johnson in buying Black lives to manage his properties.[3]

The motivations of the merchants-turned-farmers were not always easy to detect, maybe even to the factory farmers themselves. One hand extended friendship, the other was always chopping. The farmers didn't seem to see that they were digging down to the dangerous place where the People of the Great Peace had buried their weapons, and that they were weakening the Tree of Peace whose needles supply the oxygen that everyone – whether newcomer, Haudenosaunee or the animal nations – needed to stay alive. They didn't attend to the fact that they were depriving themselves and everyone else of the pinene transpired by pine needles that scientists have shown boosts the immune system and rids the lungs of toxins in human and animal bodies for as long as thirty days after one inhalation.[4]

They did not seem to understand that the Tree provided the medicine they themselves needed. Suzanne Brant, Katsi'tsiarihshion, the Tyendinaga practitioner of traditional medicine I quoted from earlier, warns: "When you gather medicine, your attitude plays a role in the effect that the medicine will have in the body. What you touch is affected by how you feel. When you gather medicines, make sure that you have a good mind, and are not sick yourself."[5] The men with the axes in their hands did not seem to know the sickness that distorted their own minds, which made them heedless to the medicine they were destroying. They seemed ignorant of the self-harm they were conducting. What's become clearer and clearer, as the generations have passed, is that the threat to the way of peace developed consistently and often undramatically, each act of chopping agreed upon by handshakes and assurances of good intent – a root here and a branch there, a land sale here and a privatization there, the assignment of an Indian agent here and the flooding of land to feed a canal-way there, a sewage drainpipe into the river here and the building of yet another suburban development there – as the Tree weakens and tips more and more heavily onto the linked arms of the chiefs. Suzanne Brant continues, "Humans no longer communicate with plants. Plants are affected by negative thought, and if they receive negative energy all the time they will shut down. It is at this time that they will leave the earth and return to the Sky World."[6]

But it seems that, with growing awareness of climate change, of the importance of keeping trees, land and rivers healthy in their natural state and according to their own laws, we're belatedly becoming aware of widespread hemorrhage, the kind of internal bleeding that happens when something has gone wrong in our living system. At first there may be only small signs of something wrong – a bit of bruising, some shortness of breath, a sense of generalized anxiety, some ache in the joints – but eventually we develop blind spots in our vision, ringing in the ears and deafness, difficulty breathing or swallowing, gastrointestinal bleeding. Perhaps we will realize in time that the mysterious illnesses, the cancers, leukemias and blood ailments are direct results of our chopping at the roots of peace.

And perhaps we won't. Perhaps we will increase the rate of our chopping, hoping we can get ahead of our worries – strip the ship masts we need from the last of the white pines so that we can sail away from these problems. Find another new world where we can stop the hemorrhage, build a new circle around a new tree of peace. Maybe on Mars. Knowing all along that the hemorrhage is in our minds, and that we'll take our axes with us, in the way we think.

Can We Restore the Linked Arms?

"Some of our people wish Canadians would move back to their original homelands," wrote the much mourned Lee Maracle (Stó:lō), who died in 2021. Her comment comes from her straight-talking, final book, *My Conversations with Canadians* (2017). This wish would be a longing to rewind history. For all of her desire to see the natural world restored to Indigenous guardianship, however, Maracle rejects this nostalgic impulse, saying, "Not me – I hope [Canadians] fall in love with the land the way I have: fully, responsibly, and committed for life."[7] At the heart of the Great Law of Peace is the generation and regeneration of *Ka'nikonhriyó'tshera't*, the Good Mind, as happened when the Peacemaker met Jigonsaseh, Ayonwátha, the leaders of the five nations and eventually Atotáhrho, when the People's good minds, unified in purpose, threw the weapons into the hole under the Tree of Peace. They then raised up a circle of leaders to protect and enhance the Tree's ability to generate the pinene, oxygen, shade and shelter needed by every living thing – from earth, air, water, plants and animals to human beings themselves.

At the heart of the Agreement to Link Arms, too, was love for the River of Life on which the vessels of the two parties floated, which is to say, love for the life cycles of Mother Earth – full, responsible and committed for life – for the future lives waiting in the soil to be born. As the 1988 version of Jake Thomas's Two Row oration put it, humans were

> created to walk upon the Earth to enjoy all nature's fruits, saying that no one will claim Mother Earth except rising faces which are about to be born. We will go by these symbols: As long as the sun shines upon this earth, as long as the water still flows, and as long as the grass grows green at a certain time of the year, that is how long our agreement will stand. Now we have symbolized this agreement and it shall be binding forever, as long as Mother Earth is still in motion. We have finished and we understand what we have confirmed and this is what our generation should know and learn not to forget.

Thomas's oration of the *Tĕkeni Teyohà:te* echoed the Peacemaker's words quoted in the epigraph to this chapter. The reason to create an agreement with other humans was to ensure a peaceful way of life within the ever-renewing cycle of living things, to provide loving, nurturing conditions for the rising faces that were about to be born. "You will have one body, the Peacemaker had said, and one head, and one heart, which means that as it became one family, when we unified, creating relatedness and kindness, each person will now be kind to one and all." This awareness, as Lee Maracle put it, of knowing oneself capable of falling in love with the earth, of having been cared for and nurtured by the generosity of earth, liberates our minds from seeing the earth as a dead object, as real estate, as property. It causes us to question our long history of thinking that chopping away the roots improves the land and grants us owners' rights to do with it as we please. For the roots are actually *how* the earth loves us. They seek out nutrients in the living soil. They cooperate through the mycorrhiza, sharing sugar with the fungi which in turn feed them the nutrients they need. They generate the new shoots, stems and leaves that photosynthesize the energies of the sun and the minerals from earth and water, transforming them into the air in our lungs. They filter atmospheric carbon that chokes the air, sequestering it once again in wood and soil, feeding nutrients to the rising faces about to be born.

The Peacemaker's prophecy predicts that, just as the Circle of Chiefs' endurance is about to give way under the weight of the sagging Tree, great-grandchildren will come running from the north and the east and the south and the west. They will come in numbers and they will lift the tree one last time. They will push it back upright once more.

I've never had much taste for prophecy. It's too easily used to manipulate people's fears and to rationalize deathbed conversions. But I hope the Peacemaker's warnings can alert us to the dangers as well as the possibilities of our times. For I do see new generations emerging from the four directions of the globe, all questioning the industries of axe-making that have defined the entire colonial era from the moment the French arrived on the St. Lawrence River and the Dutch on the Hudson River to the present. I don't know if they are emerging soon enough, if their campaigns to stop the chopping will succeed in restoring the Tree of

Peace, if the Circle of Chiefs can be restored and reinvigorated, if the two rows of the canoe and the ship can work together to nurture the River of Life that keeps us all afloat. But I do recall that the three links of the Silver Covenant Chain refer to *ka'nikonrio* (friendship), *ka'nikonhriyó'tsherа't* (good-mindedness) and *skén:nen* (peace), and that these concepts were developed to address their opposite, the presence of distrust, disrespect and violence, the very sources of hemorrhage identified in the Peacemaker's prophecy – the eyes blurred by tears of guilt and anger, the ears ringing with fear and anxiety and the throats blocked by despair, grief and violence.

Perhaps the threats of climate change, of global pandemics, of hundred-year storms, unprecedented droughts and wildfires, of heightened fear and distrust, and of plagues and pestilence have cast our minds upon the ground, making us stumble through what little remains of the woods – much like Ayonwátha did long ago. And perhaps we can still find a way through the welter if we pick up the shells exposed by the desiccation of the lakes and rivers, if we place them carefully in order on a thread of sinew, then count the beads of our human-made sorrow and loss, one by one. And maybe by actually sorting through the chaos together, bead by bead, we can steady our resolve, we can wipe the tears that bleed from our eyes, calm the ringing that deafens our ears, soothe the blockage in our throats.

Maybe, with relieved, unclouded minds we can stop our compulsive chopping, let go of the axe handle and take up our end of the *Tehontatenentshonteronhtáhkwa*, the thing by which we linked arms, remind ourselves of the promises our ancestors made to walk upon the earth and enjoy all nature's fruits, remembering that no one can claim Mother Earth except rising faces that are about to be born. Maybe we will remember that the covenant between our differentiated vessels is our true Constitution, one that was meant to ensure and endure as long as the sun shines upon this earth, as long as the water still flows and as long as the grass grows green at a certain time of the year. That is how long our agreement was meant to stand.

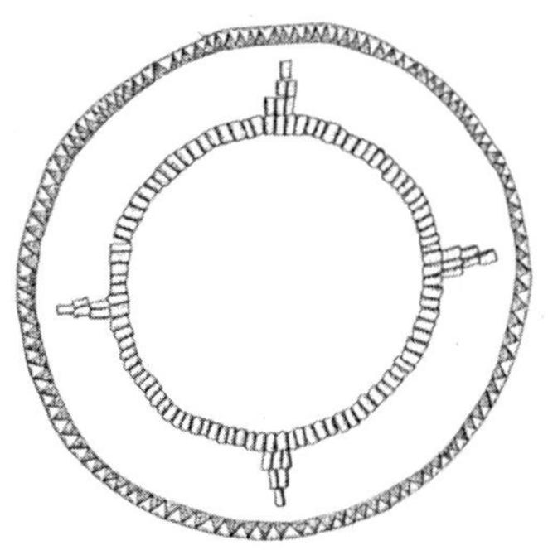

Gratitude

Grandfather of the Treaties is one of the many gifts I received from moving to a professor's job at McMaster University in Hamilton, Ontario, in 1997. I had never heard of wampum, let alone the Covenant Chain–Two Row Wampum treaty tradition, before I moved here. But the people I met in this region and the natural environment itself – the lush vitality of the Niagara Escarpment Biosphere doing its best to survive hyper-industrialization – soon taught me that I had arrived in a place of incredibly blessed, if troubled, relationships. Within weeks of my arrival, I met Haudenosaunee colleagues such as Rick Monture, who introduced me and my students to the wampum covenants that were conceived and established by ancestors of the People who live here. This book emerged through the many relationships that have continued to shape and inform my understanding of these primary agreements ever since.

First among these relationships is the Two Row Research Partnership group of reserve-based and university-based people who have met on the Grand River territory at Deyohahá:ge: Indigenous Knowledge Centre, Six Nations Polytechnic, once a month for the past ten years to discuss the teaching and relevance of the Covenant Chain–Two Row Wampum for our times. Over the years, the group included Wendi Adair, Sara Anderson, Talena Atfield, Paul Barrett, Johannah Bird, Heather Bomberry, Kosha Bramesfeld, William Coleman, Ki'en Debicki, Tracey

Deer, Sarah Dover, Thohahoken Michael Doxtater, Bonnie Freeman, Sara General, Heather George, Taylor Gibson, Abdo Habbani, Jeremy Haynes, Stanley Henry, Rick Hill, Tanis Hill, Chris Hiller, Rebecca Jamieson, Chelsey Johnson, Oznur Kaynak, Chandra Maracle, Johanne McCarthy, Rick Monture, Sandra Muse, Carlie Myke, Raphaela Pavlakos, Susie Price, Derek Sandy, Savannah Sloat, Logan Smith, Nathan Tidridge, Lene Trunjer, Trish van Katwyck, Jennifer Walker, Maggie Ward, Renae Watchman, Kevin White, Taif Zuhair, Gina Zuroski – and I'm undoubtedly forgetting to mention others who participated over the years. I'm grateful for the way these seminar friends challenged and honed my understanding. The royalties as well as all the notes and background research I conducted on this book have been given to Deyohahá:ge: with thanks.

The Two Row Research Partnership group would never have gathered were it not for the vision of the elders, honoured as official Knowledge Guardians by Six Nations Polytechnic, who urged us to establish Deyohahá:ge: on the two roads or paths of Haudenosaunee and Western knowledge systems: Tom Deer, Lottie Keye, Ima Johnson and Hubert Skye. This book aims to honour their vision.

I am grateful to the many people who engaged in conversation with me about various parts of the writing of this book. They include Phanuel Antwi, Tim Bascom and Cathleen Chittenden Bascom, Bea Coleman (my mother), Ki'en Debicki, Bonnie Freeman, Michael Gallant, Heather George, Rebecca Jamieson, Chandra Maracle, Rick Monture, Linda Staats, Paul Williams and Vanessa Watts.

Several people read and commented on parts of the book: Geoff Martin, Dave Gray, Wendy Coleman, John and Mary Terpstra.

I am eternally grateful to seven people who read and commented on six distinct manuscripts as I wrote and revised from one version to the next: they are, in order of their reading, Jane Watt, Lorraine York, Amber Meadow Adams, Rick Hill, Noelle Allen, Jen Hale and Wendy Coleman. I cannot say enough thanks to each of these for the incisiveness of their comments and their commitment to making this book the best it can be. They are not responsible for the parts I haven't found the right words for or that I'm still coming to understand.

And then there is the wider ecosystem of support near and far who encouraged me over the decade of writing this book: Phanuel Antwi; Marie and Richard Banville; Greg and Debbie Benson; Hazel Berkan; Johannah Bird; Michael and Christine Bucknor; Chandrima Chakraborty; David Chariandy and Sophie McCall; John and Phyllis Coleman; Andy Crowell; Juliet Daniel; Amber Dean; Len Findlay; Ana Fraile Marcos; Julie Gellner; Don Goellnicht; Brenda Gordon; Sidney Gordon; Beth Gray; Abdo Habbani and Fatima Bushra; Lawrence Hill; Elizabeth Jackson; Paul Lisson and Fiona Kinsella; Tim Long and Brenda Beckman-Long; Peggyanne Mansfield; Barbara Mutch and Marv Dewey; Grant, Dana and Caleb Moore; Gary and Carla Nelson; Susie O'Brien; Mary O'Connor and Gaby Moyal; Simon Orpana; Jim Peck; Marianne and Larry Penner; Rodrigo Perez; Michael Ross and Lorraine York; Armand Ruffo; Bernadette Rule; Sharon and Tim Sandvig; Dawn Styles; John and Mary Tersptra; Nathan Tidridge; Paul Ugor; Peter Walmsley and Sarah Brophy; Katie Waring; Clare Warner and Michael Opoku-Forfieh; Gary and Joy Warner; Cam and Joan Yates; Mary Jane Yates; Matt Zantingh; and Jose Zarate and Yoanna Noa Carcaces. At the heart of it all is Wendy Coleman. This ecosystem would not be complete without an expression of admiration and debt to the many Indigenous elders, writers and thinkers, especially Haudenosaunee ones, whose published work shaped my thinking in this book and that form the majority of my bibliography.

This is the second book I have published with Wolsak & Wynn under the editorship of Noelle Allen. Noelle's ready welcome for and ability to enter into the spirit of this project, her warm encouragement and practical facilitation, along with Ashley Hisson, Managing Editor, of the steps to publication, have made this project a true delight – and a much better book. Wolsak & Wynn, along with the Ontario Arts Council's recommenders grant program, helped us meet the expenses of Rick Hill's art that appears throughout this book.

Finally, I offer greetings and thanks to the larger ecosystem – the many lives of minerals, plants, animals and humans – that has made life, learning and writing possible in this Dish With One Spoon region at the Head of Lake Ontario.

Glossary

This glossary consists of notes and comments on Haudenosaunee and English terms that helped me try to use them as clearly and consistently as I could – without being a fluent speaker of *Kanyen'kéha* (Mohawk) or other Haudenosaunee languages, nor a person with a specialized legal vocabulary. Most of these notes are derived from the published and unpublished work, as well as the editorial conversations I've had with Amber Meadow Adams, Rick Hill and others. Throughout the glossary, I have tried to indicate who or where I learned these usages from. All Haudenosaunee terms are *Kanyen'kéha*, unless indicated otherwise, and spellings and commentary are from Adams's glossary in *Seyakhikwatakwénnis*, again, unless indicated otherwise. Adams's own understandings of these terms comes from studying with *Kanyen'kéha* language teachers such as Tehahenteh Frank Miller and Kanatawakhon David Maracle.

Atotarhonh – Sometimes spelled Atotáhrho, Toh-do-dah-ho, Tadodaho, from the story of the Peacemaker, "a wizard of unparalleled destructive power, [who was] transformed by forgiveness and compassion" (Adams, *Seyakhikwatakwénnis*, 36).

Ayonwátha – Also spelled Aionwahta, Hay-yonh-wa-tha or Hiawatha, the first person to be Condoled by the Peacemaker. Today, still a *Kanyen'kehàka royá:ner*'s title.

De'haĕ^{n}'hiyawă´'kho^{n}' and **O'hā'ă'** – Onondaga names for the Creator Twins as spelled in Gibson (1928); see **Tharonhyawá:kon** and **Thawískaron**, respectively, for their meanings in *Kanyen'kéha* below.

Elder and younger people – "Generally, a reciprocal affection and respect governs relationships between generations: the elder generation provides protection, guidance, patience and the benefit of deeper knowledge and experience, and the younger generation responds with attentiveness, deference, and often greater physical and emotional energy and flexibility. The greater the generational separation, the more obvious this dynamic. One's grandparent or great-grandparent (or a person of their generation) is customarily accorded great respect. It's considered unspeakably bad manners to ignore, openly dispute with, or engage in conflict with such an elder, though one is free to disagree in private. The same holds true for dealing with one's parents and the aunts and uncles of their generation" (Adams, *Seyakhhikwatakwénnis*, 18).

"Even between peers, a Haudenosaunee language speaker must distinguish between *rakhtsi'a*, my elder brother, and *ri'kenha*, my younger brother. The ethic of reciprocity by which elder and younger meet each other's different but complementary needs still shapes the elder/younger brother (or elder/younger sister) relationship. The elder/younger dynamic is not a hierarchy, but an acknowledgement that one's needs, desires, and capacities change throughout the course of one's life" (Adams, *Seyakhhikwatakwénnis*, 19).

Haudenosaunee – (Rotinonhsyón:ni in *Kanyen'kéha*) Might be better translated as "they have begun building the house and are still building it" (Adams, "Grasping the Chain," 38).

Jigonsaseh (Cayuga) – See Tsikónhsase (Mohawk).

Ka'nikonhriyó'tshera't – "Development of one's *ka'nikòn:ra*, often translated as 'mind' but encompassing character, intellect, desire, ethics, morality, imagination, habits, and knowledge, is a theme across traditional Haudenosaunee narrative. Cultivation of *ka'nikonhriyo'tshera't*, often translated as 'good mind,' is a principle upholding Haudenosaunee law. The suffix *-iyo*, as it appears in the word, goes beyond the generic niceness of the English word 'good.' It can include wisdom, flexibility, magnanimity, self-discipline, and generosity, as well as discernment, pragmatism, kindness, wit, and a sharp sense of humour. These are considered necessary qualities for our leaders, but all those who embrace

Haudenosaunee law, both within Haudenosaunee homelands and beyond them, need them, too" (Adams, *Seyakhikwatakwénnis*, 17).

Kanyen'kéha – Meaning the way or the place of flint or chert, this name describes the language spoken by the people of Kanyèn:keh (i.e., the Mohawk language).

Kanyen'kehága – Meaning the people of the way or the place of the flint or chert, this name describes the people of Kanyèn:keh (i.e., the Mohawk nation).

Ka'shatsténhsera – Often translated as "power" or "strength," this term describes raw capacity, energy, force or ability, which can be used well or badly. "It includes the verb root *-'shatste-*, which can indicate capacity of body, mind, or spirit, or ruggedness, toughness, and durability. It can also describe strictness and rigidity, and habits of demand, brutality, and violence. The spectrum of positive and negative connotations associated with *ka'shatstenhsera* reveals the deep vein of distrust running through Haudenosaunee philosophy regarding power or capacity, at least when it's not balanced by any other force" (Adams, *Seyakhikwatakwénnis*, 36).

Kaswentha – "This is the word used to denote a wampum belt, but it doesn't literally translate to that. Instead, depending on whom you ask among speakers (and also, weirdly, how you spell it), you'll get definitions ranging from 'it flows' or 'it holds something up (with flexibility, like a spine)' to 'leftover ash, embers.'" "The root *-hswenht-* describes something that both lends structure and flows. So, for example, it can describe a river, as in the geographical feature. It can describe a spine, the body part. It can also describe a fundamentally important relationship, something that both lends structure and retains flexibility and tension. Thus, it can also describe the wampum belt whose design symbolizes that relationship" (Adams, two sets of comments on my use of this term in this manuscript, 2022).

Kayanerenhtsherakó:wa – Most often rendered as the "Great Law" or "Great Peace," this is the constitution of the Haudenosaunee and the legal system the Haudenosaunee follow today. Predating the arrival of Europeans in North America by several centuries, this legal system is encoded in the story of the Peacemaker's journey. Today, it is spoken publicly every year in several Haudenosaunee languages, with English translation. "The verb root in *Kayanerenhtsherakó:wa -yan-* refers to the trace of a stride, according to *Kanyen'kéha* speaker and teacher Tehahente Frank Miller. He describes it not as a footprint, but sort of the energetic echo of a stride. A way to walk, a pace" (Adams, personal communication).

kentèn:ron – "Based on the verb root *-itenhr-*, meaning to take pity on or have compassion for someone, *kentèn:ron* is related to the term . . . for 'friendship,' *onkyatèn:ron* (literally, 'this person and I have compassion for each other'). If we imagine the three principles of Haudenosaunee law [*ka'shatstenhsera*, *ka'nikonhriyó'tshera't* and *skén:nen* – see their entries in this glossary] as they are presented in *Kayanerenhtsherakó:wa* (the Great Law of Peace . . .) as forming a circle in perpetual motion, *kentèn:ron* is the centripetal force pulling them all toward the middle, and keeping any one of them from spinning away under the external forces of conflict. Like many Haudenosaunee words, *kentèn:ron* differs from its English translations at its verb root: *-itenhr-* describes an action, something one does to help someone else . . . like the other *Kanyen'kéha* (Mohawk language) family terms described above, *kentèn:ron* describes the fundamental act that creates and sustains an emotional bond. We hold, we carry, we lend, we care for, we love" (Adams, *Seyakhhikwatakwénnis*, 36–37).

Konwatsi'tsayén:ni – Mary or Molly Brant, wife of Sir William Johnson.

Law – "Our stories are not only our laws. They carry information and rules about many other matters, including profound ecological knowledge, family structure, and economic patterns, to name just a few. Law, too, is an inadequate word for *tsi niyonkwarihò:ten* (our ways of addressing matters), which don't necessarily separate domains of spirituality, or art, or science from that of law in the way English, French, or Canadian legal systems might. For the purposes of discussing treaty relationships, however, we may use the word law as a term of common ground, with the understanding that, from a Haudenosaunee point of view, *tsi niyonkwarihò:ten* (as law) includes many more dimensions of meaning than it might for those operating within different legal systems" (Adams, *Seyakhikwatakwénnis*, 33).

Ohén:ton Karihwatéhkwen – "Opening Address, literally what we say before we do anything important" (Porter, *And Grandma Said*, 420).

Ohnehta'ko:wa – The Great White Pine, the Tree of Peace.

Onkwehón:we – "Genuine, sincere, or real person," not a racial category (Adams, personal communication, 2022).

Onkwehonwenéha – Literally meaning "in the way of genuine or real people," this term describes the way in which a Haudenosaunee (or, in some contexts, an Indigenous person) would behave. Can be rendered as "culture," "worldview," "lifeway," etc. (Adams, *Seyakhikwatakwénnis*, 85).

Orì:wa – A matter of business between people: "Many speakers of Haudenosaunee languages, when asked the word for 'treaty,' will say that the nearest equivalent we have is *orì:wa*. Usually defined as a matter of business undertaken by a group of people, *orì:wa* can refer to an agreement, an issue to be decided, an ongoing project (the word for spouse or marriage partner, *teyonkenirihwayenawàkon*, includes the root *-rihw-* and means 'they carry the business forward together') or, in the vocabulary of the Canadian legal system, a law or treaty" (Adams, *Seyakhikwatakwénnis*, 37). Rick Hill adds: "The [Wampum] Chain is the relationship, the Treaty Council is the event where issues of the Chain are addressed, *orì:wa* is an article in that event (there could be several), and if the council is successful in addressing the *orì:wa* then it is considered a completed matter. Succeeding councils might refer to the previously completed matters, or those *orì:wa* that were not properly addressed in the past" (Rick Hill, editorial comments on chapter 7, "From Proclamation to Constitution").

royá:ner – (singular, also spelled roiá:ner) Meaning "chief" (literally "he's of the good, he's good") and *rotiyaneshon* (plural, also spelled rotihianéhson) meaning "chiefs (lit. they of the good) (masculine)" (Porter, *And Grandma Said*, 423).

skén:nen – "Often translated simply as 'peace' but unifying not only the absence of conflict but also the physical health, emotional wellness, social cohesion, ecological balance, and spiritual fulfilment of a multidimensional synchronous thriving. Related to the words *owén:na*, meaning language, word, or voice, *karén:na*, meaning song or poem, and *a'én:na*, the hum of a bowstring at the arrow's release, *skén:nen* describes whole-existence vibration whose best English equivalent might be 'harmony'" (Adams, *Seyakhikwatakwénnis*, 34).

Tehontatenentshonteronhtáhkwa – They Link Arms or They Have Joined Hands: "The prefix *te-* describes something doubled, dual, or done together. The pronominal prefix *-hontate-* is reflexive, describing a group of people doing something to or with itself, or for one another. The root *-nentsh-* refers to an arm or, specifically, the forearm. The prepositional infix *-onte-* describes something attached to the end of something else. The ending *-onhtahkwa-* indicates that the action's been undertaken sometime in the past, and continuing into the present moment. All together, *Tehontatenentshonteronhtáhkwa* might be translated as 'they [males] together have attached the ends of one another's arms at some point in the past, and continue to do so now'" (Adams, *Seyakhikwatakwénnis*, 43–44).

Tékeni Teyohà:te – "Often referred to in English as the 'Two Row wampum,' has been described, and celebrated, as the first treaty established between an Indigenous nation of North America and a European nation. The verb phrase consisted of *tékeni*, the prefix *te-* describing something doubled or dual in nature, and *-keni-*, referring to two women or female actors, can be translated as the numeral two, or as two people undertaking something jointly. *Teyohà:te* includes the root *-hah-*, meaning path or way (in both literal and figurative senses) and, again, the dualic prefix *te-*, the suffix *-ate* indicating the location or placement of something. A more accurate translation might be 'the path two are on together' or 'the double path that two [travel]'" (Adams, *Seyakhikwatakwénnis*, 77–78).

"The three rows of white beads – white symbolising *skén:nen*, clarity, *kentèn:ron* and *ka'nikonhriyo'tshera't* – resemble, visually and conceptually, the links of the silver chain, and the respect, trust and friendship that connect the two brothers in both *Tehontatenentshonteronhtáhkwa* and *Tékeni Teyohà:te*. Keeping the path, this white or silver space between the parties, clear means not only keeping the white clean and the silver polished, but also the literal paths between villages or settlements, which can become overgrown with brush and thorns if not maintained" (Adams, *Seyakhikwatakwénnis*, 79). "Keeping the paths of communication clear means maintaining a direct government-to-government channel between the Haudenosaunee and the Crown, unimpeded by policy, bureaucracy, or the refusal to respond meaningfully" (Adams, *Seyakhikwatakwénnis*, 79–80).

In editorial notes on my use of these two wampum belts, Adams wrote: "First, we make you family; this is the message delivered in speech after speech delivered by Haudenosaunee speakers to European government representatives in the 17th and 18th centuries. Then, if that doesn't work the way we anticipated, we change the nature of the relationship; it becomes what's called *Tekeni Teyohate*. We're still brothers, but operating at some distance. The distance is not a void, it's filled with respect, trust, and friendship."

Thaientané:ken – Joseph Brant.

Tharonhyawá:kon – (sometimes spelled Teharonhiawá:kon) "He embraces or holds up the sky" (Porter, *And Grandma Said*, 83) and his twin brother **Thawískaron** (sometimes spelled Shawískara) in *Kanyen'kéha*. "It is not as easy to translate his name as his brother's name," writes Tom Porter, "some people say [Shawískara] has to do with ice, cold ice, in this *wísk* part . . . And some people say it means like when you come real quickly into something, like a bird dives and then just swerves off and goes another place . . . Or like you're rushing in somewhere, and you don't even . . . you just go, just rush in and go right away, something like that. It's like his visit is so short and gone. He's just there momentarily, and then he's gone . . . It bothered me for a number of years 'cause nobody could tell me what it meant . . . And then I had a dream about it . . . Whether that dream is correct or not, it came to me, so here's what it told me: Shawískara means that it's like a tornado or a big wind or hurricane comes. All of a sudden it comes there, and it comes so fast that everything not tied down starts flying around: the dust, the papers, everything . . . And that's him. He comes so fast that it just causes everything that's not tied down to be in disarray" (Porter, *And Grandma Said*, 83–84; see also **De'haĕ^{n}'hiyawă^{n}'kho^{n}'** and **O'hā'ă'**, respectively, above for Onondaga variants of these names).

Tsi Karhákta – The Edge of the Woods ceremony (Adams, *Seyakhbikwatakwénnis*, 68).

Tsikónhsase – (spelled Jigonsaseh in Cayuga) Means "she has a new face (name of first Clan Mother)" (Porter, *And Grandma Said*, 427). "Tsikonhsase, a woman who plays a major leadership role in the story [of Peacemaker and the Great Law], gently combs the snakes from Atotarhonh's hair, and massages his body back into its right shape. Hers is an act of compassion, but also done for the sake of public safety. Once Atotarhonh's body is restored to health, his thinking more easily becomes likewise healthy, and he ceases murdering and other harms to work for the good of his people" (Adams, *Seyakhbikwatakwénnis*, 67).

yakoyaner – (plural yakoyaneshon) "Usually rendered as 'Clan Mother' in English, this verb phrase shares the root *-yan-* with its counterpart, *royá:ner*. It identifies the woman at the head of an *o'tara*, who makes domestic and economic decisions, and who carries the title of the *royá:ner* who (with the consensus of her *o'tara*) she must choose and whose conduct she's responsible for. The office of *yakoyaner* predates that of *royá:ner* by centuries, if not millennia, and she carries the heaviest burden of authority and responsibility in Haudenosaunee society" (Adams, *Seyakhbikwatakwénnis*, 89).

Yethi'nihstenha Onhwentsyakekha' – "(*Yethi'* [she to us] + *nihsten* [strength, capacity, even harshness] + *ha* [living now] *Onhwentsya* [earth] + *kek* [on it] + *ha'* [here present]): she to us is exerting her capacity and strength to keep us living now (Adams's editorial notes on chapter 15, "The Family of Earth").

Notes

Part I: Good Minds

1 Following the debates that led to the United Nations Declaration on the Rights of Indigenous Peoples (UNDRIP) choosing the word "peoples" (over alternatives such as "populations") to identify Indigenous groups as distinct peoples with rights to self-determination (See UNDRIP's article 3), style guides such as Gregory Younging's *Elements of Indigenous Style* recommend using "Peoples" (capitalized) to emphasize Indigenous nations' distinct, self-determining status. Accordingly, I follow these guidelines: I use "Indigenous person" to refer to a person who identifies as First Nations, Inuit or Métis; "Indigenous Peoples" for the distinct societies of First Nations, Inuit and Métis peoples in Canada; "Indigenous People" for a single one of the distinct societies of First Nations, Inuit and Métis peoples in Canada; and "Indigenous people" for individuals who identify as First Nations, Inuit or Métis in a context where their specific identity is not at issue. But these distinctions are not easy to maintain. For example, the Haudenosaunee consist of a confederacy of six distinct nations, so I refer to "Haudenosaunee Peoples" to respect the six distinct nations, but their confederation operates on a model of unity, as being one longhouse family, so my use of "Peoples" disjoins that unity. Another problem arises from the way the English language reserves terms like "people" and "person" to refer to humans only, with the effect that concepts like "self-determination" and "distinct society" status are assumed to apply only to humans. Haudenosaunee (and many other Indigenous legal systems) would not discriminate against the rights of animals and plant peoples in this way. Considerations such as these arise from using English conventions to evoke Haudenosaunee concepts, and I am aware that my use of words like "Peoples" departs from conventions common in Haudenosaunee writers' own works. My current thinking, which may change, is that, as an English-language user who is not fluent in Haudenosaunee languages, I will capitalize words like "Peoples" because the unfamiliar English usage is a way to signal the distinct legal and ontological groundwork of Haudenosaunee civilization.

2 I'm taking this account from two main sources: Father Vimont's account in *The Jesuit Relations*, edited by Reuben Thwaites, vol. 27, 247–93, and Marie de l'Incarnation, *Word from New France: The Selected Letters of Marie de l'Incarnation*, trans. and ed. Joyce Marshall, Letter XIX, 135–51. Marie de l'Incarnation's letter was based on reports she had received about the embassy to Trois-Rivières and on Fr. Vimont's account for the *Relations*, so I have relied mostly on his account with refinements from hers. He spells the French prisoner's name "Cousture," for example, whereas she spells it "Couture." I have followed her spelling.

3 See *L'Incarnation*, Letter XIX, note 2.

4 Here is Joyce Marshall's footnote on "porcelain" from her translation of Marie

de l'Incarnation's account: "beads, made originally from shells but, after trade with Europeans began, of porcelain. They were strung in long strands and a number of these strands were then made into collars, or belts" (390n8). Paul Otto notes that the French used the word "pourcelaine" for wampum beads because the beads looked to them like those Marco Polo had introduced to Europe from China (11).

5 Vimont, *Jesuit Relations*, vol. 27, 248–49.

6 Vimont, *Jesuit Relations*, vol. 27, 251.

7 Brian Maracle, writer and *Kanyen'kéha* language teacher at Six Nations of the Grand River, writes, "Iroquois is the name that the French gave our people 450 years ago. The word is Algonquin in origin and the experts can't agree on exactly what it means. But going by one scholarly explanation, what I think happened was this: the French ask the Algonquins who their southern neighbours were and the Algonquins said 'They are *Irinakhoiw*' – 'real snakes.' . . . Naturally, we don't call ourselves 'real snakes' in our own languages" (*Back on the Rez*, 69). While "Iroquois" was subsequently taken up in anthropological literature to refer to the Haudenosaunee, I will use it only to refer to anthropological use of the term, and not to the people.

8 Vimont, *Jesuit Relations*, vol. 27, 253.

9 As with other references to Indigenous conceptual, political and social designations, such as "Peoples" or "Elder," *Elements of Indigenous Style* advises that "Wampum" and "Wampum Belts" should be capitalized. In the context of Haudenosaunee conceptions and uses of *kaswentha*, or "wampum," universal capitalization would erase the distinction between what have become the proper noun names in English for specific wampum agreements, such as the "Two Row Wampum," and references to generic elements of wampum, whether non-distinct references to wampum in general or to elements of wampum, such as the beads of which they are made. In this book, I capitalize the proper noun references to specific wampum agreements (for example, "The Dish With One Spoon Wampum Belt") but do not capitalize generic references (for example, "wampum strings").

10 Kayanesenh Paul Williams writes, "There was a time when a great speaker would 'perk up the ears' of his audience by 'driving it into them with a song.'" He goes on to quote Horatio Hale's *The Iroquois Book of Rites* (1883): "The hymn, or *karenna*, deserves a special notice. In every important council of the Iroquois a song or chant is considered a proper and almost essential part of the proceedings. Such official songs are mentioned in many reports of treaty councils held with them by the French and English authorities" (*Kayanerenkó:wa*, 121).

11 See a full discussion of the *Ohén:ton Karihwatéhkwen* in Sakokweniónkwas Tom Porter's chapter, "The Opening Address," in *And Grandma Said . . . Iroquois Teachings as Passed Down Through the Oral Tradition*, 8–26.

12 L'Incarnation, Letter XIX, 141.

13 Vimont, *Jesuit Relations*, vol. 27, 251.

14 Vimont, *Jesuit Relations*, vol. 27, 256, 255.

15 Vimont, *Jesuit Relations*, vol. 27, 259.

16 Leonard, "*Wunnáumwash*," 59–60.

17 This is an interpretation offered by Kayanesenh Paul Williams, see note 23 in Warkentin, "'Word of the Other,'" 23.

18 Vimont, *Jesuit Relations*, vol. 27, 261.

19 Vimont, *Jesuit Relations*, vol. 27, 261.

20 Seneca chief Oren Lyons called the Two Row Wampum the "grandfather of all subsequent treaties," see "Gä•sweñta' Reflections," 29; Lyons' phrasing has been echoed by Assembly of First Nations leader Ovide Mercredi and Mary Ellen Turpel, *In the Rapids*, 35.

Chapter 1: Reintroducing the Linked Arms

1 Adams, *Seyakhikwatakwénnis*, 51.

2 Adams, *Seyakhikwatakwénnis*, 48.

3 L'Incarnation, 147; my italics.

4 L'Incarnation, 147–48.

5 L'Incarnation, 141.

6 Warkentin, "'Word of the Other,'" 6.

7 Havard, "*Le rôle médiateur du wampum dans la diplomatie franco-amérindienne*," 37.

8 See *R. v. Williams*, 2023 ONCJ, 393.

9 *R. v. Derek White & Hunter Montour*, 2023, 240.

10 See Oren Lyons, "Gä•sweñta' Reflections," 29, and Assembly of First Nations leader Ovide Mercredi and Mary Ellen Turpel, *In the Rapids*, 35. Judge Sophie Bourque quotes historian Jon Parmenter's use of other terms: "the Covenant Chain alliance acted as a meta-treaty, one that he describes as 'mediatory,' that contained an *overarching pattern of relations* and the *baseline terms of agreement* between the Haudenosaunee and the British" (*R. v. Monture and White*, 2023, D.1.4, [688], 164; my italics).

11 Williams, "Chain, Naturally Understood," 68–69. In 1971 American anthropologist Francis Jennings published an article on "The Constitutional Evolution of the Covenant Chain." While the concept of this covenant was most consistently and heartily voiced by the Haudenosaunee, he noted, it was also referred to by Hudson River Valley neighbours such as Mahicans and Schaghticokes (89). The widespread use of the concept of the Covenant Chain way of making treaties, he notes, flies in the face of the idea that Europeans introduced law and civilization to "savage" peoples in what Euro-American historians habitually dismissed as the "frontier" (96).

12 Amber Meadow Adams, personal communication, 2021.

13 From the Latin phrase '*iuris dictio*,' genitive of *ius*, 'law, right' (see jurist) + *dictio* 'a saying' (from PIE root *deik- 'to show,' also 'pronounce solemnly'). Meaning

'extent or range of administrative power, domain over which a legal or judicial authority extends' is from late 14c., Meaning "judicial authority, right of making and enforcing laws" is from early 15c (*Online Etymology Dictionary*, s.v. "jurisdiction (n.)," https://www.etymonline.com/word/Jurisdiction).

14 See House Concurrent Resolution 331, October 4, 1988 – "A concurrent resolution to acknowledge the contribution of the Iroquois Confederacy of Nations to the development of the United States Constitution and to reaffirm the continuing government-to-government relationship between Indian tribes and the United States established in the Constitution." https://www.congress.gov/bill/100th-congress/house-concurrent-resolution/331.

15 "Perverse ignorance is a particular form of the defence mechanism of denial," writes Chickasaw scholar Eber Hampton. "By perverse ignorance, I mean motivated apparent ignorance about issues of culture or race" ("Towards a Redefinition of Indian Education," 36). Four years later, South Asian subaltern studies professor Gayatri Spivak wrote, "Part of mainstream education involves learning to ignore [non-Western canons of thought] absolutely, with a sanctioned ignorance" (*Critique of Postcolonial Reason*, 2).

16 Sometimes the word *kentèn:ron* (compassion, friendship) replaces the word *ka'shatsténhsera* in this list. Perhaps we can understand why in this commentary by Amber Meadow Adams on these key, interrelated words: "If we imagine the three principles of Haudenosaunee law [*ka'shatstenhsera, ka'nikonhriyó'tshera't* and *skén:nen*] as they are presented in *Kayanerenhtsherakó:wa* (the Great Law of Peace . . .) as forming a circle in perpetual motion, *kentèn:ron* is the centripetal force pulling them all toward the middle, and keeping any one of them from spinning away under the external forces of conflict. Like many Haudenosaunee words, *kentèn:ron* differs from its English translations at its verb root: *-itenhr-* describes an action, something one does to help someone else . . . like the other *Kanyen'kéha* family terms described above, *kentèn:ron* describes the fundamental act that creates and sustains an emotional bond. We hold, we carry, we lend, we care for, we love" (Adams, *Seyakhikwatakwénnis*, 36–37; for more on these words, see the glossary to this book).

Chapter 2: Introducing Wampum

1 The question marks here indicate words in Goldenweiser's handwriting that the translator-editor was not able to translate confidently.

2 Gibson, *Concerning the League*, 133–53.

Chapter 3: Introducing Myself

1 I have written about my upbringing in Ethiopia in *The Scent of Eucalyptus: A Missionary Childhood in Ethiopia* (Fredericton: Goose Lane, 2003).

2 See Lenore Keeshig-Tobias (Anishinaabe), "Stop Stealing Native Stories," and Gregory Younging's (Opaskwayak Cree) review of these events in *Elements of Indigenous Style*, 122–24.

3 Perhaps the most (in)famous "expert" of Haudenosaunee history and culture was the American anthropologist William Fenton. For sixty years, beginning in the 1930s, Fenton was known as the "Dean of Iroquois Studies" by his colleagues, authoring over two hundred publications on the Iroquois, including five monographs, and several edited collections, articles and chapters. Onondaga scholar Theresa McCarthy explains that for much of that time he controlled the orientation of research, the peer reviewing of publications, the flow of grant money and the management of museum collections (*In Divided Unity*, 60). Kayanesenh Paul Williams and others interested in repatriating Haudenosaunee wampum ran into conflict with Fenton, who insisted that the Haudenosaunee were not sufficiently familiar with their own culture to be custodians of their ancestral wampum, which he believed should remain under the care of the New York State Museum. He argued that Haudenosaunee scholars like John Mohawk, Oren Lyons and Rick Hill disrespected his superior knowledge. Fenton "had made his reputation as a scholar of Haudenosaunee history and culture," Williams explains, which is why "a living Confederacy was a constant challenge to his authority" (*Great Law*, 98n49 and 425n391).

4 Linda Tuhiwai Smith, *Decolonizing Methodologies*, 1.

5 See "Caledonia Land Claim: Historical Timeline" and "Caledonia Land Dispute." As a measure of how wide the alarm was over the Caledonia dispute, it's revealing to know that a U.S. Border Patrol vehicle was found patrolling the protest site, and observing the OPP's "management" of the situation, in June 2006.

6 "Respect is not an indifferent relationship, . . . a serene contemplation," writes Emmanuel Levinas, in an arresting phrase (*Entre Nous*, 34). "The respected one is not the one to whom, but with whom justice is done" (35).

7 With this in mind, all this book's proceeds will go to Deyohahá:ge: Indigenous Knowledge Centre, which is, after all, the learning community that facilitated, stimulated and helped to develop my understandings as presented here.

8 See Six Nations Polytechnic, *Deyohahá:ge: Indigenous Knowledge Centre 10th Anniversary*, video, 31:57, March 24, 2021, https://www.youtube.com/watch?v=EFo5-RFNVTU, and Daniel Coleman, Ki'en Debicki and Bonnie M. Freeman, eds., *Deyohahá:ge: Sharing the River of Life* (Waterloo: Wilfrid Laurier University Press, 2025).

9 Wolfe, "Settler Colonialism," 390, 388.

10 The Yellowhead Institute studied one hundred Canadian court injunctions to track their characteristics: "The sad final tally was that 76 percent of injunctions filed against First Nations by corporations were granted, while 81 percent of injunctions filed against corporations by First Nations were denied. Perhaps most tellingly, 82 percent of injunctions filed by First Nations against the government were denied" (Pasternak et al., 30).

11 See Barrera, "Beyond the Barricades," and Antonacci, "'Endless Cycle.'"

12 I am not comfortable with any of these terms for describing myself: "white," "settler" or "Canadian." No one is truly "white" or "black" or "red," yet these colour terms function as shorthand "types" in a racial register that, illusory as it is,

still generates real-world hierarchies of privilege and power. As Ruth Frankenberg says, "whiteness is a location of structural advantage" (1). And, despite the featherlight implication of the word "settle," the same is true of those we refer to as "settlers" or non-Indigenous "newcomers" who have come to dominate government and social hierarchies in the Americas. "Settler," too, is a location of brutally enforced, structural advantage. Anishinaabe writer Patty Krawec notes that whereas "immigrants" "come to a place and become part of the existing political system" (4), "settlers" have never become part of the political systems that existed in Turtle Island when they arrived. As for the third of the three terms, "Canadian" derives from the Huron-Iroquoian word "kanata," meaning "village" or "settlement," so the name "Canada" borrows the term for an Indigenous community to identify a nation-state that has consistently constructed for itself a position of structural advantage over the villages and existing political systems it is named after – so this term, too, remains a troubling way to identify myself. Tyson Yunkaporta, a senior lecturer in Indigenous Knowledges at Deakin University's Geelong Waurn Ponds Campus who belongs to the Apalech clan in the far north of Queensland, Australia, uses the term "Second Peoples" to refer to those of us in countries like Australia or Canada who live within European-derived dominant culture with its linear conception of time and history (see "First Law," in *Sand Talk*, 29–37). Perhaps, given my book's investigation of the way settler colonial cultures in what is called Canada and the United States emerged through their encounter with the Covenant Chain–Two Row Treaty tradition, "Second Peoples" would be a good way to reposition us within our "younger sibling" status in one of the two rows vis-à-vis "First Peoples" in Turtle Island's constitutional history.

13 It would take more room than I have to provide a full sense of this remarkable productivity in Haudenosaunee cultural expression. A very cursory gesture to recent influential Haudenosaunee artists and scholars (with apologies to more people I have not included than ones I have) would note the dynamic work of the 1970s and 1980s conducted by Bob Antone, José Barreiro, Oren Lyons, John Mohawk, Leon and Audrey Shenandoah, Jake Thomas and the circle of writers and thinkers associated with *Akwesasne Notes*. It would also include artists such as Vincent Bomberry, Elizabeth Doxtater, John Kahionhes Fadden, Eric Gansworth, David General, Rick Hill, Arnold Jacobs, Peter Jemison, Chandra Maracle, Alan Michelson, Shelly Niro, Jolene Rickard, Raymond Skye and Santee Smith. As for writers and scholars, a foreshortened twenty-first century list would include Percy Abrams, Amber Meadow Adams, Taiaiake Alfred, Darren Bonaparte, Katsi Cook, Ki'en Debicki, Tom Deer, Bonnie Freeman, Sara General, Taylor Gibson, Mishuana Goeman, Susan Hill, Kahente Horn-Miller, Beverley Jacobs, Norma Jacobs, Keith Jamieson, Penelope Kelsey, Brian Maracle, Dawn Martin-Hill, Theresa McCarthy, Rick Monture, David Newhouse, Brian Rice, Marilyn Schindler, Audra Simpson, Scott Manning Stevens, Sandra Styres, Lina Sunseri, Vanessa Watts, Kevin White, Kayanesenh Paul Williams and Adrianne Lickers Xavier. These and other Haudenosaunee artists, writers and thinkers created the ferment in which I have written this book, so it's appropriate that they make up the majority of my bibliography.

Chapter 4: Oral Histories of the Agreement

1 Jake Thomas said that if you are a wampum keeper reciting the message of a wampum, "you don't try to use your own ideas, because if you do, you keep people confused. The thing that I have heard is only what I go by" (Muller, *Holding Hands*, 10–11). Wampum speakers like Thomas kept themselves as much as possible to verbatim accuracy.

2 I'm influenced here by Kayanesenh Paul Williams, who writes, "To function, a law preserved in memory rather than writing must place emphasis on principles rather than details" (*Kayanerenkó:wa*, 85).

3 Foster was a non-Haudenosaunee linguist who worked at the time for what was then called the Canadian Museum of Civilization.

4 Muller, "Two Mystery Belts," 149.

5 From Michael Foster's notes courtesy of Rick Hill.

6 While sometimes translated to mean "original people," Amber Meadow Adams explained to me that "Onkwehón:we" means something more like "genuine, sincere, or real person." It is not a racial category as the Thomas-Miller version suggests by setting it in opposition to "white man" (personal correspondence).

7 From Hill, "Oral Memory."

8 Jake Thomas participated in several trips to Ottawa to present the Covenant Chain–Two Row history to the governor general and other parties between 1981 and 1983. Muller may indicate a different translator to the photograph from Rick Hill that is supplied because she is describing a different day's oration in the same series.

9 Muller, *Holding Hands*, 208–9.

10 Some have specified 1613 as the date for when the Haudenosaunee and Dutch agreed to the Covenant Chain–Two Row treaty. The Two Row Renewal Campaign of 2013 took the occasion of that date's four hundredth anniversary to send Haudenosaunee and ally paddlers down the Mohawk and Hudson Rivers as "a statewide advocacy and educational campaign to polish the chain of friendship established by the Two Row (between the Haudenosaunee and Dutch immigrants) and continued with the French, British and United States. Environmental cleanup and preservation were the core components of our campaign" (http://honorthetworow.org/ [site discontinued]; see also Hallenbeck, "Returning to the Water"). While it is clear that Dutch traders had established trade in and around Fort Orange (today, Albany) within five or so years of Hudson's 1609 voyage, the 1613 date is based on a document that ostensibly records the agreement in writing but whose authenticity has been disputed (see Gehring and Starna, "Revisiting the Fake Tawagonshi Treaty"). I don't rely on the 1613 date here because it is clear that Haudenosaunee protocols for linking arms and treaty-making long preceded Dutch arrival in the region. Whatever the exact date, it is undisputed that the Haudenosaunee and Dutch had established trading relationships in the early seventeenth century and that Haudenosaunee wampum protocols for how to create and maintain such relationships governed

them and subsequent British administrations up and down the region for centuries.

11 Hill, "Oral Memory," 153.

Chapter 5: What Could "Covenant" Mean to Dutch and British Ears?

1 In his history of the formation of Dutch identity from the sixteenth century onward, Simon Schama says that "years of crisis and prolonged military endeavor [in the movement toward independence from Spain] were likely to imprint on the Dutch mentality an awareness of their symbolic embodiment of the resistance to Catholic absolutism" (53), and he anchors this embodiment in Dutch understanding of *verbont* (covenant) theology summarizing William the Silent in 1573 insisting that "'*een vaste verbont*' – an unshakeable union – made with the King of Kings . . . self-evidently superseded any earthly allegiance to a mere king of Spain . . . The covenant between God and his Chosen People had destroyed the unrighteous in favor of a new and godly order" (45).

2 Johnston, *Covenant Chain of Peace*, 129.

3 John 14:14–15.

4 Althusius quoted in Johnston, *Covenant Chain of Peace*, 146–47.

5 McCoy and Baker quoted in Johnston, *Covenant Chain of Peace*, 148–49.

6 Williams, "Algebra of Federal Indian Law," 227–36.

7 Dennis, *Cultivating a Landscape of Peace*, 126.

8 In this sense, conversion was the religious rationale within New France's more intimate practice of assimilation, whereby Indigenous people were welcomed into the French family. Métis historian Dr. John Andrew Morrow voices a common French-Canadian assessment of the history of French-Indigenous relations when he writes, "In New France, there was no 'war against the Indians' . . . The encounter between the French and the aboriginal inhabitants of the Americas was distinct . . . As Samuel de Champlain said: 'Our sons shall wed your daughters and we shall be but one people.' That was not the case in the United States or English Canada where racism generally prevented intermixing. In Canada, the French were concerned with coexistence with Indigenous people . . . Alliances were made. Territories were delineated. And, in the process, a new nation of people was created: the Métis, who served as a bridge between cultures and languages" ("Indigenous and Muslim Perspectives"). What places the Haudenosaunee in sharp contradiction to this view is their Two Row insistence on staying in their own vessel and refusing to become "sons" or "daughters" in the French family, and especially not converting to the Catholic faith. There were exceptions among communities of Mohawks who became known as "praying Indians" for their having become Catholics and settling in Catholic communities known today as Kanesatake and Kahnawà:ke near Montreal. And, as Sir William Johnson's common-law marriage to Konwatsi'tsayén:ni Mary Brant demonstrates, there were marriages between Haudenosaunee and

British colonials that produced "Métis" children, but such relationships were understood within the framework of autonomously linked arms, rather than assimilation or conversion. Despite multiple efforts by the Haudenosaunee to extend the covenant of friendship to the French (such as during Kiotsaeton's visit to Trois-Rivières), however, the Confederacy's overall insistence on being "brothers" rather than "sons," expressed in their disinterest in conversion, kept them at odds with New France and its Indigenous allies.

9 Dennis, *Cultivating a Landscape of Peace*, 154–63.

10 Dennis, *Cultivating a Landscape of Peace*, 191–93.

11 Dennis, *Cultivating a Landscape of Peace*, 166–67.

12 Dennis, *Cultivating a Landscape of Peace*, 169.

13 Shorto, *Island in the Center of the World*, 95–98.

14 Shorto, *Island in the Center of the World*, 267–68, 273.

15 Shorto, *Island in the Center of the World*, 304.

Chapter 6: Tracing *Kaswentha*'s Flow

1 Jake Thomas, 1981 oration.

2 Adams, "Where the Roots Touch," 43–48.

3 Amber Meadow Adams puts it this way: "If Tehontatenentshonteronhtáhkwa is a story about how and why people connect, Tékeni Teyohà:te (the Two Row) is about what's in the space they cross when connecting" ("Where the Roots Touch," 51).

4 As Hill puts it in "Oral Memory of the Haudenosaunee," "Many of today's Iroquois people live in the whiteman's vessel. Many traditionalists call them 'sellouts' and have turned their backs on these people. Thomas's and Miller's interpretation of the Two Row takes a kinder view of those Indians in the whiteman's vessel – saying in effect that Indians should retain an Indian value system no matter where they go" (158).

5 Venables, "Polishing the Silver Covenant Chain," 3.

6 Treaty Minutes, *Pennsylvania Council Minutes* (June 16, 1744, 4: 706–9). Cited in Williams and Nelson, "*Kaswentha*," 92–93.

7 Amber Meadow Adams writes, "That this agreement was meant to be maintained through regular re-enactment – that it constituted a relationship, rather than a discrete event – emerges when the Haudenosaunee began to describe it in terms of being a 'chain' of covenants. The word that describes a chain in *Kanyen'kéha* . . . literally [means] 'they link arms together.' The act of linking arms was – and still is – performed in several Haudenosaunee ceremonies." This is an important corrective, she explains, to William Fenton's assertion that the concept of "chain" postdated European arrival, since the iron links were not available in the Haudenosaunee world (Adams, "Covenant Chain in Passamaquoddy," 16–17).

8 Mary Louise Pratt writes, "A 'contact' perspective emphasizes how subjects are

constituted in and by their relations to each other. It treats the relations among colonizers and colonized, or travelers and 'travelees,' not in terms of separateness or apartheid, but in terms of copresence, interaction, interlocking understandings and practices, often within radically asymmetrical relations of power" (*Imperial Eyes*, 7). When Canesatego met with the British governors in 1744, the Haudenosaunee represented a power with which the British were eager to ally themselves.

9 Gibson, *Concerning the League*, 433–34.

10 See Sub-Chief Jock Hill's contemporary narration of the Dish With One Spoon Wampum in *Sewatokwa'tshera't: The Dish with One Spoon* (Dawn Martin-Hill, dir.) and Alan Corbiere's narrative of the Anishinaabe Friendship Belt ("'Their Own Forms of Which They Take the Most Notice,'" 57).

11 Richter, "Rediscovered Links in the Covenant Chain"; Parmenter, "Meaning of Kaswentha," 89; Venables, "Polishing the Silver Covenant Chain," 3. Judge Sophie Bourque in her recent Quebec Superior Court case *R. v. Monture and White* (November 2023) based her decision that the Covenant Chain is a treaty right as defined in Section 35(1) of the Canadian Constitution on evidence that the Haudenosaunee held ten documented treaty council meetings with the British commissioners in Albany between 1664 and 1760 at the capitulation of Quebec, and that afterward, when the British administrative centres moved north after the Revolutionary War, that Covenant Chain councils were moved to Quebec City (5, 32, 185).

12 Williams, *Linking Arms*, 122.

13 Gwyn, "Johnson, Sir William."

14 Graymont, "Konwatsi'tsayén:ni [Mary Brant]."

15 See for example James E. Doan's essay on Johnson in the *Dictionary of Irish Biography*, originally published October 2009, last revised April 2021, https://www.dib.ie/biography/johnson-sir-william-a4300.

16 An editor's footnote spells this name "Canaseraga."

17 *Papers of Sir William Johnson*, Vol. 1, 157–59.

Chapter 7: From Proclamation to Constitution

1 *R. v. Williams*, 2023 ONCJ, 7.

2 *R. v. Monture and White* (November 2023), D.2.5, sections 1050–52, 233.

3 Jacobs' talk took place on March 7, 2022, as part of the "On Treaty Recognition Week" series of talks at Wilfrid Laurier University. She was citing Monture-Angus's *Thunder in My Soul.*

4 In a section entitled "D.2.6 Extinction of the Covenant Chain, or breaking the chain" in *R. v. Monture and White,* Judge Bourque writes, "[1071] Canadian law requires the consent of both parties for the extinction of a treaty. Not only is there no evidence that the Haudenosaunee consented to the extinguishment of the Covenant Chain, but the evidence points to the contrary . . . [1077] Breaking the Covenant Chain cannot result from mere negligence or dysfunction. To

do that requires an explicit gesture from the parties expressing their intent to sever the relationship . . . [1084] The Covenant Chain relationship and Treaty between the Crown and the Mohawks of Kahnawà:ke has not disappeared and is not broken, despite being tested over recent centuries. In the era of reconciliation, the Covenant Chain is uniquely well suited for this important task" (236–38).

5 Fifteen years ago in 2009, during negotiations between the Six Nations Confederacy Council and the federal government over the lands disputed at Douglas Creek Estates near Caledonia, the government negotiators wrote in a draft statement that was later rescinded: "We take the view that, whatever the nature of the early relations between the Hodinöhsö:ni and European societies, the relationship between Canada and the Six Nations of the Grand River has evolved into one between governments within a federal state. Canada does not believe that a protracted debate over the historical significance of the Covenant Chain or the Two Row Wampum would be constructive, since the historical record suggests that it would be difficult, if not impossible, for the parties to reach a common understanding of these symbols" (Hill, *War Clubs and Wampum Belts*, 70). Such a view missed the point that as subjects of the Crown treaties, the negotiators have a responsibility to address past injustices that have been ignored for too long. We cannot move forward in restoring the linked arms of peace, friendship and respect if the path is clogged by crawling insects or dust on the Covenant Chain.

6 In "Trans-Systemic Constitutionalism in Indigenous Law and Knowledge," Sa'ke'j Henderson writes that we need a wide variety of people, including artists, scholars and legal workers, among a wide swath of Canadians to learn to think between Indigenous epistemologies and legal traditions and European ones so that a new grundnorm can develop in which Indigenous culture, beliefs and laws can influence our courts' and parliamentarians' understandings of what constitutes evidence, what narrative traditions inform the basis for ethics and law, and how Indigenous ecological thinking and spirituality can reshape Canadian constitutionalism.

7 Gwyn, "Johnson, Sir William."

8 In a letter dated February 17, 1763, Johnson explained his mandate to John Tabor Kemp, Attorney General of New York: "The nature of my office is Expressed in General terms in his Majestys Commission to me, but the intent and meaning of the Government relative thereto is more particularly signified in the several Letters I have received from the Lords of Trade who consider it as the sole & only Channel through which Indn. affrs. of wt. nature soever are to be transacted, and for that purpose that I am to be supported by Authority in all matters relative thereto in which the good of his Majestys Service is any wise concerned & therefore I apprehend the Govt, is to take such matters into Consideration as I shall be under the necessity of layg. before them" (*Papers of Sir William Johnson*, vol. 4, 45–46).

9 Personal communication, February 7, 2023. Many of Rick Hill's thoughts on Johnson were communicated in editorial comments he offered in the draft version of this chapter.

10 Rick Hill commented on this paragraph, "It is important to remember that the

Haudenosaunee objected to this line as it cut right through their traditional homelands. This objection resulted in a separate Treaty of Fort Stanwix in 1768 to redefine that line to the satisfaction of the Haudenosaunee leadership. It is also important to realize that the Haudenosaunee did not give up sovereignty or access to their lands east of that line, which included Oneida, Onondaga and Mohawk territory."

11 See Williams, "Royal Proclamation," 9. Williams generously shared this unpublished article with me, and it has significantly influenced my current understanding of Johnson and the Royal Proclamation's influence on Canadian jurisprudence. He continues to refine and develop a far-reaching and in-depth analysis of the legal impact of the Royal Proclamation upon Canadian law, as for example in the legal council he provided on *R. v. Monture and White* (2023). That is his expertise, and it is not mine. My purpose here is to convey in broad strokes the flow of Covenant Chain–Two Row procedures and thinking that runs through the Royal Proclamation to the 1982 Constitution Act of Canada.

12 See for example Flanagan, *First Nations? Second Thoughts*, 6–7.

13 Williams, "Royal Proclamation," 26.

14 Judge Sophie Bourque: "[21] The relationship developed and evolved through council meetings, a vital component of the Haudenosaunee diplomatic system . . . [23] From 1664 to 1755, the Albany Commissioners held the authority to hold councils and to negotiate agreements and treaties with the Haudenosaunee . . . Initially, these Commissioners were primarily traders of Dutch descent. However, in 1755, Sir William Johnson took on the role of British Superintendent of Indian Affairs, becoming the key figure in negotiating treaties . . . [28] The Mohawk and the British continued to hold council meetings well into the nineteenth century" (*R. v. Monture & White*, 34–35).

15 See *Papers of Sir William Johnson*, vol. 4, 50–61; 140–44,

16 *Papers of Sir William Johnson*, vol. 4, 56.

17 *Papers of Sir William Johnson*, vol. 4, 56–57.

18 The agreement reads, "That if any English, Dutch, or Indian (under the protection of the English) do any wrong, injury or violence to any of ye said Princes, or their Subjects, in any sort whatsoever, if they complained to the Governor at New York or to the Officer in Chief at Albany, if the person so offending can be discovered, then that person shall suffer punishment and all due satisfaction shall be given, and the like shall be done for all other English Plantations.

"That if any Indians belonging to any of the Sachims aforesaid, do any wrong, injury or damage to the English, Dutch, or Indians under the protection of the English, if complaint be made to ye Sachims, and the person be discovered who did the injury, then the person so offending shall be punished and all just satisfaction shall be given to any of His Majesties subjects in any Colony or other English plantation in America" (*Documents Relative to the Colonial History of the State of New York* [hereafter referred to as *NYCD*], London Docs, vol. 1, 67–68; cited in Williams and Nelson, *Kaswentha*, 124).

19 "The King's subjects were forbidden from taking possession of any of the lands that the Proclamation reserved for the Nations or Tribes of Indians. It follows

logically that the Indians were not considered to be among the King's subjects" (Williams, "Royal Proclamation," 35).

20 Dunning wrote, "The Royal Proclamation of 1763 had great impact throughout Canada. It was regarded as of high constitutional importance. It was ranked by the Indian people as their bill of rights equivalent to our own bill of rights in England eighty years before. To my mind the Royal Proclamation of 1763 was equivalent to an entrenched provision in the constitution of the colonies in North America. It was binding on the Crown 'so long as the sun rises and the river flows.' I have no doubt that all concerned [in Canadian Confederation in 1867] regarded the royal proclamation of 1763 as still of binding force. It was an unwritten provision [of the 1867 British North America Act] which went without saying. It was binding on the legislatures of the Dominion and the provinces just as if there had been included in the statute a sentence: 'The aboriginal peoples of Canada shall continue to have all their rights and freedoms as recognized by the royal proclamation of 1763' . . . Its force as a statute is analogous to the status of the Magna Carta which has always been considered to be the law throughout the empire . . . There is nothing so far as I can see, to warrant any distrust by the Indians of the Government of Canada. But, in case there should be, the discussion in this case will strengthen their hand so as to enable them to withstand any onslaught. They will be able to say that their rights and freedoms have been guaranteed to them by the Crown, originally by the Crown in respect of the United Kingdom, now by the Crown in respect of Canada, but, in any case, by the Crown. No Parliament should do anything to lessen the worth of these guarantees. They should be honored by the Crown in respect of Canada 'so long as the sun rises and the river flows.' That promise must never be broken" (*The Queen [ex parte the Indian Association of Alberta et al.] v. Secretary of State for Foreign and Commonwealth Affairs*, [1982] All E R 118 (Court of Appeal). [1982] QB 892, [1981] 4 CNLR 86; cited in Williams, "Royal Proclamation," 58–59). It can help us understand Lord Dunning's statement if we remind ourselves that the famous provisions of the Magna Carta (1215) arose from the nobles forcing King John to acknowledge laws that limited the king's arbitrary powers so that nobles had a right to a fair trial by a court of their peers. Key among these new limitations were a reduction of the number and extent of "King's Forests," land preserves reserved exclusively for his use and pleasure.

21 Williams, "Royal Proclamation," 9–10.

22 *Papers of Sir William Johnson*, vol. 4, 297.

23 *Papers of Sir William Johnson*, vol. 4, 20.

24 Williams, "Royal Proclamation," 19–20.

25 This is Kayanasenh Paul Williams' interpretation, "Chain, Naturally Understood," 94n70. See also William Starna's article questioning the authenticity of this version of the seal, hand-drawn by Rufus Grider, likely in the 1890s ("Sir William Johnson's Seal or Rufus Grider's Imagination?").

26 Corbiere, "'Their Own Forms of Which They Take the Most Notice,'" 60–62.

27 Rick Hill, editorial correspondence on this passage in my manuscript, February 7, 2023. Hill adds, "The reality of the Treaty of Fort Niagara was it was actually three different treaties made at the same time. One was with the Haudenos-

aunee speaking nations at Fort Niagara to renew the Covenant Chain; a second treaty was made with the Chenusiio Senecas who were responsible for the Devil's Hole victory and this resulted in the gifting of a four-mile tract of land on either side of the Niagara River corridor; and a third treaty was made with the Anishinaabemowin-speaking nations held at Fort George near present-day Niagara-on-the-Lake, Ontario. Johnson realized that he could not hold one council with all these different nations, as he feared old animosities would lead to outright conflicts during the treaty council." The ongoing significance of the 1764 Niagara Treaty can be witnessed in the Commemoration of the 250th Anniversary of the Treaty of Niagara, held August 1–2, 2014, at Old Fort Niagara (August 1) and the site of the Indian Council House on The Commons at Niagara-on-the-Lake (August 2). The two-day event was co-organized by the Association of Iroquois and Allied Indians, the Chiefs of Ontario and the Six Nations Legacy Consortium, and descendants of the original twenty-four Indigenous "signatory" nations to the treaty were in attendance along with the Honourable David Zimmer, Ontario Minister of Aboriginal Affairs, Deputy Minister David de Launay and the Honourable David C. Onley, Lieutenant Governor of Ontario. As part of his address to the assembled nations commemorating the Treaty of Niagara, Minister Zimmer presented each of the twenty-four nations that gathered 250 years ago with two strings of wampum to evoke the two row wampum relationship (see Tidridge, *Queen at the Council Fire* and Tidridge, "The Queen at the Council Fire," Crown in Canada, https://www.canadiancrown.com/queen-at-the-council-fire.html).

28 Rick Hill, editorial correspondence on this passage in my manuscript, February 7, 2023.

29 Borrows, *Recovering Canada*, 255n108.

30 Adams, "Covenant Chain in Passamaquoddy," 49–50.

31 Adams, "Covenant Chain in Passamaquoddy," 9.

32 Adams, "Covenant Chain in Passamaquoddy," 11.

33 Gwyn's entry on Johnson in *Dictionary of Canadian Biography* reads, "He accepted a 130,000-acre grant from the Mohawks of Canajoharie (near Little Falls, N.Y.). For £300, New York currency, he bought about 100,000 acres on the Charlotte Creek, a tributary of the Susquehanna River though as a result of boundary limits set by the Fort Stanwix agreement of 1768 he was obliged to abandon his purchase. In 1765, less than three months after a treaty had been concluded with Pontiac, designed in part to allay Indian fears for their land, Johnson purchased some 40,000 acres from the Oneidas. In all this he acted no differently from dozens of other speculators in Indian lands. He was distinguished only by the great advantages he possessed through his office and through his long intimacy with the Indians. He was indeed one of their principal exploiters; his actions speak louder than any words of his. He was a typical imperial servant, in an area where he had few competitors able to match his intelligence and interest."

34 Albert James Williams-Myers writes that Johnson had some sixty enslaved people working for him, making him the largest slaveholder in the county and likely in the province (*Long Hammering*, 24, 29–30).

35 Gwyn's entry reads, "Johnson served himself at least as well as he served his king. From April 1755 until his death some £146,546 came into his hands as superintendent, an annual average of £7,700. From it he received his salary, as well as salaries for his son John and sons-in-law Guy Johnson and Daniel Claus. He arranged for the crown to rent his store and pay his storekeeper's wages and he charged the crown two and one-half per cent commission on all goods he supplied to the Indians as superintendent. Perhaps the principal item in value furnished to the Indians was rum."

36 *Papers of Sir William Johnson*, vol. 4, 231.

37 *Papers of Sir William Johnson*, vol. 4, 235; my italics.

38 *R. v. Monture and White*, 2023, C.2 [586], 133.

39 *Calder* (1973) 34 DLR (3d) 145 at 203; cited in Williams, "Royal Proclamation," 41.

Chapter 8: Race and the Other Theology

1 Hill and Tidridge, "Crown, the Chain, and Peacebuilding," 15.

2 See APTN, January 24, 2012, http://aptn.ca/news/2012/01/24/chiefs-cabinet-ministers-mps-arrive-for-historic-gathering/ [page discontinued].

3 *The Final Report of the Truth and Reconciliation Commission of Canada*, vol. 6, *Canada's Residential Schools: Reconciliation* (Montreal & Kingston: McGill-Queen's University Press, 2015), 39.

4 President Barack Obama, "Remarks by the President at Tribal Nations Conference," White House, President Barack Obama, November 13, 2013, https://www.whitehouse.gov/the-press-office/2013/11/13/remarks-president-tribal-nations-conference.

5 The role and function of the Crown in Canada's constitution is too large a topic for me to address adequately here. For a recent set of discussions of the Crown, see D. Michael Jackson, ed., *Royal Progress: Canada's Monarchy in the Age of Disruption* (Toronto: Dundurn Press, 2020). In their contribution to this volume, Rick Hill and Nathan Tidridge explain that, historically, "the 'Crown' meant the King or Queen of the United Kingdom, but has come to mean the various governmental agencies and officials making agreements on behalf of the sovereign" (2). Later in the volume, Judith Guichon, twenty-ninth lieutenant governor of British Columbia from 2012 to 2018, writes, "The monarch in our constitutional monarchy represents sober second thought and wisdom; not the next political cycle but rather enduring truths and the historical evolution of our nation through generations" (34). This makes governors general and lieutenant governors more than the ceremonial figureheads most Canadians consider them to be. "Like hereditary chiefs of many First Nations," she writes, "the Crown is represented by sober, apolitical, elder statespersons, ready to advise elected politicians when necessary to act as an adjudicator, and this represents a constraint" (38). Perry Bellegarde, National Chief of the Assembly of First Nations

between 2014 and 2021, further explains in his chapter in the same volume, "While the government of the day has to operationalize the treaty obligations held by the Crown, the Queen's representatives are the caretakers and witnesses to this immutable relationship. The Crown-First Nations treaty relationship is not founded in colonialism or rights denial, but rather the equality and sovereignty of peoples and our agreement to share the land without dominating one another . . . Treaties between the British Crown and First Nations are what made the Canadian Constitution possible" (21).

6 Brooklyn Neustaeter, "Pope Francis Apologizes for Catholic Church's Role in Canadian Residential School System," CTV News, April 1, 2022, https://www.ctvnews.ca/canada/pope-francis-apologizes-for-catholic-church-s-role-in-canadian-residential-school-system-1.5843937.

7 Williams, "Algebra of Federal Indian Law," 254.

8 Williams, "Algebra of Federal Indian Law," 232.

9 Williams, "Algebra of Federal Indian Law," 228–29.

10 Williams, "Algebra of Federal Indian Law," 235. In *The "Doctrine of Discovery" and* Terra Nullius*: A Catholic Response*, the Conference of Canadian Catholic Bishops repudiates these "doctrines" of colonialism and supply an appendix commenting on church laws during the "Age of Discovery." Citing Innocent IV's commentary on *Quod super his*, they explain, "Pope Innocent IV (1243–54) considered the conditions under which war could be waged against non-Christians, and concluded that these could not be deprived of their property or lordship simply because they were not Christian. However, if a nation violently prevented peaceful missionaries from entering that land, then Christian soldiers could be sent to ensure the security of the missionaries, even deposing the non-Christian ruler if he were intent on persecuting Christians within his borders" (8).

11 Williams, "Algebra of Federal Indian Law," 238–39. Catholic legal opinions were not entirely consistent throughout the early years of colonial exploration and expansion. So, for example, Dominican priest and theologian Francisco de Vitoria argued in *On the Indians* (1532) that "the law of nations, on the other hand, expressly states that goods which belong to no owner pass to the occupier. Since the goods in question here [lands encountered by Columbus and obviously occupied by Indigenous Peoples] had an owner, they do not fall under this title" (cited in Canadian Conference of Catholic Bishops, *The "Doctrine of Discovery" and* Terra Nullius, 12). And in 1537, Pope Paul III issued the bull *Sublimis Deus*, which stated, "We define and declare . . . that . . . the said Indians and all other people who may later be discovered by Christians, are by no means to be deprived of their liberty or the possession [*dominio*] of their property, even though they be outside the faith of Jesus Christ; and that they may and should, freely and legitimately, enjoy their liberty and the possession of their property; nor should they be in any way enslaved; should the contrary happen, it shall be null and have no effect" (cited in Canadian Conference of Catholic Bishops, *"Doctrine of Discovery" and* Terra Nullius, 14).

12 Gomes Eanes de Azurara, *The Chronicle of the Discovery and Conquest of Guinea*, 2 vols, 82–83, quoted in Jennings, *Christian Imagination*, 19.

13 Cited in Jennings, *Christian Imagination*, 32.

14 Jennings, *Christian Imagination*, 108, 109 and 114.

15 Jennings, *Christian Imagination*, 59.

16 Williams, "Algebra of Federal Indian Law," 245.

17 Williams, "Algebra of Federal Indian Law," 246.

18 See Long March to Rome, http://longmarchtorome.com/, for a petition for the Church to reject the papal bulls that add up to the Doctrine of Discovery, and Canadian Conference of Catholic Bishops, *The "Doctrine of Discovery" and* Terra Nullius, for the Conference of Canadian Catholic Bishops' official repudiation of Doctrine of Discovery and *terra nullius*, in 2016.

19 L'Incarnation, 147.

Chapter 9: Distorting "Protection"

1 Bird, "Federal Power and Federal Duty," 4. (Bird is citing the words of legal scholar Charlotte Bell in relation to the Royal Proclamation's protection against land frauds and abuses by colonists.)

2 Bird, "Federal Power and Federal Duty," 9.

3 Bird, "Federal Power and Federal Duty," 3–4.

4 As William Johnson explained in 1755, "That memorable and important act by which the Indians put their Patrimonial and conquered lands under the Protection of the King of Great Britain their Father is not understood by them as a cession or surrender as it seems to have been ignorantly or wilfully supposed by some, they intended and look upon it as reserving the Property and Possession of the soil to themselves and their heirs. This property the Six Nations are by no means willing to part with and are equally averse and jealous that any Forts or Settlements should be made thereon either by us or the French" (Johnson, *NYCD*, XXXIII 18, cited in Hill, *Clay We Are Made Of*, 120).

5 Bird admits that he is mystified as to where this authority over Indigenous land and Peoples comes from: "Section 91(24) of the Constitution Act, 1867 provides the Parliament of Canada with 'exclusive Legislative Authority' in relation to the classes of subjects 'Indians, and Lands reserved for the Indians.' There is little evidence to indicate why the Fathers of Confederation opted to assign the federal government exclusive legislative authority in this domain, but the most plausible explanation appears to be the nation-to-nation relationship that characterized dealings between Aboriginals and the Crown in British North America since contact. From the outset of Crown-Aboriginal relations in British North America, the Crown found itself responsible for protecting Aboriginals and their lands from the encroachment of settlers and exploitation by colonial governments. A renowned articulation of this responsibility and relationship is found in the Royal Proclamation of 1763, wherein King George III decreed that Aboriginals living under British rule 'should not be molested or disturbed' by colonial governments or settlers with respect to lands 'reserved to them'" (4). It seems to me the distortion, the sleight of hand, reveals itself even in the sympathetic Bird's transmogrification of "people with whom we are connected" into "Aboriginals living *under* British rule." This twisting occurs when

protection from encroachment turns from authority over settler colonials who are encroaching into authority over Indigenous allies who are being encroached upon. At the same time, this distortion confiscates the land being protected and places it (and its inhabitants) *under* the management-and-soon-"ownership" of the Crown. *Kanyen'kehàka* law professor Patricia Monture-Angus wrote in 1995, "The irony lies in the fact that the connection in section 91(24) between Indians and land is not a recognition of how we see ourselves as being of this land. It merely creates two separate subjects of federal authority to legislate" (*Thunder in My Soul*, 163).

6 Cited in Williams, "Royal Proclamation," 58.

7 *Secretary of State* (1982) All E R 118 (Court of Appeal). [1982] QB 892, [1981] 4 CNLR 86.

8 *Calder v. Attorney General of British Columbia*, [1973] SCR 313, 151, as cited in Williams, "Royal Proclamation," 62.

9 Quoted in Woo, "Canada's Forgotten Founders," 6.

10 Simcoe Papers, 1, 364, June 22, 1793; quoted in Williams and Nelson, *Kaswentha*, 80.

11 *Logan v. Styres*, [1959] 20 DLR 416 at 422]; quoted in Williams and Nelson, *Kaswentha*, 79.

12 Sinclair, *I, Candidate for Governor*, 109; italics in original.

13 See Graymont, "Konwatsi'tsayén:ni [Mary Brant]."

14 For the Mississaugas of the New Credit version of the history of the Anishinaabe Mississaugas in this region and the fallout from the Halidmand's Niagara Purchase, see *A Sacred Trust: (Part One) A Brief History of the Mississaugas of the New Credit First Nation*, directed by David A. Moses, 2017, video, 13:04, https://mncfn.ca/culture-history/a-sacred-trust/.

15 "The Haldimand Proclamation," Local History, Waterloo Public Library, https://www.wpl.ca/services/local-history/; my italics.

16 In 1821 Ahyonwaeghs John Brant (1794–1832, Joseph Brant's son, elected in 1823 to the provincial legislature and appointed superintendent of the Grand River in 1828) and Robert Johnson Kerr went to England to lobby on behalf of the Six Nations. According to Rick Hill in *History as Told Through Haudenosaunee Wampum Belts*, "The two delegates argued that the transfer of the valley from the Mississaugas to the Six Nations had actually been made by an agreement between those groups prior to Haldimand's proclamation and that the parties to this agreement had understood that the entire valley was being transferred. Brant and Kerr also remarked that it was absurd to maintain that titles were invalid because the king had not purchased the lands from the original proprietors" (233).

17 According to Statistics Canada, "In 1784 the whole littoral of the River of St. Lawrence, from Lake St. Francis to Lake Ontario, the shores of Lake Ontario as far as and including the Bay of Quinté, the neighbourhood of the town of Niagara, then called Newark, and part of the shores of the Detroit River, were colonized by about 10,000 United Empire Loyalists who, assisted by Government aid, took possession of land which had been laid out for their reception" ("Upper

Canada & Loyalists [1785 to 1797]," Statistics Canada, last updated August 26, 2015, https://www150.statcan.gc.ca/n1/pub/98-187-x/4151286-eng.htm).

18 See Brant, "Letter 10 December 1798," 12–14.

19 Leroy Hill, "What's Happening in Caledonia?"; Six Nations Lands and Resources Department, *Land Rights*; Monture, *Teionkwakhashion/We Share*, 125; DeVries, *Conflict in Caledonia*, 37.

Chapter 10: Canada Strong-Arms the Canoe

1 See Roberta Jamieson's testimony to the 1983 Penner Commission quoted in Williams and Nelson, *Kaswentha*, 432, and Williams and Nelson's own commentary, 111. In *The Clay We Are Made Of*, Susan Hill (Mohawk, Wolf clan) says that the Grand Indian Council's primary concerns were the threat of an Ottawa-imposed band council system that would replace their traditional governments and the status of women conveyed in the act's clauses about marrying in and out (191–92). The council remained active for at least the next thirty years. Hill provides a table of twelve written statements of concern sent by the council to Ottawa over different provisions of the Indian Act between November 1887 and March 1920 (216–17).

2 National Archives of Canada, (Date 1872), RG10, Volume number: 1862, Microfilm reel number: C-11103, File number: 239.

3 See Monture, "'Beneath the British Flag.'"

4 Please refer to Part I, 315n1 for my usage of "Peoples" and "people."

5 For a full discussion of the reasons why many Indigenous Peoples have rejected the "Queen's invitation" to accept Canadian citizenship, see Henderson, "*Sui Generis* and Treaty Citizenship."

6 Woo, "Canada's Forgotten Founders," 6; Titley, *Narrow Vision*, 110ff.

7 Ahenakew, *Voices of the Plains Cree*, 80–85; McLeod, "Embodied Memory," 250.

8 See Montgomery, "Six Nations Indians and the Macdonald Franchise."

9 Quoted in Titley, *Narrow Vision*, 116.

10 There are too many instances of this logic throughout Confederation-era race thinking to cite here. A telling example appears in the poem "The Onondaga Madonna" by D.C. Scott, who is renowned as one of the "Confederation Poets" but is also notorious in his role as Deputy Superintendent of Indian Affairs between 1913 and 1932 for enforcing the removal of Indigenous children from their families into the residential schools. Scott infamously described the "tragic savage lurking in [the] face" of an Onondaga mother whom he describes as descending from "a weird and waning race." Chillingly, the Residential School policy and Indian Act he enforced aimed to reduce Indigenous Peoples into a "waning race" until, as he put it in 1922, "there is not a single Indian in Canada that has not been absorbed into the body politic" (see "Duncan Campbell Scott," CanLit Guides, November 5, 2013, last updated August 19, 2016,

https://canlitguides.ca/canlit-guides-editorial-team/poetry-and-racialization/duncan-campbell-scott/).

11 See E. Brian Titley on Scott's suppression of Dr. Peter H. Bryce's 1905 and 1907 reports on health conditions in the schools (*Narrow Vision*, 83–87); Titley is also interviewed on this matter in the documentary film *Duncan Campbell Scott*. The recent revelations of unmarked graves on the sites of former residential schools give evidence of the deaths Scott knew about and suppressed.

12 *Duncan Campbell Scott*, directed by James Cullingham.

13 Woo, "Canada's Forgotten Founders," 7; Titley, *Narrow Vision*, 114–16.

14 Hill, *Clay We Are Made Of*, 232–36. Very often Six Nations people refer to this system as the "elected band council" system. I have dropped the term "elected" because I think it functions as part of the propaganda deployed by Canadian government officials to contrast the idea of a "progressive" *elected* council with the idea of a "regressive" *traditional* Confederacy council. Given the very low participation in band council elections ever since 1924 (an average of 15 percent voter turnout, as I note later on in this chapter), it's hardly the case that the band council is elected by the People of Six Nations. By contrast, the Confederacy Council chiefs are selected by each clan's *Yakoyaner* or Clan Mother on the basis of consensus among the clan, a form of what John Mohawk calls a truly participatory (as opposed to representative) democracy (see Akwesasne Notes, ed., *Basic Call to Consciousness*, 38).

15 This is why Jake Thomas travelled to Ottawa in 1981 to recite the agreement to Governor General Edward Schreyer, the queen's representative, not to then–Prime Minister Pierre Trudeau.

16 Rick Hill comments on this photo in *Two Row*, 21.

17 Quoted in Monture, "'Beneath the British Flag,'" 135.

18 Woo, "Canada's Forgotten Founders," 7; Titley, *Narrow Vision*, 117; Smith, "Deskaheh (Levi General)."

19 See "Deskaheh: An Iroquois Patriot's Fight for International Recognition" (41–47) and "The Last Speech of Deskaheh" (48–54), the text of the radio speech Levi General made on March 10, 1925, in Rochester, NY, in Akwesasne Notes, ed., *A Basic Call to Consciousness*. See also Rick Monture, *Teionkwakhashion/We Share*, 107–40, for a chapter-long discussion of Deskaheh's campaign in England and Geneva. Deskaheh's mission to the League of Nations directly addressed the Eurocentrism of the "Law of Nations" theory, outlined in the previous chapter, which had refused Indigenous participation in the practice of arbitrating *European* nations' control over Indigenous lands throughout the colonial world.

20 Akwesasne Notes, ed., *Basic Call to Consciousness*, 49.

21 Titley, *Narrow Vision*, 119.

22 Woo, "Canada's Forgotten Founders," 8.

23 Monture, "'Beneath the British Flag,'" 135.

24 See Smith, "Deskaheh (Levi General)."

25 McCarthy, *In Divided Unity*, 180.

26 Hill, *Clay We Are Made Of*, 236.

27 Woo, "Canada's Forgotten Founders," 9.

28 Dickason, *Canada's First Nations*, 344.

29 Akwesasne Notes, ed., *Basic Call to Consciousness*, 45.

30 Woo, "Canada's Forgotten Founders," 9.

31 Forester, "Six Nations Elected Council Agreed to 'Publicly Support' McKenzie Meadows Development."

32 Akwesasne Notes, ed., *Basic Call to Consciousness*, 53.

33 Hill, *Two Row Wampum Belts*, 22–23.

34 DeVries, *Conflict in Caledonia*, 10; *Sewatokwa'tshera't: The Dish with One Spoon*; McCarthy, *In Divided Unity*, 191ff.

35 Quoted in McCarthy, *In Divided Unity*, 185.

36 Quoted in McCarthy, *In Divided Unity*, 188.

Part III: Linking Arms: Face-to-Face Ethics

1 Gibson, *Concerning the League*, xxxviii–xlix.

2 Gibson, *Concerning the League*, xlii.

3 These first gestures at the Edge of the Woods also function as the opening movement of a much longer Haudenosaunee ceremony known as the Condolence, which has at least fifteen "episodes" or "burdens" whose purpose is to console those who have lost a chief or clan leader. Each of the fifteen burdens is weighted and conveyed by wampum. To this day, travel and grief are closely associated, for a person never knows when they will see their loved ones again, and why would they journey at all, but for the need to visit those who have lost a family or clan member and who are in mourning? At the Edge of the Woods, the mourners greet those who have endured the dark woods and dangerous rivers in order to comfort them, to console those who had come to console them. At the signal of the travellers' Prologue, the hosts (often those who are in grief) build a fire, arrange themselves by clan or family and speak words of greeting to "condole" those who arrive tired from the journey. (For more on Condolence, see Hill, "Restorative Aesthetic of Greg Staats," and "First Words" in Taiaiake Alfred's *Peace, Power, Righteousness*.)

Chapter 11: Clearing Ethical Space

1 In "The Haudenosaunee Imagination and the Ecology of the Sacred," Dan Longboat – Roronhiakewen (He Clears the Sky) and Joe Sheridan call this "old-growth mind," explaining how Haudenosaunee and Indigenous philosophy more generally understand human thinking and imagination as shaped and trained within and by the ecosystem, with its sentience, intelligence, wisdom, spirit and dispersed forms of knowledge.

2 McKay, *Deactivated West 100*, 98.

3 Machado, *Times Alone*, 143.

4 I am taking the spellings of the pronoun stems here from our textbook in Tom Deer's class, Nora Deering and Helga Harries Delisle's *Mohawk: A Teaching Grammar* (1976; Kahnawà:ke, QC: Kenien'kehaka Raotitiohkwa Cultural Center, 1995), 87, 255.

5 In "Guswenta Space," David Newhouse writes, "We need preparation to enter Guswenta space, a preparation of the intellect and the emotion. . . . Working in the Guswenta space requires patience and perseverance. It also requires a structure of dialogue and discussion" (118–19).

6 Leduc, ed., *Ǫ da gaho dę:s,* 7. I will return to Gae Ho Hwako's development of this concept later in this chapter.

7 Johanne McCarthy, in Two Row Research Partnership meeting, Deyohahá:ge:, Six Nations Polytechnic, November 30, 2023.

8 Levinas, *Entre Nous*, 17.

9 Levinas, *Humanism*, xii.

10 Ermine, "Ethical Space of Engagement," 194.

11 Ermine, "Ethical Space of Engagement," 197.

12 Ermine, "Ethical Space of Engagement," 197.

13 Ermine, "Ethical Space of Engagement," 194. Ermine revealingly borrows, for Indigenous-Canadian relations, a term originally used to describe the "solitudes" of Anglophone and Francophone Canada and made famous by Hugh MacLennan's 1945 novel entitled *Two Solitudes*. MacLennan took the phrase from Rainer Maria Rilke's *Letters to a Young Poet*: "Love consists in this, that two solitudes protect and touch and greet each other," which places these two "solitudes" in a relationship of love that *protects* each other's solitude, each one's distinct dignity.

14 Ermine, "Ethical Space of Engagement," 202.

15 Quoted in Lippard's Plate 40 caption (*Lure of the Local*).

16 Tracey Deer's documentary film, *Club Native* (2008), traces the exclusion of various long-time residents of the urban Kahnawà:ke reserve from official membership by the band council on the basis of non-Indigenous ancestry or marriage to non-Indigenous partners. More recently, questions about "Pretendians" – high-profile scholars and artists making claims to Indigenous ancestry – have caused Indigenous Studies units at Canadian universities, including my own McMaster University, to establish "Ancestry" committees, which are tasked to ensure the legitimacy of Indigenous experts' claims to Indigeneity.

17 Palmer, *To Know as We Are Known*, 31–32.

18 See Kawennakon (Bonnie Whitlow), "Kentyohkwa, Sewatahonhsi:yohst! (A Call to Listen Closely!)," in *Ǫ da gaho dę:s*, ed. Leduc, 15.

19 Leduc, ed., *Ǫ da gaho dę:s,* 278.

20 Gae Ho Hwako, *Ǫ da gaho dę:s,* 7–8.

21 Williams, *Linking Arms Together*, 81–82.

Chapter 12: Putting "First" Encounters Back in the Flow

1 Hobbes published *Leviathan* in 1651, eighty years after the Haudenosaunee met Cartier on the St. Lawrence and thirty years after they met Henry Hudson on the Hudson River. Written during the English Civil War (1642–51), Hobbes's book famously argues that civil war and what he represented as a violent state of nature ("the war of all against all") could be avoided only by establishing strong, unified government. Having never heard of the Peacemaker's *Kayanerenhtserakó:wa* or of Ayonwátha's invention of wampum, Hobbes points to the "savage people in many places of America" as examples of disorganized populations who "have no government at all, and live at this day in that brutish manner" (*Leviathan*, 79).

2 In a brilliant article entitled "The Unexamined," Australian cultural critic Ross Chambers defines "privilege" by its capacity to avoid examination. Speaking of race privilege, for example, he writes that "we can encapsulate the secret of whiteness's unmarked, unexamined quality in a single portmanteau word, in(di)visibility" (146), whereby white privilege avoids critique by remaining *invisible*, by being considered normative and indistinct, an *undividable* aggregate of individuals, rather than a distinctive or marked group. This kind of normative privilege is thus not seen as an "interest group." The same is true, he says, of any social group that defines the social norm, whether that be males in the domain of gender, heterosexuals in the domain of sexuality or the bourgeoisie in late-twentieth-century Euro-American social class. Considered from Chambers' perspective, then, categories of privilege depend upon avoiding scrutiny, upon socially sanctioned self-ignorance, upon not seeing ourselves as others outside our category see us.

3 Allen, "Danger of Fetishizing Radical Distinctiveness."

4 Williams, "Chain, Naturally Understood," 68. According to Sa'ke'j Henderson, to properly interpret constitutional treaty rights requires what he calls "trans-systemic legal synthesis." He says, "Trans-systemic analysis is designed to promote a more profound and coherent understanding of fundamental epistemologies that mould the jurisprudential consciousness and legal principles of Canadian law rather than simply teaching the logic of a single system of law . . . Trans-systemic legal synthesis establishes the premises to understand, respect, and substantially converge and reconcile the Eurocentric legal traditions of common law and civil law with the distinct, constitutionalized legal traditions of the Aboriginal peoples" ("Trans-Systemic Constitutionalism," 66–67).

5 Kayanesenh Paul Williams draws attention to the race thinking that lies at the base of this European-based timeline: "After 1982, Canadian courts embarked on a new effort to define and refine the Aboriginal and treaty rights that the new Constitution Act had recognized. The first cases referred back to the right of discovery, in the sense that they declared that Aboriginal rights were to be determined according to which practices were integral to the distinctive Indigenous society 'at the time of first contact with Europeans.' Since the first Asians, Africans, Australians or Amerindians an Indigenous people met would have no similar impact on their rights, it soon became clear that this aspect of Canadian law was, at its core, racist. It presumes that, no matter how scruffy, lost or out-

numbered the European might be, he would still have a determinative impact on a nation's Aboriginal rights" ("Royal Proclamation," 54).

6 Borrows, *Recovering Canada*, 66.

7 Quoted in Borrows, *Recovering Canada*, 74.

8 Goldie, *Fear and Temptation*, 168.

9 Gibson, *Concerning the League*, 458–60. Also cited in Williams, *Kayanerenkó:wa*, 339–40.

10 Hill, *History as Told*, 26.

11 Hill, *History as Told*, 16.

12 See Dickson and Watson, "Remains of 215 Children Found Buried."

13 See Jennifer Brant, "Missing and Murdered Indigenous Women and Girls in Canada" in *The Canadian Encyclopedia* online for a discussion of statistics, demographics and debates about the conduct of the independent national inquiry into the matter since it was launched in 2016. https://www.thecanadianencyclopedia.ca/en/article/missing-and-murdered-indigenous-women-and-girls-in-canada.

14 "IV – Aboriginal Right" of Opening Summary, 18.

15 Bourque, *R. v. Monture and White*, 18.

16 Bourque, *R. v. Monture and White*, 20.

17 Bourque, *R. v. Monture and White*, 233.

18 Bourque, *R. v. Monture and White*, 240.

Chapter 13: Exhausting Inquiry

1 Hawthorn Report, 264.

2 Hawthorn Report, 335.

3 Hawthorn Report, 13. Alan Cairns, a member of the Hawthorn research team, went on to publish a book-length development of this approach to Indigenous status in Canada entitled *Citizens Plus: Aboriginal Peoples and the Canadian State* (Vancouver: UBC Press, 2000).

4 Hawthorn Report, 234; my italics.

5 "Ours is an Industrial Growth Society," write Americans Joanna Macy and Molly Brown, taking their understanding of this term from the work of Norwegian eco-philosopher Sigmund Kvaløy Setreng (1934–2014). "Our political economy requires ever-increasing extraction and consumption of resources." Macy and Brown go on to explain that they use Kvaløy Setreng's term because they understand it to be "a more inclusive term than capitalism, because it also applies to state-controlled industrial economies premised on growth" (*Coming Back to Life*, 2).

6 This shared assumption is strikingly evident between the right-wing Tom Flanagan's *First Nations? Second Thoughts* and left-wing Frances Widdowson and

Albert Howard's *Disrobing the Aboriginal Industry: The Deception Behind Indigenous Cultural Preservation*. A special advisor to Prime Minister Stephen Harper, Flanagan could not be further removed on the political spectrum from Widdowson, a professor of policy studies at Mount Royal University, and Howard, her husband and co-author, who identify themselves as Marxian cultural materialists. By placing their conservative-capitalist and Marxist views beside each other, we can see their common assumptions: (1) both books picture all human societies as engaged in an evolutionary race, with some societies lagging behind while others are surging forward into the vanguard of progress and (2) they conceive of this evolutionary timeline as always measured by industrial economic growth. With this timeline guiding their thinking, they can only see Indigenous peoples as stuck in a primitive past and Western industrial and technological economies guiding the way to the future. The vacuity and bias of this Western myth of social evolutionary progress is at the centre of what British political historians David Graeber and David Wengrow, in *The Dawn of Everything: A New History of Humanity*, call the centuries-long "Indigenous critique" of the persistent myth of progress ("Wicked Liberty: The Indigenous Critique and the Myth of Progress," 27–77).

7 Akwesasne Mohawk elder F. Henry Lickers writes in his contribution to the Haudenosaunee Environmental Task Force's book *The Words That Come Before All Else: Environmental Philosophies of the Haudenosaunee* that newcomers arrived in Haudenosaunee territory from Europe having "lived with strife and imbalance for centuries. They did not see or understand their place in Creation and believed that the world was theirs. To our people, we saw them as being sick. They needed to be taught and nurtured, so that they would get better and understand their place in Creation. They brought sickness and diseases, which our people never saw before. These were diseases not only of the body but also of the spirit. They had no concept of place, little concept of family, and very little concept of Nation or Confederacy. They believed that they could buy or sell Mother Earth as if she was a commodity for sale, and they saw the beauty of the land as goods for their use" (158).

8 Penner Report, v.

9 Williams and Nelson, *Kaswentha*, 431–32.

10 Williams and Nelson, *Kaswentha*, 435.

11 Williams and Nelson, *Kaswentha*, 439.

12 Penner Report, 12.

13 Penner Report, 13.

14 Penner Report, 41.

15 Penner Report, 44; my italics.

16 Penner Report, 44.

17 Canada, "Commission's Terms of Reference," 699.

18 Reynolds, *People to People*, 2; my italics. The fuller mandate was "to examine the links between an adequate land base, jobs, and income and design effective processes for settling land disputes; to look at how treaties have been interpreted and implemented and to propose ways to make sure they are honoured; to

study the nature and causes of poverty, substandard housing, unemployment, ill health, substance abuse, suicide rates and family violence among Aboriginal communities" (2). Throughout this overview of RCAP, I cite *People to People: Nation to Nation: A Consultation Document Summarizing the Main Findings and Recommendations of the Royal Commission on Aboriginal Peoples* by Anthony Reynolds, Executive Director of the RCAP from 1993 to 1996.

19 RCAP's Indigenous leaders were Georges Erasmus (former national chief of the Assembly of First Nations), Paul Chartrand (Métis professor in the Department of Native Studies at the University of Manitoba), Mary Sillett (former president of the Inuit women's association, Pauktuutit) and Viola Robinson (former president of the Native Council of Canada).

20 See Reynolds, *People to People*, 2–3. Among these studies was *Kaswentha*, the aforementioned research report of over three hundred pages submitted to RCAP by Six Nations Confederacy lawyer Kayanesenh Paul Williams and Arihote Curtis Nelson, who had combed through more than three hundred years of written records of British, Canadian and American negotiations of the Covenant Chain–Two Row agreement with Haudenosaunee people.

21 The concept and application of reconciliation is continuing to evolve in significance and application. In sections 492–95 of *R. v. Monture and White*, Judge Bourque outlines an evolution in Canadian law of three different concepts of *reconciliation*: first was reconciliation as tolerance where, in cases like *Sparrow*, *Van der Peet* and *Gladstone*, "reconciliation is an accommodation of Indigenous peoples' way of life within the laws of Canadian society" [493]. The next "stage can be described as 'reconciliation as consistency.' Reconciliation . . . is about reconciling Aboriginal and common law perspectives, about translating these rights in a way that is consistent with European conceptions of law. Aboriginal legal traditions are translated so that they become comprehensible to the common and civilian system" [494]. Currently, she writes, we have "reconciliation as a constitutional and legal relationship, with jurisdictional implications . . . It is no longer a vertical relationship between a people and the Crown, but a horizontal relationship between equivalent humans" [495] (113–14). Judge Bourque placed her determination that the Covenant Chain is a treaty as recognized under Section 35(1), within this current and emerging understanding of reconciliation as a legal relationship between equals.

22 Reynolds, *People to People*, 18–19.

23 Reynolds, *People to People*, 15.

24 Reynolds, *People to People*, 13.

25 Case in point: *R. v. Monture and White* (November 2023), the case I have mentioned several times throughout this book because it determined that the Covenant Chain represents a procedural Indigenous right recognized under Section 35(1), was immediately appealed to the Superior Court of Quebec, and will no doubt be further appealed to the Supreme Court. The resistance to legal reconciliation in Canada is predictable, strong and consistent.

26 National Inquiry into Missing and Murdered Indigenous Women and Girls, *Reclaiming Power and Place*, 54.

27 National Inquiry into Missing and Murdered Indigenous Women and Girls, *Reclaiming Power and Place*, 54; my italics.

28 Truth and Reconciliation Commission of Canada, *Honouring the Truth*, 326.

29 Truth and Reconciliation Commission of Canada, *Honouring the Truth*, 326.

30 National Inquiry into Missing and Murdered Indigenous Women and Girls, *Reclaiming Power and Place*, Vol. 1a, 586.

31 Hawthorn Report, 234.

32 Truth and Reconciliation Commission of Canada, *Honouring the Truth*, 18.

Chapter 14: Undoing Unilateral Multiculturalism

1 "Many speakers of Haudenosaunee languages, when asked the word for 'treaty,' will say that the nearest equivalent we have is *orì:wa*. Usually defined as a matter of business undertaken by a group of people, *orì:wa* can refer to an agreement, an issue to be decided, an ongoing project (the word for spouse or marriage partner, *teyonkenirihwayenawàkon*, includes the root *-rihw-* and means 'they carry the business forward together') or, in the vocabulary of the Canadian legal system, a law or treaty" (Adams, *Seyakhikwatakwénnis*, 37). If treaty is "an ongoing project" undertaken by a group of people, the kind of common agreement one takes on in marriage, say, then any rights attached to it has more to do with *participation* in carrying that project forward than it does any individual rights *derived from* participation in that process.

2 See *R. v. Monture and White*, 148ff.

3 *R. v. Monture and White*, D.1.6.7 Oswegatchie Treaty, [727] 171. See *Papers of Sir William Johnson*, vol. XIII, 163ff.

4 Par. 30, quoted in Henderson, "Trans-Systemic Constitutionalism," 58.

5 Henderson, "Trans-Systemic Constitutionalism," 59.

6 Henderson, "Trans-Systemic Constitutionalism," 51–52.

7 If a trans-systemic understanding of law seems unfamiliar to Canadians, this is, once again, a result of the widespread ignorance of our own history of pluralist constitutional origins. Law professors Helge Dedek and Armand de Mestral, for example, describe the evolution of their "Trans-systemic Law Program" at McGill University as having its roots in the Quebec Act's requirement that French civil law – the *Coutume de Paris* – would determine private disputes in that province, while British common law would guide matters adjudicated by the Crown. The result was that the province needed lawyers who were conversant in both systems. Beginning in 1968, then, McGill increasingly trained its law students in comparative methods. Over time, Dedek and Mestral observe, lawyers trained in this comparative way are loosened away from "positivist" interpretations of national legal codes and inclined to more "systemic" understandings of the principles by which different legal systems operate. Sounding very much like Henderson, they write, "law teaching from a trans-systemic perspective is much more easily aligned with the broader social sciences and the humanities; the search for general principles becomes more necessary and the study of law is less likely to be dominated by the professionalist ethic" (907). Their article was published in a special issue on "Transnationalizing Legal Ed-

ucation" in the *German Law Journal* in 2009, so it's understandable that their writing would focus on challenges to monolithic nation-state law in an increasingly globalized world economy and specifically in relation to the European Union. But it is revealing that, unlike Henderson, they make no reference to Indigenous law in their article. Once again, the two founding nations theory blinds even Canadians interested in trans-systemic law to legal systems deriving from non-Western sources.

8 Borrows, *Canada's Indigenous Constitution*, 260.

9 Borrows, *Canada's Indigenous Constitution*, 250–52.

10 Borrows, *Canada's Indigenous Constitution*, 247.

11 Borrows, *Canada's Indigenous Constitution*, 248.

12 Locke, section 41, "Chapter V: Of Property," 122.

13 Borrows, *Canada's Indigenous Constitution*, 258.

14 Daniel Victor, "Dead Whale Found with 88 Pounds of Plastic Inside Body in the Philippines," *New York Times*, March 18, 2019, https://www.nytimes.com/2019/03/18/world/asia/whale-plastics-philippines.html.

Part IV: Covenant Chain–Two Row Ecologies

1 This sequence appears about fifty pages into the 380-page "Iroquoian Cosmology: Second Part, with Introduction and Notes" that Tuscarora ethnologist J.N.B. Hewitt translated in 1900 from John Arthur Gibson's Onondaga language telling of the Creation Story (491–506). It was then published in the *Forty-Third Annual Report of the Bureau of American Ethnology to the Secretary of the Smithsonian Institution*, 1925–1926. Gibson uses the Onondaga names De'haĕn'hiyawă''khon' and O'hā'ā' for the twin brothers. In accordance with my practice of using *Kanyen'kéha* terms, I am following the spellings here of Grand River *Kanyen'kéha* language teacher Brian Maracle ("First Words," 24). The *Kanyen'keháka* elder Sakokweniónkwas Tom Porter from Akwesasne spells these names "Teharonhiawá:kon" and "Shawískara" and translates them respectively as "He Holds Up the Heavens" and "Ice" or, less literally, "Big Wind" or "Hurricane" (83–84).

Chapter 15: The Family of Earth

1 Adams, "Where the Roots Touch," 48.

2 In *Reading the Wampum*, Seneca scholar Penelope Kelsey calls this grounding "Iroquois normative" (3).

3 Lickers in Haudenosaunee Environmental Task Force, *Words That Come Before All Else*, 156.

4 Pessoa, *Little Larger Than the Entire Universe*, 64.

5 Pessoa, *Little Larger Than the Entire Universe*, 34.

6 This translation is from Amber Meadow Adams, personal correspondence, May 9, 2022.

7 Haudenosaunee Environmental Task Force, *Words That Come Before All Else*, 21–22. Because I'm focusing here on what Salli Benedict says about mothers and mothering, I don't focus on her father, Ernie Benedict, who shared in the mothering work of nurturing earth-sustaining Indigenous traditions. Partnering with Ray Fadden-Tehanetorens, as far back as the 1950s, he rallied Mohawk youth to form the Akwesasne Mohawk Counsellor Organization, encouraging young people to value their traditions. "The two men's travels would lead them to develop the unity caravans of the early 1960s and then to the formation of the White Roots of Peace, which lit the flames of Aboriginal nationalism across the continent, changing the way mainstream society viewed 'Indians.'" (Dianne Meili with files from Doug George–Kanentiio, "Ernie and Salli Benedict [footprints]," *Windspeaker Publication* 29, no. 8 [2011], https://ammsa.com/publications/windspeaker/ernie-and-salli-benedict-footprints.)

8 David Maracle, *Karoron Ne Owennahshonha*, 322, emphases in original.

9 Haudenosaunee Environmental Task Force, *Words That Come Before All Else*, 22.

10 Haudenosaunee Environmental Task Force, *Words That Come Before All Else*, 22.

11 Haudenosaunee Environmental Task Force, *Words That Come Before All Else*, 22–23.

12 Haudenosaunee Environmental Task Force, *Words That Come Before All Else*, 133.

13 Quoted in Cook, "Women Are the First Environment." Another version of this talk can be found at Katsi Cook, "Women as the First Environment: A Broader Ecological Perspective from a Mohawk Midwife Elder," video, 1:18:31, posted December 20, 2020, https://www.youtube.com/watch?v=5Ervsv9L-UA.

14 Cook, "Women Are the First Environment."

15 See Office of Response and Restoration, "Alcoa Aluminum Factories Settle $19.4 Million" and Bonvillain, *Native Nations*, 100.

16 ICT Staff, "Mohawk Akwesasne Mourn Salli 'Kawennotakie' Benedict," *ICT*, June 4, 2011, updated September 13, 2018, https://ictnews.org/archive/mohawk-akwesasne-mourn-salli-kawennotakie-benedict.

17 Tom Schmidt, "In Memory of Salli Benedict, 1954–2011," Donaldson Funeral Home, posted November 30, 2011, http://donaldsonfuneralhome.frontrunnerpro.com/book-of-memories/1135474/Benedict-Salli/view-condolences.php.

18 "Our stories are not only our laws," writes Amber Meadow Adams. "They carry information and rules about many other matters, including profound ecological knowledge, family structure, and economic patterns, to name just a few. Law, too, is an inadequate word for *tsi niyonkwarihò:ten* (our ways of addressing matters), which don't necessarily separate domains of spirituality, or art, or science from that of law in the way English, French, or Canadian legal systems might" (*Seyakhikwatakwénnis*, 33).

19 ICT Staff, "Mohawk Akwesasne Mourn Salli 'Kawennotakie' Benedict."

20 Haudenosaunee Environmental Task Force, *Words That Come Before All Else*, 2.

21 Adams, *Seyakhikwatakwénnis*, 44–45.

22 Cook, "Women Are the First Environment."

23 Haudenosaunee Environmental Task Force, *Words That Come Before All Else*, 38.

Chapter 16: Divided Home

1 Shawn Jeffords, "Environmental Groups Critical of Ontario Government Forestry Plan," *Hamilton Spectator*, February 5, 2020.

2 I quote this particular article because it so clearly highlights how central the trade-off between *economy* and *ecology* is to Canadian politics. But it would not be difficult to cite different examples every month. When I was revising this chapter in June 2022, for example, the *Hamilton Spectator* printed an opinion piece by Gretchen Fitzgerald, national programs director for the Sierra Club Canada Foundation, about the federal government's approval of the Bay du Nord offshore oil project off Newfoundland and Labrador and its issuing of a call for bids for oil exploration for an area one-third larger than the size of New Brunswick. "It's time to kick this habit," Fitzgerald writes. "It's time to break the cycle of approving oil and gas projects and then responding to the victims of climate change disasters" (Fitzgerald, "Climate Dysfunction on Full Display," *Hamilton Spectator*, June 6, 2022. https://www.thespec.com/opinion/contributors/2022/06/06/climate-dysfunction-on-full-display.html).

3 Mia Rabson, "Canada Produces More Greenhouse Gas Emissions Than Any Other G20 Country, New Report Says," *Toronto Star*, November 14, 2018.

4 In "The Haudenosaunee Imagination and the Ecology of the Sacred," Joe Sheridan and Dan Longboat – Roronhiakewen (He Clears the Sky) observe that Western people see imagination as a property of individuals divided from and competing against their environment. By contrast, Haudenosaunee (and Indigenous philosophy, more generally) understand human thinking as shaped and trained within an ecosystem, with its sentience, intelligence, wisdom, spirit and knowledge dispersed among the species of that ecosystem: "The conceit that imagination is a function of intelligence and that mind is a solely human capacity is akin to reasoning that the food chain possesses a human ruler because that very metaphor is unguided by the primal experience of human dependence on the rest of Creation. The Western imagination, lest we forget, is also the agent of evil when it thinks only with the narcissism of individualism. Feeding on broken fragments of cosmology and finally on itself, imagination no longer is the creative ecology of intelligences in their places but becomes a nonspatial entity limping on the singularity of a receding future bereft of the eternal" (374).

5 See "Mycorrhiza," *Microbiology from A to Z*, Artis-Micropia, Accessed 14 June 2022. https://www.micropia.nl/en/discover/microbiology/mycorrhiza/ (site discontinued).

6 Haudenosaunee Environmental Task Force, *Words That Come Before All Else*, 155–56.

7 Sheridan and Longboat, "Haudenosaunee Imagination and the Ecology of the Sacred," 369, 371–72.

8 Haudenosaunee Environmental Task Force, *Words That Come Before All Else*, 155–56.

9 Haudenosaunee Environmental Task Force, *Words That Come Before All Else*, 156.

10 Gibson, "Iroquoian Cosmology," 503; my italics.

11 Gibson, "Iroquoian Cosmology," 580.

12 Haudenosaunee Environmental Task Force, *Words That Come Before All Else*, 70.

13 Haudenosaunee Environmental Task Force, *Words That Come Before All Else*, 71.

14 Gibson, "Iroquoian Cosmology," 582.

15 Hill, editorial comments on this chapter, July 13, 2023.

16 Haudenosaunee Environmental Task Force, *Words That Come Before All Else*, 79.

17 See RCAP on the doctrine of extinguishment (Reynolds, *People to People*, 9) and Borrows, *Canada's Indigenous Constitution*, 11–21.

18 Potawatomi ethno-botanist Robin Wall Kimmerer writes, "The essence of the gift is that it creates a set of relationships. The currency of the gift economy is, at its root, reciprocity. In Western thinking, private land is understood to be a 'bundle of rights,' whereas in a gift economy property has a 'bundle of responsibilities' attached" (Kimmerer, *Braiding Sweetgrass*, 28).

19 Kimmerer, *Braiding Sweetgrass*, 30, 376.

20 Hill, editorial comments on this passage, July 7, 2023. For more, see "Meet the People," Akwesasne Mohawk, National Museum of the American Indian, video, 5:21, https://americanindian.si.edu/environment/akwesasne/People.cshtml.

21 Kimmerer, *Braiding Sweetgrass*, 149.

22 Kimmerer, *Braiding Sweetgrass*, 187.

23 Akwesasne Notes, ed., *Basic Call to Consciousness*, 124.

24 Akwesasne Notes, ed., *Basic Call to Consciousness*, 124–25.

25 Hill, editorial comments on this passage, July 7, 2023.

Chapter 17: Awe and Respect

1 "Respect" implies optics (from the Latin "specere," to look at). *Oxford English Dictionary*: "Respect: v. . . . 2. To regard, consider, take into account. b. To heed, pay attention to; to observe carefully. . . . 4. To treat or regard with deference, esteem, or honour; to feel or show respect for. b. To esteem, prize, or value (a thing). c. To treat with consideration; to refrain from injuring or interfering with; to spare."

2 Haudenosaunee Environmental Task Force, *Words That Come Before All Else*, 137.

3 There is some distortion for modern ears in the English Bible's repetition of the word "fear" in these passages. Several commentaries on the Hebrew word

"Yirah" offer "awe" as an English alternative. Central to the concept of "yirah," says one Jewish-Christian commentary, "Awe . . . has to do with beholding something that is beyond one's capabilities and understanding'" ("Hebrew Meaning of Yirah: What Connects Fear and Awe?," Fellowship of Israel Related Ministries, July 20, 2021, https://firmisrael.org/learn/hebrew-meaning-of-yirah-what-connects-fear-and-awe/).

4 Hobbes, *Leviathan*, 78.

5 The *Oxford English Dictionary* explains that "awe" comes to English from Scandinavian languages, meaning "originally: a feeling of fear or dread, mixed with profound reverence, typically as inspired by God or the divine. Subsequently: a feeling of reverential respect, mixed with wonder or fear, typically as inspired by a person of great authority, accomplishments, etc., or (from the 18th century) by the power or beauty of the natural world." It then supplies the example from the 1535 Coverdale Bible: "Let the whole earth stonde in awe of him" (Psalms 96:9).

6 These Mohawk language translations are from Adams, *Seyakhikwatakwénnis*, 17, 36, 34.

7 Lyons, "Spirituality, Equality, and Natural Law," 12.

8 Berry, *Dream of the Earth*, 134–35.

9 Berry, *Dream of the Earth*, 25.

10 Steve Buist, "Protest Over 'Disgusting' Pollution Prompts City to Close Waterfront Trail," *Hamilton Spectator*, November 16, 2015, https://www.thespec.com/news/hamilton-region/protest-over-disgusting-pollution-prompts-city-to-close-waterfront-trail/article_34c51652-dc89-58ac-a032-3facb48b8c4b.html.

11 For an overview of the spill, see Matthew Van Dongen, "Sewergate: A Chedoke Creek Sewage Spill Timeline," *Hamilton Spectator*, November 18, 2019.

Chapter 18: Dish With One Spoon–Land Back

1 Pierce, "A Manifesto for Speculative Relations," 25.

2 On Claus, see Hill, *War Clubs and Wampum Belts*, 24 and Elbourne, "Broken Alliance," 500; on Jarvis, see Leighton and Burns, "Jarvis, Samuel Peters."

3 See Taekema, "Six Nations Traditional Government Wants Moratorium."

4 "Governance back," write Aimée Craft, Rachel Plotkin and Max McQuaig for the David Suzuki Foundation, "is about honouring and restoring Indigenous relationships to lands and waters and reclaiming Indigenous decision-making authority. The initiatives profiled in this report take diverse approaches to achieve this, including Indigenous-municipal alliances, self-government agreements, land trusts, governance reclamations by legislative grant, cultural easements, declarations, Indigenous protected and conserved areas and partnerships to restore compromised environments" (*Governance Back*, 26). Rick Hill adds, "One could say that the relationships don't need to be 'restored,' as they have been ongoing; however, there is a need to share our view of land with non-In-

digenous people as seen through our understanding of how to relate to land" (editorial comments on this passage, July 7, 2023).

5 *Conserve*: "'to keep safe, preserve from loss or decay,' late 14c., from Old French *conserver* (9c.), from Latin *conservare* 'to keep, preserve, keep intact, guard' . . . archaic form of classical Latin cum 'together, together with, in combination'" + "*servare* 'to guard, keep, watch'" (*Online Etymological Dictionary*, s.v. "conserve [v.]," https://www.etymonline.com/word/conserve).

6 Rick Hill, editorial comments on this passage, July 7, 2023.

7 See Page and Daniel, dirs., *There's Something in the Water*. In Chapter Three, I cited a Yellowhead Institute study of one hundred court injunctions that found that 76 percent of injunctions filed against First Nations by corporations were granted, while 81 percent filed against corporations by First Nations were denied. In addition, 82 percent of injunctions filed by First Nations against the government were denied (Pasternak et al., *Land Back*, 30). Canadian law is heavily slanted not just to the protection but to the promotion of corporate extraction.

8 *R. v. Monture* cites the expert witness of law professor Mark Walters regarding the legal orders assumed in Haudenosaunee law: "[768] For the Haudenosaunee, their ideas about normative ordering were inseparable from ideas about nature itself: earth, water, sky and the land. Their ideas about law and order are, therefore, grounded in their understanding of the place of people in relationship with land, water and nature in general" (178).

9 See how Judge Gethin Edward applied the Two Row Wampum concept in *R. v. Williams* (2023).

10 See the work of Mohawk scholar Dr. Dawn Martin-Hill, a colleague at McMaster, in two interrelated projects, *Ohneganos* and Co-Creation of Indigenous Water Quality Tools, on the health of the Grand River watershed and its impact on Six Nations Reserve. See Sonia Verma, "Empowering Communities to Shape Sustainable Water Solutions," Brighter World, McMaster University, December 10, 2020, https://brighterworld.mcmaster.ca/articles/empowering-communities-to-shape-sustainable-water-solutions/; Alexandra Shimo, "While Nestlé Extracts Millions of Litres from Their Land, Residents Have No Drinking Water," *Guardian*, October 4, 2018, https://www.theguardian.com/global/2018/oct/04/ontario-six-nations-nestle-running-water; and Brent Patterson, "Six Nations of the Grand River Challenges Nestle's Plan to Keep Taking Water from Its Territory," Council of Canadians, January 25, 2018, https://canadians.org/analysis/six-nations-grand-river-challenges-nestles-plan-keep-taking-water-its-territory/. In 2021, Nestlé Waters North America changed its name to BlueTriton, which in November 2024 announced its intention to discontinue operations in January 2025 (see Diego Pizarro, "Local Water Advocates Hail Closure of Southern Ontario Bottling Plant as a Win for Conservation," CBC News, November 21, 2024, https://www.cbc.ca/news/canada/kitchener-waterloo/blue-triton-closing-aberfoyle-water-bottling-facility-1.7388736).

11 See Joe Pavia, "Ohsweken Waits for Funding to Deliver Clean Water to More People," CBC News, July 30, 2017, https://www.cbc.ca/news/canada/kitchener-waterloo/indigenous-water-supply-1.4226347.

12 Borrows, *Recovering Canada*, 140. There are practical concerns to be addressed here. In my view, Canada desperately needs Indigenous leadership to influence and shape Canadian affairs. But Indigenous communities already experience regular departures of talented leaders who seek incomes and opportunities in broader Canadian society, often in government. This is why I have adapted Borrows's "Indigenous control of Canadian affairs" with the phrase "Indigenous governance in Canadian affairs." By supporting the resurgence of Indigenous knowledge, languages, philosophies and technologies, Canadians can support the consolidation of knowledgeable Indigenous "elder brothers" whose understanding and experience can teach us Canadians principles and procedures for how to conduct our affairs – ecological, economic, political, let alone familial, spiritual and cultural.

13 Borrows, *Recovering Canada*, 149.

14 Saul, *Fair Country*, 105.

15 Reynolds, *People to People*, 18–19.

16 See Sub-Chief Jock Hill's contemporary narration of the Dish With One Spoon Wampum in *Sewatokwa'tshera't: The Dish with One Spoon*, and Alan Corbiere's narrative of the Anishinaabe Friendship Belt, "'Their Own Forms of Which They Take the Most Notice,'" 57.

17 According to V.P. Neimanis, "Crown land is the term used to describe land owned by the federal or provincial governments. Authority for control of these public lands rests with the Crown, hence their name. Less than 11% of Canada's land is in private hands; 41% is federal crown land and 48% is provincial crown land. . . . Surface and subsurface rights to the mineral, energy, forest and water resources may be leased to private enterprise – a very important source of government income in Canada. National and provincial parks, Indian reserves, federal military bases and provincial forests are the largest and most visible allocations of crown land." (Neimanis, "Crown Land," *Canadian Encyclopedia*, May 18, 2011; last edited December 16, 2013; site accessed November 7, 2023, https://www.thecanadianencyclopedia.ca/en/article/crown-land.)

18 Ontario Ministry of Natural Resources, "Disposition of Public Land to Other Governments and Government Agencies," January 24, 2006, https://files.ontario.ca/environment-and-energy/crown-land/mnr_e000096.pdf.

19 Ojibwe Anishinaabe writer Patty Krawec explains, "Settlers and migrants and the forcibly displaced get worried when Native people start talking about Land Back. What about their house? Where will they go? Unable to imagine any scenario other than what settler colonialism unleashed upon us, people assume that Land Back means evictions, relocations, and elimination. In some cases, that might be appropriate . . . But wholesale eviction was never what we intended. Remember, from the earliest treaties [such as the Covenant Chain and Two Row Wampum], we offered a way to live together in peace, friendship, and respect. And although we are often, and I think reasonably, looking for change in ownership, at its core, Land Back means profoundly changing our relationship with land" (*Becoming Kin*, 131).

20 Brett Forester, "OPP Spent More than $16M Policing 1492 Land Back Lane: Records," APTN News, March 30, 2021, https://www.aptnnews.ca/national

-news/opp-spent-more-than-16m-policing-1492-land-back-lane-records/ and Brett Forester, "OPP Try and Alter Figures to Manipulate $21M Cost of Policing Occupation in Caledonia," APTN News, May 31, 2022, https://www.aptnnews.ca/national-news/opp-try-and-alter-figures-to-manipulate-21m-cost-of-policing-occupation-in-caledonia/. The latter article indicates "In 2006, following a similar occupation that also continues today [Douglas Creek Estates], the province paid $30 million in policing costs, $20 million in legal settlements, and $15 million to buy out that developer."

Chapter 19: Linked Arms–Land Back

1 Johanne McCarthy (Onondaga, Beaver Clan), discussion during Two Row Research Partnership meeting, Deyohahá:ge:, Six Nations Polytechnic, November 30, 2023. Glen Coulthard, mentioned above, has developed the term "grounded normativity" to encapsulate the impact of these laws on Indigenous thinking. With Anishinaabe writer Leanne Betasamosake Simpson, he explains, "Grounded normativity houses and reproduces the practices and procedures, based on deep reciprocity, that are inherently informed by an intimate relationship to place. Grounded normativity teaches us how to live our lives in relation to other people and nonhuman life forms in a profoundly nonauthoritarian, non-dominating, nonexploitive manner. Grounded normativity teaches us how to be in respectful diplomatic relationships with other Indigenous and non-Indigenous nations with whom we might share territorial responsibilities or common political or economic interests. Our relationship to the land itself generates the processes, practices, and knowledges that inform our political systems, and through which we practice solidarity. To willfully abandon them would amount to a form of auto-genocide" (Coulthard and Simpson, "Grounded Normativity," 254).

2 Lyons, "Spirituality, Equality, and Natural Law," 12.

3 Watts, "Indigenous Place-Thought," 21. See also Sheridan and Longboat's discussion of "old-growth" understanding of place-nurtured Indigenous thinking and imagination as "animate realism" ("Haudenosaunee Imagination and the Ecology of the Sacred," 369).

4 Watts, "Indigenous Place-Thought," 23.

5 Watts, "Indigenous Place-Thought," 23.

6 Venne quoted in Watts, "Indigenous Place-Thought," 27.

7 Watts, "Indigenous Place-Thought," 33.

8 Watts, "Indigenous Place-Thought," 33.

9 Beverley O'Neil, "Energy Companies that Want to Do Projects on Indigenous Lands Must Be Open to Collaboration," *Hamilton Spectator*, October 6, 2020.

10 King and Yesno, "Reclamation," in Pasternak et al., *Land Back*, 48.

11 King and Yesno, "Reclamation," in Pasternak et al., *Land Back*, 44.

12 See Deer, "Developer Offers to Give Land Back" and also Valiante, "'I Filled a Void.'"

13 Deer, "Developer Offers to Give Land Back" and Valiante, "'I Filled a Void.'"

14 Bankuti, "Oka Denied on Pines Land Legal Maneuver."

15 McDermott and Bell, *Indigenous Perspectives on Conservation Offsetting*, 19.

16 Hill, "'Traveling Down the River of Life Together," 40–41.

17 See "About Us," Joint Stewardship Board, Accessed June 24, 2022, http://jointstewardshipboard.com/about-us/.

18 Of course, these three strings evoke the three wampum strings of the "Edge of the Woods" ceremony discussed earlier in this book (see especially the opening to Part Three), with its function to clear the tears from the eyes, the ringing from the ears and the blockage from the throats of those who are in mourning so that they can regain good, clear minds in order to make good decisions about choosing new leaders who can negotiate peaceful relations for the future.

19 McDermott and Bell, *Indigenous Perspectives on Conservation Offsetting*, 22.

20 See Weinberg, "The Red Hill Expressway," 135.

21 See Teviah Moro, "Studies into Red Hill Widening Suspended to Bring Indigenous Delegates into the Fold," *Hamilton Spectator*, June 14, 2022, https://www.thespec.com/news/hamilton-region/2022/06/14/hamilton-suspends-studies-into-red-hill-valley-parkway-widening-to-present-pitch-to-joint-stewardship-board.html.

22 See Matthew Van Dongen, "Hamilton Votes Down Study of Indigenous Council Seat," *Hamilton Spectator*, July 13, 2024, https://www.thespec.com/news/council/hamilton-votes-down-study-of-indigenous-council-seat/article_89b276f0-5458-57e7-806b-f8875272a1b1.html.

23 The struggle over how to implement Linked Arms land and water governance came back in the Hamilton news in relation to Chedoke Creek, which runs west of the Red Hill Creek into Cootes Paradise, the marsh at the Head of Lake Ontario on Hamilton's west side. After one of its Combined Sewer Overflow tanks had leaked an estimated twenty-four billion litres of contaminated water into the creek over four years (in the scandal known as "sewergate" discussed in Chapter 17), the City was ordered by the province's Ministry of the Environment to dredge the creek in an effort to restore water health in the marsh and, downstream, Hamilton Harbour. As the City prepared to begin dredging in summer 2022, the Confederacy Council's Haudenosaunee Development Institute (HDI) insisted that the City should consult with them before commencing any intervention on 1701 Albany (Nanfan) Treaty lands. The dispute put the dredging on hold for a year, until the City agreed to appoint HDI representatives to monitor the dredging process, which then recommenced in July 2023. Once again, we have an example of consultation after the fact. But the capacity of HDI to intervene and the willingness of City Council to be convinced of the importance of Haudenosaunee monitors for this environmental project indicates a reluctant but rising awareness of how a Linked Arms approach can provide new understandings of jurisdiction in our watershed. See Bobby Hristova, "Chedoke Creek Clean Up Resumes After Months-Long Delay," *CBC News*, July 18, 2023, https://www.cbc.ca/news/canada/hamilton/chedoke-creek-dredging-resumes-1.6909757.

Part V: Conclusion

1 "I really want to emphasize that this is the reader's digest form," Porter says. "I've heard it myself recited for ten days, on three different occasions in my life. In fact for two of those, I was asked to be the interpreter, in the afternoons, for it. At the time it was scary because there were no notes. It was almost like a simultaneous recitation, in the afternoon . . . So it meant that I had to listen to all the Mohawk language of the recital, from eight or nine o'clock in the morning until one o'clock, with no breaks, no stops, from eight to one. That's the Great Law in the Mohawk language. Then after we had eaten, in the afternoon, I had to repeat what he said, recite it, with no tape recorder, and no writing either. It was really frightening for me. I was familiar with it, but I had never actually done it. But on two occasions, or maybe it was three times, I did it. So I have a pretty good familiarity with it" (Porter, *And Grandma Said*, 272–73).

2 Porter, *And Grandma Said*, 307–9; italics in original.

3 There are many sources for Brant's and Johnson's owning of slaves. Allen and Conn's entry in *The Canadian Encyclopedia* says Brant may have owned as many as thirty slaves. Julian Gwyn's entry on Johnson in the *Dictionary of Canadian Biography* indicates Johnson used "white indentured and black slaves" to till the two hundred acres of his home farm.

4 Beresford-Kroeger, *To Speak for the Trees*, 194–95.

5 Haudenosaunee Environmental Task Force, *Words That Come Before All Else*, 80.

6 Haudenosaunee Environmental Task Force, *Words That Come Before All Else*, 81.

7 Maracle, *My Conversations with Canadians*, 81.

Bibliography

Abley, Mark. *Spoken Here: Travels Among Threatened Languages.* New York: First Mariner Books, 2005.

Adams, Amber Meadow. *Seyakhikwatakwénnis ne Tehontatenentshonteronhtáhkwa; Grasping the Chain Again* (*R. v. Derek White & Hunter Montour*, S.C. 505-01-137394-165 and CM-2018-000545), Expert Report, June 4, 2021.

———. "Where the Roots Touch: tsi niyothahinen ne Tehontatenentshonteronhtáhkwa." In *Deyohahá:ge: Sharing the River of Life*, edited by Daniel Coleman, Ki'en Debicki and Bonnie M. Freeman, 35–51. Waterloo: Wilfrid Laurier University Press, 2025.

Ahenakew, Edward. *Voices of the Plains Cree.* Edited by Ruth M. Buck. Regina: Canadian Plains Research Centre, University of Regina, 1995.

Ahmed, Sara. *Strange Encounters: Embodied Others in Post-Coloniality.* London: Routledge, 2000.

Akwesasne Notes, ed. *Basic Call to Consciousness.* Summertown, TN: Native Voices, 2005.

Alfred, Taiaiake. *Peace, Power, Righteousness: An Indigenous Manifesto.* Toronto: Oxford University Press, 1999.

———. "Sovereignty." In *Sovereignty Matters: Locations of Contestation and Possibility in Indigenous Struggles for Self-Determination*, edited by Joanne Barker, 33–50. Lincoln: University Nebraska Press, 2005.

Allen, Chad. "The Danger of Fetishizing Radical Distinctiveness." *Different Knowings Speaker's Series.* September 2, 2011. Video, 3:37. https://www.youtube.com/watch?v=2y_fFkfBlpM.

Allen, Robert S., and Heather Conn. "Joseph Brant." In *The Canadian Encyclopedia.* Last edited October 22, 2019. https://www.thecanadianencyclopedia.ca/en/article/joseph-brant.

Antonacci, J.P. "'Endless Cycle': Battle Over Land Rights in Caledonia Continues 15 Years Later," *Hamilton Spectator*, March 6, 2021: A1, A8–A10.

Bankuti, Marcus. "Oka Denied on Pines Land Legal Maneuver," *The Eastern Door*, May 15, 2023. https://easterndoor.com/2023/05/15/oka-denied-on-pines-land-legal-maneuver/.

Bardeau, Phyllis Eileen Wms. *Definitive Seneca: It's in the Word.* Edited by Jaré Cardinal. Salamanca, NY: Seneca-Iroquois Museum Publisher, 2011.

Barrera, Jorge. "Beyond the Barricades." CBC News, November 25, 2020. https://newsinteractives.cbc.ca/longform/1492-land-back-lane-caledonia-six-nations-protest.

Battiste, Marie. "Print Culture and Decolonizing the University: Indigenizing the Page: Part 1." In *The Future of the Page*, edited by Peter Stoicheff and Andrew Taylor, 111–23. Toronto: University of Toronto Press, 2004.

Baxter, Peter, and Peter Spirer, dirs. *Spirit Game: Pride of a Nation*. Toluca Lake, CA: One Bowl Productions, 2017.

Bélanger, Damien-Claude, ed. *FLQ Manifesto.* Peterborough, ON: Trent University, 2007. Accessed November 29, 2018. http://faculty.marianopolis.edu/c.belanger/quebechistory/docs/october/documents/FLQManifesto.pdf.

Beresford-Kroeger, Diana. *To Speak for the Trees: My Life's Journey from Ancient Celtic Wisdom to a Healing Vision of the Forest.* Toronto: Random House Canada, 2019.

Berry, Thomas. *The Dream of the Earth.* San Francisco: Sierra Club Books, 1988.

Bird, Brian. "Federal Power and Federal Duty: Reconciling Sections 91(24) and 35(1) of the Canadian Constitution." *Appeal: Review of Current Land and Law Reform* 16 (2011): 3–14. Accessed March 17, 2022. CanLIIDocs 228, https://canlii.ca/t/2bwr.

Blackstock, Cindy. "First Nations Child and Family Services: Restoring Peace and Harmony in First Nations Communities." In *Child Welfare: Connecting Research, Policy, and Practice*, edited by Kathleen Kufeldt and Brad McKenzie, 331–42. Waterloo, ON: Wilfrid Laurier University Press, 2003.

Bonvillain, Nancy. *Native Nations: Cultures and Histories of Native North America.* 2nd ed. Lanham, MD: Rowman & Littlefield, 2017.

Borrows, John. *Canada's Indigenous Constitution*. Toronto: University of Toronto Press, 2010.

———. *Recovering Canada: The Resurgence of Indigenous Law.* Toronto: University of Toronto Press, 2002.

Bosman, William. *A New and Accurate Description of the Coast of Guinea.* 1705. London, 1967.

Brant, Joseph. "Letter 10 December 1798." In *An Anthology of Canadian Native Literature in English*, 3rd ed., edited by Daniel David Moses and Terry Goldie, 12–14. Toronto: Oxford University Press, 2005.

Cairns, Alan C. *Citizens Plus: Aboriginal Peoples and the Canadian State*. Vancouver: UBC Press, 2000.

———. *Reconfigurations: Canadian Citizenship and Constitutional Change: Selected Essays by Alan C. Cairns*. Edited by Douglas E. Williams. Toronto: McClelland & Stewart, 1995.

Cairns, Alan, and Tom Flanagan. "An Exchange." *Inroads: A Journal of Opinion* 10 (2001): n.p. http://www.inroadsjournal.ca/linkpgs/aboutinroads.htm.

"Caledonia Land Claim: Historical Timeline." CBC News. November 1, 2006.

"Caledonia Land Dispute." *Wikipedia*. September 1, 2016.

Canada. "The Commission's Terms of Reference." In *Looking Forward, Looking Back: Report of the Royal Commission on Aboriginal Peoples*, 699–702. Ottawa: Minister of Supply & Services, 1996.

Canadian Conference of Catholic Bishops. *The "Doctrine of Discovery" and* Terra Nullius*: A Catholic Response*. Ottawa: Concacan Inc., 2016. https://www.cccb.ca/wp-content/uploads/2017/11/catholic-response-to-doctrine-of-discovery-and-tn.pdf.

Cardinal, Harold. *The Unjust Society*. 1970. Toronto: Douglas and McIntyre, 1999.

Chambers, Ross. "The Unexamined." In "The White Issue." Special issue, *The Minnesota Review* 47 (1996): 141–56.

Chandler, Justin. "Broken Promises, Unceded Land: The History Behind the Land Back Lane Protest." *TVO*, January 5, 2021. https://www.tvo.org/article/broken-promises-unceded-land-the-history-behind-the-land-back-lane-protest.

Coleman, Daniel, Ki'en Debicki and Bonnie M. Freeman, eds. *Deyohahá:ge: Sharing the River of Life*. Waterloo: Wilfrid Laurier University Press, 2025.

Cook, Katsi. "Women Are the First Environment: Interview with Mohawk Elder Katsi Cook." Interview by Leslee Goodman. Braided Way: Faces and Voices of Spiritual Practice, November 3, 2018. https://braidedway.org/women-are-the-first-environment-interview-with-mohawk-elder-katsi-cook/.

Corbiere, Alan. "'Their Own Forms of Which They Take the Most Notice': Diplomatic Metaphors and Symbolism on Wampum Belts." In *Anishnaabewin Niwin: Four Rising Winds*, edited by Alan Ojig Corbiere, Mary Ann Naokwegiig Corbiere, Deborah MacGregor and Crystal Migwans, 47–64. M'Chigeeng, ON: Ojibway Cultural Foundation, 2013.

———. *Red Skin, White Masks: Rejecting the Colonial Politics of Recognition*. Minneapolis: University of Minnesota Press, 2014.

Coulthard, Glen, and Leanne Betasamosake Simpson. "Grounded Normativity / Place-Based Solidarity." *American Quarterly* 68, no. 2 (2016): 249–55.

Craft, Aimée, Rachel Plotkin and Max McQuaig. *Governance Back: Exploring Indigenous Approaches to Reclaiming Relationships with Land*. Toronto: David Suzuki Foundation, 2022. https://davidsuzuki.org/science-learning-centre-article/governance-back-exploring-indigenous-approaches-to-reclaiming-relationships-with-land/.

Cruikshank, Brigadier General E. A. "The Reserve of the Six Nations Indians on the Grand River and the Mennonite Purchase of Block 2." In *The Fifteenth Annual Report of the Waterloo Historical Society Reports*, 303–52. Waterloo: Chronicle Press, 1927. https://www.whs.ca/wp-content/uploads/2015/11/1927.pdf.

Cullingham, James, dir. *Duncan Campbell Scott: The Poet and the Indians*. Peterborough, ON, and Montreal, QC: Tamarack Productions and the National Film Board of Canada, 1995.

Debicki, Kaitlin, and Wenda Debicki. "Our Fires Are Connected: The Story of a Two Row Wampum Family." In "Re:Creation," edited by Johannah Bird. Special Issue, *Hamilton Arts & Letters* 12, no. 1 (2019): n.p. https://samizdatpress.typepad.com/hal_magazine_issue_12-1/hal-magazine-issue-twelve1-cover.html.

Dedek, Helge, and Armand de Mestral. "*Born to Be Wild*: The 'Trans-systemic' Programme at McGill and the De-Nationalization of Legal Education." *German Law Journal* 10, no. 7 (2009): 889–911.

Deer, Ka'nhehsí:io. "Developer Offers to Give Land Back to First Nation Where Oka Crisis Happened." CBC News, July 11, 2019, accessed October 20, 2020. https://www.cbc.ca/news/indigenous/kanesatake-pines-gregoire-gollin-1.5204242.

Deer, Tracey, dir. *Club Native*. Montreal: National Film Board of Canada, 2008.

Deering, Nora, and Helga Harries Delisle. *Mohawk: A Teaching Grammar*. 1976. Reprinted by Kenien'kehaka Raotitiohkwa Cultural Center, 1995.

Dennis, Matthew. *Cultivating a Landscape of Peace: Iroquois-European Encounters in Seventeenth-Century America*. Ithaca, NY: Cornell University Press, 1993.

DeVries, Laura. *Conflict in Caledonia: Aboriginal Land Rights and the Rule of Law*. Vancouver: UBC Press, 2011.

Dickason, Olive Patricia. *Canada's First Nations: A History of Founding Peoples from Earliest Times*. 3rd ed. Toronto: Oxford University Press, 2002.

Dickson, Courtney, and Bridgette Watson. "Remains of 215 Children Found Buried at Former B.C. Residential School, First Nation Says." CBC News, May 27, 2021. https://www.cbc.ca/news/canada/british-columbia/tk-emlúps-te-secwépemc-215-children-former-kamloops-indian-residential-school-1.6043778.

Elbourne, Elizabeth. "Broken Alliance: Debating Six Nations Land Claims in 1822." *Social and Cultural History* 9, no. 4 (2012): 497–525.

Elliott, Alicia. "Boundaries Like Bruises." In *A Mind Spread Out on the Ground.* Toronto: Doubleday Canada, 2019.

Environmental Literacy Council. "Aluminum." Accessed January 18, 2020. https://enviroliteracy.org/special-features/its-element-ary/aluminum/.

Ermine, Willie. "The Ethical Space of Engagement." *Indigenous Law Journal* 6, no. 1 (2007): 193–203.

Etinson, Adam Daniel. "Aboriginal Oral History Evidence and Canadian Law." *Central European Journal of Canadian Studies* 6 (2008): 97–104.

Fenton, William N. "The New York State Wampum Collection: The Case for the Integrity of Cultural Treasures." *Proceedings of the American Philosophical Society* 115, no. 6 (December 30, 1971): 437–61.

———. "Return of Eleven Wampum Belts to the Six Nations Iroquois Confederacy on Grand River Canada." *Ethnohistory* 36, no. 4 (Autumn 1989): 392–410.

Flanagan, Tom. *First Nations? Second Thoughts.* 2nd ed. Montreal and Kingston: McGill-Queen's University Press, 2008.

Forester, Brett. "Six Nations Elected Council Agreed to 'Publicly Support' McKenzie Meadows Development, Help Stop Protests as Part of Accommodation Deal." *APTN National News*, August 11, 2020. https://www.aptnnews.ca/national-news/six-nations-elected-council-agreed-to-publicly-support-mckenzie-meadows-development-help-stop-protests-as-part-of-accommodation-deal-court-docs/.

Foster, Michael K. "The Reading of the Friendship (Covenant) and Two Rows Belts at the Governor General's, scheduled for 4:00 PM on 26 Feb. 81." Unpublished notes from Foster's personal collection, reproduced by Rick Hill.

Francis of Assisi. "The Canticle of the Creatures." Franciscan Seculars. Accessed December 27, 2019. http://franciscanseculars.com/the-canticle-of-the-creatures/.

Frankenberg, Ruth. *White Women, Race Matters: The Social Construction of Whiteness.* Minneapolis: University of Minnesota Press, 1993.

Freeman, Bonnie M. "The Spirit of Haudenosaunee Youth: The Transformation of Identity and Well-Being Through Culture-Based Activism." PhD diss., Wilfrid Laurier University, 2015.

Gates, Henry Louis, Jr. "Writing, 'Race' and the Difference It Makes." *Critical Inquiry* 12, no. 1 (Autumn 1985): 1–20.

Gehring, Charles T., and William A. Starna. "Revisiting the Fake Tawagonshi Treaty of 1613." *New York History* 90 (Winter 2012): 95–101.

Gibson, John Arthur. *Concerning the League: The Iroquois League Tradition as Dictated in Onondaga by John Arthur Gibson*. 1912. Newly Edited and Translated by Hanni Woodbury in Collaboration with Reginald Henry and Harry Webster on the basis of A.A. Goldenweiser's manuscript. Winnipeg: Algonquian and Iroquoian Linguistics, 1992.

———. "Iroquoian Cosmology: Second Part, with Introduction and Notes." Translated and edited by J.N.B. Hewitt. In *Forty-Third Annual Report of the Bureau of American Ethnology to the Secretary of the Smithsonian Institution, 1925–1926*, 449–819. Washington: United States Government Printing Office, 1928.

Goldie, Terry. *Fear and Temptation: The Image of the Indigene in Canadian, Australian, and New Zealand Literatures*. Kingston and Montreal: McGill-Queen's University Press, 1989.

Government of Canada. "Multiculturalism." Accessed November 26, 2018. https://www.canada.ca/en/services/culture/canadian-identity-society/multiculturalism.html.

———. *Statement of the Government of Canada on Indian Policy, 1969* [a.k.a. the White Paper]. Ottawa: Indian and Northern Affairs Canada, 1969. https://publications.gc.ca/site/eng/9.700112/publication.html.

Graeber, David, and David Wengrow. *The Dawn of Everything: A New History of Humanity*. Toronto: Penguin Random House, 2021.

Graymont, Barbara. "Koñwatsiˀtsiaiéñni (Gonwatsijayenni) (Mary Brant, Molly Brant)." In *Dictionary of Canadian Biography*, vol. 4. University of Toronto/Université Laval, 2003–. Accessed February 9, 2022. http://www.biographi.ca/en/bio/konwatsitsiaienni_4E.html.

Gwyn, Julian. "Johnson, Sir William." In *Dictionary of Canadian Biography*, vol. 4. University of Toronto/Université Laval, 2003–. Accessed February 9, 2022. http://www.biographi.ca/en/bio/johnson_william_4E.html.

Hale, Alan S. "St. Regis Mohawk Tribe Joins Lawsuit Against Monsanto over PCB Contamination." *Cornwall Standard-Freeholder*, November 26, 2018, accessed January 21, 2020. https://www.standard-freeholder.com/news/local-news/st-regis-mohawk-tribe-joins-lawsuit-against-monsanto-over-pcb-contamination.

Hallenbeck, Jessica. "Returning to the Water to Enact a Treaty Relationship: The Two Row Wampum Renewal Campaign." *Settler Colonial Studies* 5, no. 4 (2015): 350–62. http://dx.doi.org/10.1080/2201473X.2014.1000909.

Hampton, Eber. "Towards a Redefinition of Indian Education." In *First Nations Education in Canada: The Circle Unfolds*, edited by Marie Battiste and Jean Barman, 5–46. Vancouver: UBC Press, 1995.

Haudenosaunee Confederacy. "Joint Stewardship Board." Accessed October 22, 2020. https://www.haudenosauneeconfederacy.com/departments/joint-stewardship-board/.

Haudenosaunee Environmental Task Force. *Words That Come Before All Else: Environmental Philosophies of the Haudenosaunee.* Edited by James W. Ransom. Akwesasne, ON: Native North American Travelling College, 1999.

Havard, Gilles. "*Le rôle médiateur du wampum dans la diplomatie franco-amérindienne (XVIIe–XVIIIe siècles).*" Translated as "The Mediating Role of Wampum in French-Native American Diplomacy (17th–18th Centuries)" by Saskia Brown. *Gradhiva: Revue d'anthropologie et d'histoire des arts* 33 (2022): 23–39.

Hawthorn, H.B., ed. *A Survey of the Contemporary Indians of Canada: A Report on Economic, Political, Educational Needs and Policies* [a.k.a. the Hawthorn Report]. 2 vols. Ottawa: Indian Affairs, 1967.

Henderson, James (Sa'ke'j) Youngblood. *First Nations Jurisprudence and Aboriginal Rights: Defining the Just Society.* Saskatoon: Native Law Centre of Canada, University of Saskatchewan, 2006.

———. "Sui Generis and Treaty Citizenship." *Citizenship Studies* 6, no. 4 (2002): 415–40. https://doi.org/10.1080/1362102022000041259.

———. "Trans-Systemic Constitutionalism in Indigenous Law and Knowledge." In *Critical Collaborations: Indigeneity, Diaspora, and Ecology in Canadian Literary Studies*, edited by Smaro Kamboureli and Christl Verduyn, 49–68. Waterloo, ON: Wilfrid Laurier University Press, 2014.

Hill, Leroy. "What's Happening in Caledonia?" Speech at McMaster University, Hamilton, ON, February 12, 2007.

Hill, Richard "Rick" W., Sr. *Being Hodinöhsö:ni': A User's Guide.* Ohsweken, ON: Deyohahá:ge: Indigenous Knowledge Centre, Six Nations Polytechnic, 2013. Draft document.

———. *History as Told Through Haudenosaunee Wampum Belts.* Report submitted to Deyohahá:ge: Indigenous Knowledge Centre, Six Nations Polytechnic, March 2017.

———. "Linking Arms: The Haudenosaunee Context of the Covenant Chain." In *Mamow Be-Mo-Tay-Tah: Let Us Walk Together*, edited by José Zárate and Norah McMurtry, 17–24. Toronto: Canadian Ecumenical Anti-Racism Network, Canadian Council of Churches, 2009.

———. "Oral Memory of the Haudenosaunee: Views of the Two Row Wampum." In *Indian Roots of American Democracy*, edited by José Barreiro, 149–59. Ithaca, NY: Akwe:kon Press/Cornell University Press, 1992.

———. "The Restorative Aesthetic of Greg Staats." *Greg Staats Liminal Disturbance.* Hamilton: McMaster Museum of Art, 2012. Exhibition catalogue.

———. "*Rotihnahon:tsi* and *Rotinonhsón:ni*: Historic Relationships Between African Americans and the Confederacy of Six Nations." In *IndiVisible: African-Native American Lives in the Americas*, edited by Gabrielle Tayac, 99–107. Washington: Smithsonian Institution, 2009.

———. *Two Row Wampum Belts and the Silver Covenant Chain.* Ohsweken, ON: Deyhahá:ge: Indigenous Knowledge Centre, Six Nations Polytechnic, 2016. Draft document.

———. *War Clubs and Wampum Belts: Hodinöhsö:ni Experiences of the War of 1812.* Brantford, ON: Woodland Cultural Centre, 2012.

Hill, Richard W., Sr., and Daniel Coleman. "The Two Row Wampum-Covenant Chain Tradition as a Guide for Indigenous-University Research Partnerships." *Cultural Studies ↔ Critical Methodologies* 19, no. 5 (2019): 339–59.

Hill, Richard W., Sr., and Nathan Tidridge. "The Crown, the Chain, and Peacebuilding: Diplomatic Traditions of the Covenant Chain." In *Royal Progress: Canada's Monarchy in the Age of Disruption*, edited by D. Michael Jackson, 1–18. Toronto: Dundurn Press, 2020.

Hill, Susan. *The Clay We Are Made Of: Haudenosaunee Land Tenure on the Grand River.* Winnipeg: University of Manitoba Press, 2017.

———. "'Traveling Down the River of Life Together in Peace and Friendship, Forever': Haudenosaunee Land Ethics and Treaty Agreements as the Basis for Restructuring the Relationship with the British Crown." In *Lighting the Eighth*

Fire: The Liberation, Resurgence, and Protection of Indigenous Nations, edited by Leanne Betasamosake Simpson, 23–45. Winnipeg: Arbeiter Ring Publishing, 2008.

Hobbes, Thomas. *Leviathon, or the Matter, Forme, and Power of Common Wealth Ecclesiasticall and Civill.* London: Andrew Cooke, 1651.

Jacobs, Beverley. “Legal Foundations of Haudenosaunee Assertions of Sovereignty: How Ancestral Laws of the Land Ensure Abundance for All and Define Healthy Relationships Between Us Confirmation.” Zoom lecture hosted by Wilfrid Laurier University, March 7, 2022.

Jennings, Francis. “The Constitutional Evolution of the Covenant Chain.” *Proceedings of the American Philosophical Society* 115, no. 2 (April 22, 1971): 88–96.

Jennings, Willie James. *The Christian Imagination: Theology and the Origins of Race.* New Haven, CT: Yale University Press, 2010.

Johnson, William. *The Papers of Sir William Johnson*. Edited by James Sullivan, Alexander Clarence Flick, Almon W. Lauber, Milton W. Hamilton and Albert B. Corey. 14 vols. Albany: University of the State of New York, Division of Archives and History, 1921–1965.

Johnston, Charles M. “The Six Nations in the Grand River Valley, 1784–1847.” In *Aboriginal Ontario: Historical Perspectives on the First Nations.* Edited by Edward S. Rogers and Donald B. Smith, 167–81. Toronto: Dundurn, 1994.

Johnston, Charles M., ed. *The Valley of the Six Nations: A Collection of Documents on the Indian Lands of the Grand River.* Toronto: Champlain Society for the Government of Ontario, University of Toronto Press, 1964.

Johnston, Louise. *The Covenant Chain of Peace: Metaphor and Religious Thought in Seventeenth Century Haudenosaunee Council Oratory.* PhD thesis, Faculty of Religious Studies, McGill University, 2004.

———. “Polishing the Silver Covenant Chain: An Address by Sir William Johnson to the People of Kahnawake and Kanesatake, 1762.” *Historical Papers: Canadian Society of Church History* (August 1997): 79–95. http://historicalpapers.journals.yorku.ca/index.php/historicalpapers/article/view/39414/35741.

Joint Stewardship Board. “About Us.” Accessed October 22, 2020. http://jointstewardshipboard.com/about-us/.

Justice, Daniel Heath. “Indigenous Writing.” In *The World of Indigenous North America*, edited by Robert Warrior, 291–307. New York: Routledge, 2014.

Keeshig Tobias, Lenore. “Stop Stealing Native Stories.” *Globe and Mail*, January

26, 1990, A7. Reprinted in *Introduction to Indigenous Literary Criticism in Canada*, edited by Heather Macfarlane and Armand Garnet Ruffo, 34–36. Peterborough, ON: Broadview Press, 2016.

Kelsey, Penelope Myrtle. *Reading the Wampum: Essays on Hodinöhsö:ni' Visual Code and Epistemological Recovery*. The Iroquois and Their Neighbors. Syracuse, NY: Syracuse University Press, 2014.

Kimmerer, Robin Wall. *Braiding Sweetgrass: Indigenous Wisdom, Scientific Knowledge, and the Teachings of Plants*. Minneapolis: Milkweed Editions, 2013.

———. "The Rights of the Land: The Onondaga Nation of Central New York Proposes a Radical New Vision of Property Rights." *Orion Magazine* (November/December 2008): 1–7.

Krawec, Patty. *Becoming Kin: An Indigenous Call to Unforgetting the Past and Reimagining Our Future*. Minneapolis: Broadleaf Books, 2022.

Kvaløy Setreng, Sigmund. "Norwegian Ecophilosophy and Ecopolitics and Their Influence from Buddhism." In *Buddhist Perspectives on the Ecocrisis: With a Declaration on Environmental Ethics by H. H. the Dalai Lama*, edited by Klas Sandell. Wheel Publication, no. 346/348. Kandy, Sri Lanka: Buddhist Publication Society, 1987. https://www.bps.lk/olib/wh/wh346_Sandell-etal_Buddhist-Perspectives-on-the-Ecocrisis.pdf.

Lagace, Naithan, and Niigaanwewidam James Sinclair. "The White Paper, 1969." In *The Canadian Encyclopedia*. Historica Canada. Article published September 24, 2015; last modified June 10, 2020. https://www.thecanadianencyclopedia.ca/en/article/the-white-paper-1969.

Leduc, Timothy B., ed. *Ǫ da gaho dę:s: Reflecting on Our Journeys / Gae Ho Hwako (Norma Jacobs) and the Circles of Ǫ da gaho dę:s*. Montreal and Kingston: McGill-Queen's University Press, 2022.

Leighton, Douglas, and Robert J. Burns. "Jarvis, Samuel Peters." In *Dictionary of Canadian Biography*, vol. 8. University of Toronto/Université Laval, 2003–. Accessed July 6, 2021. http://www.biographi.ca/en/bio/jarvis_samuel_peters_8E.html.

Leonard, Kelsey. "*Wunnáumwash*: Wampum Justice." In *Deyohahá:ge: Sharing the River of Life*, edited by Daniel Coleman, Ki'en Debicki and Bonnie M. Freeman, 52–66. Waterloo: Wilfrid Laurier University Press, 2025.

Levinas, Emmanuel. *Entre Nous: On Thinking-of-the-Other*. Translated by Michael

B. Smith and Barbara Harshav. New York: Columbia University Press, 1998.

———. *Humanism of the Other.* 1972. Translated by Nidra Poller. Urbana and Chicago: University of Illinois Press, 2003.

L'Incarnation, Marie de [Marie Guyart]. *Word From New France: The Selected Letters of Marie de l'Incarnation*, translated and edited by Joyce Marshall. Toronto: Oxford University Press, 1967.

Lippard, Lucy. *The Lure of the Local: Senses of Place in a Multicentered Society.* NY: New Press, 1997.

Locke, John. "Chapter V: Of Property." In *Two Treatises of Government*, 115–26. Vol. 5 of *The Works of John Locke*, A New Edition, Corrected, in Ten Volumes, Prepared by Rod Hay. London: Thomas Tegg; W. Sharpe and Son, 1823.

Lyons, Oren. "Gä•sweñta' Reflections." Excerpts from the writing and speeches of Oren Lyons, Onondaga Nation Faithkeeper, assembled and edited by Rick Hill. In *Deyohahá:ge: Sharing the River of Life*, edited by Daniel Coleman, Ki'en Debicki and Bonnie M. Freeman, 29–34. Waterloo: Wilfrid Laurier University Press, 2025.

———. "Spirituality, Equality, and Natural Law." In *Pathways to Self-Determination: Canadian Indians and the Canadian State*, edited by Leroy Little Bear, Menno Boldt and J. Anthony Long, 5–21. Toronto: University of Toronto Press, 1984.

Machado, Antonio. *Times Alone: Selected Poems of Antonio Machado.* Translated by Robert Bly. Middletown, CT: Wesleyan University Press, 1983.

Macy, Joanna, and Molly Brown. *Coming Back to Life: The Updated Guide to the Work that Reconnects.* Gabriola Island, BC: New Society Publishers, 2014.

Maracle, Brian. *Back on the Rez: Finding the Way Home.* Toronto: Penguin Canada, 1996.

———. "First Words." In *Our Story: Aboriginal Voices on Canada's Past*, 12–31. Toronto: Random House, 2004.

Maracle, David Kanatawakhon. *Karoron Ne Owennahshonha: A Mohawk Thematic Dictionary.* London, ON: Kanyn'keha Books/Graphic Services, University of Western Ontario, 2001.

Maracle, Lee. *My Conversations with Canadians.* Toronto: BookThug, 2017.

Martin-Hill, Dawn, dir. *Sewatokwa'tshera't: The Dish with One Spoon.* Ohsweken, ON: Haudenosaunnee Confederacy, 2007. DVD, 77 min.

McCarthy, Theresa. *In Divided Unity: Haudenosaunee Reclamation at Grand River.* Tucson: University of Arizona Press, 2016.

McDermott, Larry, and Anne Bell. *Indigenous Perspectives on Conservation Offsetting: Five Case Studies from Ontario, Canada*. Toronto: Ontario Nature; Lanark, ON: Plenty Canada; Peterborough, ON: Indigenous Environmental Studies and Sciences Program at Trent University, 2017.

McKay, Don. *Deactivated West 100*. Kentville, NS: Gaspereau, 2005.

McLeod, Neal. "Embodied Memory: Universal Citizenship and Indigenous Cree Identity." In *Human Welfare, Rights, and Social Activism: Rethinking the Legacy of J.S. Woodsworth*, edited by Jane Pulkingham, 244–65. Toronto: University of Toronto Press, 2010.

Mercredi, Ovide, and Mary Ellen Turpel. *In the Rapids: Navigating the Future of First Nations*. Toronto: Viking, 1993.

Mohawk, John. *Iroquois Creation Story: John Arthur Gibson and J.N.B. Hewitt's Myth of the Earth Grasper*. Buffalo, NY: Mohawk Publications, 2005.

Montgomery, Malcolm. "The Six Nations Indians and the Macdonald Franchise." *Ontario History* 57, no. 1 (1965): 13–25.

Monture, Rick. "'Beneath the British Flag': Iroquois and Canadian Nationalism in the Work of Pauline Johnson and Duncan Campbell Scott." In "'Race' Into the Twenty-First Century," edited by Daniel Coleman and Donald Goellnicht. Special issue, *Essays on Canadian Writing* 75 (2002): 118–41.

———. *Teionkwakhashion Tsi Niionkwariho:ten / We Share Our Matters: Two Centuries of Writing and Resistance at Six Nations of the Grand River*. Winnipeg: University of Manitoba Press, 2014.

Monture-Angus, Patricia. *Thunder in My Soul: A Mohawk Woman Speaks*. Halifax: Fernwood, 1995.

Morrow, John Andrew. "Indigenous and Muslim Perspectives on Colonization, Treaties, and Decolonization." John Andrew Morrow (blog), February 17, 2022, accessed January 26, 2024. https://johnandrewmorrow.com/2022/02/17/indigenous-and-muslim-perspectives-on-colonization-treaties-and-decolonization/.

Muller, Kathryn V. "Holding Hands with Wampum: Haudenosaunee Council Fires from the Great Law of Peace to Contemporary Relationships with the Canadian State." PhD thesis, Queen's University, 2008.

———. "The Two 'Mystery' Belts of Grand River: A Biography of the Two Row Wampum and the Friendship Belt." *The American Indian Quarterly* 31, no. 1 (Winter 2007): 129–64.

National Inquiry into Missing and Murdered Indigenous Women and Girls. *Reclaiming Power and Place: Executive Summary of the Final Report.* Vancouver: Privy Council Office, 2019. https://www.mmiwg-ffada.ca/final-report/.

———. *Reclaiming Power and Place: The Final Report of the National Inquiry into Missing and Murdered Indigenous Women and Girls*, Volume 1a and Volume 1b. Vancouver: Privy Council Office, 2019. https://www.mmiwg-ffada.ca/final-report/.

Newhouse, David. "Guswenta Space: An Invitation to Dialogue." In *Deyohahá:ge: Sharing the River of Life*, edited by Daniel Coleman, Ki'en Debicki and Bonnie M. Freeman, 109–20. Waterloo: Wilfrid Laurier University Press, 2025.

OED Online, *Oxford English Dictionary*, 3rd ed. Oxford: Oxford University Press, 2015; last modified December 2021.

Office of Response and Restoration. "Alcoa Aluminum Factories Settle $19.4 Million for Pollution of St. Lawrence River Watershed, Most Will Fund Restoration of Tribal Culture, Recreational Fishing, and Habitat." National Oceanic and Atmospheric Administration's Office of Response and Restoration, March 27, 2013, accessed January 20, 2020. https://response.restoration.noaa.gov/about/media/alcoa-alumium-factories-settle-194-million-pollution-st-lawrence-river-watershed-most-w.

O'Neil, Beverley. "Indigenous Peoples – Connected to the Land: Proposed Projects on First Nations Lands Must be Respectful, Collaborative." *Hamilton Spectator*, October 6, 2020.

Otto, Paul. "'This Is that Which . . . They Call Wampum': Europeans Coming to Terms with Native Shell Beads." *Early American Studies: An Interdisciplinary Journal* 15, no. 1 (Winter 2017): 1–36.

Page, Elliot, and Ian Daniel, dirs. *There's Something in the Water.* Two Weeks Notice, 2019.

Palmer, Parker. *To Know as We Are Known: Education as a Spiritual Journey*. 2nd ed. San Francisco: HarperSanFrancisco, 1993.

Parker, Arthur C. *Parker on the Iroquois: Iroquois Uses of Maize and Other Good Plants, the Code of Handsome Lake, the Seneca Prophet, the Constitution of the Five Nations*. Edited by William N. Fenton. Syracuse: Syracuse University Press, 1968.

Parmenter, Jon. *The Edge of the Woods: Iroquoia, 1534–1701.* Lansing: Michigan State University Press, 2010.

———. "The Meaning of *Kaswentha* and the Two Row Wampum Belt in

Haudenosaunee (Iroquois) History: Can Indigenous Oral Tradition Be Reconciled with the Documentary Record?" *Journal of Early American History* 3 (2013): 82–109. https://doi.org/10.1163/18770703-00301005.

Pasternak, Shiri, Hayden King and Riley Yesno. *Land Back: A Yellowhead Institute Red Paper.* Toronto: Yellowhead Institute, 2019. https://redpaper.yellowheadinstitute.org/.

Pessoa, Fernando. *A Little Larger Than the Entire Universe: Selected Poems.* Edited and translated by Richard Zenith. New York: Penguin Classics, 2006.

Pierce, Joseph M. "A Manifesto for Speculative Relations." In *Five Manifestos for the Beautiful World*, edited by Cynthia Sharpe, 8–37. Toronto: Alchemy by Knopf Canada, 2024.

Porter, Tom (Sakokweniónkwas). *And Grandma Said . . . Iroquois Teachings as Passed Down Through the Oral Tradition.* Self-published, Xlibris, 2008.

Pratt, Mary Louise. *Imperial Eyes: Travel Writing and Transculturation.* New York: Routledge, 1992.

"Rally Organizer Arrested at Caledonia Occupation Site." CBC News, December 16, 2006, accessed September 1, 2016. https://www.cbc.ca/news/canada/rally-organizer-arrested-at-caledonia-occupation-site-1.589173.

Red Jacket. *The Collected Speeches of Sagoyewatha, or Red Jacket.* Edited by Granville Ganther. Syracuse, NY: Syracuse University Press, 2006.

R. v. Monture and White (505-01-137394-165), November 1, 2023, Judge Sophie Bourque, J.S.C., Quebec Superior Court, Longueuil QC. https://canlii.ca/t/k0wzd.

R. v. Williams (ONCJ 393), June 29, 2023, Judge Gethin Edward, Ontario Court of Justice, Cayuga, ON. https://canlii.ca/t/k06c9.

Reynolds, Anthony. *People to People: Nation to Nation: A Consultation Document Summarizing the Main Findings and Recommendations of the Royal Commission on Aboriginal Peoples.* Ottawa: Government of Canada, 1997.

Richter, Daniel K. "Rediscovered Links in the Covenant Chain: Previously Unpublished Transcripts of New York Indian Treaty Minutes, 1677–1691." *Proceedings of the American Antiquarian Society* 92 (1982): 45–85.

Robie, Harry W. "Kiotsaeton's Three Rivers Address: An Example of 'Effective' Iroquois Oratory." *American Indian Quarterly* 6, nos. 3/4 (Autumn–Winter, 1982): 238–53.

Royal Proclamation. October 7, 1763. Reproduced by William F. Maton Sotomayor.

Canadian Constitutional Documents. http://www.solon.org/Constitutions/Canada/English/PreConfederation/rp_1763.html.

Rushforth, Brett, and Paul W. Mapp. *Colonial North America and the Atlantic World: A History in Documents.* London and NY: Routledge, 2009.

Saul, John Ralston. *The Comeback: How Aboriginals Are Reclaiming Power and Influence.* Toronto: Penguin Random House, 2014.

———. *A Fair Country: Telling Truths About Canada.* Toronto: Penguin Canada, 2009.

Schama, Simon. *The Embarrassment of Riches: An Interpretation of Dutch Culture in the Golden Age.* New York: Alfred A. Knopf, 1987.

Sheridan, Joe, and Dan Longboat – Roronhiakewen (He Clears the Sky). "The Haudenosaunee Imagination and the Ecology of the Sacred." *Space and Culture* 9, no. 4 (November 2006): 365–81.

Shorto, Russell. *The Island in the Center of the World: The Epic Story of Dutch Manhattan and the Forgotten Colony that Shaped America.* New York: Vintage, 2004.

Simpson, Audra. *Mohawk Interruptus: Political Life Across the Borders of Settler States.* Durham, NC: Duke University Press, 2014.

Sinclair, Upton. *I, Candidate for Governor, and How I Got Licked.* 1934. Berkeley: University of California Press, 1994.

Six Nations Lands and Resources Department. *Land Rights: A Global Solution for the Six Nations of the Grand River.* Ohsweken, ON: Self-published booklet, 2015.

Smith, Donald W. "Deskaheh (Levi General)." In *Dictionary of Canadian Biography,* vol. 15. University of Toronto/Université Laval, 2003–. Accessed September 22, 2016. http://www.biographi.ca/en/bio.php?id_nbr=8103.

Smith, Linda Tuhiwai. *Decolonizing Methodologies: Research and Indigenous Peoples.* London: Zed Books, 1999.

Somerville, Alice Te Punga. "'Reach across an ocean to find the right words': Māori-Aboriginal Literary Connections." Keynote paper presented at the Canadian Association for Commonwealth Literature and Language Studies conference, Wilfrid Laurier University, Waterloo, ON, May 28, 2012.

Special Committee on Indian Self-Government. *Indian Self-Government in Canada: A Report of the Special Committee* [a.k.a. the Penner Report]. Ottawa: Queen's Printer for Canada, 1983.

Spivak, Gayatri C. *A Critique of Postcolonial Reason: Toward a History of the Vanishing Present.* Boston: Harvard University Press, 1999.

Starna, William A. "Sir William Johnson's Seal or Rufus Grider's Imagination? A Short Story on Historical Authenticity." *Pennsylvania History: A Journal of Mid-Atlantic Studies* 90, no. 1 (Winter 2023): 35–47.

Taekema, Dan. "Six Nations Traditional Government Wants Moratorium on Development of Haldimand Tract." CBC News, April 20, 2021. https://www.cbc.ca/news/canada/hamilton/haldimand-tract-development-moratorium-1.5993081.

Tehanetorens (Ray Fadden). *Wampum Belts of the Iroquois*. Summertown, TN: Book Publishing, 1999.

Terpstra, John. *Daylighting Chedoke*. Hamilton, ON: Wolsak and Wynn, 2018.

Thomas, Jacob, with Terry Boyle. *Teachings from the Longhouse*. Toronto: Stoddart, 1994.

Thwaites, Reuben Gold, ed. *The Jesuit Relations and Allied Documents*. Cleveland: Burrows Brothers Company, 1898.

Tidridge, Nathan. *The Queen at the Council Fire: The Treaty of Niagara, Reconciliation, and the Dignified Crown in Canada*. Toronto: Dundurn Press, 2015.

Titley, E. Brian. *A Narrow Vision: Duncan Campbell Scott and the Administration of Indian Affairs in Canada*. Vancouver: University of British Columbia Press, 1986.

Trevor-Roper, Rupert. *The Rise of Christian Europe*. London: Thames and Hudson, 1965.

Trudeau, Pierre Elliott. "Multiculturalism." Speech to the House of Commons, October 8, 1971. Canada History. Accessed November 29, 2018. https://canadahistory.ca/sections/documents/leaders/Trudeau/On%20Multiculturalism.html.

Truth and Reconciliation Commission of Canada. *Honouring the Truth, Reconciling for the Future: Summary of the Final Report of the Truth and Reconciliation Commission of Canada*. Ottawa: Truth and Reconciliation Commission of Canada, 2015. https://nctr.ca/records/reports/.

Tuck, Eve, and K. Wayne Yang. "Decolonization Is Not a Metaphor." *Decolonization: Indigeneity, Education & Society* 1, no. 1 (2012): 1–40.

Tully, James. *Strange Multiplicity: Constitutionalism in an Age of Diversity*. Cambridge: Cambridge University Press, 1995.

Valiante, Giuseppe. "'I Filled a Void': How a Developer Wants to Help Settle Centuries of Grievances in Oka." *Global News*, July 31, 2019. Accessed October 20,

2020. https://globalnews.ca/news/5709978/developer-help-settle-centuries-grievances-oka/.

Venables, Robert. "Polishing the Silver Covenant Chain: A Brief History of Some of the Symbols and Metaphors in Haudenosaunee Treaty Negotiations." November 2008. Onondaga Nation, October 4, 2010. Updated July 11 and October 4, 2010; and February 26 and March 10, 2011. https://www.onondaganation.org/history/2010/polishing-the-silver-covenant-chain-a-brief-history-of-some-of-the-symbols-and-metaphors-in-haudenosaunee-treaty-negotiations/.

Walcott, Rinaldo. "Disgraceful: Intellectual Dishonesty, White Anxieties, and Multicultural Critique Thirty Years Later." In *Queer Returns: Essays on Multiculturalism, Diaspora, and Black Studies*, 79–110. Toronto: Insomniac Press, 2016.

Wallace, Paul A.W. *The White Roots of Peace: The Iroquois Book of Life*. Port Washington, NY: Ira J. Friedman, 1946.

Warkentin, Germaine. "'The Word of the Other': Aboriginal Sign Systems and the History of the Book in Canada." *Book History* 2 (1999): 1–27.

Watts, Vanessa. "Indigenous Place-Thought and Agency Amongst Humans and Non-Humans (First Woman and Sky Woman Go on a European World Tour!)." *Decolonization: Indigeneity, Education & Society* 2, no. 1 (2013): 20–34.

Weinberg, Paul. "The Red Hill Expressway, One-Way Streets and Hamilton's Car Culture." In *Reclaiming Hamilton: Essays from the New Ambitious City*, edited by Paul Weinberg, 103–39. Hamilton: Wolsak and Wynn, 2020.

Widdowson, Frances, and Albert Howard. *Disrobing the Aboriginal Industry: The Deception Behind Indigenous Cultural Preservation*. Montreal and Kingston: McGill-Queen's University Press, 2008.

Williams, Kayanesenh Paul. "The Chain, Naturally Understood." In *Deyohahá:ge: Sharing the River of Life*, edited by Daniel Coleman, Ki'en Debicki and Bonnie M. Freeman, 67–105. Waterloo: Wilfrid Laurier University Press, 2025.

———. *Kayanerenkó:wa: The Great Law of Peace*. Winnipeg: University Manitoba Press, 2018.

———. "The Royal Proclamation: Clearing the Waters." Unpublished paper, September 2014.

Williams, Paul Kayanesenh, and Arihote Curtis Nelson. *Kaswentha*. Research report prepared for the Royal Commission on Aboriginal Peoples. January

1995. In *For Seven Generations: An Information Legacy of the Royal Commission on Aboriginal Peoples*. Ottawa: Libraxus, 1997.

Williams, Robert A., Jr. "The Algebra of Federal Indian Law: The Hard Trail of Decolonizing and Americanizing the White Man's Indian Jurisprudence." *Wisconsin Law Review*, no. 2 (1986): 219–300.

———. *Linking Arms Together: American Indian Treaty Visions of Law and Peace, 1600–1800*. New York: Oxford University Press, 1997.

Williams-Myers, Albert James. *Long Hammering: Essays on the Forging of an African American Presence in the Hudson River Valley to the Early Twentieth Century*. Trenton: NJ: Africa World Press, 1994.

Wilson, Shawn. *Research Is Ceremony: Indigenous Research Methods*. Black Point, NS, and Winnipeg: Fernwood, 2008.

Windle, Jim. "Police Take Brantford Supremist Rally Seriously." *Tekawennake News*, January 16, 2008. https://rabble.ca/babble/anti-racism-news-and-initiatives/police-take-brantford-supremacist-rally-seriously (page discontinued).

Wolfe, Patrick. "Settler Colonialism and the Elimination of the Native." *Journal of Genocide Research* 8, no. 4 (December 2006): 387–409.

Woo, Grace Li Xiu. "Canada's Forgotten Founders: The Modern Significance of the Haudenosaunee (Iroquois) Application for Membership in the League of Nations." *Law, Social Justice, and Global Development* 2003, no. 1 (April 2003). http://www2.warwick.ac.uk/fac/soc/law/elj/lgd/2003_1/woo/.

Younging, Gregory. *Elements of Indigenous Style: A Guide for Writers by and about Indigenous Peoples*. Edmonton: Brush Education, 2018.

Yunkaporta, Tyson. *Sand Talk: How Indigenous Thinking Can Save the World*. Melbourne: Text Publishing Company, 2019.

Index

A

Adams, Amber Meadow, 11–12, 146, 321n6, 343n18; on Haudenosaunee Creation Story, 46, 213, 228; on Two Row agreement, 70, 98, 323n3, 323n7
Adams, Mary, 248–49
Akwesasne, 57, 95, 199, 243, 282, 320n13; basket-making, 223, 248–49; toxins in land, water and humans, 35, 222–27, 229, 258
Albany (Nanfan, 1701), Treaty of, 120, 163, 272, 288
Albany (1664), Treaty of, 92–93, 116
Alexander VI, Pope, 65, 109
Allen, Chad, 166–67
Althusius, Johannes, 63–64
aluminum toxicity, 223–24, 226
Anishinaabe, 95, 170, 276, 332n14; community decision-making and law, 204–5; treaty tradition, 18, 76, 119, 163–65
Antone, Bob, 183, 184–85, 320n13
Assembly of First Nations, 103, 131, 183–84, 317n10, 317n20, 329n5
Atotarhonh, The One Who Lives Alone, 23–25, 132, 257, 300
Ayonwátha (Hiawatha), He Keeps Awake, 25, 61, 132, 152, 164, 254, 300–302; calming troubled minds, 42–43, 68, 141–43, 254; condolence story of, 27–32
Azurara, Gomes Eanes de, 109–10, 150, 178

B

band council system, 129–30, 140, 182, 184–85, 333n1. *See also* Six Nations Confederacy Council
Beaver Wars, 4, 172
Benedict, Ernie, 343n7
Benedict, Kawennotakie Salli, 220–23, 227, 248, 268, 270, 343n7
Benedict, Les, 225–26
Berry, Thomas, 259–60
Bird, Brian, 115, 331n1, 331n5
Bird, Johannah, 276
Borrows, John, 86, 273–75, 279, 348n12; and constitutional law in Canada, 201, 202, 203–4, 206; on "distinctive culture test," 168–69; on flow of Covenant Chain–Two Row tradition in Canada, 104; on Indigenous control of Canadian affairs, 273–75, 348n12; on wampum and colonial diplomacy, 97
Bourque, Sophie, 17, 175, 317n10, 324n4, 324n11, 326n14, 340n21. See also *R. v. Monture and White*
Brant, Joseph Thaientané:ken, 78, 119, 121–23, 298, 351n3
Brant, Konwatsi'tsayén:ni Mary (Molly), 78–79, 88–89, 98, 99, 119, 322n8
Brant, Suzanne Katsi'tsiarihshion, 244, 298–99
British colonization on Turtle Island: adaptation to wampum diplomacy, 2, 13–14, 18–20, 78–81; adoption of Two Row agreement, 68–69, 297; colonial law and racial hierarchy, 111–13, 155; colonies' tenuous security after Seven Years War, 89, 94; Indian agents and theft and fraud, 124, 133, 266–67, 299; and Indigenous nations as allies, not subjects, 84, 123–24, 130, 135, 185; interference in Haldimand Tract, 121–24; and turn against Indigenous allies, 45; need to link arms with former French allies, 88. *See also* Albany (Nanfan, 1701), Treaty of; Fort Niagara, Treaty of; Fort Stanwix, Treaty of; protection; Royal Proclamation
British North America: and Covenant Chain as multicultural constitution, 77–81, 302; shaped by Covenant Chain–Two Row principles, 14, 20, 94, 114–24; shift in Indigenous relations after War of 1812, 119
British North America Act, 94, 114–16, 174, 327n20, 331n5

Brown, Molly, 338n5
Brûlé, Étienne, 172
Bush, Wendy, 262, 264

C

Cairns, Alan, 338n3
Caledonia land disputes, 16, 33, 37–38, 47, 103–4, 164, 319n5, 325n5; Kahnonstaton (Douglas Creek Estates), 36, 43, 123, 246; Land Back Lane (McKenzie Meadows), 123, 137–38, 246, 267–68, 278–79; origins in Plank Road construction, 36, 43, 123–24, 137; police involvement, costs of, 33–34, 36–37, 47, 278
Canada, 103, 196–200, 340n25: Confederation of, 115, 183, 193, 281, 331n5, 333n10; constitution and Covenant Chain–Two Row Wampum tradition, 15–17, 20, 98, 100, 116–25, 152–53, 164, 174–76, 279, 302; constitutional reform, 177, 185–89, 213–14; extraction economy of, 124, 138, 194, 270–71, 319n10, 347n7; façade of peace, order and good government, 35, 114, 136, 151; and influence of Haudenosaunee law and diplomacy, 19–20, 21, 82, 105, 317n13; influence of Royal Proclamation on, 84, 90, 100–102, 104–5, 114, 167, 326n11, 327n20; myth of two solitudes, 152, 166, 336n13; and role of governor general, 49, 57–58, 85–88, 103–5, 147, 321n8, 329n5, 334n15. *See also* British North America Act; Canadians; Crown land; Dish With One Spoon; Doctrine of Discovery; Indian Act; Indigenous sovereignty or self-determination; protection; Supreme Court of Canada
Canadian Army, 35, 86, 130, 188. *See also* Ontario Provincial Police; police
Canadian Conference of Catholic Bishops, 330n11, 331n18
Canadian martyrs, story of, 1, 11
Canadians: divided minds of, 231–39; forgetting/learning Indigenous histories, 20–21, 37–38, 43–44, 164–67, 175–78, 203; history, ignorance/denial of, 37–38, 164–67; misunderstanding treaty agreements, 246; responsibilities of, 42–43, 83–101, 207, 265, 270, 285, 300, 325n6
Canajoharie: and Brant family, 78, 99; land swindle, 89–93, 121, 124, 328n33
Canandaigua Treaty Belt (George Washington Belt), 97
Canesatego, 105, 107, 150, 166, 181, 269, 323n8; recitation of the Two Row, 72–78, 80–81, 171, 212
capitalism. *See* Industrial Growth Society
Cardinal, Harold, 273, 274
Cartier, Jacques, 14, 19, 42
Catholic Church, 61–64, 65, 106, 108–9, 287, 330n11. *See also* Alexander VI; Doctrine of Discovery; Francis; Innocent IV; Jesuits
Cayenquiragoa and Canajoharie land swindle, 91–93
Cayuga (*Gayogohó:no*), in Haudenosaunee Confederacy, 2, 15, 165, 294; language, 25, 40, 48, 49, 147, 158–59. *See also* Deskaheh, Levi General; Jigonsaseh; Thomas, Jacob (Jake)
Chambers, Ross, 337n2
Champlain, Samuel de, 3, 14, 150, 322n8
Charlottetown Accord, 177, 188, 189
Charter of Rights and Freedoms, 82–95, 101, 129, 156, 167, 184, 276
Cherokee nation, 98, 170, 198
Chrétien, Jean, 139–40, 163, 180, 188
Christianity: and covenant theology, 62–64, 106, 322n1; fear of the Lord theology, 253, 255–56, 260; and racial hierarchy, 110–13; and St. Francis's creation theology, 214–17. *See also* Catholic Church
Claus, Daniel, 98, 329n35
Claus, William, 98, 266–67
Coleman, William, 40
colonialism, 45, 127–28, 130–32, 225–27, 301; and myth of First Encounters, 162–76, 193, 330n10. *See also* settler colonialism
Columbus, Christopher, 65, 111, 154–55, 330n11
Condolence Ceremony and wampum, 27–32, 67, 254, 335n3
Confederacy Council: and circle of fifty chiefs, 70, 74, 121, 155, 295, 302
Cook, Katsi Tekatsi'tsiah:khwa, 225–26, 320n13, 343n13
Corbiere, Alan, 96
Coulthard, Glen, 268, 349n1

Couture, Guillaume, 3, 6, 12–13, 43, 113, 145, 315n2
covenant, English-language meanings of, 61–68, 111, 157
Covenant Chain, 11, 184, 199, 302; silver chain instead of rope, 74–76, 80; well-suited for era of reconciliation, 271, 293, 324n4, 340n21
Covenant Chain–Two Row Wampum tradition, 17, 41–42, 45–46, 126, 138, 158–61, 183–84; as alliance of reciprocity, 43, 69; disavowal of, 17, 123, 162; embedded in Charter of Rights and Freedoms, 83–101; linking arms, respecting differences, 69, 152–54, 157; as multicultural constitution in North America, 77–81, 170; symbols of, 19, 53–56, 60, 76, 95–97, 147, 159, 300, 325n5; three principles at the heart of, 21, 175, 258. *See also* Covenant Chain; grandfather of the treaties; Linked Arms; Two Row Wampum
Craft, Aimée, 272, 275, 346n4
Creation story, Haudenosaunee, 46, 70, 126, 208–11, 236, 238–45, 253, 255, 264
Crown land: definition and extent of, 116, 125, 162, 174, 348n17; redesignate as Dish With One Spoon, 276–79
cultural appropriation, 35

D

decolonization, 179–81, 268–69
Dedek, Helge, 341n7
deer, 203, 209, 210, 259, 288, 290–91
Deer, Tom, 40, 146, 304, 320
Deer, Tracey, 40, 304–5
Dennis, Matthew, 66–67
Descartes, René, 67, 235, 283
Deskaheh, Levi General, 133–35, 138, 139, 152, 183, 334n19
Deyohahá:ge: Indigenous Knowledge Centre, 26, 39–40, 319n7
Dish With One Spoon, 77, 126, 145, 171–72, 324n10; and Crown Land, 276–79
Doctrine of Discovery, 102, 125, 330n11; and chattel slavery, 68, 109–10, 150, 178–79, 298; and justification in papal bulls, 65, 108–9, 136, 331n18; need to repudiate, 113, 193, 331n18; Pope Alexander VI and "Inter Caetera," 65, 109; Pope Innocent IV, 65, 108–9, 146, 150, 165, 330n10; and racial and religious superiority, 106–113, 116–17, 139, 148; and terra nullius, 162–63, 169, 175, 193, 330n10. *See also* Catholic Church
Douglas Creek Estates. *See* Caledonia land disputes
Doxtater, Thohahoken Michael, 304
Dunning, Lord, 94, 101, 327n20
Dutch, 13–14, 18–20, 59, 73–74, 185, 301; adaptation to wampum diplomacy, 13–14, 18–20, 59, 297; negotiating the Two Row agreement, 50–59, 64–65, 150, 321n10; and political influence of covenant theology, 63–68, 322n1; prayer beads analogous to wampum string, 61–62

E

Earth. *See* Mother Earth
Edge of the Woods: ceremony, 5–9, 14, 141–45, 149, 169, 205, 335n3, 350n18; fear of, 24, 147, 164, 171, 175, 230, 254, 298
Edward, Gethin, 17, 84, 347n9
Ermine, Willie, 151–53, 157, 166, 336n13

F

family and widening conceptions of our relatives, 220–22, 227–28, 237
fear and religious awe, 253, 256–57, 345n3, 346n5
Fenton, William, 44, 57, 319n3
First Nations University of Canada, 34
Flanagan, Tom, 338n6
Forester, Brett, 348n20
Fort Niagara, Treaty of, 94–100, 192, 327n27
Fort Stanwix, Treaty of, 325n10, 328n33
Foster, Michael K., 49, 57–58, 60, 321n3, 338n6
Francis, Pope, 106
Francis of Assisi, 214–16, 230
Frankenberg, Ruth, 319n12
Franklin, Benjamin, 72
Freeman, Bonnie, 40, 320n13
French colonization, 9–12, 88; adaptation to wampum diplomacy, 13–14, 18–20, 32, 43; influence of religious

rationale on colonial project, 66–67, 322n8; involvement in fur trade and conflict, 2, 79, 172, 297, 301

G

General, Arnie, 39
General, Levi. *See* Deskaheh
genocide of Indigenous life and culture, 45, 132, 140, 151, 178, 192, 268, 349n1
George Washington Belt, 97
Gibson, John Arthur, 25–32, 75, 142, 241, 294–95, 342n1; and oration of Creation Story, 208–11, 212, 241
gift economy, 231, 246–50, 286, 287, 345n18
Glenbow Museum and cultural appropriation, 35
Goldenweiser, Alexander, 25, 31, 142
Goldie, Terry, 170
Gollin, Grégoire, 286–87
Good Mind, 2, 16, 24, 214, 240, 258, 300; seeking a future built of, 44; united in friendship and peace, 44, 59, 187. See also *ka'nikonhriyó'tshera't*
Gradual Enfranchisement Act, 139, 150
Graeber, David, 338n6
grandfather of the treaties, 17–18, 19, 98
Grassy Narrows and mercury poisoning, 35
Great Chain of Being and covenant theology, 63–65
Great Law of Peace, 24, 27–32, 30, 77, 171, 300, 351n1; three principles of, 15, 24, 152–53, 165, 213, 300, 318n16. *See also* Edge of the Woods
Great White Pine. *See* Tree of Peace
Guswenta space and rows of three white beads, 147, 153, 157–60, 235, 275

H

Haldimand, Frederick, 119–21, 332n14
Haldimand Proclamation, 120, 163, 174, 246, 266–67, 332n16
Haldimand Tract, 118–24, 137, 246, 265–68, 278, 332n16; and construction of Plank Road, 36, 43, 123–24, 137–38. *See also* Caledonia land disputes; Six Nations of the Grand River
Hamilton (Ontario): Joint Stewardship Board, 288–93; and pollution, 260–64, 282; and Red Hill Valley and Parkway, 288–93, 350n23
Hamilton, Meagan, 291
Hampton, Eber, 21, 318n15
Harper, Elijah, 188
Harper, Stephen, 103–4, 338n6
Haudenosaunee, 21, 31–32, 73–75, 244; citizenship and passports, 71, 103, 134; and different relationships with Dutch and French, 66–68, 297; and diplomatic protocols, 18–20, 176; and ecological imagination, 344n4, 347n8; fur trade involvement, 2, 4, 69, 90, 96, 169, 172; games, 26–27, 103, 251; meaning of name, 1, 14–15, 316n7; and nature as guide, 254–55; negotiating the Two Row Wampum with the Dutch, 58–59, 64–65, 150, 321n10; reminding Canada of alliance, 49, 183–86. *See also* Covenant Chain–Two Row Wampum tradition; Creation story, Haudenosaunee; Great Law of Peace; Hill, Rick; Indigenous sovereignty or self-determination; *ka'nikonhriyó'tshera't*; Kiotsaeton; Land Back; Six Nations Confederacy Council; Six Nations of the Grand River; Thomas, Jacob (Jake); Tree of Peace
Haudenosaunee Confederacy Council, 12, 20, 118, 123–24, 126, 136, 165, 288–90; Joint Stewardship Board, 288–93
Haudenosaunee Environmental Task Force, 220, 225, 229–30, 339n7, 343n7
Havard, Gilles, 14
Hawthorn Report and Harry B. Hawthorn, 177, 178, 179–81, 188, 194, 269
Henderson, James Sa'ke'j Youngblood, 86, 201–2, 325n6, 333n5, 337n4, 341n7
Hewitt, J.N.B., 210, 242, 342n1
Hiawatha. *See* Ayonwátha (Hiawatha), He Keeps Awake; Hiawatha Belt
Hiawatha Belt, 172–74
Hill, Karen, 40
Hill, Rick, 40, 49, 88, 172–73, 319n3, 320n13, 325n10, 332n16; on basket-making and black ash trees, 248, 250; on Covenant Chain and

Dish With One Spoon Wampum, 88, 96–97; on the "Crown," 329n5; on Indigenous jurisdiction, land and earth's rules, 270, 346n4; on Orì:wa as treaty and meeting protocols, 310; on writing and memory, 26
Hill, Susan, 116, 288–89, 320n13, 333n1
Hill, Tanis, 40
Hobbes, Thomas, 163, 180, 205–6, 241, 243, 254, 257, 284, 337n1
Honour the Two Row Campaign, 16
Howard, Albert, 338n6
Hudson, Henry, 58–59, 112
Hupačasath First Nation, 285–86
Huron Peace Belt, 172
Huron-Wendat-Algonquin alliance, 2, 172
Hwako, Gae Ho (Norma Jacobs), 147, 158–59, 320n13

I

Incarnation, Marie de l' (Marie Guyart), 12, 13, 42
Indian Act, 45, 71, 125–35, 139, 152–54, 162, 179; and definitions of an Indian, 154–57, 169–70, 333n10; enfranchisement tool in, 128–29, 131, 152. *See also* band council system; Canada; protection; Six Nations of the Grand River
Indian Advancement Act, 150
Indian Residential Schools, 21–22, 35, 103, 178, 190, 266, 333n10, 334n11. *See also* Canada; Catholic Church
Indian Self-Government in Canada: A Report of the Special Committee. See Penner Report
Indigenous Knowledge and appropriation of, 35–36, 319n3
Indigenous Peoples and language usage in this book, 128, 315n1
Indigenous resurgence, 26, 44, 49, 284–85, 301, 320n13, 348n12
Indigenous sovereignty or self-determination: and benefits to all Canadians, 192, 272, 348n12; connected to bioregions, 183–84, 269, 275; and "governance back," 269–70, 282–93, 346n4; in Penner Report, 185–86, 190; in RCAP, 182, 190–91; as source of law in Canada, 201–2. *See also* Royal Proclamation
Industrial Growth Society: and Canada's relations with Indigenous Peoples, 180–81, 195, 269; in contrast to gift ecology, 245, 247, 277; and economic "improvement," 21, 206, 236, 237, 258, 271, 298–301, 338n5; and economy vs. ecology, 231–52, 344n2; and extraction, 119, 255–56, 269–73, 277, 285–86, 338n5; and hydroelectric plants, 229; and imagination, 344n4; resource extraction, toxicity and sexual violence in, 194, 223–24, 228; and storyline of scarcity, 238–40, 247, 251. *See also* Mother Earth
Innocent IV, Pope, 65, 108–9, 146, 150, 165, 330n10
Islam and fear of Allah, 256–57

J

Jack and Charlie v. The Queen, 203–4, 207
Jacobs, Beverley, 86, 272, 320n13, 324n3
Jacobs, Jack, 253, 255
Jacobs, William, 126–27, 131, 151
Jamieson, Rebecca, 40
Jennings, Francis, 317n11
Jennings, Willie James, 110–11
Jesuits, 1–2, 4, 66–67, 109–11. *See* Catholic Church
Jigonsaseh, 25, 132, 144, 254, 300
Johnson, Aidan, 262
Johnson, Guy, 98, 329n35
Johnson, Ima, 40
Johnson, John, 98, 329n35
Johnson, John Smoke, 117–18
Johnson, William, 66–67, 78–79, 87, 105, 133, 150, 322n8, 325n8; formulating the Royal Proclamation, 82, 85, 87–95; and linking arms between Crown and Indigenous nations, 181, 198–99, 297; setting precedent for guarantee of collective rights, 199; version of Two Row agreement, 79–81; and wealth, land and slavery, 98–100, 351n3
Johnston, David, 103
Johnston, Louise, 62–64, 67
Judaism, 256
Judaism and fear of the Lord, 253, 256–57

K

Kahnawà:ke, 95, 199, 322n8, 324n4, 336n16

Kahnonstaton (Douglas Creek Estates). *See* Caledonia land disputes
Kamloops and Cowessess Indian Residential Schools, 174, 265–66
Kanesatake, 85, 95, 286–87, 322n8. *See also* Oka Crisis
ka'nikonhriyó'tshera't, 6, 24–25, 31, 143, 235, 258, 275, 300, 302, 318n16. *See also* Good Mind; Haudenosaunee
kaswentha, 3–4, 27–32, 170; origin and purpose of, 19, 20, 27–32, 78. *See also* Guswenta space; wampum
Katsi'tsiarihshion, Suzanne Brant, 244–45
Kayanerenhtsherakó:wa. *See* Great Law of Peace
Kelsey, Penelope, 342n2
kentèn:ron (friendship). See *ka'nikonhriyó'tshera't*
Keye, Lottie, 40
Kimmerer, Robin Wall, 247–49, 345n18
King, Hayden, 286
Kiotsaeton, 20, 44, 48, 58, 88, 105, 113, 150; hanging cords of wampum, 32, 171; peace mission to Trois-Rivières, 2–9, 11–13, 141, 145, 152; words of, forming Canada's history plays, 42
Krawec, Patty, 319n12, 348n19
Kvaløy Setreng, Sigmund, 338n5

L

LaFrance, Brenda, 243
Land Back, 39, 265–79, 280–93, 300, 346n4, 348n19, 349n1
Laskin, Bora, 101
Laurier, Wilfrid, 131, 171
League of Nations, 127, 134–36, 139, 152, 334n19
Leduc, Timothy, 158
Leonard, Kelsey, 8
Levinas, Emmanuel, 149–50, 319n6
Lickers, Henry, 214, 237, 238–40, 248, 339n7
Linked Arms, 9, 20–21, 39, 45, 50–60; about making family together, 234, 239–40, 252, 300. *See also* Covenant Chain–Two Row Wampum tradition
Locke, John, 180, 241, 243, 291; on labour and property, 205–6, 245–46
Logan v. Styres, 118, 163
Longboat, Dan – Roronhiakewen (He Clears the Sky), 237, 335n1, 344n4, 349n3
Longboat, Sheri, 291
Lyons, Oren, 18, 49, 258, 260, 282, 317n10, 319n3, 320n13

M

Macdonald, John A., 131, 270
Machado, Antonio, 145–46
Macy, Joanna, 338n5
Maracle, Brian, 316n7, 320n13, 342n1
Maracle, Kanatawakhon David, 221, 306
Maracle, Lee, 34, 300–301
Marshall, John, 106–7, 112
Martin-Hill, Dawn, 38, 40, 320n13, 347n10
McCarthy, Johanne, 148, 282, 304, 349n1
McCarthy, Theresa, 319, 320n13
McKay, Don, 144–45, 150
McKenzie Meadows. *See* Caledonia land disputes
McLachlin, Beverley, 169
McMaster University, 11, 36, 38–40, 255, 336n16, 347n10; jointly funding Indigenous Knowledge Centre, 40; police barracked at, 33–34, 39, 43, 47, 174
McQuaig, Max, 346n4
Meech Lake Accord, 177, 188
Meegwun, NaWalka Geeshy (Lyndon George), 292
Mercredi, Ovide, 18, 317n20
Mestral, Armand de, 341n7
Mi'kmaq, 270–71
Miller, Huron, 49
Missing and Murdered Indigenous Women and Girls, National Inquiry (MMIWG), 177, 178, 190–92, 194, 338n13
Mississaugas of the Credit, 119–21, 293, 332n14, 332n16
Mohawk people (*Kanyen'kehá:ka*), 2, 26, 230; diplomacy with Dutch and British, 68, 70, 85, 102, 120, 133; in Haudenosaunee Confederacy, 15, 25, 30, 97, 165, 294; land and river, 3, 16, 58–59, 78, 80, 89, 199, 225, 226; language, 14–15, 17, 48, 146, 158, 198, 200, 220–21, 295. *See also* Akwesasne; Haudenosaunee; Kanesatake; Kiotsaeton; Thomas, Jacob (Jake)
Mohawk, Sotsisowah John, 250–51, 319n3, 320n13, 334n14

Mohawk Institute (Mush Hole), 266–67
Monture, Rick, 38–39, 40, 255, 303, 320n13, 334n19
Monture-Angus, Patricia, 86–87, 331n5
Morgan, C.E., 136
Morrow, John Andrew, 322n8
Mother Earth, 207, 225–26, 268, 274, 296; building a better relationship with, 230, 252, 302; in European cultures, 214–20; and liberation theologies, 250–51; as living being, 24, 205–6, 212–14, 223, 283–85, 298–300; medicines of, 244–45; and "mothering" in *Kanyen'kéha* (Mohawk), 220–22. *See also* Creation Story, Haudenosaunee; Tharonhyawá:kon ("Earth-Holder"); Thawískaron ("Flint")
Muller, Kathryn V., 57
multiculturalism, 77, 196–207, 341n1. *See also* Covenant Chain–Two Row Wampum tradition; trans-systemic or "multi-juridical" law
Myers, Segwalise Mike, 183–84, 186

N

Nanfan (Albany, 1701), Treaty of, 120, 163, 272, 288
Nelson, Arihote Curtis, 85, 183, 340n20
Newhouse, David, 147, 320n13, 336n5
New York, 67, 74, 89, 92–94, 323n8
Neyaashiinigmiing, the Chippewas of Nawash, 204–5

O

Official Languages Act, 198
Ohnehta'ko:wa. *See* Haudenosaunee; Tree of Peace
Oka Crisis, 35, 188, 286–87
Oliver, Frank, 117, 128, 139
Oneida (*Onyota'a:ká:*), 13, 31, 43, 141, 152; in Haudenosaunee Confederacy, 2, 15, 165, 294; land, 57, 73–74, 325n10, 328n33. *See also* Ayonwátha (Hiawatha)
O'Neil, Beverley, 285
Onkwehón:we (Onkwehonweh), 50–60, 69–70, 81, 111, 212, 321n6
Onondaga (*Onoñda'gega'*), in Haudenosaunee Confederacy, 2, 15, 80, 165, 173, 294; land, 16, 79–80, 95, 325n10; language, 25, 142–43, 255, 342n1. *See also* Canesatego; Gibson, John Arthur
Ontario Provincial Police, 22, 33, 36, 47, 174, 278. *See also* Canadian Army; police
orality and oral narrative, 48, 321nn1–2
Oswegatchie, 95, 199
Ottawas (*Odawa*), 89

P

Palmer, Parker, 157
Parmenter, Jon, 77, 317n10
Peacemaker, 15, 24–25, 58, 66, 77, 132, 164, 171; and Great White Mat, 75–76, 100, 153; meeting Jigonsaseh, Ayonwátha and Atotarhonh, 24–25, 254, 300; warning to keep watch on peace, 295–97, 301–2
Pearson, Lester B., 179
Penner Report (*Indian Self-Government in Canada*), 177, 181–89, 190–91
Pessoa, Fernando, 216–19, 228, 230
Pierce, Joseph M., 265
Place-Thought, 283–84
Plank Road, 36, 43, 123–24, 137
police: presence at Oka/Kanesatake, 35, 188; violence against Black and Indigenous people, 22. *See also* Caledonia land disputes; Canadian Army; Ontario Provincial Police
Pontiac's War, 89, 94
Porter, Sakokweniónkwas Tom, 295–97, 312–13, 342, 351
Powless, Irving, Jr., 49
Pratt, Mary Louise, 323n8
protection, 81, 114–25, 161; of creation, 214, 225–26, 248, 264, 291; in Royal Proclamation, 89–94, 99, 186, 280, 326n18, 331n4; referred to in Canadian law, 126, 132, 196–98; paternalistic notions of, 131–33, 140, 151, 281, 331n5, 347n7; of rights to hunt, trap and fish, 163. *See also* Albany (Nanfan, 1701), Treaty of; Charter of Rights and Freedoms; Covenant Chain–Two Row Wampum tradition; Linked Arms; Mother Earth; Royal Proclamation

Q

Quebec Act, 198

R

Ransom, James W., 229–30
Reynolds, Anthony, 339n18, 340n20
Richmond, Don, 58
Richter, Daniel K., 77
Rickard, Jolene, 153–54, 320n13
Royal Commission on Aboriginal Peoples (RCAP), 177, 182, 189–93, 276, 280, 339n18, 340nn19–20, 345n17
Royal Proclamation, 174; and calls in Canada for a New Royal Proclamation, 190, 192, 280–81; as an Indigenous Magna Carta, 92–94, 101, 327n20; and Indigenous protection, not subjection, 90–95, 114, 127, 139, 197, 277; language, terms, subjects of, 280, 326n19; setting terms of Crown's responsibilities, 82, 117, 281, 331n5. *See also* British colonization on Turtle Island; Covenant Chain–Two Row Wampum tradition; Johnson, William; protection
R. v. Monture and White (2023), 4, 25, 84, 175–76, 292, 317, 324n11, 326n11, 340n21, 347n8
R. v. Van der Peet (1996), 168–69, 175, 201, 340n21
R. v. Williams (2023), 17, 84, 176, 292, 347n9

S

Saul, John Ralston, 275
Schama, Simon, 322
Schreyer, Edward R., 49, 334
Scott, Duncan Campbell, 130–34, 151–52, 333n10, 334n11
Second Peoples, as younger siblings to First Peoples, 319n12
Seneca (*Onödowa'ga:'*), 89, 93, 206, 327n27; in Haudenosaunee Confederacy, 2, 15, 165, 294; land of, 97, 229
settler colonialism, 41, 84, 125, 155, 162–65, 170, 268, 278, 319n12, 348n19. *See also* colonialism
Sheridan, Joe, 237, 335n1, 344n4, 349n3
Shorto, Russell, 67–68
Simcoe, John Graves, 118, 121, 127–28, 139, 163
Simpson, Leanne Betasamosake, 349n1
Sinclair, Upton, 119
Six Nations Confederacy. *See* Haudenosaunee Confederacy Council; Six Nations Confederacy Council; Six Nations of the Grand River
Six Nations Confederacy Council, 122, 135–39, 152, 155–56, 267, 325n5, 334n14
Six Nations of the Grand River, 17, 273, 325n5, 347n10; band council, 133, 135–36, 138–39, 155, 182, 185, 288, 293; and expropriated trust funds, 124, 137, 139, 150, 152, 156, 266–67; and Grand Indian Council, 126, 131, 333n1. *See also* Caledonia land disputes; Haldimand Tract; Haudenosaunee; Six Nations Confederacy Council
Six Nations Polytechnic, 38–40
skén:nen (peace, clarity). See *ka'nikonhriyó'tshera't*
Skye, Hubert, 40
Smith, Linda Tuhiwai, 36
Soldier Settlement Act, 130–33
Somerville, Alice Te Punga, 162–63
Spivak, Gayatri, 318n15
Staats, Linda, 40
Supreme Court of Canada, 17, 85, 168, 203

T

Tehahenteh Frank Miller, 306
Tehanetorens, Ray Fadden, 187, 343n7
Tehontatenentshonteronhtáhkwa ("The thing by which they link arms"). *See* Covenant Chain–Two Row Wampum tradition; Linked Arms
Tékeni Teyohà:te (Deyohahá:ge: "the two roads or paths"). *See* Two Row Wampum
Terpstra, John, 262–63
Thanksgiving Address, 5–6, 12, 58, 113, 184, 216, 242–44, 293
Tharonhyawá:kon ("Earth-Holder"), 46, 70, 126, 208–11, 212, 213, 236, 240–44, 247, 255–56, 281. *See also* Creation Story, Haudenosaunee; Mother Earth; Thawískaron; protection
Thawískaron ("Flint"), 46, 70, 208–11, 219, 232, 236, 240–41, 247, 255. *See also* Creation Story, Haudenosaunee; Mother Earth; Tharonhyawá:kon; protection
Theysmeyer, Tys, 262–64

Thomas, David, 47, 58
Thomas, Jacob (Jake), 26, 49, 71, 80, 107, 200, 321n1; on Haudenosaunee and Dutch encounter, 47–56, 59–61, 69, 81, 111, 150, 158; oration at Grand River ceremony (1988), 57–58, 212, 252, 300–301; oration at Rideau Hall (1981), 57–58, 147
Tidridge, Nathan, 96, 327n27; on the "Crown," 329n5
Titley, E. Brian, 334n11
Trans Mountain pipeline, 232, 270, 281, 286
trans-systemic or "multi-juridical" law, 202, 325n6, 337n4, 341n7
Treaties, 18, 76; as ongoing relationship not individual transaction, 18, 73–78, 168, 272, 341n1; and phrase "as long as the sun shines . . .," 53, 86, 100, 230, 247, 300, 302. *See also* Albany (Nanfan, 1701), Treaty of; Covenant Chain–Two Row Wampum tradition; Fort Niagara, Treaty of; Fort Stanwix, Treaty of; Linked Arms; Two Row Wampum
Tree of Peace, 12, 70, 95, 137, 173, 295–302
Trudeau, Justin, 104, 233, 270
Trudeau, Pierre Elliott, 196, 334n15; patriation of the Constitution, 49, 71, 83; and White Paper, 138, 150, 174, 180–82, 273, 334n15
Truth and Reconciliation Commission (TRC), 177, 190–94
Tuck, Eve, 268
Tully, James, 201
Tuscarora (*Skarure'*), 15, 229. *See also* Haudenosaunee; Hewitt, J.N.B.
Two Row Research Partnership, 40, 148
Two Row Wampum, 16, 78–81, 186–88; Dutch and British respecting Haudenosaunee prior claim, 11, 73–74; embedded in Charter of Rights and Freedoms, 83–101; and orations by Jacob (Jake) Thomas, 47–60, 69–70; path of peace between the vessels, 70, 173, 274, 289, 323n4; and "repolishing" the agreement, 16–17, 21, 75, 77, 80, 103, 133, 148, 153; as supplement to Covenant of Linked Arms, 46, 184; two separate paths as story of division, 45, 70, 72, 235. *See also* Covenant Chain–Two Row Wampum tradition; Land Back; Linked Arms; *R. v. Monture and White*; *R. v. Williams*; Thomas, Jacob (Jake)

U

United Empire Loyalists, 122, 332n17
United Nations Declaration on the Rights of Indigenous Peoples (UNDRIP), 193, 315n1
United States, 97, 132, 138; and Revolutionary War, 14, 97–100, 119, 123, 130, 324n11; political foundations influenced by Haudenosaunee, 20, 72–75, 318n14
United States Supreme Court, 106–7

V

Venables, Robert, 72, 77
Venne, Sharon H., 284
Villebrun, Kristen, 262, 264
Vimont, Barthélemy, 3–4, 7, 9, 32, 42, 48

W

Wabanaki Confederacy, 18, 98, 170, 198
Wampanoag, 31–32
wampum, 6–14, 19, 27–32, 49, 67, 136–37, 164–65, 316n9; Circle Wampum, 95, 295; and condolence, 27–32, 67, 254, 335n3; and Covenant Chain Wampum Belt, 96–97, 173; and Dish With One Spoon Belt, 76, 172; Fire of the Valley, 289–90; First Sighting of the People with Pale Faces, 173; Friendship Belt, 58, 76, 103; Hiawatha (Ayonwátha) Belt, 172–73; Huron Peace Belt, 172; iconography of, 17, 76, 171–74; named by French as "Colliers de pourcelaine," 3, 5, 22, 59, 315n4; and white beads as path of peace, 70, 76, 143, 152, 157, 172–73, 235, 274–75, 312. *See also* Guswenta space; *kaswentha*; Kiotsaeton; Two Row Wampum
Warkentin, Germaine, 13
Watts, Vanessa, 283–85, 320n13
Wengrow, David, 338n6
Western societies, 235, 239–40, 250, 254, 283–84, 318n15, 344n4; and ideas of law and land, 60, 246, 282, 341n7, 345n18; and need for sacred

awe, fear, 256–57, 259–60, 264, 345n3, 346n5; and race thinking, 102–13, 117, 155, 338n6. *See also* Doctrine of Discovery; Industrial Growth Society
White, Doug, 86, 272
whiteness, 110–12, 154, 168, 201, 267, 319n12, 337n2; and "white settler" term, 43, 319n12
White Paper (*Statement of the Government of Canada on Indian Policy*, 1969), 138, 150, 163, 174, 180–82, 273, 334n15
Widdowson, Frances, 338n6
Williams, Kayanesenh Paul, 49, 228, 316n10, 319n3; legal advice in *R. v. Monture and White*, 84–86; Kaswentha report to RCAP, 183, 340n20; on race thinking in European "discoveries," 337n5; on Royal Proclamation and continuous treaty tradition, 90, 94–95, 104; on treaties as relationship not transaction, 18, 168, 201, 321n2
Williams, Robert A., Jr., 65, 77, 108, 111, 160
Williams, Skyler, 17, 84
Williams-Myers, Albert James, 328n34
Wolfe, Patrick, 41
Woodbury, Hanni, 25, 31
Words Before All Else, 5–6, 12, 59, 241

Y

Yang, K. Wayne, 268
Yerxa, Leo, 187–88
Yesno, Riley, 286
Yethi'nihstenha, 129, 213, 220–27, 229, 269, 271, 282. *See also* Mother Earth
Younging, Gregory, 315n1, 348n19

Daniel Coleman is a recently retired English professor who is grateful to live in the traditional territories of the Haudenosaunee and Anishinaabe in Hamilton, Ontario. He taught in the Department of English and Cultural Studies at McMaster University. He has studied and written about Canadian Literature, whiteness, the literatures of Indigeneity and diaspora, the cultural politics of reading, and wampum, the form of literacy-ceremony-communication-law that was invented by the people who inhabited the Great Lakes–St. Lawrence–Hudson River Watershed before Europeans arrived on Turtle Island.

Daniel has long been fascinated by the poetic power of narrative arts to generate a sense of place and community, critical social engagement and mindfulness, and especially wonder. Although he has committed considerable effort to learning in and from the natural world, he is still a bookish person who loves the learning that is essential to writing. He has published numerous academic and creative non-fiction books as an author and as an editor. His books include *Masculine Migrations* (1998), *The Scent of Eucalyptus* (2003), *White Civility* (2006; winner of the Raymond Klibansky Prize), *In Bed with the Word* (2009) and *Yardwork: A Biography of an Urban Place* (2017, shortlisted for the RBC Taylor Prize).